To Dare Mighty Things

To Dare Mighty Things

U.S. DEFENSE STRATEGY SINCE THE REVOLUTION

Michael O'Hanlon

Yale
UNIVERSITY PRESS
New Haven & London

Published with assistance from the foundation established in memory of Calvin Chapin of the Class of 1788, Yale College.

Yale University Press books may be purchased in quantity for educational, business, or promotional use. For information, please e-mail sales.press@yale.edu (U.S. office) or sales@yaleup.co.uk (U.K. office).

Set in Adobe Garamond Premier Pro type by IDS Infotech Ltd.
Printed in the United States of America.

Library of Congress Control Number: 2025938752
ISBN 978-0-300-27993-1 (hardcover)

A catalogue record for this book is available from the British Library.

Authorized Representative in the EU: Easy Access System Europe, Mustamäe tee 50, 10621 Tallinn, Estonia, gpsr.requests@easproject.com

For Bob Kagan, who taught and teaches me so much, and for Suzanne Maloney, who toils so hard for all of us while also being one of the best Iran scholars in the world, and for Strobe Talbott, and the memory of Martin Indyk and of my brother Bill, best brother ever

Far better is it to dare mighty things, to win glorious triumphs, even though checkered by failure, than to take rank with those poor spirits who neither enjoy much nor suffer much, because they live in the gray twilight that knows not victory nor defeat.

—THEODORE ROOSEVELT, address to the Hamilton Society, Chicago, April 1899

Contents

Maps

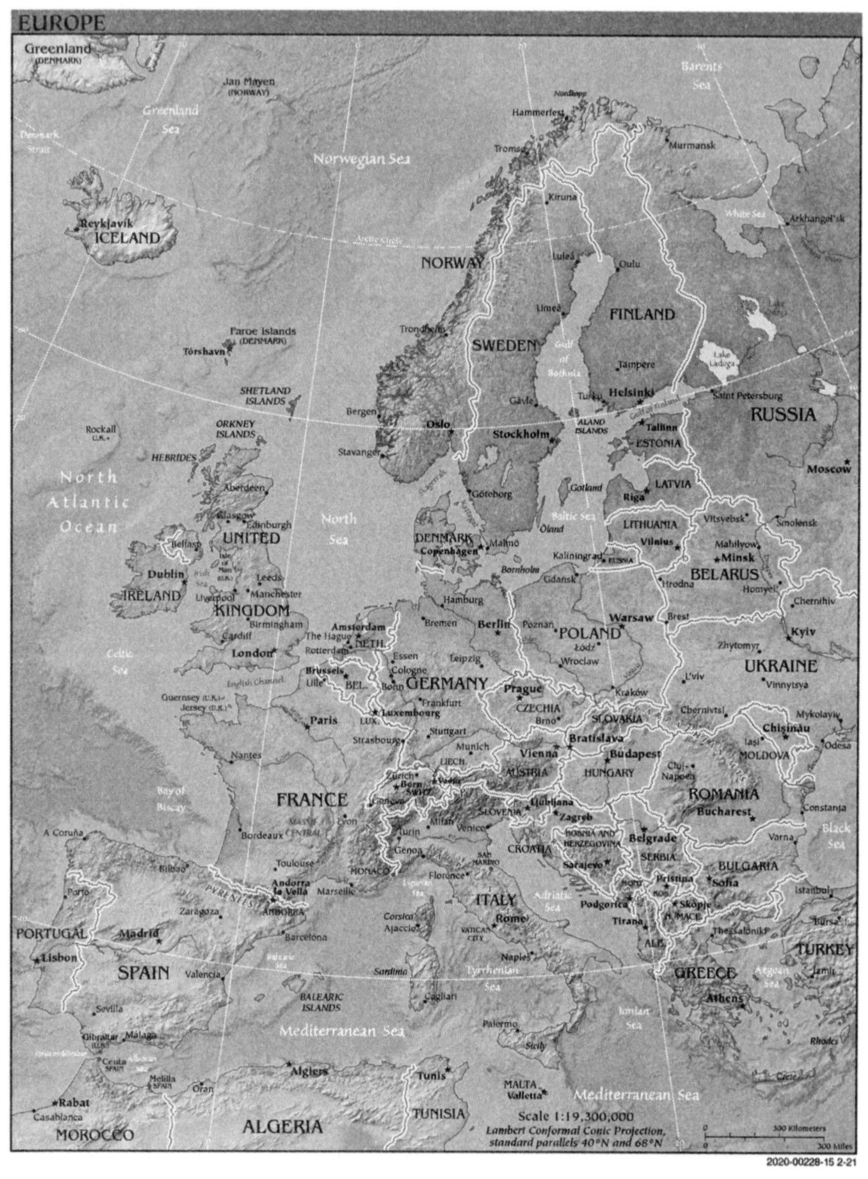

Map of Europe. *The World Factbook 2024.* Washington, D.C.: Central Intelligence Agency, 2024. https://www.cia.gov/.

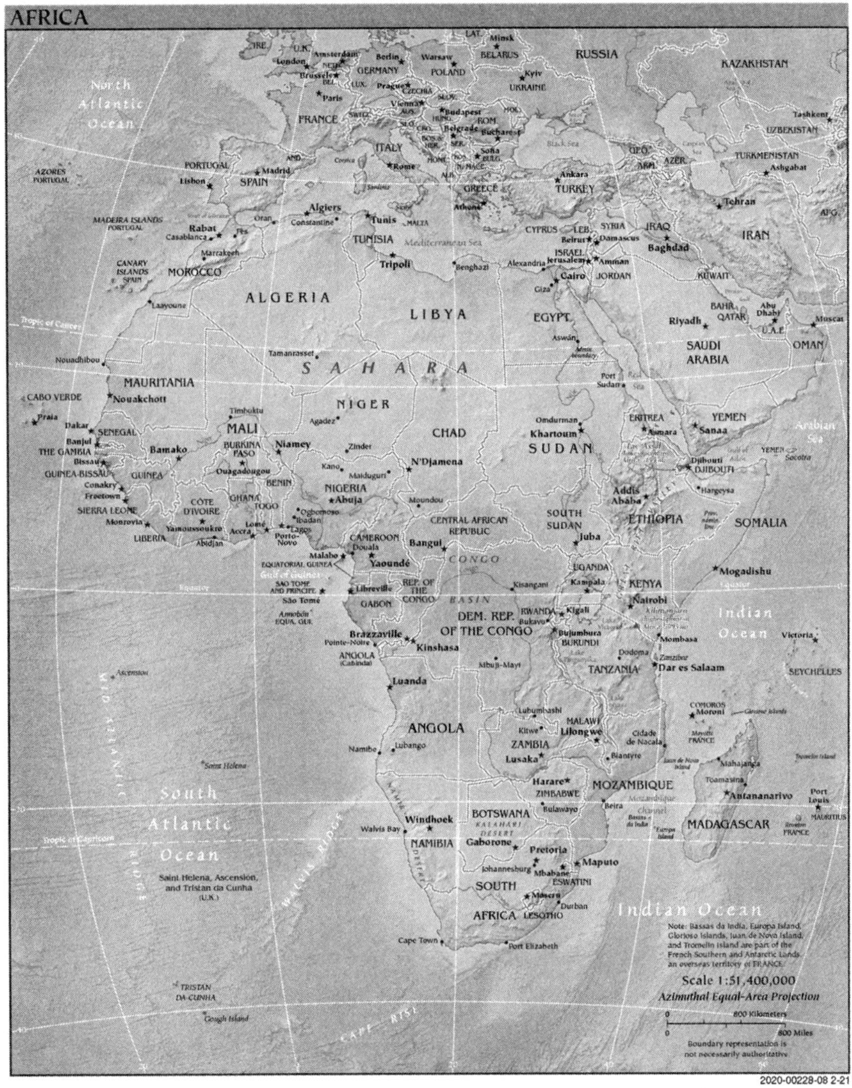

Map of Africa. *The World Factbook 2024.* Washington, D.C.: Central Intelligence Agency, 2024. https://www.cia.gov/.

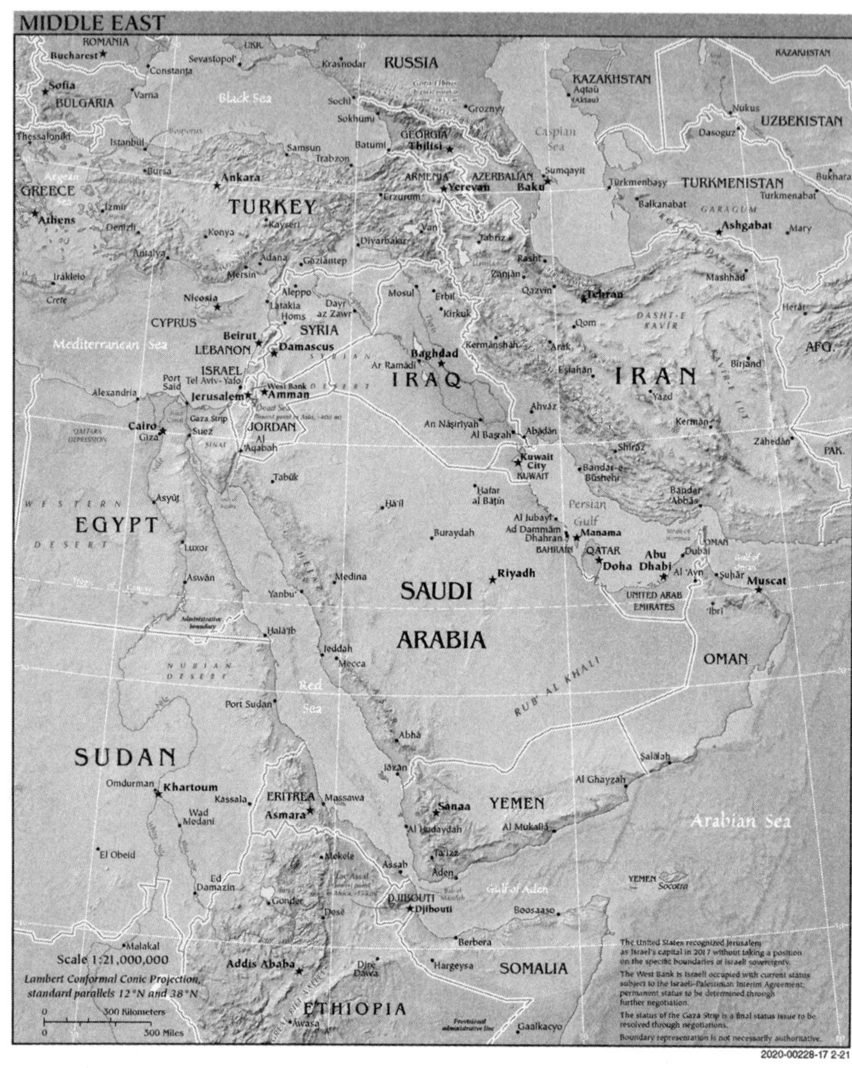

Map of the Middle East. *The World Factbook 2024.* Washington, D.C.: Central Intelligence Agency, 2024. https://www.cia.gov/.

Map of Southeast Asia. *The World Factbook 2024.* Washington, D.C.: Central Intelligence Agency, 2024. https://www.cia.gov/.

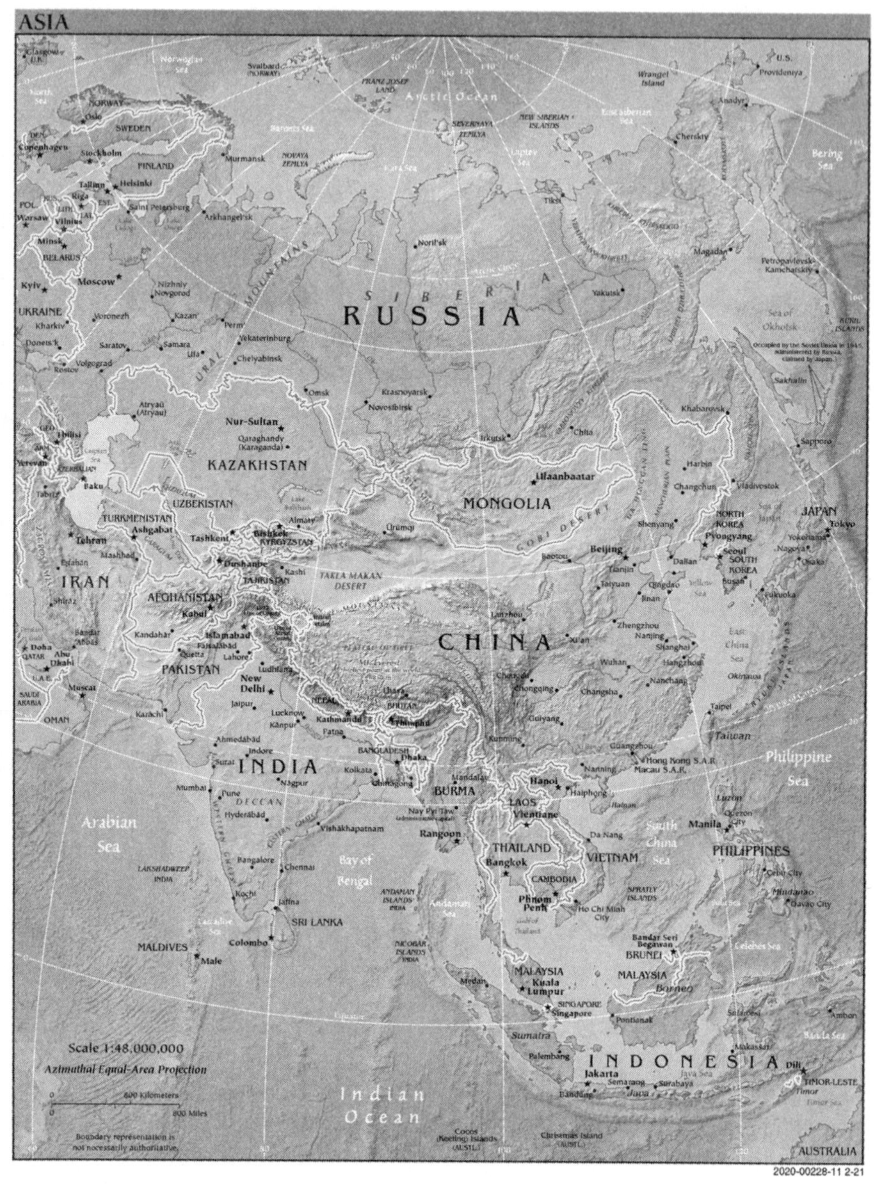

Map of Asia. *The World Factbook 2024.* Washington, D.C.: Central Intelligence Agency, 2024. https://www.cia.gov/.

Graphs

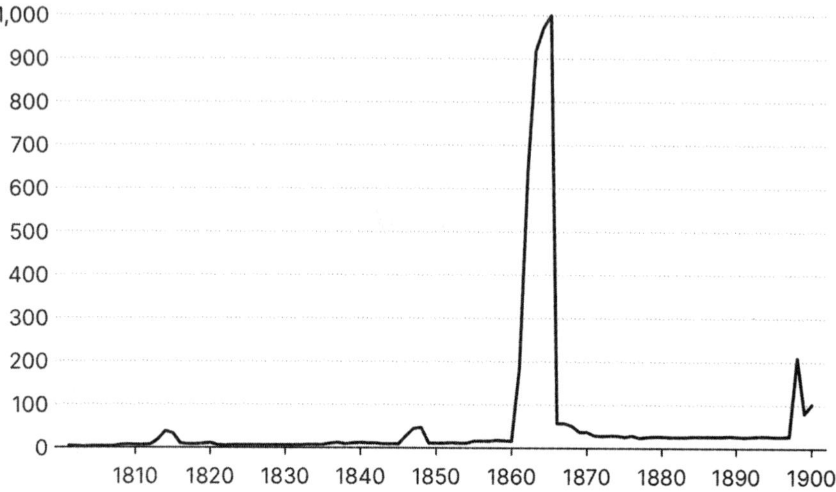

Active-Duty Army, 1801–1900. The *y*-axis represents thousands of soldiers. *Source:* U.S. Bureau of the Census, *Historical Statistics of the United States, Colonial Times to 1957* (Washington, D.C., 1960), 736–37, https://www2.census.gov/library/publications/1960/compendia/hist_stats_colonial-1957/hist_stats_colonial-1957-chY.pdf.

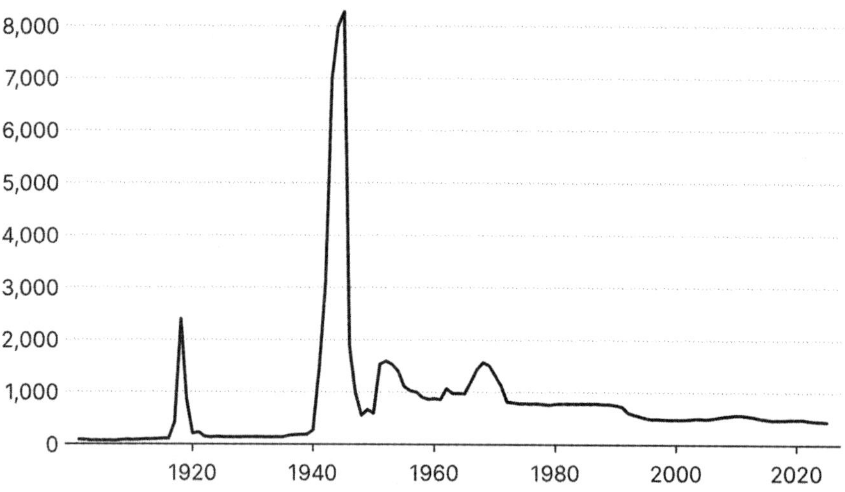

Active-Duty Army, 1901–2025. The *y*-axis represents thousands of soldiers. *Source:* U.S. Bureau of the Census, *Historical Statistics of the United States, Colonial Times to 1957* (Washington, D.C., 1960), 736–37, https://www2.census.gov/library/publications/1960/compendia/hist_stats_colonial-1957/hist_stats_colonial-1957-chY.pdf; Office of the Under Secretary of Defense (Comptroller), *National Defense Budget Estimates for Fiscal Year 2025* (Washington, D.C.: Department of Defense, April 2024), 288–90, https://comptroller.defense.gov/Portals/45/Documents/defbudget/FY2025/fy25_Green_Book.pdf. *Note: Figures before 1948 include the Army Air Corps.*

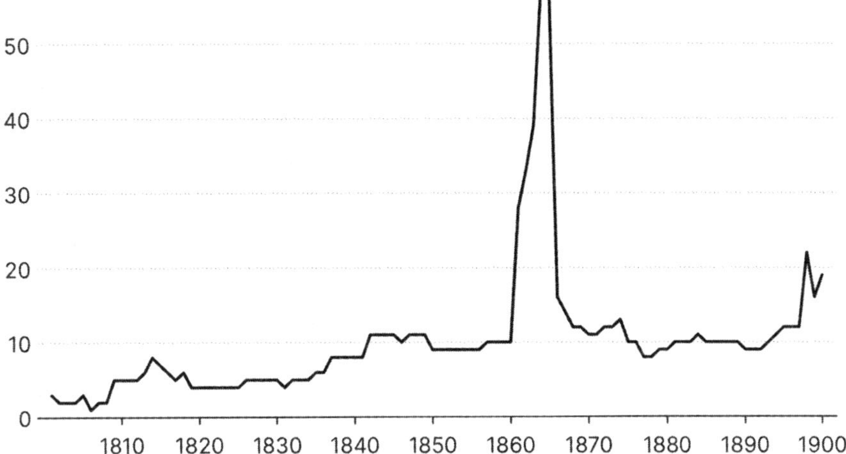

Active-Duty Navy, 1801–1900. The *y*-axis represents thousands of sailors. *Source:* U.S. Bureau of the Census, *Historical Statistics of the United States, Colonial Times to 1957* (Washington, D.C., 1960), 736–37, https://www2.census.gov/library/publications/1960/compendia/hist_stats_colonial-1957/hist_stats_colonial-1957-chY.pdf. *Note: Does not include U.S. Marine Corps.*

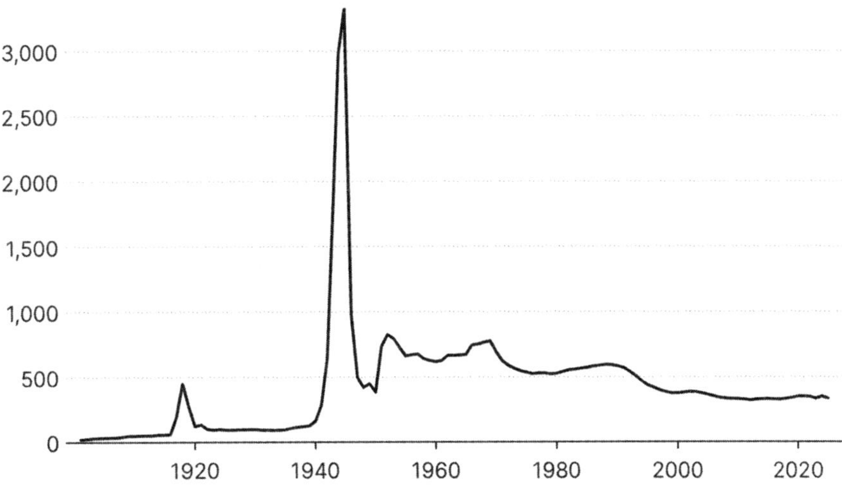

Active-Duty Navy, 1901–2025. The *y*-axis represents thousands of sailors. *Source:* U.S. Bureau of the Census, *Historical Statistics of the United States, Colonial Times to 1957* (Washington, D.C., 1960), 736–37, https://www2.census.gov/library/publications/1960/compendia/hist_stats_colonial-1957/hist_stats_colonial-1957-chY.pdf; Office of the Under Secretary of Defense (Comptroller), *National Defense Budget Estimates for Fiscal Year 2025* (Washington, D.C.: Department of Defense, April 2024), 288–90, https://comptroller.defense.gov/Portals/45/Documents/defbudget/FY2025/fy25_Green_Book.pdf. *Note: Does not include U.S. Marine Corps.*

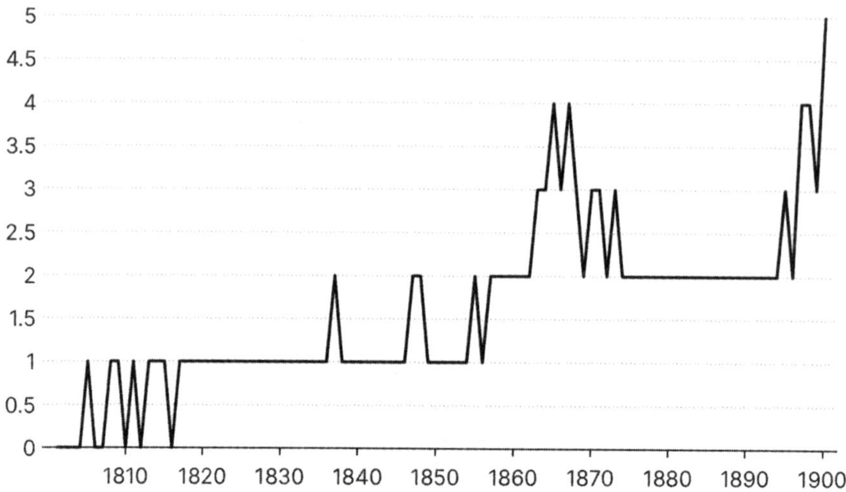

Active-Duty Marine Corps, 1801–1900. The *y*-axis represents thousands of Marines. *Source:* U.S. Bureau of the Census, *Historical Statistics of the United States, Colonial Times to 1957* (Washington, D.C., 1960), 736–37, https://www2.census.gov/library/publications/1960/compendia/hist_stats_colonial-1957/hist_stats_colonial-1957-chY.pdf. *Note: Rounded to the nearest thousand.*

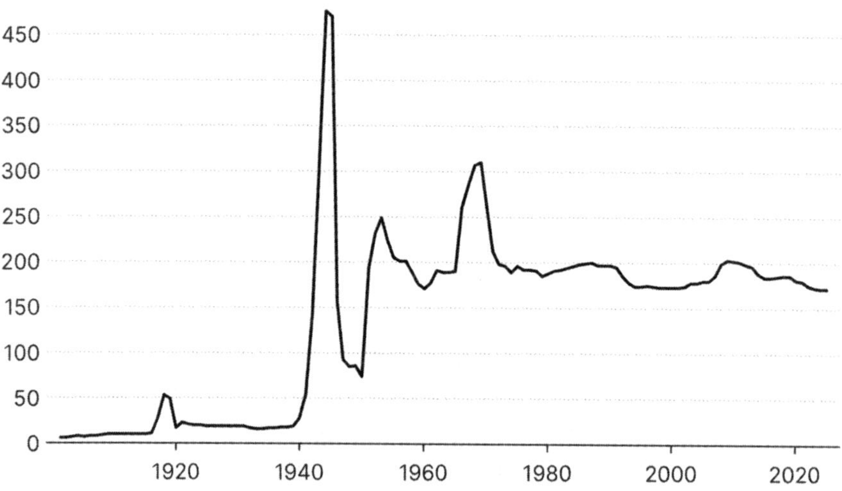

Active-Duty Marine Corps, 1901–2025. The *y*-axis represents thousands of Marines. *Source:* U.S. Bureau of the Census, *Historical Statistics of the United States, Colonial Times to 1957* (Washington, D.C., 1960), 736–37, https://www2.census.gov/library/publications/1960/compendia/hist_stats_colonial-1957/hist_stats_colonial-1957-chY.pdf; Office of the Under Secretary of Defense (Comptroller), *National Defense Budget Estimates for Fiscal Year 2025* (Washington, D.C.: Department of Defense, April 2024), 288–90, https://comptroller.defense.gov/Portals/45/Documents/defbudget/FY2025/fy25_Green_Book.pdf.

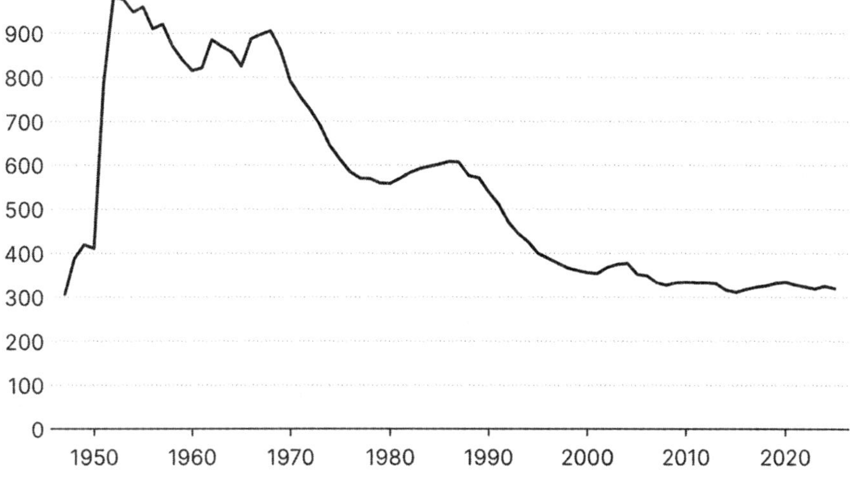

Active-Duty Air Force, 1947–2025. The *y*-axis represents thousands of airmen. *Source:* Office of the Under Secretary of Defense (Comptroller), *National Defense Budget Estimates for Fiscal Year 2025* (Washington, D.C.: Department of Defense, April 2024), 288–90, https://comptroller.defense.gov/Portals/45/Documents/defbudget/FY2025/fy25_Green_Book.pdf. *Note: Does not include the U.S. Space Force, established in 2019. The Space Force had approximately 7,000 Guardians in 2021, 8,000 in 2022, 9,000 in 2023, 9,000 in 2024, and 10,000 in 2025.*

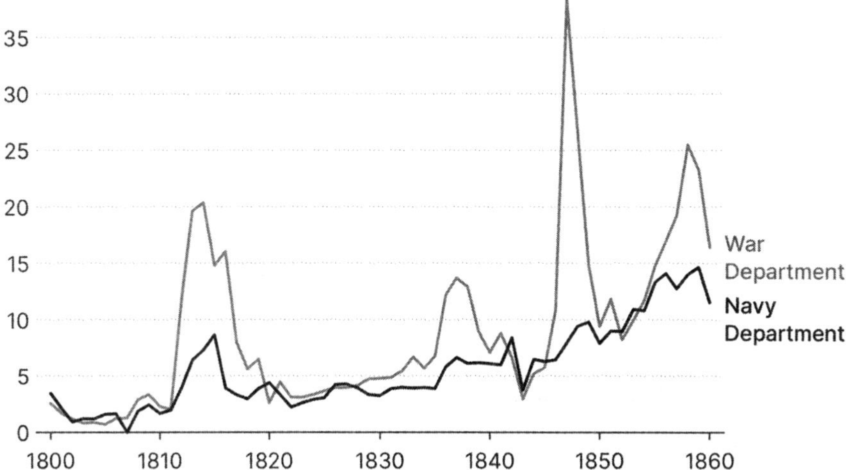

U.S. national defense expenditures, 1800–1860. Annual spending in nominal dollars (not adjusted for inflation, millions of USD). *Source:* Treasury Department, *Annual Report of the Secretary of the Treasury on the State of the Finances for the Fiscal Year Ended June 30, 1940* (Washington, D.C., 1941), 646–47, https://fraser.stlouisfed.org/title/annual-report-secretary-treasury-state-finances-194/annual-report-secretary-treasury-state-finances-fiscal-year-ended-june-30-1940-5586. *Note: $1 in 1800 was equivalent in consumer purchasing power to about $25 in 2024; $1 in 1825 was equivalent to about $32 in 2024; $1 in 1850 was equivalent to about $40 in 2024.*

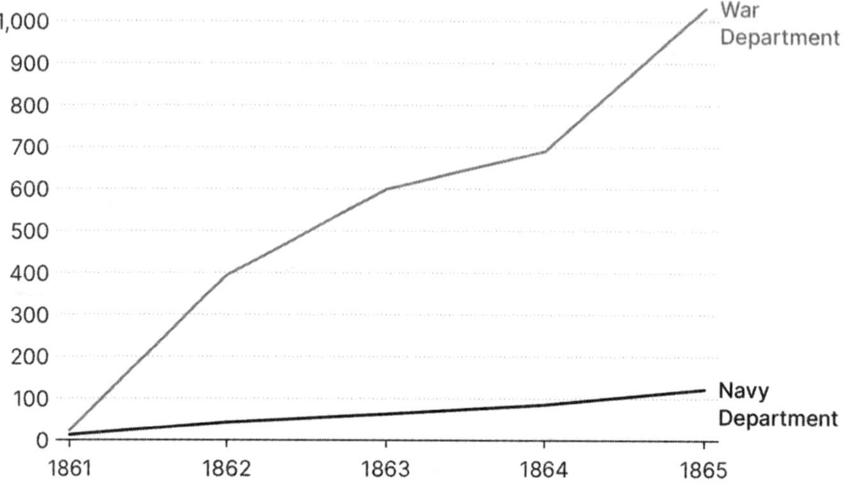

U.S. national defense expenditures, 1861–65. Annual spending in nominal dollars (not adjusted for inflation, millions of USD). *Source:* Treasury Department, *Annual Report of the Secretary of the Treasury on the State of the Finances for the Fiscal Year Ended June 30, 1940* (Washington, D.C., 1941), 647, https://fraser.stlouisfed.org/title/annual-report-secretary-treasury-state-finances-194/annual-report-secretary-treasury-state-finances-fiscal-year-ended-june-30-1940-5586. *Note: $1 in 1863 was equivalent in consumer purchasing power to about $25 in 2024.*

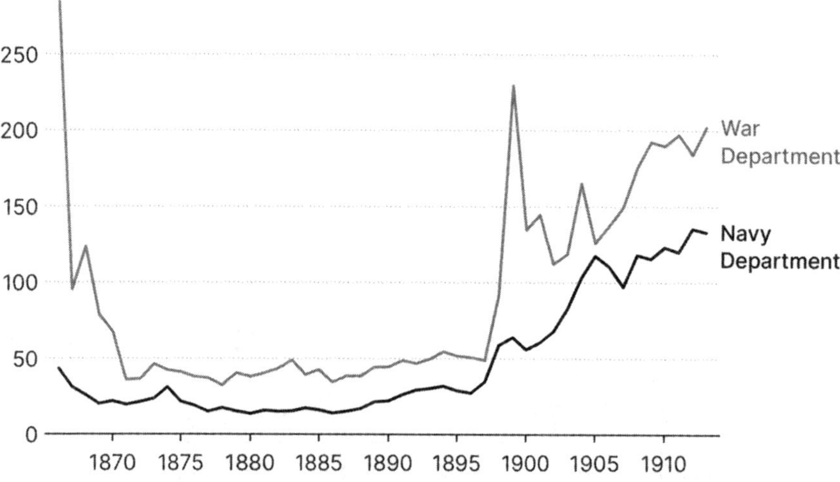

U.S. national defense expenditures, 1866–1913. Annual spending in nominal dollars (not adjusted for inflation, millions of USD). *Source:* Treasury Department, *Annual Report of the Secretary of the Treasury on the State of the Finances for the Fiscal Year Ended June 30, 1940* (Washington, D.C., 1941), 647–48, https://fraser.stlouisfed.org/title/annual-report-secretary-treasury-state-finances-194/annual-report-secretary-treasury-state-finances-fiscal-year-ended-june-30-1940-5586. *Note: $1 in 1875 was equivalent in consumer purchasing power to about $29 in 2024; $1 in 1900 was equivalent to about $38 in 2024.*

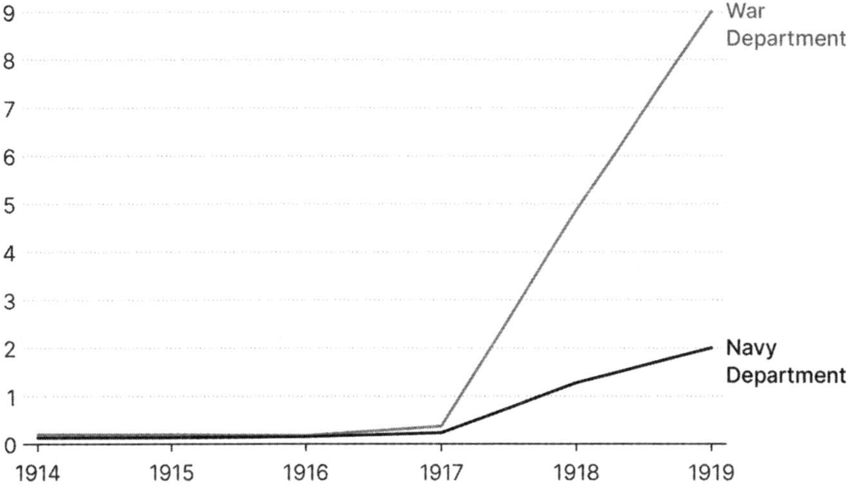

U.S. national defense expenditures, 1914–19. Annual spending in nominal dollars (not adjusted for inflation, billions of USD). *Source:* Treasury Department, *Annual Report of the Secretary of the Treasury on the State of the Finances for the Fiscal Year Ended June 30, 1940* (Washington, D.C., 1941), 648–49, https://fraser.stlouisfed.org/title/annual-report-secretary-treasury-state-finances-194/annual-report-secretary-treasury-state-finances-fiscal-year-ended-june-30-1940-5586. *Note: $1 in 1916 was equivalent in consumer purchasing power to about $29 in 2024.*

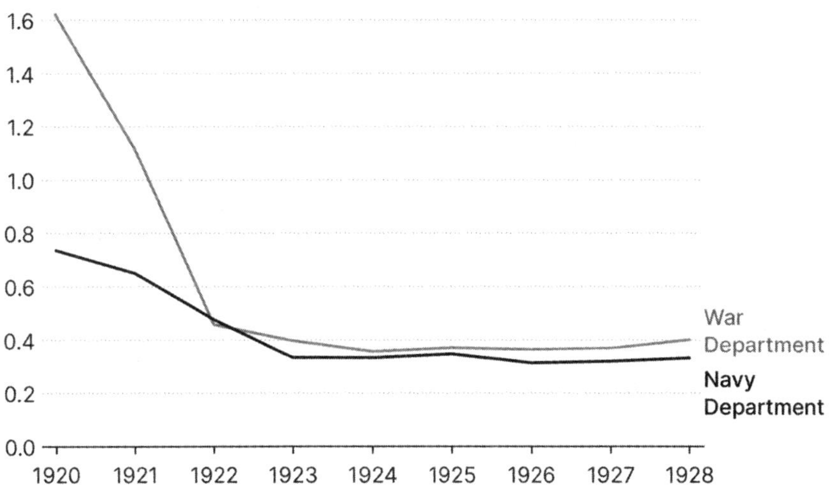

U.S. national defense expenditures, 1920–28. Annual spending in nominal dollars (not adjusted for inflation, billions of USD). *Source:* Treasury Department, *Annual Report of the Secretary of the Treasury on the State of the Finances for the Fiscal Year Ended June 30, 1940* (Washington, D.C., 1941), 649, https://fraser.stlouisfed.org/title/annual-report-secretary-treasury-state-finances-194/annual-report-secretary-treasury-state-finances-fiscal-year-ended-june-30-1940-5586. *Note: $1 in 1925 was equivalent in consumer purchasing power to about $18 in 2024.*

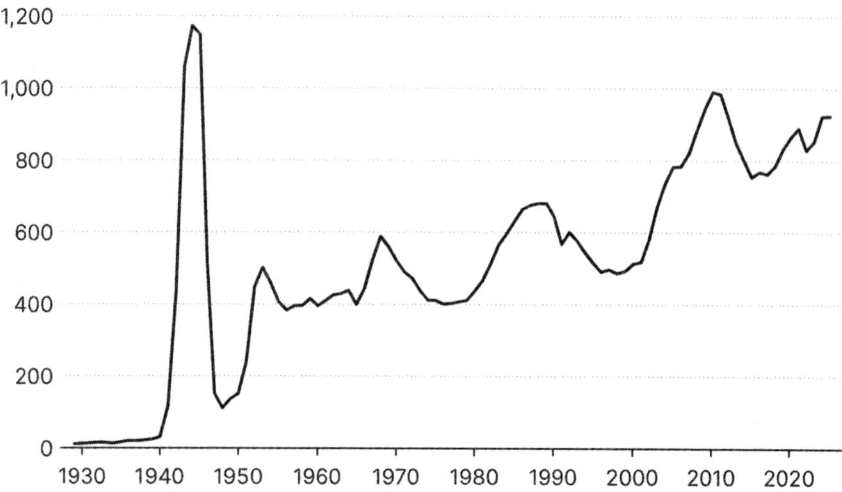

U.S. national defense expenditures, 1929–2025. Annual spending in FY 2025 constant dollars (billions of USD). *Source:* U.S. Bureau of the Census, *Historical Statistics of the United States, Colonial Times to 1957* (Washington, D.C., 1960), 718–19, https://www2.census.gov/library/publications/1960/compendia/hist_stats_colonial-1957/hist_stats_colonial-1957-chY.pdf; *Office of the Under Secretary of Defense (Comptroller), National Defense Budget Estimates for Fiscal Year 2025* (Washington, D.C.: Department of Defense, April 2024), 279–81, 294, https://comptroller.defense.gov/Portals/45/Documents/defbudget/FY2025/fy25_Green_Book.pdf; U.S. Bureau of Economic Analysis, "Table 1.1.5. Gross Domestic Product," accessed December 9, 2024, https://apps.bea.gov/iTable/?reqid=19&step=2&isuri=1&categories=survey&_gl=1*eza1mr*_ga*MTU0NjA0ODA4My4xNzMzMTYzMzI3*_ga_J4698JNNFT*MTczMzc3NTU1Ni44LjEuMTczMzc3NTYwMC4xNi4wLjA.#eyJhcHBpZCI6MTksInN0ZXBzIjpbMSwyLDMsM10sImRhdGEiOltbImNhdGVnb3JpZXMiLCJTdXJ2ZXkiXSxbIk5JUEFfVGFibGVfTGlzdCIsIjUiXSxbIkZpcnN0X1llYXIiLCIxOTI5Il0sWyJMYXN0X1llYXIiLCIyMDI0Il0sWyJTY2FsZSIsIi05Il0sWyJTZXJpZXMiLCJBIl1dfQ==; U.S. Bureau of Economic Analysis, "Table 1.1.9. Implicit Price Deflators for Gross Domestic Product," accessed December 9, 2024, https://apps.bea.gov/iTable/?reqid=19&step=3&isuri=1&1921=survey&1903=13#eyJhcHBpZCI6MTksInN0ZXBzIjpbMSwyLDMsM10sImRhdGEiOltbIk5JUEFfVGFibGVfTGlzdCIsIjEzIl0sWyJDYXRlZ29yaWVzIiwiU3VydmV5Il0sWyJGaXJzdF9ZZWFyIiwiMTkyOSJdLFsiTGFzdF9ZZWFyIiwiMjAyNCJdLFsiU2NhbGUiLCIwIl0sWyJTZXJpZXMiLCJBIl1dfQ==. *Note: This graphic presents data calculated using different methods across various time periods. For 1929 to 1939, expenditures were determined by summing the War and Navy Departments' expenditures and converting them to FY 2025 constant dollars using a GDP deflator. For 1940 to 2023, expenditures were derived from the percentage of GDP allocated to national defense, multiplied by GDP for each year, and then converted to FY 2025 constant dollars using a GDP deflator. For 2024 to 2025, expenditures in FY 2025 constant dollars were calculated using a conversion factor of 1.26 from FY 2017 dollars.*

War	Years	Total U.S. Deaths
Revolutionary War	1775-1783	4,435
War of 1812	1812-1815	2,260
Mexican War	1846-1848	13,283
Civil War (Union forces only)	1861-1865	364,511
Spanish-American War	1898-1901	2,446
World War I	1917-1918	116,516
World War II	1941-1945	405,399
Korean War	1950-1953	36,574
Vietnam War	1964-1973	58,220
Persian Gulf War	1990-1991	383
Iraq War	2003–2011	4,492
Afghanistan War	2001–2021	2,459

U.S. Fatalities in Key Conflicts. *Source:* Defense Casualty Analysis System (DCAS), "Conflict Casualties," Defense Manpower Data Center (DMDC), Washington, D.C., accessed November 2024, https://dcas.dmdc.osd.mil/dcas/app/conflictCasualties. *Note: Excluding the Revolutionary War and the War of 1812, deaths include those from other causes, such as accidents, disease, and infections.*

To Dare Mighty Things

CHAPTER I

American Ways of War and (Relative) Peace

Over its 250 years as a nation, how has the United States developed and implemented defense strategy? What big themes, what American story, can describe the nation's approaches to war and peace—the ways it has built, modernized, postured, and employed its armed forces—since the founding of the Republic? How has the United States sought to establish and balance ends, ways, and means in its decisions on defense or military strategy?[1]

Much of this history is a story of success. The United States won its independence, then pursued its internal growth and development while surviving a civil war, then led the way to coalition victories in two world wars, and then worked with allies to pursue victory without large-scale combat in the Cold War. Undergirding the global order since 1945, it has also contributed to the most peaceful and prosperous and democratic period in human history, albeit one under serious stress today. Although it has retained a large standing military backed up by a robust defense industry throughout this latter period, it has avoided becoming what Princeton professor Aaron Friedberg calls a "garrison state" or a hypermilitarized economy in the process.[2] Generally speaking, it has found approaches to defense strategy and military policy that have not broken the bank—at least not relative to the monumental nature of some of the tasks it has attempted. Its geographic location, protected by oceans and bordered by generally friendly neighbors, has helped enormously in this process, as has its wealth of resources, as have the diversity and industriousness of its people.

Yet even as the United States has, as Theodore Roosevelt stated when he addressed the Hamilton Society in 1899, "dared mighty things" with its development and employment of national military power, it has also made many mistakes. Its foreign policy record is indeed checkered with failure, to again borrow Roosevelt's words. It has often been motivated by less than peaceful or noble goals; even when its goals and values were on solid ground, its approach to pursuing them has often failed. America has arguably been the greatest force for good in international politics in the history of the modern human race. Yet it has also been a "dangerous nation," as historian Robert Kagan entitled one of his books (quoting John Quincy Adams).[3] It nearly ripped itself in two over the issue of slavery and states' rights. It sought to avoid entanglement in Eurasian wars but ultimately failed in that goal spectacularly on two separate occasions in the twentieth century and had to enter those world wars once they were already fully blazing. From 1945 onward, the United States has compiled a notably mediocre record of success and failure in its major wars. The story of America's grand strategy, and its defense strategy, has been complex and checkered to say the very least.

That story also reveals patterns and tendencies—an American strategic culture, almost a national DNA—that are important to understand going forward. Only if Americans understand their strengths as well as their characteristic weaknesses can we minimize future failure and danger. In ancient times, the Chinese strategist Sun Tzu wisely admonished those who thought of matters of war and peace to know themselves as well as their potential enemies.[4] The United States spends $100 billion a year in its intelligence budget alone attempting to understand the outside world, including its enemies and rivals, but we tend to spend much less time and effort trying to understand ourselves.[5]

GRAND STRATEGY VERSUS DEFENSE STRATEGY

Two big conceptual frameworks run through these pages and should be clearly defined up front: *grand strategy,* on the one hand, and *defense strategy,* on the other. The latter term is used interchangeably with *military strategy;* unlike the modern Pentagon, I do not make any bureaucratic or semantic distinction between those two, since my goal is to keep language simple and clear.

In this book, I employ the term *grand strategy* to mean the big idea, or core theory of the case, for how the United States should ensure its security and promote its power. Others, such as Professor Joshua Rovner in his fine book on the subject, define grand strategy solely in relation to security. But my take on humans, and nations, is that they also seek power and influence, above and beyond what they may need just to be safe from attack by others. Certainly, that seems true of the United States historically.[6] Grand strategy involves much more than military instruments of national power. It also tends to be a general concept, as opposed to a detailed road map.

By contrast, *defense strategy* provides military tools for promoting that grand strategy in any period. Defense strategy encompasses military budgets, military personnel, force structures, deployments abroad, modernization strategies, warfighting concepts, and actual military operations, including in wars. I also define it to include the creation of specific treaty partners and obligations, as with NATO (North Atlantic Treaty Organization) or the U.S.-Japan or U.S.–South Korea alliances. Deciding when and where to risk American lives in the protection of overseas interests is a crucial matter where grand strategy meets the road of practical commitments.

Defense strategy may support grand strategy well or badly. The link between the two may be explicit or implicit, especially for the first two-thirds of the nation's history, when it was less common than today to issue formal strategies of either type.

Indeed, this book focuses less on formal documents and publicly announced or articulated strategies than it does on American behavior. Declared strategies often have purposes besides simply clarifying the nation's actual objectives. They can also be cheerleading documents or political tracts or public relations documents that explain how the country wishes its strategies to be understood rather than what they actually are. This is not to accuse U.S. policy makers of dishonesty. Rarely has the country deliberately dissembled about its core objectives in foreign policy. But rarely, too, have official American foreign policy documents been written for the exclusive purpose of laying out existing or intended strategies in the clearest possible light. And for the country's first 150-plus years, seldom were such documents written at all. Primarily in the post–World War II era has the country issued National Security Council memoranda, presidential decision documents, national security strategies, quadrennial defense reviews, national defense strategies, national military strategies, regional security strategies, and the like. As such, in this book, I am more interested in studying what the United States *does* on the global stage than in analyzing it what it says or claims it is doing. Economists talk about *revealed preference*—how an economic actor's actual behaviors in the marketplace give away its true priorities. Similarly, my focus here is on what might be called the revealed grand strategies and revealed defense strategies of the United States through history. Official documents contribute to understanding defense strategies, but they are not the same.

Defense strategy, comprising military budgets and modernization plans and force postures and war-fighting concepts, is the main subject of this book. But that strategy can be understood only in the context of broader grand strategy—of overarching national security goals and purposes. Both concepts thus receive considerable attention throughout these pages.[7] The emphasis, however, is on defense strategy. There is a large literature on American grand strategy, but less on the history of U.S. defense strategy in this more granular sense. It is in regard to that history that I hope this book will make its main contribution. In these pages, I also wrestle with the legacy of the so-called forever wars of the twenty-first century as well as the return to great power rivalry over the past one to two decades in ways that other books on the general subject, most written in earlier periods, could not.

GRAND STRATEGY AND DEFENSE STRATEGY IN AMERICA'S FIRST 250 YEARS

Once it had its independence, the United States benefited greatly from its location. In that sense, compared with other nations, it never really needed a *defense* strategy per se after 1783. No hostile foreign power ever credibly threatened to take away its original territory or its sovereignty. Once the American colonies won the Revolutionary War and became a nation, geography gave the new republic natural protection. With oceans to the east and west and big and nonaggressive territories that would later become Canada and Mexico to the north and south, geostrategically the nation was born with a silver spoon in its mouth. Yes, American blood has been shed numerous times on American soil since Yorktown in 1781. But the War of 1812 was likely avoidable, if the nation had really wanted to avoid it. The Civil War was terrible, but it consisted of Americans fighting Americans, so it was not really a defensive war. The wars of expansion of the nineteenth century were mostly conflicts brought on by Americans against others—Native Americans, Mexicans, Spaniards, Canadians. They consisted primarily of offensive, not defensive, uses of military force. The Pearl Harbor attacks in 1941 occurred, not because Japan wanted Hawaii for itself, but because Japan wanted to persuade the United States to let it act as it pleased in East Asia. Obviously, Americans would not oblige. The 9/11 attacks were a response to U.S. policy in the Middle East rather than an attempt by al Qaeda to defeat the United States comprehensively in war or to take any of its territory. In literal terms, the United States has not really needed a defense strategy. Its "defense" strategy has usually been one designed to expand the country and shape the world, not simply to protect the nation and its citizens in their homeland.

Indeed, U.S. defense strategy for the first half of the nation's history to date more resembled offense strategy, because the grand strategy that it served was one of expansionism. The esteemed late British strategist Colin Gray defined *military strategy* as "the use that is made of force and the threat of force for the ends of policy." Those ends centered on growing the country through the nineteenth century.[8] In the words of modern political science, the U.S. approach was akin to offensive realism—with the building up of American power the central goal. Yet America has never really been purely realist; it has always been ideological in its underlying motivations. Inspired by such concepts as Manifest Destiny that conflated the pursuit of territory and power for the young nation with the spreading of individual rights and democracy, U.S. grand strategy and defense strategy emanated from a sense of higher purpose, not just self-interest. For at least a historical moment, that attitude led Americans to be tempted to pursue empire—notably, with the taking of the Philippines in 1898—but for the most part, Americans did not find that they relished controlling overseas colonies. They were, however, enthusiastic about expansionism, and that expansionism succeeded dramatically, at least when measured against its goals. Moreover, it did so at very low cost. Leaving aside the Civil War, the U.S. military typically numbered only a few tens of thousands of federal soldiers, marines, and sailors, even as the nation's population grew into the many tens of millions during the nineteenth century.

Then, around the turn of the twentieth century and for the next forty years, the most frequent goal of U.S. grand strategy was to try to stay out of Eurasia's wars. This was largely a grand strategy of quasi-isolationism, or perhaps more precisely, regionalism (since the United States never really took a break from intervening in North and Central America militarily) that relied on America's geography to protect the country.[9] Of course, it failed catastrophically with the outbreak of the world wars and the ultimate decision of the United States to enter both. As such, grand strategy had to shift from quasi-isolationism to maximal interventionism, backed up by the world's greatest technological and manufacturing prowess.

Yet an important theme that emerges, when viewed through the prism of *defense strategy*, is that the peacetime quasi-isolationism was a matter of degree. Even in this period, the United States colonized the Philippines and kept a wary eye on any European or Asian powers that would seek too much advantage in the Americas or in East Asia. It began to develop strong military institutions. Its long-latent naval ambitions came increasingly to the fore, as it started to build a European-style blue-water navy. As its technology and industry grew in the late nineteenth and early twentieth centuries, the nation created the raw economic muscle that would allow it to pursue military might if and when it so chose. Indeed, in the prelude to the Pearl Harbor attack, Japanese admiral Isoruku Yamamoto was always wary that an awakened America—a country he knew well from earlier stints of study in the United States—could soon become a formidable adversary, given the nation's latent strengths and congenital assertiveness.[10]

Ultimately, of course, the United States twice failed to stay removed from conflict in Europe and East Asia. That peacetime defense spending was generally well under 1 percent of gross domestic product (GDP) was of little solace when it had to rise to some 14 percent in World War I and to some 35 percent of national economic output in World War II. Casualties were also very high in these wars—far higher than in any previous American war except the Civil War (even if considerably less than losses of the main belligerents in Europe and Asia).

In 1945, the United States may have hoped to return to relative minimalism in its national security policies. But by then, the country had undergone a profound transformation in how it saw its role in the world, as the scholar and strategist Stephen Wertheim has insightfully argued.[11] With this new strategic mindset established, the descent of the Iron Curtain in Europe soon disabused Americans of the thought that they could retreat back to their Western Hemispheric fortress yet again.

Since World War II, and especially since 1949–50, American grand strategy has sought to protect a community of generally like-minded allies, as well as the international "commons" of sea and airspace that are crucial for worldwide trade and investment. Yes, containment was a constant watchword of the grand strategy for forty years. But there has also been a more proactive and positive element of grand strategy ever since the end of World War II.

This stretch of continuity in grand strategy since World War II may be changing under President Donald Trump. Yet after his first full term in the White House, the main elements of the strategy had not changed even if much of the rhetoric around it clearly did. Trump remains a disruptive and potentially revolutionary national leader, to be sure, but as of this writing at least, he has not yet caused a revolution in American national security policy—or at least no systematic withdrawal from the world.

U.S. defense strategies have had global goals—and a global military footprint—for eighty years. The American armed forces cost the nation roughly

5–10 percent of GDP during most of the Cold War, and 3–5 percent of GDP ever since. At the broadest level, this grand strategy has succeeded: there has been no World War III and no need to hypermilitarize the American economy. But implementation of the grand strategy has been plagued by many failures of defense strategy, especially in Vietnam and Afghanistan, with a mediocre result to date in Iraq as well. U.S. casualties in these conflicts and in Korea did not reach the levels of the world wars or the Civil War, but they have reached well into the tens of thousands. There was a silver lining even in these failed efforts; by showing how hard it would fight in faraway places such as Vietnam and Afghanistan, the United States likely left little doubt in the minds of other would-be adversaries about its willingness to fight for more important interests in more strategic locations. The credibility of NATO, of the U.S.-Japan alliance, and of other security partnerships was buttressed by a United States that demonstrated resoluteness even when it could not muster successful wartime defense strategies.

In summary: expansionism, then quasi-isolationism or regionalism twice interrupted by world wars, then internationalism with forward engagement and interventionism. These are the three broad themes running through the annals of U.S. grand strategy, the three big ideas. They have determined the objectives of what various defense strategies would seek to achieve. Of these three themes, only the last has been largely altruistic, though perhaps it is more accurate to say that it has been informed by enlightened self-interest. It is also the only one that the country has consciously and forthrightly acknowledged. Expansionism and quasi-isolationism were never the declared grand strategies of the nation. No National Security Strategy codified them into formal doctrine in the way the United States now typically attempts to formalize contemporary grand strategy and then, within that broader framework, to derive and explain national defense strategy as well. In earlier eras, grand strategies needed to be inferred primarily from how the nation actually behaved and how it budgeted, built, postured, and modernized its armed forces and its alliances. Arguably, even today in a world rich in formal national security documents, America's grand strategy should be interpreted based more on what the country does than on what it says, though both words and deeds have importance.

DARING MIGHTY THINGS

I come away from this book project convinced that there has been a steadier strategic theme throughout U.S. history than I previously believed. This nation has always been restless, chomping at the bit, bursting at the seams, daring and doing mighty things. Some look at its history and see a long streak of isolationism, at least until World War II. Yes, isolationist currents have a long history in American foreign policy, and they may be strengthening again today.[12] But I am more struck by the American polity's consistent assertiveness on matters of national security. This intense energy and activism goes back to the Revolution itself. It then picked up steam again in the 1790s and animated the country's behavior throughout the nineteenth and twentieth centuries as well as the twenty-first century to date. The manifestations of that assertiveness have changed. However, the underlying national energy and ambition, and the willingness to use military power in pursuit of the country's goals spoken or unspoken, have not changed much at all. President Trump may wind up changing the country's long-standing commitment to alliances and the so-called rules-based liberal order; he will not, I predict, fundamentally change our proclivity toward activism and assertiveness.

America has never really been a status-quo country. Americans often tell ourselves that we are a peaceful people who prefer to stay out of world affairs unless we absolutely cannot avoid involvement, but this is not true.[13] Nor is this empirical reality a bad thing. The world would likely be a much less stable, democratic, and prosperous place had the United States really been an isolationist nation. But we need to know ourselves to make good decisions about future policy—and, sometimes, to restrain an itchy trigger finger (just as we should try to avoid the opposite strategic sin of isolationism).

I am skeptical that there is an American way of war—that is, a typical way the nation sends its men and women into combat, or a preferred type of fighting that correlates well with the American strategic character and culture and tends to produce the country's best outcomes. For example, some might claim that especially since becoming a large and industrialized nation, the United States has preferred to apply overwhelming or decisive force in traditional fights against other nations' militaries while doing less well in more diffuse counterinsurgency and stabilization wars. That is surely true to a degree. Operation Desert Storm to liberate Kuwait from Iraq in 1991 was an excellent example of the kind of war the United States prefers to fight, if fight it must. The protracted conflicts in Iraq and Afghanistan this century, by contrast, were operations that the United States and coalition partners handled less well. But there are numerous counterexamples. The Kosovo War of 1999, the rapid overthrow of the Taliban in conjunction with Northern Alliance indigenous forces in Afghanistan in 2001, the overthrow of Saddam Hussein in Iraq in 2003, the protracted intelligence-driven campaigns against al-Qaeda leadership early in the twenty-first century, and the more recent operations against ISIS in Iraq and Syria from roughly 2014 through 2019 featured more limited uses of force. Precision strikes, as well as excellent tactical war-fighting skills by American and allied forces, were more important than sheer mass. Moreover, with the remarkable surge in Iraq in 2007 and 2008, the United States showed that at least under certain conditions it could do very well in complex internal conflicts. These questions and others are considered in more depth in the Conclusion, where I summarize and draw on more than forty historical cases of peacetime and wartime defense strategies of the United States to tease out historical patterns and national proclivities.

The main chapters of this book take a chronological approach to understand the history of American defense strategy. They include two distinctive types of historical periods: those of war and those of relative peace. The goals of defense strategy during wartime were generally to win wars while minimizing costs and risks. The goals of defense strategy during peacetime have generally been, or at least should have been, to prevent future war but to be ready for conflict if it came anyway and to handle military missions short of major war effectively (since even in relative peacetime, America has rarely been peaceful). The chapters flow like this:

The Revolution and the Seeds of American Strategic Culture, 1775–1815
The Nineteenth Century and Expansionism
The Great Transformation: From Quasi-Isolationism to Internationalism, 1901–1945
The Cold War: From Primacy to Parity, Hyperactivism to Patience, 1946–1989
The Post–Cold War Era: From the End of History to Its Return, 1990–2014
The Return of Great Power Rivalry Since 2015

Thus, the first two chronological chapters address the eras of the nation's expansionism, as well as the creation of its foundational military institutions (the Marine Corps, Army, and Navy originally in 1775; the Department of War in 1789 and the separate Department of the Navy in 1798).[14] The third then covers the period of the nation's greatest strategic schizophrenia. The fourth, fifth, and sixth have been dominated by a combination of internationalism, engagement (including with forward-stationed American military forces in key littoral regions of Eurasia), and interventionism.

The final chapter of the book looks back and draws lessons. Perhaps the most important for defense strategy is this: the United States has a good record in war but far from an unblemished one; more than one-third of its defense strategies in major wars have failed in their main objectives, by my count. By contrast, the country's defense strategies in times of (relative) peace have been much more successful, when measured against what I argue are the three correct metrics for assessing such a defense strategy: deterrence of possible future war, quality of preparation for such major war should it occur anyway, and effectiveness in more limited military operations during the period in question. The United States tends to do better strategically when it keeps its powder dry. That is a sweeping generalization that cannot be a perfect guide to decision-making at all times, of course. But it is still a striking finding when America's 250-year military history is examined as a strategic whole.

And perhaps the central broad observation about grand strategy that emerges from the history is this: America and Americans are highly assertive on the global stage. The nation has dared mighty things and often achieved them. It has, in my view, been a major force for good in world affairs over the preponderance of its history. But it has rarely turned the other cheek. It has been at least as inclined toward offense as toward defense in making military strategy and policy. Its leaders *and* its people are a highly self-confident and highly activist bunch. These national strategic characteristics can produce much good; they can also be dangerous. We need to know ourselves well enough to understand the potential for both kinds of outcomes and to make judicious decisions about matters of war and peace with this self-awareness fully in mind.

CHAPTER II

The Revolution and Its Aftermath, 1775–1815

By 1797, George Washington had again hung up his public-service cleats and returned permanently to Mount Vernon—or so he thought. In fact, the nation would nearly call him back to action one more time, as it considered rebuilding a substantial federal army that he would again be asked to lead.

In those days, the United States and France were engaging in a quasi-war in the Caribbean, where privateers with Paris's blessing and encouragement were interrupting American shipping because it was seen as too helpful to Great Britain. (Naturally, Britain and France were again at war against each other.) So the United States not only resolved to build a significant navy but also considered reestablishing a full-fledged federal army with 10,000 or more troops as insurance against a hypothetical French invasion. No such standing federal army had been retained after the Revolutionary War was won during the previous decade. When President John Adams asked Washington to take command of that new army, the revered hero agreed to do so only on the condition that Alexander Hamilton would be his deputy (technically the inspector general, but effectively the army's field commander).[1]

Adams and Vice President Thomas Jefferson were horrified. Linked in the administration by the peculiarities of early American democracy that saw the runner-up for president awarded the nation's number-two position, they were rivals and agreed on little in those days (though they would later become famous long-distance pen pals before both dying on the same day, July 4, 1826). But unlike Washington—and also unlike many twenty-first-century American theater afficionados who worshipped the musical Hamilton*—the two men shared a contempt for Washington's protégé, whom they saw as vainglorious and even dangerous to the young republic. What, they feared, might Hamilton do with a splendid and well-resourced army if given the reins? Civilian control of the military was a work in progress in those early days of the United States, and it would be risky to entrust any such powerful force to the egotist Hamilton, they felt. He might use it against future insurrectionists in the States, the Spanish in Florida, or some other victim. Thus, when Adams saw the chance for peace with France in 1799, he jumped at it. The modest American naval buildup continued and wound up being useful for challenging the Barbary pirates during the Jefferson administration. But Adams nixed the idea of a substantial federal army and put Hamilton back in his place.*[2]

During the Revolution, American defense strategy went through three main phases. It began with an almost instinctual backlash against British power, especially in and around Boston in 1775. It then emphasized an unsuccessful attempt at direct defense and confrontation with Redcoats and Hessians, primarily in New York in 1776. And it then evolved into a much more successful form of flexible defense laced with elements of quasi-guerrilla warfare as well as opportunistic offense. This counterpunching approach, together with French intervention, produced success and independence for the thirteen colonies.

Once victorious, the country reverted to a minimalist type of military posture for a time. National security debates took a back seat to the more foundational debate about what kind of country Americans wanted to build together. In this period, Alexander Hamilton was a hero, arguing for a strong central bank and federal assumption of state debts from the Revolution. But debates over grand strategy as well as defense strategy intensified dramatically in the 1790s. The new nation would soon be fixated on the goals of expanding its own territory as well as its economy. Because contemporary Americans think of the natural borders of the country as the Atlantic and Pacific Oceans, plus Canada and Mexico, we often tend to think of the expansionism of the late eighteenth and nineteenth centuries as domestic policy. But at the time it was in fact foreign policy, of a sort, and constituted the foundation of the American defense debate for more than a century.[3]

THE BACKDROP TO THE AMERICAN REVOLUTION

The Revolutionary War was the main existential struggle in American history. The very creation of the United States hinged on its outcome. Only the Civil War, which threatened to divide the country in two, and World War II, which had the potential to rip the entire planet apart and perhaps even lead to a direct attack on the U.S. mainland if Adolf Hitler had realized his greatest dreams, could possibly claim to approach the same category of vital importance.

Yet at another level, the Revolutionary War was a war of choice. Patrick Henry's exhortation to "give me liberty or give me death" notwithstanding, the British were not mistreating most colonists so badly in the years leading up to April 1775, and they certainly were not threatening mass murder or genocide against them. Indeed, the colonists and the Crown had been joined in a common mission of territorial expansion in North America for decades by that point, with a sense of joint purpose.[4] The status quo was not so horrible, and the protagonists were not initially archenemies of each other. Even after open conflict broke out, many on both sides hoped it could be quickly contained. Thomas Paine's *Common Sense,* which made the case for independence, was written largely in 1775 and published in January 1776 because the debate over whether independence was even the right goal for the colonies continued even after the Battles of Lexington and Concord.[5] The escalation to all-out military and political battle did not really occur until the summer of 1776.

Nonetheless, the Revolutionary War ultimately did become a major life-and-death struggle. The ideological case for creating a new form of human government strengthened with time and made the conflict much more than a fight over self-rule, at least in the eyes and minds of many of the colonists.[6] It became a noble quest for a new kind of country and new empowerment of the human spirit.

Relative to the size of the country at that time, the conflict also became a big and bloody struggle. A substantial fraction of the adult population ultimately participated. Its costs were only a couple billion dollars in modern-day equivalent terms, but the burden on the emergent nation was considerable. So were the casualties.[7] Rebel fatalities may have totaled around 5,000 from the direct effects of combat, with many thousands more dying from disease, often when on prison ships after being captured.[8] The enemy, a combination of Redcoats, Hessians, other foreign mercenaries, and Loyalist colonists, probably suffered losses in that same general range.[9]

The thirteen colonies were lightly populated, and largely rural, meaning that the war would not be primarily one about taking and defending key cities.[10]

America was a vast land with a spread-out citizenry; its 2.5 million people numbered less than a fourth of the population of the British Isles.[11] Most of the colonies in New England and the mid-Atlantic region resembled their namesake states of today in size and shape. But Maine and Vermont did not yet exist, and Florida was still held by Spain. Virginia as well as Georgia and both Carolinas extended all the way to the Mississippi, though western regions were sparsely settled.[12]

The weaponry of the day featured muskets and artillery, as well as sailing ships with heavy cannons. Rebel forces often struggled to have enough weaponry and ammunition, but they developed supply lines from France and elsewhere that ultimately sufficed.[13] The opposing armies were large but not enormous. Rebel troop strength, including militias plus regular army, may have peaked at around 40,000, with a total of 100,000 or more colonists fighting against the British at some point during the war.[14] Railroads and the telegraph did not yet exist; communications were often carried out by horseback. Most soldiers excepting cavalry (or "dragoons") moved by foot, though supply trains were often pulled by horse.

THE EVOLUTION OF STRATEGY

When the war began in 1775, the colonies had no defense strategy to guide them. How could they? The war was barely expected. Certainly, its likely longevity and character were unforeseen. The idea that a simmering struggle between the Crown and colonists in which a few lives here and there had been lost during the early 1770s would explode into an all-out war lasting years and killing thousands would prove an enormous shock. In the war's early months, there were still hopes for a negotiated peace of some sort, reflected in the initial reluctance of the colonists to build a sizable standing army with long-term enlistments.[15] Independence was not declared until fifteen months into the fighting. The grand strategists of the conflict in the Continental Congress and the Continental Army, especially George Washington, would need time to develop their ideas about how to fight the war.

Indeed, that Continental Army was very much a work in progress throughout the war. It was preceded, and outnumbered, by the combined strength of the colonies' state and local militias. Military conscription was instituted by some colonies but was plagued with abuses, evasions, and workarounds. Leaders including General Washington were often frustrated with the quality of their troops, especially in the war's early stages.[16] Successful ways of fighting the

British for this initially ragtag aggregation of rebel fighters had to be developed over the long revolution—especially its first two and a half years. America's Founders are often lionized for their political vision and for the republic they built, founded on the Declaration of Independence and the Constitution they wrote. All that is as it should be. But led by Washington, and with key input from other military leaders including Charles Lee and Horatio Gates and Nathanael Greene and others, they also collectively felt their way to one of the best military paradigms in the nation's history over those years, employing savvy combinations of insurgent, defensive, and offensive warfare.[17] They did lots of hit-and-run fighting and lots of ambushing, frequently avoiding big open-field confrontations after the tragic Battle of New York in 1776. Yet they also did well in a number of other big battles, when the time and place and geography were right—especially at Saratoga in the early fall of 1777 and Yorktown in the early fall of 1781, but also near the Delaware River in late 1776–early 1777, at Monmouth, New Jersey, in June 1778, and at Cowpens and Guilford Courthouse in the Carolinas toward war's end.[18]

As noted, the basic American approach to the Revolution went through three main strategies. It began as resistance in and around Boston. Next, after the British regrouped and repositioned, the rebels tried their collective hand at open-field fighting and large force-on-force engagements in and around New York City in the summer and early fall of 1776. That period did not go well for Washington and his troops. Then, after realizing that he could not defend New York or Philadelphia or any other single point where the British might attack, Washington gradually shifted priority to the survival of his army, with the ultimate goal of using the colonies' vast territorial expanses as sanctuary in which militias and armies could grow and hide and find sustenance—while also awaiting their chances to deliver violence. Washington began to figure that concept out at the very end of 1776. By Saratoga the next fall, this strategy was well established and promised the way to ultimate victory and independence.

That first defense strategy, resistance against British operations and positions in and near Boston, worked better than might have been expected. The rebel performance at Lexington and Concord on April 19, 1775, was pitched and passionate. Once their fighting retreat back to Boston was done, the British all told wound up losing nearly 300 of their 1,800-strong force to casualties or capture.[19] In late spring at Breed's Hill next to Bunker Hill, just north of Boston on the Charlestown peninsula, the rebels established a position on June 16. They were forced to give it up the next day—but again, they made the British suffer a severe cost, with some 1,000 out of roughly 2,500 British troops winding up as casualties. (Losses were also heavy for the rebels, but substantially fewer, at around 400 out of their initial strength of around 1,000.) Even in tactical defeat, therefore, the patriots gained a further boost of morale and confidence.[20] Around the same time, the Continental Congress created the Continental Army, placed George Washington in command, and authorized a strength of ten companies of soldiers (totaling perhaps a couple thousand troops) to accompany various state militias supporting the rebel cause. Many British had doubted the tenacity and fighting prowess of the colonists, as well as their ability to find strong leaders amid their ranks—but the doubters were beginning to be proven wrong.[21]

Not everything would go the rebels' way in the early going. In particular, rebel forays into Canada failed badly. Moving northward along the Lake Champlain axis in the west and Maine in the east, rebel forces numbering around 1,000 sought to use this pincer approach to take Montreal and then Quebec. Perhaps that would be enough to convince those living in the future Canada to join the anti-British fight.[22] The rebels succeeded in the Montreal part of the plan. However, when attacking Quebec during a snowstorm on December 31, 1775, American forces under General Richard Montgomery and Colonel Benedict Arnold were unable to defeat the British defenders. General Montgomery was killed in the action, Benedict Arnold was wounded, and the assaulting party suffered a major defeat. For the rest of that winter and the following spring, rebel forces sought to strengthen their ranks with reinforcements from the colonies, in the hope of attacking again. Alas, enough British and Hessians arrived to keep the balance favorable to the Crown. The great Canadian adventure was not to be. Ultimately, the rebel forces gave up their efforts to take Quebec, relinquished their positions in Montreal and elsewhere, and returned home.[23]

But the rebels regained momentum back in Boston in the early spring of 1776. The cold and snow and ice of New England allowed artillery from Fort Ticonderoga on Lake Champlain to be sledded all the way to Boston. Forces under General Washington quickly and stealthily placed them in improvised fortifications on Dorchester Heights, south of Boston, on the night of March 4, 1776. That brought rebel cannons within range of British positions and ships. Understanding his predicament, British general William Howe chose to relocate rather than fight. He departed with his troops and some Loyalists for Nova Scotia on March 17, where he spent the spring receiving reinforcements from Britain, building up his forces, and planning his next move.[24]

To ascribe the lofty term *strategy* to what the rebels were doing in these early stages of the war would be a stretch. What they were doing was shooting at the bad guys wherever they found them, with whatever weapons and in whatever formations they could. To be sure, there was some chance that these early wins could have produced an overall victory, if London had quickly decided that the costs of combat were not worth the stakes. But that was an unlikely prospect. Beyond pushing Howe out of Boston, the rebels did not really have a military plan yet. First would have to come a political decision about objectives. That would be settled soon, with the Declaration of Independence in early July 1776, fifteen months into the fight. But then they would have to develop a viable military means of achieving that independence.

After their defeat in Boston in early 1776, the British developed a bit of a plan themselves. Their focus turned to New York City by summer of that year, starting with Long Island and then moving to Manhattan. There, they would proceed to rout Washington and his forces in several significant battles, then chase the rebels southward through New Jersey, as Washington and the Continentals fled for their lives.

The British would eventually also employ other forces, some going northward from New York and others heading southward from Canada, to try to establish control of the Hudson River and the broader Lake Champlain region. The goals in New York City and New Jersey were largely to destroy rebel armies while seizing choice real estate that could serve as a staging base for their armies and navies. The goal in upstate New York was to sever New England from the rest of the colonies out of a belief that, since New England was the hotbed of revolution, isolating it would fundamentally weaken the rebels. If that could be achieved, they hoped, rebels to the south, animated by less revolutionary fervor than the New Englanders, might give up the fight. London always held out hope in this phase of the fight that many if not most colonists were in fact Loyalists and could be persuaded to come back around to support the Crown with the right mix of incentives (and the right dose of iron knuckles). Such was Britain's strategic thinking. At the tactical and campaign levels of warfare, the Crown also hoped that it could translate its superior naval capabilities into an ability to control coastal cities in the colonies and employ its superior armies to decimate the colonists' forces on the fields of battle. It was partially right about the first advantage but ultimately wrong about the second.[25]

In this 1776 phase of the war, Washington chose direct defense mixed with some direct attack as the essence of his military strategy. Total British manpower in the New York area under General Howe would soon reach 45,000, including soldiers, Hessians, and sailors. Having guessed correctly that the British would target New York, General Washington had brought some 20,000 men to the region.[26] But Washington got most other things wrong—not only in overall defense strategy but in tactical decision-making about where and how to set up his forces and engage the enemy in battle. John Adams wryly and rightly observed, "In general, our generals were outgeneraled."[27]

Fortunately, Washington and his fellow officers started to learn. As Washington biographer Ron Chernow put it, these defeats "had shown [Washington] the futility of trying to defend heavily fortified positions along the seaboard and forced him out into the countryside, where he had mobility and where the British Army, deprived of the Royal Navy, operated at a disadvantage."[28] Perhaps he drew from his experience in fighting the French and Indian War in the 1750s, learning certain methods from the Native Americans.[29] By late 1776, Washington was starting to think about tactics, campaigns, and strategy differently.

After the defeats in New York, by December 1776, Washington and his rebel forces reached Trenton on the east side of the Delaware River. There, they confiscated all the boats they could find to deprive the British of a timely means of crossing the river—buying themselves a few weeks until its waters froze. They hoped to protect themselves while also potentially shielding the city of Philadelphia (though out of caution, on December 13 the Continental Congress temporarily relocated from Philadelphia to Baltimore anyway).

As British forces reached the vicinity and considered their options, Washington struck, in what amounted to the beginning of a new phase of the war. This rebel brand of fighting would seek to avoid open-field combat except when specific opportunities for attack arose.[30] Washington sent some of his force across the Delaware back to the New Jersey side on Christmas night, leading to the first Battle of Trenton on December 26. Washington did it again a few days later, leading to the second Battle of Trenton on January 2, 1777. After that second successful offensive, rather than retreat across the Delaware yet again to return to Pennsylvania territory, Washington snuck around British forces, going north and east to strike a garrison at Princeton on January 3.[31]

The blend of defense, evasive action, and opportunistic offense would not always work for the rebels. With the return of warm weather, British forces returned to New York, then loaded up on ships to sail southward all the way to the Chesapeake Bay. Once inside the bay, they sailed northward, disembarked, and started to march on Philadelphia. All of that took a while, but by September, the British neared Philadelphia. And Washington came out to meet them in what became the Battle of Brandywine. Alas, it quickly became another clear British win. Rebel casualties wound up at about 900, while British losses were around 550. Philadelphia fell to the British later that same month. Luckily for Washington and the rebels, the British victory was far from decisive. Philadelphia was of limited importance (as the British realized the next year when they withdrew); Washington also managed to save much of his army despite the defeat.[32]

Washington's approach at Brandywine—accepting a big force-on-force fight—was not so brilliant. But the turning point of the war was about to take place in central New York, at Saratoga. The famous battle there was the culmination of campaigns that had developed over the preceding summer. In June 1777, British general John Burgoyne started to move southward from Canada, boasting a total force just shy of 10,000 personnel (and wagons full of creature comforts for himself). He had his eye on taking Albany. There, he hoped to rendezvous with Redcoats moving northward along the Hudson from New York City, giving the British full control of the water system of Lake Champlain–Lake George–the Hudson River from Canada to New York City. He hoped that a third British force coming from Lake Ontario and points westward might even contribute as well. But as the summer unfolded, Burgoyne found himself unable to handle all the challenges of the complex topography of the region, including rebel ambushes and delaying tactics that made good use of the hills, forests, lakes, and marshes (rebels often felled trees to block paths, for example). Patriot ranks were strengthened by various militias over the spring and summer. Washington had recognized the importance of the theater for the overall war and directed reinforcements as well as some of his best commanders to the effort.[33] Burgoyne, by contrast, did not get help. British forces approaching from the west, often aided by Native Americans from various tribes of the Iroquois Nation (who fought mostly but not entirely on the British side), petered out. Nor did Burgoyne get help from the south. Because General Howe had taken some 15,000 Redcoats out of the overall troop strength the British had based in New York City to pursue Washington and Philadelphia, British general Henry Clinton had only about 7,000 troops (and unclear instructions) to draw on when he sailed up the Hudson.[34] His midsize force never was able to make it more than about halfway up the Hudson, turning back well short of Albany.[35]

Alone, stuck deep in the American hinterland, and increasingly encircled, Burgoyne still attacked—at Freeman's Farm and Bemis Heights, near Saratoga—in mid-September and mid-October 1777, respectively. Rebel forces under General Horatio Gates made good use of the natural terrain, combined with smart defensive tactics, to stymie the British. Isolated and low on provisions, the British ultimately surrendered on October 17.[36] This ability to turn defense and ambush into opportunistic offense had become a key element of the new American strategy.

With the win at Saratoga, the Americans had established military momentum. They also now gained political and strategic momentum. Early in 1778, France would join the war in support of the rebels.[37] By June 1778, Britain and France were formally at war with each other. That meant the British now had other things to worry about in other places. So they decided to vacate Philadelphia and return to New York. Rebel forces, learning of the British retrograde action, set out in pursuit from Valley Forge. The result was the Battle of Monmouth on June 28. It was effectively fought to a draw, but that was better than what had happened in New York or at Brandywine. By now, Washington was better at picking when and where and how to fight. In addition, the Continental Army had improved technically, largely due to drilling under the tutelage of the Prussian Baron von Steuben at Valley Forge over the preceding winter.[38] With France in the war, fighting to a draw was not such a bad overall outcome. The battle also permanently solidified support for General Washington's military leadership throughout the young United States.[39]

So by this point, American defense strategy had reached its third phase and would not change again. But it would play out in one new theater in the British southern campaign. There, in 1780, London initiated a major operation under General Charles Cornwallis that it hoped would inspire and empower Loyalist subjects of the king. A similar theory had not worked out so well up north. But perhaps it could work in the Carolinas and Georgia—and then spread northward, even? With a new southern campaign, the British also hoped to deprive the fledgling United States of access to ports and tighten the economic squeeze on the rebellious colonies.

It started out well for the Crown. Rebel forces in Charleston under General Benjamin Lincoln were ultimately trapped and forced to surrender on May 12, 1780. Some 5,500 rebels were taken prisoner, the most to be captured on the American side in a single engagement during the entire war. As spring and summer unfolded, British forces built on this initial coastal success and established a series of outposts throughout much of South Carolina.[40]

But with their mix of defense, evasiveness, and offense, rebel forces would first survive, then defeat the British in the south. The momentum shifted in October 1780, at the Battle of Kings Mountain near Charlotte, North Carolina. The rebels, under General Nathanael Greene, also benefited from a topography of forests, swamps, and rivers that many of them, as locals, knew well.[41] Then British forces caught up with a large chunk of rebel forces, resulting in the

Battle of Cowpens, South Carolina, in January 1781. But Daniel Morgan's rebel forces employed excellent tactics, including multiple disguised fighting positions and feigned retreats, as well as the clever and timely use of horse cavalry to complement infantry. The British suffered "a devil of a whipping," in Morgan's memorable phrase.[42] British forces did a bit better at Guilford Courthouse, North Carolina, in March, where rebel forces ultimately retreated. But at a strategic level, the outcome was another setback for the British, since casualties were considerable on both sides and Cornwallis could not easily replace his fallen troops.

Then Cornwallis decided to give it a try in Virginia in May 1781. Unfortunately for him, General Washington as well as his French counterparts the Marquis de Lafayette and the Comte de Rochambeau had figured out what Cornwallis was up to—and how he might be boxed in. They sent ground reinforcements to pin Cornwallis down; Admiral François de Grasse of the French navy was directed to bottle off possible escape routes on the Chesapeake Bay. With their 17,000 troops providing roughly a two-to-one advantage in ground strength, and boasting naval superiority as well, these combined French-American forces then lay siege to the British position in the Battle of Yorktown. Cornwallis was ultimately forced to surrender his 8,000-strong forces to Washington on October 19, 1781, in what proved the last big battle of the war.

The evolution of colonist/American strategy during the Revolutionary War was impressive. As famed historian Russell Weigley argued in *The American Way of War,* Washington was both a traditionalist and an innovator. He really wanted to command a classic army, in organization, training, and even tactics. Yet he also came to realize that his strategic approach had to be largely defensive.[43] In addition, his available forces would be largely militia of uneven and generally rough-hewed ability. He and his forces did fine in New England in 1775 and into early 1776. But they were battered in New York in the summer and early fall of 1776—and much of it was Washington's fault.

However, Washington was a learner. Running barely ahead of British pursuit from New York toward Philadelphia in the fall of 1776, Washington gradually figured out how to combine an overarching campaign of withdrawal with limited, tactical offensives. The key early successes were in the crossings of the Delaware in the last days of 1776 and first of 1777. With his smallish and often ragged forces, Washington knew he could not win big slugfests against the British. That meant he could not protect the colonies' major cities or even reliably win major engagements fighting on the tactical defensive. He had to be elusive, cherishing the survival of his army more than the territory or people he was protecting—even as he continually sought to turn that army into a more professional, disciplined, seasoned force throughout the war.[44]

In these basic strategic approaches, Washington had some commonalities with twentieth-century proponents of people's war and insurgency such as Mao Zedong and Ho Chi Minh—and with Fabius Maximus of ancient Rome.[45] So did other rebel leaders—Nathanael Greene, Francis Marion, Daniel Morgan.[46]

Over 250 years, the United States has had a number of major military accomplishments and victories. But for panache, creativity, adaptability, and ultimate importance for the nation, few rival the American Revolution, and few military leaders rival Washington.

AFTER THE WAR

Once the war was over, entirely new security issues emerged for the young nation. The American grand strategy amounted to expansionism first and foremost—just as it would throughout most of the nineteenth century. Yet grand strategy also included an element of vigilance toward the European powers, with the United States trying not to be taken advantage of by any of them, especially Britain and France at various times, yet also attempting to avoid involvement in their messy and often highly militarized affairs.

To begin to understand the country's sequence of events after 1783, there is no better place to start than with George Washington. Even after the Revolution was won, he made at least two more crucial contributions to the nation's early traditions on strategic culture. First, like the ancient Roman Cincinnatus, he resigned his commission, put down his sword, and went back to his plow. Indeed, he also went back to his compass as well as his sextant, not only devoting energies to his farm at Mount Vernon but exploring in westward directions on a major mission in 1784 (animated by interest in his personal properties "out west" and by the idea of a grand waterway project that might someday connect the East and the Potomac River to the Great Lakes region and the Mississippi River).[47] Washington like many other ambitious Americans was thinking of power, to be sure, but power measured in territory and economic development in the first instance, rather than military strength. If such a famous general as Washington, having defeated the mighty British and become world famous in the process, could choose civilian and commercial interests over military rank and power, that would speak volumes about where the nation would direct its passions and purpose in the years and decades to come. If the general with the most impressive winning streak on the planet saw America's interior as more interesting than its potential power projection activities to the north, south, or east, that would do much to shape America's "grand strategy."[48]

Second, Washington stayed true to the idea that while the federal government needed to be strong enough to hold together and protect the union, it must adamantly avoid the proclivities of the Old World. His Farewell Address of 1796 contained the following important passage: "Hence, likewise, they will avoid the necessity of those overgrown military establishments which, under any form of government, are inauspicious to liberty, and which are to be regarded as particularly hostile to republican liberty. In this sense it is that your union ought to be considered as a main prop of your liberty, and that the love of the one ought to endear to you the preservation of the other."[49] In other words, Washington saw large standing militaries as a threat to the internal health of the nation—indeed, to the very idea of America. A country that prioritized military spending and military forces over other matters would centralize power, use that power to embark on pointless adventures abroad, and most of all, subvert its own national character and weaken its commitment to the protection of the rights of the individual.

Of course, it would not prove quite as simple as disarming and ignoring the outside world.[50] Washington might warn against permanent alliances, Jefferson against entangling alliances, but permanent peace, with European powers or others, could not be taken for granted, either.[51] Tensions would remain with Britain, especially until the signing of Jay's Treaty in 1794 (with ratification to follow the next year)—about the time when tensions would start to grow with France. Indeed, foreign policy wound up dominating a good chunk of Washington's second term as president. That was not quite what he had expected when persuaded to run for reelection.[52] (Tensions with Britain would of course come back in the early nineteenth century, leading to the War of 1812.)[53]

Sensing that it would prove challenging to prevent the United States, like other countries, from becoming militaristic, the founders apportioned powers between the Congress and the Executive to create a system of mutual restraints. Hence the system of checks and balances that: (1) described Congress's powers before those of the Executive (Congress being the focus of Article I, the Executive Branch of Article II); (2) gave Congress power of the purse and the rights and responsibilities to raise armies and maintain navies; and (3) gave Congress exclusive power to declare war, by the mechanism of majority vote in each house.

Otherwise, during these early years of the Republic and through at least Washington's first term as president, most military matters were of secondary importance. Other debates for the new nation mattered more, largely those centered on war debt, on federal revenue, and on the strength of the central government. Ultimately, Alexander Hamilton and company won the debate in favor of federal acceptance of state debt as reflected in the Assumption Act of 1790. These "Federalists" also succeeded in creating a strong national bank and the Treasury Department; the feds now had powers of taxation as well as the sole prerogative to issue currency within the United States.[54] From a long-term national security perspective, these decisions about finance and about the nature of the union were absolutely crucial as Americans determined what kind of nation they would build.

These financial matters also had more immediate security implications. Objections to taxes led in some cases to resistance. Shays' Rebellion in western Massachusetts in 1787 was in large part a response to Massachusetts taxes; suppressing it required the call-up of state militia and led to several battlefield deaths. It was fortunate that this operation did not require much if anything in the way of federal forces, since there were few to be found on American soil.[55] What remained of a U.S. Army amounted to fewer than 1,000 soldiers in all, manning forts along the East Coast and in the western territories, where fighting with Native Americans was common (and where Britain did not quickly evacuate some of the positions it had previously held, raising the specter of a renewal of conflict with the former colonial power). As the Shawnee (or Northwest) Confederacy of Native American tribes strengthened and had battlefield success against settlers in the late 1780s and early 1790s, the army was doubled in size. Under General Anthony Wayne, it was more successful in combat, including at the Battle of Fallen Timbers in 1794. That led to the Treaty of Greenville in 1795 that gave lands in what are now Ohio, Indiana, Illinois, and Michigan to the United States.[56] Expansionism as a defining feature of American policy was alive and well. But doubling a force of fewer than 1,000 soldiers still did not make for much of a federal army.

Nor was there a remaining navy, since Revolutionary War ships had been dispensed with.[57] Indeed, the Navy effectively ceased to exist until 1794, when six frigates were authorized for just under $700,000 (some $20 million in today's dollars).[58] The authorizing legislation makes for an entertaining read and should perhaps provide some solace to modern-day Department of Defense officials who believe that contemporary Congresses have developed a tendency to micromanage. Not only did the Congress of 1794 appropriate funds for the ships, but it specified their exact crew sizes and composition, and even the rations allowed each sailor (a few highlights: four ounces of cheese on Mondays, six ounces of molasses on Wednesdays, and a quart of beer daily unless distilled spirits were available instead!).[59] Three of the frigates would be completed promptly. They constituted the fledgling U.S. naval capability that would be employed against French-sponsored privateers in the Caribbean at the very end of the decade (and then again by President Jefferson against Barbary pirates early in the following century).[60]

The showdown with France was remarkable given the crucial French role in helping the United States gain its independence from Britain just a decade before. By the late 1790s, France had had a revolution, and the United States had also reached a fuller peace accord, the Jay Treaty, with Britain. Moreover, France and Britain were again at loggerheads with each other. All of that led, in 1798, to what President Adams called a "half war" against France—otherwise known as the "quasi war"—since Paris authorized and abetted privateers in the Caribbean to attack American shipping (because some of it was helping France's nemesis). Thus the renewed U.S. interest in developing a navy, as well as better coastal defenses, to deal with the French threat. (Earlier increases in naval budgets in the 1790s were originally motivated by the Barbary pirates in the Mediterranean Sea and eastern Atlantic, not France or Britain.)[61] Overall, the U.S. Navy soon totaled more than fifty vessels of various shapes and sizes.[62] A separate Department of the Navy was created during Adams's presidency (to go along with the existing Department of War), and the U.S. Marine Corps was reestablished to deploy on the new ships.[63]

For a while in this period, the U.S. government even seemed inclined to build a substantial army with at least 10,000 soldiers. President Adams went so far as to ask George Washington to come out of retirement to command that new federal army, as noted before. Thankfully for Adams, before this effort could progress very far, he was able to conclude a peace with France that made the army unnecessary for the moment. That latter development was much to the chagrin of Washington's number two in command, Alexander Hamilton, and other uber-federalists who, as noted at the beginning of this chapter, might have had various ideas in mind for how to use such an army (perhaps taking Florida from Spain?!). Hamilton actually wound up the highest-ranking general in the U.S. military after Washington again stepped down, for a few months—though Adams chose not to designate him commanding general of the army.[64] The Hamilton-Adams relationship became highly acrimonious, even though they were both Federalists.[65] Indeed, vigorous debate, often highly personal and bitter, characterized the nation's politics as well as its national security policies from early days.

Michigan senator Arthur Vandenberg, in a famous speech from 1947, argued that politics should stop at the water's edge.[66] But that has rarely described the reality of American foreign policy-making. And it certainly did not describe the 1790s.

Even if no large central army would be built, federal powers over land forces would grow in the 1790s. The Whiskey Rebellion of 1791–94 in western Pennsylvania and continued danger in the nation's western frontiers contributed to the strategic and political pressure. Legislation including the Uniform Militia Act of 1792, the Calling Forth Act of 1792, and a revised Calling Forth Act of 1795 strengthened the president's authorities to use state militia for various national purposes. Yet federal combat capability remained minimal. Even Washington's modest ideas from the early 1780s for a standing federal force of some 2,600 soldiers failed to come to fruition.[67]

BARBARY PIRATES IN DISTANT WATERS AND EARLY-CENTURY DEFENSE POLICY

The United States had on-again, off-again problems with pirates from West Africa and the Mediterranean through the 1790s and into the 1800s. They were minor in one sense. But they foreshadowed bigger debates over the American navy that would intensify in the decades to come.

Raiding by the Barbary pirates, based out of the statelets of Morocco, Algiers, Tunis, and Tripoli, against American shipping had led to the decision in 1794 to build six frigates for the U.S. Navy; construction of half of them was suspended for a time once an accord ended the raiding in 1796. But as noted, the quasi-war with France brought back the imperative for greater naval capability.

Resumption of Barbary predatory behavior in the early years of the new century led President Jefferson to send a raiding party to the Mediterranean. He did so again in following years, by then armed with legislation passed in early 1802 by which Congress encouraged such action (though just as in 1798 regarding the quasi-war with France, Congress did not actually declare war).[68] This set of congressional actions established a precedent, to become common after World War II, whereby Congress would take action short of a formal declaration of war to authorize an American president to use force.

Jefferson's commanders were armed not just with greater congressional authorities but also with a healthy mix of combat ships to blockade Tripoli. Their coercive efforts resulted in a settlement, achieved in 1805 by Commodore John Rodgers. The resulting accord included ransom to free American hostages previously kidnapped, but no further tribute.[69] The fights were more on the scale of skirmishes than major battles at sea, with casualty totals often in the low dozens or so, but these faraway fights kept naval matters on American minds and set the stage for bigger naval debates—and ambitions—in the nation's future.[70]

The successful use of naval power to protect American shipping rights did not, however, imply or create a major consensus in favor of a naval buildup anytime soon. Jefferson's own real vision for an American navy was, in keeping with his overall political philosophy, different from those of Adams or other Federalists. The third American president favored a navy dominated by more than 200 gunboats that could defend American ports, swarming to counter any unfriendly battleships that might enter American waters but otherwise posing little to no capacity for open-ocean or other faraway operations themselves. Many of these were built. Meanwhile, any progress toward a bigger navy with larger ships—frigates and "ships of the line" (with as many as seventy-four guns)—was effectively suspended under both Jefferson and his successor, President James Madison.[71] As historian Adam Millett trenchantly put it about the period leading up to the War of 1812, "Of military preparations there were none of consequence, since Congress was divided on the wisdom of war."[72]

As for the federal army, it typically did not exceed 3,000 to 4,000 soldiers in total during the first few decades of the new republic and was, as noted, even smaller than that in the late 1700s. Only on the eve of the outbreak of the War of 1812 did it climb even toward 6,000 troops.[73]

THE WAR OF 1812

Most Americans today, when asked about the War of 1812, have a hard time explaining what it was about, what caused it, or which side actually won. That is for good reason. Its causes were murky; its outcomes were, in historical perspective, relatively unnoteworthy.

But the War of 1812 provides powerful evidence in support of my main observation in this book about the American strategic character—its highly assertive and self-confident nature throughout the nation's history, all the way up until today. Picking a fight with the world's number-one power was not for the fainthearted. Yet that is exactly what the young United States did. Yes, it had real grievances with Britain. But the grievances were not existential, and they were not beyond the power of diplomacy to address.

Whatever the war's proximate causes, there were those who sought to transform it into a conflict with grand purposes and outcomes. Some Americans wanted to take Canada from Britain, pushing the former colonial master out of North America once and for all. Some British may have dreamed about reversing the outcome of the Revolutionary War. The British Empire was far from over at this point in history and was in fact still growing. And after the defeat of Napoleon in Europe in 1814, the British were poised for a dominant century from Africa to India and beyond. The fact that the war petered out was not foreordained, given the capacities of the powers involved in the fight.

The war was intense at times, though most of its geographic scope was rather limited.[74] The United States lost somewhat more than 2,000 killed in action, with several thousand more wounded, out of a population of something more than 7 million.[75] It eventually fielded about 35,000 soldiers in the regular army and another 35,000 in state militias that were called to federal service during the war.[76]

The war broke out after a period in which the British carried out a policy of impressment—stopping American ships on the high seas to force American sailors to crew its naval vessels. London had also imposed tariffs and boycotts against American commerce. After all, the Americans were trading with—and thereby helping—France, as Napoleon sought to dominate much of Europe. In American eyes, they were simply staying out of silly European wars while they tried to practice their innate right of conducting commerce and pursuing prosperity; to Britain, they were aiding and abetting the enemy.

Yet the conflict was avoidable. Many of the offending British policies that caused American anger were lifted by a new British government just before Congress voted, at President Madison's request, to declare war.[77] But by that time, war fervor ran strong in America, at least in some sectors. Moreover, the British change in policy was not immediately known in the United States since undersea telegraph did not yet exist. As such, Britain's change of policy came too late to defuse the crisis.[78] Once Americans realized they had a diplomatic option to end the crisis, they were no longer interested in invoking it.

Whatever confidence the Americans might have felt, based on the growth and development of their nation, was not justified by the state of military preparations, however. Several decades later, historian Henry Adams wrote, "No serious preparations for war had yet been made when the war began."[79] The British seagoing fleet outnumbered America's by roughly 600 to 16, for example.[80] That lack of initial preparedness would prove to be a consistent theme in much if not most American history, especially through 1941.

Despite the war fervor in some swaths of the country, the War of 1812 was controversial at home. The Federalist Party, and with it much of the region of New England, was strongly against the war. Votes on the declaration of war were by far the closest of any such votes in American history: 79–49 in the House, 19–13 in the Senate. Indeed, the skepticism would prove justified in some ways. The Treaty of Ghent ending the conflict in 1814 left things essentially as they had been before the war, in terms of policies and territorial boundaries, making the fighting seem largely pointless. Importantly, however, impressment did cease after the war.[81]

There were perhaps four main military campaigns—that is, sequences of events and operations over a given period and geographic region, in pursuit of strategic goals—during this war.[82] None reflected major changes or innovations in defense strategy, weaponry, or tactics. As such, their place in the broader story of this book is of limited consequence. But it is still worth understanding the basic sequencing of events.

The first campaign occurred from the general region of Detroit to Lake Champlain. Fighting along this axis took place throughout the war. There were some noteworthy battles, such as Oliver Hazard Perry's victory for the Americans in the Battle of Lake Erie on September 10, 1813.[83] In this fighting, the United States tried to seize parts of British-controlled Canada—at a minimum, to gain leverage against Britain for any postwar settlement, but for some including Kentucky senator Henry Clay, perhaps even to keep permanently. Even today, a Canadian government website contains the following depiction of the campaign along the U.S.-Canada border: "Believing it would be easy to conquer Canada, the United States launched an invasion in June 1812. The Americans were mistaken."[84] Touché! A combination of Canadian volunteers, Native Americans, and British soldiers fended off the invasion.

The second campaign took place at sea. Again, this did not constitute, on either side, a major evolution in the conduct of warfare. Most of the action took place in Atlantic waters near U.S. coasts. Sometimes the engagements were farther out at sea. When Napoleon abdicated in the spring of 1814, Britain devoted more assets to the campaign.

At this point, London also decided to launch raids along the Eastern Seaboard in what could be described as a third campaign. Those included the burning of the White House and Congress in August 1814 as well as the subsequent failed attack on Baltimore that led to the writing of "The Star-Spangled Banner" in September. (The same Canadian government information website depicts the torching of Congress and the White House as retaliation for U.S. attacks on Toronto the year before.) Through these operations, the British sought to impose economic pain on the United States, threaten the government, and instill a more general fear in the population. But given the size and scale of the United States, the overall impact of operations was not enough to win the war.[85]

The fourth campaign took place in the South and involved additional British attempts at raiding coastal regions. It culminated in Andrew Jackson's historic and decisive defense of New Orleans in early 1815 that tied a nice bow on an otherwise inconclusive conflict and set Jackson up for an eventual run for president. However, and perhaps fittingly given the confused character of this conflict, that victory technically came after the war was over. The two sides had already agreed to terms by the time of the battle, even if the word had not yet reached the belligerents in Louisiana.[86]

With the end of this war, the United States stopped fighting the major powers of Europe for a while. And it gained a greater self-confidence as well, despite the lack of tangible gains to show for the three years of combat. That the Americans could hold their own against the British on the North American landmass should have been no huge surprise, since they had done so (albeit with French help) some three decades before, at a time when the country was smaller and weaker. Alexander Hamilton had never been able to pursue his dreams of leading a big American army against Spain in Florida or in Louisiana, but Jefferson had managed as president to acquire the Louisiana Purchase from France, roughly doubling the country's size. The United States was also now three times as populous as at the time of the Revolution. So success in ground fighting was not a shock. However, that the Americans held their own against the British in a number of encounters on water (in freshwater along the border with Canada and to some extent in the Atlantic) constituted a significant step forward in the evolution of U.S. military power. As Russell Weigley put it, wittily and pithily, "To have emerged from combat against the premier world power of the era with the status quo ante bellum preserved was not a bad result for a war fought practically without a strategic design."[87]

Others besides Weigley made similar observations. Importantly, one of them was a young Theodore Roosevelt, who, twenty years before reaching the pinnacle of power, had written a history of the War of 1812 that celebrated U.S. accomplishments and underscored the importance of naval power for a great nation. America's first substantial war of the nineteenth century would do much to set the intellectual and strategic backdrop for its last war of that same century—and those that would follow.[88]

BARBARY PIRATES ONE MORE TIME

Despite Jefferson's earlier successes against them, the Barbary pirates had never gone away for good. And once the War of 1812 was over, the United States was in a position to do something more decisive about the problem.

Washington decided to send a naval squadron under Commodore Stephen Decatur to settle matters with Algiers. At this point, by contrast with earlier periods, America had more resources and a stronger navy. The strengthened United States Navy and Marine Corps were able to coerce the pirate fiefdoms to agree to end the practices of hostage taking and tribute paying that had been at the heart of their business model for decades.[89]

Comparing the way the pirate problem was handled, first in the 1790s and then under Jefferson and then under Madison, one sees American power and confidence on a more or less continuous rise. Thus, while the War of 1812 was not a remarkable turning point one way or another, the early decades of the nineteenth century were already revealing a young nation with growing capability and growing swagger.

CONCLUSION

Taking a step back on this period in early U.S. history, one big theme that emerges is a clear desire on the part of the young United States to stay out of what it saw as the largely pointless wars of the European powers, and to avoid the militarism and large standing militaries of those countries, as it sought to build a new kind of nation centered on protecting the rights of the individual and advancing its own prosperity.

Yet . . . there was still a tension, and complexity, to American strategic thought in this period that foreshadowed many of the big debates and policy changes of future decades. Although militarily weak, the new nation was not willing to back down in the face of threats by foreign powers, whether erstwhile allies or not. The early Americans retained a great interest in expanding the size and sweep of the United States itself—taking territory routinely from Native American tribes and nations while also denying North American lands to European powers as much as possible along the way.[90] Already in the 1790s, Vermont and Kentucky and Tennessee were added to the Union; additional states would soon follow, as would the mammoth Louisiana Purchase from France in 1803.[91] Equally notably, the U.S. decision to go to war against the world's strongest power in 1812, when diplomacy might well have resolved the core disputes, reflected a growing confidence and assertiveness in the thirty-six-year-old nation that would only grow with time.

The United States did not have that much of a defense capability during most of its first four decades. But it was already developing a distinctively American mindset toward strategic and military matters as well as its place in the world. It was becoming a dangerous nation.

CHAPTER III

From 1815 Until 1900

Strategies for Offense, Not Defense

Abraham Lincoln was arguably America's greatest president, and he wound up leading the Union to victory in one of America's three most important wars of its 250-year history (the others, by my reckoning, being the Revolution and World War II). Yet his early mistakes in the war, and those of the country he led, make vivid America's long-standing proclivity to go into combat underprepared. The United States has a good record in war, but not a stellar one, and its defense strategies during times of major conflict have often failed, especially in the early going of combat operations.

When asked shortly after his inauguration, and just before the Confederate attack on Fort Sumter that started the war on April 14, 1861, what he was thinking by way of military preparations, Lincoln told a confidant, "My policy is to have no policy."[1] Lincoln thought his main goal should be to persuade the "silent majority" of Southerners who did not, in Lincoln's estimation, wish to secede that they should not do so. As such, he refused to take military planning seriously, out of fear that it would anger and drive away the South. Also in April, his former political nemesis from Illinois, Stephen Douglas (now near his death), visited the White House and told Lincoln that a Union army of at least 200,000—several times what Lincoln advocated—would be needed (actual Union strength would exceed 1 million within a year).

Yet Lincoln was not naive. By luring the South into attacking first, he effectively chose war over the alternative of accepting the creation of the Confederacy and the dissolution of the Union. He was well aware of the gravity of the choice, yet he also displayed few doubts or regrets about the decision thrust upon him once things came down to that. His patient approach had the desirable effects of keeping the border states on the Union side (and dissuaded Britain from favoring the South). As Lincoln put it, while he hoped that God would be on his side, "I must have Kentucky."[2]

As the conflict's first months passed and it became increasingly clear that the country was in for a real war, Lincoln did undertake a huge military buildup. But then he struggled to find a general who would make good use of Union forces. General George McClellan was Lincoln's main problem in this regard, though hardly his only one. Lincoln thought McClellan had a bad case of the "slows." He also wrote McClellan at one point when the field commander was too pensive and inactive asking whether, if McClellan had no plans to use the Army of the Potomac anytime soon, Lincoln might "borrow it." Alternatively, he offered to come to the field to "hold McClellan's horse" for him or do whatever else might help get the young general going.[3]

After going through two more mediocre commanders, Lincoln finally found Ulysses S. Grant, after Grant's exploits in the western theater of combat in 1862 and 1863. When Lincoln's secretary of war asked the president what advice they should together give Grant, Lincoln replied that the two of them had been doing a pretty poor job of managing the war so far from Washington and maybe they should give Mr. Grant a chance to make his own calls. And of course, when rumors of Grant's purported proclivity to drink "more than his station in life requires" were floated, Lincoln asked what kind of whiskey Grant drank and suggested that a flask of it be sent to each of his other generals as well.[4]

In the end, the experiences of Lincoln and Grant were completely atypical of nineteenth-century America in regard to the size of the armed forces they wielded and the existential stakes for which they fought. But Lincoln's track record was also typical of America's leaders through much of its history—start slowly before ginning up the nation's war machine and finding a better way forward as the combat continued. Lincoln also certainly dared mighty things. Indeed, when Theodore Roosevelt coined that phrase in 1899, his speech made explicit reference to Lincoln as the kind of person Americans in the public arena should wish to emulate.[5]

During the preponderance of the nineteenth century, the United States did not have a defense strategy. It had an offense strategy. It expanded from a country hugging part of the Eastern Seaboard of North America to a nation stretching from the Atlantic to the Pacific. It achieved this growth with a military that was generally very modest in size. It did fight a lot—in the U.S.-Mexico War of 1846–48, in the Spanish-American War of 1898 (plus ensuing efforts to subdue insurgency in the Philippines), against Native Americans throughout the century, and of course in the Civil War. But with the exception of the Civil War, the associated military buildups and expenditures were generally modest in size and scale. They also did not tend to begin much before the wars themselves began.[6]

From a technical military perspective, what is most striking about nineteenth-century military strategy, and the broader grand strategy that guided it, was its ruthless efficiency. Depending on one's perspective, the expansionism of the nation over the nineteenth century can be seen as good—creating the greatest economic power on earth, with enough latent military potential that it would be able to lead military rescues of Europe and East Asia twice in the following century. Or the nation's growth can be seen as aggressive and greedy—taking land from Spaniards, Mexicans, and Native Americans. What is incontestable, however, is that it was one of the largest territorial expansions of any country in history over a relatively short period of time, and it was achieved with rather small armed forces, especially by comparison with the powers of Europe. Federal ground forces except during the Civil War ranged from 10,000 to 35,000 strong into the 1890s, growing to about 100,000 by century's end.[7] By comparison, individual European militaries typically boasted strengths of 200,000 to 800,000.[8] Even as late as 1913, all U.S. government spending as a percentage of GDP stood at 8 percent, whereas the average across western Europe and Japan was closer to 12 percent, the difference being largely the result of modest U.S. military budgets.[9]

Viewed historically, American expansionism has a feel of inevitability about it. The French seem to have realized as much when, rather than resist too hard, they sold the huge Louisiana Purchase territory to Thomas Jefferson's America in 1803. Admittedly, Napoleon needed the funds for other ambitions closer to home. But it likely occurred to French leaders that were the Louisiana Territory not sold to the Americans, at some point they simply might take it.

Indeed, none of the nation's founders or early leaders had ever opposed expansionism. They felt varying degrees of obligation to find a way to justify it and to explain why it was acceptable to push Native Americans off their lands. But even the likes of Washington and Jefferson favored the general idea of national growth. Manifest Destiny was coined as a phrase to explain and justify this behavior. Some interpreted American expansionism as a "lust for dominion," to quote one notable contemporary, Gouverneur Morris, an author of the Constitution.[10] Yet as Robert Kagan argues, it was about much more than money. Americans believed their whole experiment in democracy, and promotion of the rights of the individual, to be a higher calling that justified a quest to build a larger and greater nation.[11] Not only Americans themselves but peoples around the world would benefit from the example created by this experiment.

A similar attitude drove early American policy toward Asia, where commercial interests, missionary motivations, and a desire to prevent European powers from dominating China and Japan led to U.S. assertiveness. In 1821, the United States established a permanent Pacific squadron, based mostly in North American waters but making the occasional foray to Hawaii; in 1835, it added an East Asia squadron for that side of the world's greatest ocean.[12] These naval capabilities were not big at first—but they would grow. By century's end, the United States would have become not only the dominant North American land power but a maritime and a Pacific power as well.

DECADES OF EXPANSION AND THE U.S.-MEXICO WAR OF 1846–48

For most of the period after the War of 1812 and until the Civil War, the United States enjoyed a period in which it faced few threats, spent little on its military in general, maintained only modest Army and Navy (and Marine Corps) forces—and fought against others for the most part when it chose to, not when it had to.

First up after the War of 1812 were the Barbary pirates from the city-states of North Africa once more. They were up to their plunderous ways yet again; equipped with a bigger navy and growing national self-confidence from having gone toe-to-toe with the British a second time, the United States was now ready for more decisive action against them.

The story can be summarized by telling the story of one impressive, and lucky yet also unlucky, young American naval officer of the day—Stephen Decatur, thirty-six years old in 1815. Decatur captures much about the America of this period, with its burgeoning capacities, its derring-do, and its growing hankerings to enter into the ranks of the great powers. Decatur had become a national hero in 1804 as a lieutenant when, by clever ruse, he led his men in boarding the *Philadelphia,* a vessel that pirates had captured earlier from the United States. Reclaiming the ship after hand-to-hand combat, he then had it set afire, given the damage it had suffered: at least it would no longer be in the pirates' hands. Later that year, avenging the death of his brother, he boarded another enemy ship, nearly losing his life in the ensuing struggle before felling his foe. In that encounter, he memorably benefited from the self-sacrificing heroism of one of his men, who put his own neck between a Turkish officer's scimitar and its intended target. Decatur was captured by the British during the War of 1812 but was released under the terms of the Treaty of Ghent. After declaring a state of war against the pirates and gaining congressional authorization to use force, President Madison sent Decatur along with Commodore William Bainbridge to settle scores and end the piracy for good. Well equipped with not only American but captured British vessels, and sporting the same panache and spirit as a decade before, Decatur obliged, with menacing appearances in Algiers, Tripoli, and Tunis. He secured the release of American hostages, ended the practice of paying ransoms, and returned home yet again a hero. With an honorarium from Congress for his previous successes, Decatur and his wife bought a gorgeous home near the White House (known to this day as Decatur House) and became prominent in the Washington social scene.

Tragically, the good life was not to last long. An ongoing rivalry with another naval officer, James Barron, of whom Decatur thought poorly and had sought to keep out of the Navy, led to a duel in 1820. Both men were shot, but Decatur got the worse of it. President James Monroe hastened to Decatur House on hearing the word of the duel and watched his friend bleed away. The ensuing funeral several days later brought 10,000 mourning Americans to honor the fallen hero. Decatur had a combination of bravery, bravado, skill, and ambition that made him an excellent metaphor for the America of his day, even as his life ended far too soon at age forty-one.[13]

To the extent that military strategy was debated in the years after the War of 1812, the thinking about ground forces focused largely on the hypothetical problem of a ground invasion of the United States by a European power. A report of the Fortifications Board in 1821 led to construction of various coastal batteries along the nation's Atlantic and Gulf of Mexico coasts. These were manned by modest ground forces, intended to buy time for mobilization of militia in the event of a crisis.[14] The degree to which these efforts were viewed as a serious concern of the nation is debatable; budgetary allocations were modest, and the identity of the would-be attacker was difficult to discern.

The real military action for the first few decades after the War of 1812 was farther west, on the frontier, against Native Americans. Military forces and operations were generally organized on a case-by-case basis in ad hoc fashion. But they were relentless, and deadly serious, in purpose. Indeed, the United States created a Bureau of Indian Affairs in 1831—and placed it in the War Department![15] (Treatment of Native Americans got no better, however, once the bureau was moved over to the Department of the Interior in 1849.)[16] The ongoing westward expansion of the United States created a tragic pattern of Native Americans being defeated in battle, then persuaded to move westward as part of the terms of surrender, then again finding themselves in the crosshairs of settlers some years later even after having relocated.

There are too many battles, campaigns, and tragedies to recount here. That said, two intrepid scholars, R. Ernest Dupuy and Trevor N. Dupuy, *did* attempt to count them—and came up with a list of 943 battles fought by the white man against Native Americans between 1768 and 1889.[17] Most of these were fought by local militias or by militias called to temporary federal service.[18] Some of the most famous colonial-era conflicts included the Jamestown Massacre and King Philip's War and Pontiac's War. After the American Revolution (in which numerous Native American tribes participated, on both sides), key struggles included the Battle of Fallen Timbers (in present-day Ohio in 1794); the Battle of Tippecanoe (in present-day Indiana in 1811); the Seminole Wars (in Florida in 1817–18 and between 1835 and 1842); the Trail of Tears, or forced migration westward of thousands of Native Americans (from the eastern United States to lands west of the Mississippi between 1830 and 1850); the Black Hawk War (in today's Illinois in 1832); the Gold Rush battles (in California and the Pacific Northwest, from 1849 onward); the Grattan incident (in Wyoming in 1854); the Sand Creek Massacre (in Colorado in 1864, during the Civil War); Red Cloud's War (in Wyoming in 1865–67); Custer's Last Stand at the Battle of Little Bighorn (today's Montana in 1876); and the killing of Sitting Bull followed by the massacre of many of his supporters at Wounded Knee (South Dakota in 1890).[19]

To get a feel for some of these fights, consider the Battle of Tippecanoe. The conflict was sparked largely by the ambitions of Governor William Henry Harrison, and its aftermath would create a glowing reputation for Harrison that ultimately helped vault him to the presidency in 1841 (though he would catch cold soon after giving his inaugural address and die a month later). Harrison had helped win the Battle of Fallen Timbers in the Ohio Territory in the late eighteenth century and became governor of the Indiana Territory in 1801, keeping that position for a dozen years. (Note the base word of the name *Indiana;* it was originally designated as territory that the Native Americans could keep, until of course U.S. settlers changed their minds.) Harrison sought more land for settlers through a combination of purchases and treaties with local tribes but ultimately decided on a military showdown with the local Shawnee leader

Tecumseh. The fight took place near Tippecanoe Creek on November 7, 1811, giving Harrison not only his reputation as a formidable frontiersman but a new nickname to boot. His force of regular soldiers and Kentucky volunteers, though far from their home base, fended off a nighttime ambush and won the day with their superior weaponry. Much about the fighting was impressive—less in terms of sophisticated logistics or tactics than in the boldness and toughness of the fighters on both sides. U.S. forces also used indirect methods, including the cutting of supply lines from the British to the Native American tribes, to weaken the Indians economically and militarily. This concept of isolating Native Americans by cutting them off from lines of sustenance proved popular, given that the alternative was often to try to chase down their highly mobile and geographically savvy and tenacious forces.

During the War of 1812, with a new position in the U.S. Army, Harrison would again encounter Tecumseh's warriors, this time fighting in cahoots with the British. In the ensuing Battle of the Thames in 1813, Tecumseh would perish. Without his compelling and charismatic leadership, the Shawnee Confederacy that he had forged to resist settler expansion all the way from the Ohio Valley to the Gulf of Mexico would soon fade away.[20]

Yet the signature military operation of the period from 1815 until 1860 was the U.S.-Mexico War of 1846–48. It was America's ultimate war of choice, with the clear aim of territorial conquest. Former general and president Ulysses S. Grant, writing in his memoirs around 1885, regarded the war "as one of the most unjust ever waged by a stronger against a weaker nation."[21] Certainly many Mexicans feel that way. Another interpretation, however, is that it was virtually inevitable. It was fought over sparsely settled territories that, while legally part of the still-new Mexican nation, seemed a natural extension of the United States to most Americans.[22]

In terms of defense strategy, the U.S.-Mexico War highlighted the economic clout and technological innovation of a nation that was on the verge of becoming a world-class industrial power. To be sure, the United States had employed technology in earlier battles against Britain, and also against Native Americans. But by the mid-1840s, the United States had the railroads and boats to mount big logistics operations and what could perhaps be termed the nation's first major amphibious assault, en route to Mexico City in 1847.

The U.S.-Mexico War also featured several relatively decisive campaigns that achieved big things in a relatively modest period of time with relatively modest casualties. Alas, in this sense it may have fostered a certain naivete about the nature of contemporary war that contributed to the utter shock with which the bloodiness of the Civil War would greet the country less than two decades later. Many of the key protagonists in the Civil War cut their teeth in fighting Mexico; a number may have drawn the wrong lessons.

The combat began after the United States became interested in annexing the Republic of Texas—about a decade after Texas had fought for and gained its independence from Mexico. Mexico was led for much of its first quarter-century by President Antonio López de Santa Anna. Exiled before the war, Santa Anna would return to Mexico to lead the country's military against the United States. The immediate catalyst for combat was the decision of President James Polk to provoke a showdown over the U.S.-Texas border. He sent U.S. forces into disputed lands north of the Rio Grande that Mexico claimed, provoking a Mexican attack.[23] Congress promptly gave Polk the declaration of war that he requested by overwhelming majorities in both houses in May 1846. Polk quickly put it to use—and for much larger purposes than the settlement of a border dispute. Within two years, much of the American Southwest and West would wind up becoming part of a rapidly expanding United States.

More than in most of its wars, the United States had a fairly clear instinct about how to proceed in this fight. It wanted to put general pressure on Mexico, including with major threats to its army and its capital, designed to force America's southern neighbor into a peace treaty that would cede large tracts of land to the United States. It also wanted simply to seize and confiscate as much of that land as it could, from modern-day New Mexico and Arizona to California and lands farther north such as Nevada.

This general set of objectives was pursued through three major military campaigns. First and foremost was the set of operations to seize the larger version of Texas (all land north of the Rio Grande) and to protect that land grab by pushing proximate Mexican forces southward within their own country. Another campaign took place in America's current western states. The final major effort involved a big operation to threaten and ultimately seize Mexico City, so that the United States could force the Mexican government to give up all the lands it had refused to sell to the United States in 1845.[24] Logistics throughout the war were very challenging, given the harsh climate and topography. Most soldiers walked (unless a part of their initial movement could be done by ship). Horses and mules pulled supply wagons; cavalry rode on horseback. Communications were carried out by horseback or when possible by ship.

The first campaign was led by Zachary Taylor. He took the disputed parts of Texas and then moved into northern Mexico. Taylor's troops won initial battles in early May 1846 at Palo Alto, where just over 2,000 Americans defeated a

Mexican force of almost 4,000, and then at Resaca de la Palma, near the Texas-Mexico border.[25] After receiving reinforcements, Taylor then crossed the Rio Grande later in May and started to move south. The Battle of Monterrey followed in late September and produced a mixed result, with some 500 Americans killed and wounded (out of a force around 6,000 strong), while Mexico lost 350 to 400 out of 7,000 troops. Then the Mexicans built up reinforcements. General Santa Anna, with more than 20,000 fighters, tried to force an American retreat. That led to the Battle of Buena Vista in late February 1847, a more clear-cut win for outnumbered U.S. forces.[26] The Americans suffered only about half as many casualties as did Mexican troops.[27] Yet even if the battle was a win in that sense, it effectively spelled the end of any prospect of Taylor moving more deeply into Mexico.

Out west, things were heating up as well. A force led by Stephen Kearny departed from Fort Leavenworth, Kansas, in the spring of 1846 and proceeded westward to Santa Fe. Kearny then took a modest share of his original 1,600-strong force westward, arriving in San Diego in December after surviving the Battle of San Pasqual. Once in San Diego, Kearny's troops joined forces with another contingent under Admiral Robert Stockton, whose shipborne forces had already helped take control of key towns in northern California earlier in the year. American troops in the broader western theater were assisted by the legendary frontiersman Kit Carson as well as John Frémont of the U.S. Topographical Engineers.[28] In January 1847, Stockton and Kearny moved from San Diego with a combined strength of perhaps just over 500 personnel and, after prevailing in the Battles of San Gabriel and La Mesa, took Los Angeles.[29]

What proved the conclusive campaign of the war took place in the spring and summer of 1847. It was led by General Winfield Scott, who had begun the war as the nation's top general in Washington but increasingly found himself anxious to get in on the battlefield action. Scott persuaded Secretary of War William Marcy and President Polk to put him in command of what would soon become the war's decisive effort.

Scott put around 10,000 troops on Navy ships in New Orleans and sailed south. He came ashore in Veracruz, east of Mexico City, in March 1847. After laying siege to Veracruz, Scott's forces moved into the Mexican highlands, en route to the nation's capital. A key milestone toward their ultimate goal was achieved at Cerro Gordo in mid-April, where U.S. Army engineers including Robert E. Lee created paths through rough mountainous terrain that allowed the Americans to surprise Mexican forces. Though U.S. forces were outnumbered against Santa Anna's army by roughly 8,500 to 12,000, they carried the day.

Yet those forces were not quite enough to take Mexico City. That would require reinforcements from the United States, so an assault would not be possible before late summer.[30] By August, Scott's strength reached about 14,000. Mexican forces had also grown over the summer and were now twice as large as his own, but Scott attacked anyway, winning battles at Contreras and Churubusco on August 20. Mexican casualties were around 4,000; U.S. losses were only a quarter as great. After a short truce lasting the last week of August and first week of September, the Americans continued their assault, taking the fort of Chapultepec on September 13. There they inflicted nearly 2,000 more Mexican casualties, again suffering only about a quarter as many themselves. Santa Anna and his armies fled the scene. Scott took control of Mexico City, and effectively ended the war, the next day.[31]

To again quote Russell Weigley, who admired Scott and his preference for maneuver and precision over sheer mass, "Scott was a bold strategist. His march from Veracruz into the interior was one of the most daring movements of American military history, for he had to capture the enemy's capital while separated from his naval support not only by the fever coast but also by more than 200 miles of mountainous, guerrilla-infested roadway."[32]

The U.S.-Mexico War gave the United States a glimpse into what it would be like to have a larger nineteenth-century military. By war's end, roughly 100,000 total troops had served, about a quarter in the regular army and the rest in state militias or volunteer units of one kind or another that came under temporary federal control.[33] That was a much larger force than had typified the young nation's ground forces before. The army had grown to more than 10,000 soldiers temporarily in the 1830s in difficult fights against the Seminoles in Florida but otherwise stayed below that level for decades. That was the case even though formal federal plans for a more robust system of forts out west, to go along with the coastal fortifications in the East and South, really required substantially larger forces than were ever devoted to the task.[34] In theory, under a plan created by Secretary of War John Calhoun in 1820, the U.S. Army could have grown from 6,000 to 12,000—and if necessary, double that—based on a system with enough cadres of officers to grow the ranks fast.[35] But that was just a plan. Actual regular army strength tended to stay in the single-digit thousands throughout the period of 1815 to 1860. Even on the eve of war with Mexico, it totaled only some 6,000.

Despite this history, and the efficiency of Scott's taking of Mexico City and winning the war with modest-sized maneuver forces, dreams of big armies and great battles were starting to seep into the minds of American strategists. The thinking was not quite Clausewitzian in any literal sense; that great Prussian writer's works from the early nineteenth century would not be translated into English until 1873. But a French strategist named Antoine-Henri Jomini captured some of the same kind of thinking, and his writings did reach West Point (where the U.S. Military Academy had been founded in 1802) well before the Civil War. He wrote about large mobilizations of men, industrial-scale production of weaponry, and major logistical planning that would culminate in decisive battles—fighting à la Napoleon. American writers to include Dennis Mahan (the father of the famous naval strategist of future years Alfred Thayer Mahan), Henry Halleck, and Sylvanus Thayer promoted this way of thinking into the midcentury years. Unfortunately for those who would fight the Civil War subsequently, these strategists were not as strong in foreseeing or appreciating ongoing trends in technology such as the invention and spread of the rifle. Thus, the intellectual stage was being set for the carnage that would characterize America's bloodiest war of all time from 1861 until 1865.[36]

As for the Navy, after the glory days of the War of 1812, it struggled a bit for the next few decades. As two esteemed historians put it, "The dozen or so victorious naval duels between American and British cruisers upon the ocean, the spectacular exploits of famous privateers, Perry's victory upon Lake Erie, Macdonough's upon Lake Champlain, and the rout of the British Army at the Battle of New Orleans, all contributed to the rise of a legend that the United States had once more defeated the world's greatest naval power."[37] Yet the Navy was then relegated to moving Army soldiers to Veracruz, an important but clearly supporting function, in 1847. With the nation's main energies still focused westward, support languished. Nor was any perceived threat great enough to warrant sustained buildups of large warships (or to sustain consistent funding for coastal defenses after the aforementioned report of the Fortifications Board from 1821).[38] As historian Craig Symonds put it, "The day-to-day duties of the U.S. Navy involved dealing with smugglers, pirates, and the illegal slave trade, and deploying ships of the line to deal with such issues was like hitting a tack with a sledgehammer."[39] Nor did the Marine Corps, tied closely to the Navy in its main missions, grow much above 1,000 personnel or so throughout this period 1815–60.[40]

But even if the Navy was not actually growing consistently through midcentury, there was churn beneath the surface that kept the idea of a bigger and stronger navy alive in many minds. The acquisition of western territories not easily reachable by land from the eastern United States put a premium on maritime movement. Growing interest in Pacific commerce, with Commodore Matthew Perry's opening to Japan in 1853 a prominent milestone, created another argument for a naval force. American swagger played a role, too, as with the Monroe

Doctrine of 1823 that told European powers to keep their hands off the Western Hemisphere, since it was the natural right of the United States to exercise preponderant influence in both North and South America.[41] Two decades later, President John Tyler would later effectively extend the Monroe Doctrine several thousand miles westward, to Hawaii.[42] Ideas were germinating, even if they were not yet consistently winning political or budgetary debates in Washington.

Ship technology was also advancing fast in this period. The age of steam and of iron ships began to arrive. So did underwater propellers and more powerful as well as accurate naval guns firing explosive shells. Under several key leaders, to include military engineer Simon Bernard, Captain Charles Stewart, and Perry, as well as Secretary of the Navy Benjamin Stoddert and a successor, Abel Upshur (who gave his life to the cause, dying when a new type of gun on the U.S.S. *Princeton* exploded in a trial), the United States developed some rudiments of a respectable navy. It established squadrons for the Mediterranean, the Caribbean, the South Atlantic, and even the Pacific Ocean. It created the U.S. Naval Academy in 1845 as it took debates about naval technology and warfare seriously and studiously.

Again, throughout the first half of the nineteenth century, the U.S. Navy remained far from world class, especially in size.[43] Budgets throughout this period were typically in the single-digit millions per year—in the broad range of $100 million in today's dollars. Naval buildups proceeded in fits and starts; the United States would not really seek to develop a navy characteristic of a major power until toward the end of the century.[44]

Yet enough did happen in this midcentury period that, once the Civil War began and the Union inherited the fruits of all these halting efforts at naval modernization in preceding decades, it would have a major advantage over the Confederacy. That would make a fairly effective blockade possible throughout the war. In fact, an aging Winfield Scott would favor centering the Union war effort on blockade and related operations—with a squeezing strategy known by the nickname Anaconda—before being overruled by Lincoln and others who believed it likely to be too slow for what the situation required after war broke out. It is to that war that we turn next.

THE AMERICAN CIVIL WAR

The American Civil War nearly ripped the country in two. It probably came closer to doing so than most appreciate. Thus, apart from the Revolution itself, it was the nation's only truly existential war in its history. For four years, American grand strategy changed fundamentally: from the century's general pattern of expansionism to simple political survival. For the Union and President Lincoln, the goal was to preserve—and eventually, once it had been broken in two, to restore—the Union. For the Confederacy, by the time Lincoln was elected, grand strategy focused on the successful pursuit of independence. The fight was not about improving terms of any compromise; it was about breaking up or sustaining the Union. Thus, the grand strategies and goals of the two sides were diametrically opposed and mutually incompatible. The magnitude of the war was beyond anything seen before in North America. As Williamson Murray and Wayne Wei-Siang Shieh have argued, it combined the innovations of the Napoleonic Revolution (and mass mobilization) with those of the Industrial Revolution (and mass production of new weaponry) in a way and on a scale not previously witnessed anywhere.[45]

At the level of defense strategy—the military mechanics of how to pursue these respective grand strategies—thinking was less clear. Little had been prepared or planned by way of defense strategy by either side before the war broke out. Thus, lots of thinking had to go into military strategy, operations, and tactics—as well as raising and organizing forces—in the course of the fighting. Lincoln's, and Grant's, central idea was that Confederate military forces needed to be destroyed, principally through direct battlefield action, supplemented by economic strangulation that employed the North's overwhelming advantages in infrastructure, industry, and naval power. But developing the means and finding the generals (and admirals) to effect this defense strategy would take great time and effort by America's sixteenth president.[46]

The Civil War lasted almost exactly four years. It had two major theaters, in addition to the coastal and maritime dimension. In the east, General Robert E. Lee led Confederate forces for most of the war. Several generals, featuring George McClellan early on and winding up with George Meade under Ulysses S. Grant, led Union forces in that region. The two sides battled in regions stretching from northern Virginia to Richmond and environs as well as the Shenandoah Valley. The eastern theater also included famous battles at Antietam in Maryland in September 1862 and Gettysburg, Pennsylvania, in July 1863.

The western theater centered on Kentucky and Tennessee to Mississippi and Louisiana. Union forces made more consistent progress here than in the east, even from the war's relatively early days. They gradually expanded their control of the Mississippi River, taking New Orleans in the spring of 1862 and Vicksburg in July 1863.

The eastern and western theaters converged by the end of the war. Union victories in southeastern Tennessee allowed for General William Tecumseh

Sherman's attacks on Atlanta in the summer of 1864, and then his March to the Sea that fall, followed by his northward sweep into the Carolinas.

The majority of battles lasted one to three days and were fought in daylight.[47] Deployed forces in major battles typically numbered in the tens of thousands of soldiers, sometimes exceeding 100,000. The Union built a million-man army by 1864, with some 600,000 soldiers in the field.[48] By war's end, several hundred thousand Americans had died—by some estimates as many as three-quarters of a million, more than in all the rest of the nation's wars combined (even though the combined population of North and South in the 1860s was less than 10 percent of today's almost 350 million citizens).

I believe that Civil War defense strategy can be understood by dividing the war into seven main land campaigns—that is, seven main sequences of events, each across a given geographic zone or theater. The seven main campaigns of the Civil War are:

McClellan's movements south with the main Union army toward Richmond in 1862;
Stonewall Jackson's campaign in the Shenandoah Valley that same year, culminating in the Second Battle of Manassas in late August;
Lee's subsequent unsuccessful movements northward, featuring the Battles of Antietam in September 1862 and Gettysburg in July 1863 (though interrupted by defeat at Antietam, then by winter);
Ill-fated Union attacks against the South in the Virginia theater in the winter of 1862–63 and spring of 1863;
Grant's and other Union leaders' much more successful western campaign, with a notable early encounter at Shiloh in Tennessee in April 1862 as well as the taking of New Orleans that same year and culminating in the surrender of southern forces at Vicksburg on the Mississippi River in July 1863 (at the same time as Gettysburg);
Following battles the year before at Chattanooga, Tennessee, and Chickamauga, Georgia, Sherman's taking of Atlanta and fabled March to the Sea in 1864; and
The conclusive clockwise movement of Meade and Grant through Virginia, leading to the taking of Richmond and the surrender of Lee at Appomattox.

The general naval blockade of the South by the North that occurred throughout the war might be considered an eighth campaign.[49]

As for the military or defense strategies that these campaigns were designed to serve, the Confederacy's was arguably the more cogent and consistent of the two. The Confederacy's main military goal was to fight long and hard enough to convince Northern leaders and voters that preserving the Union was not worth the trouble. Although it is difficult to believe now, looking back with 160 years of hindsight, this strategy almost worked. Thus, the Confederate military strategy was defensive in overarching concept. But in practical terms, it featured important elements of offensive warfare at the campaign and tactical levels. Many of its leaders were also very good tacticians, understanding how to use maneuver, ruse, and well-prepared defensive fortifications to win fights even with smaller forces than the opponent. Confederate generals including Lee, Stonewall Jackson, and J. E. B. "Jeb" Stuart believed in the idea of the attack (of those three, only Lee survived the war). Confederacy president Jefferson Davis, himself a West Point graduate and former U.S. secretary of war before the South seceded, also subscribed to "offensive-defensive" thinking.[50] They were Napoleonic in their military philosophies, believing that outcomes in wars would usually be decided in great culminating battles.[51] This may seem in retrospect an unwise strategy for a polity outnumbered more than 3:1 in white males. But it had its logic, even if it proved a flawed logic. Confederate leaders hoped to create a momentum that would have psychological effects in both North and South—discouraging the former, encouraging the latter—and persuading border states such as Kentucky and Maryland as well as foreign powers in Europe to support the Southern cause until Northern voters or leaders simply said, "Enough."[52]

Although this approach ultimately failed, a series of Confederate battlefield wins early in the war seemed to offer promise. The First Battle of Manassas, on July 21, 1861, began the string of major victories. There, in a well-advertised encounter treated almost like a fair or sporting event by observers from Washington, D.C., about 20,000 forces on each side engaged in a bloody exchange that ultimately went the Confederates' way, as some Union forces fled the battlefield. After a fall and winter of mobilization on both sides, General George McClellan's idea to undertake a major amphibious movement down the Chesapeake and attack Richmond as well as Lee's forces from the east got bogged down in swamp, mud, and McClellan's own tendencies to dither. Union forces did not perform badly at the Battle of Seven Pines and Seven Days' Battles in late spring and early summer of 1862, but McClellan ran out of verve after these engagements, and his forces were soon withdrawn northward from the theater. Later that summer, at the Second Battle of Manassas, Lee and Jackson again outgeneraled Union forces and carried the day.

The early run of successes was about to be interrupted, however, as the most controversial aspect of Lee's strategy, his aggressiveness—together with some bad luck—got him into trouble. His attack plans were discovered by Union forces just before the Battle of Antietam in Maryland in September 1862. But this setback did not become a major turning point; McClellan failed to exploit the opportunity produced by Lee's defeat there.

A few months later, McClellan's successor as general in chief of Union forces, Ambrose Burnside, then conducted one of the war's worst tactical operations at the Battle of Fredericksburg, Virginia, in December 1862. Running his forces across a field into enemy fire, he produced a staggering Union defeat and restored the battlefield momentum to the Confederacy. Once the ensuing winter ended, the fights again went the South's way, notably in Virginia at the Battle of Chancellorsville in May 1863 when Lee divided his forces and sent Stonewall Jackson on an improbable move through dense forest to attack the Union flank. Again, the South won the day—in terms of casualty counts, military panache, and which side "owned" the battlefield once the gunpowder cleared away. In some ways, this was the high-water mark of the Confederate war effort.

Or at least, Lee seemed to have won big at Chancellorsville. But if it was victory, it was victory of a type Lee could not afford too many times. The result wound up much more mixed than it appeared. Jackson died after being accidentally shot in the arm by his own men and then suffering an amputation that led to infection and death. As Lee said, even before Jackson's passing, "He has lost his left arm but I have lost my right arm."[53] Truer words were rarely spoken. Moreover, as the North ginned up its population base and industry for extended conflict, the kind of tactical victory that the Confederacy won at Chancellorsville was not the type it could easily afford. Even if the Union suffered 50 percent more casualties in a given battle, it could withstand such losses more easily given its population base, which was more than three times larger in available male fighters.

Yet Lee did not appear to see it that way, and his offense-defense thinking led him to perhaps his biggest blunder of the war. Confident after Chancellorsville, he pursued an even greater ambition in Pennsylvania at Gettysburg—hoping to shock the Union with a major attack on its own soil. But there Lee failed, taking heavy casualties and being forced to return home. Afterward, the South would never really regain military momentum in the war.

Lee perhaps should not have sought battle at Antietam and Gettysburg. Arguably the better strategy would have resembled Stonewall Jackson's campaign in the Shenandoah Valley culminating at Second Manassas in the late summer of 1862, in which Jackson used ruse and maneuver as much as pitched battle. (That is not to say that Jackson always shrank from a fight; in fact, he got his nickname by standing firm and tall at the First Battle of Manassas the year before.) Or perhaps the better template was provided by Confederate general Joe Johnston in Georgia in the summer of 1864, where he defended Atlanta for a time against Sherman with a series of delaying actions and limited engagements. Grant himself believed that a strategy like Johnston's might have been the South's best bet.[54]

For Lincoln, and the Union, military strategy would have to shift as the Confederacy proved more obdurate and tougher than initially expected. The essential first goal of the Union had to be political, not military per se: portraying the South as the aggressor. In this way, Lincoln hoped, other Southerners would rethink their support for the cause and become more apt to view the promoters of secession as rabble-rousers who should be discredited. He also sought to maximize sympathies in the North, border states, and foreign countries for the Union cause—so that Northern citizens and politicians would support whatever wartime efforts proved necessary, and so that border states as well as European powers would not join or support the Confederacy. Lincoln was quite Clausewitzian, recognizing the interplay between politics and military operations and seeking to use the latter to shape the former. In reflecting on the start of the war at Fort Sumter, where Northern forces sought to reinforce a United States military base on Confederate soil rather than evacuate it, Confederate president Jefferson Davis understood Lincoln's basic mindset: "It was cunningly attempted to show that the South, which had been pleading for peace and still stood on the defensive, had by this [bloodless] bombardment inaugurated a war against the United States."[55]

Once the fighting got going, Lincoln needed a military strategy, too. Three main ideas were initially in play. One was that of Lincoln's top uniformed officer, General Winfield Scott, who as noted favored a patient strategy of blockading and squeezing the South to weaken its economy and eventually force its capitulation. There might be limited offensive operations against ports and railroads, but otherwise this strategy would imply less fighting. General Scott called this the Anaconda strategy (General David Petraeus, an avid fan of Civil War history, would employ the same term to describe the approach of the surge in Iraq more than 140 years later). Another possible military strategy focused on taking Richmond, Virginia, the capital of the Confederacy for most of the conflict, in the hope that the Confederate government would either be captured, discredited, or demoralized and thereby defeated. A third emphasized the importance of defeating Lee's main army, since once that was done, the South would be defenseless and, unless it chose to undertake guerrilla-like resistance, would then be forced to give up the fight. The first of these possible military strategies viewed the Confederate economy as the South's center of gravity. The second saw its government as the center of gravity; the third saw the Confederate military as the main objective.

Lincoln himself believed that destroying Lee's army must be the main Union goal. So he included elements of Anaconda in the Union strategy but did not rely on it.[56] Yet it is notable that most Union successes, such as they were, in 1862 and much of 1863 occurred in the western theater of the war and supported the general logic of Anaconda. The Battle of Shiloh in April 1862 in Tennessee was inconclusive, but in broader terms it weakened the South's hold on Tennessee and made it harder for Confederate forces to reclaim Kentucky. It thus bounded and weakened the Confederacy's northwestern flank and deprived it of resources. The taking of Memphis and New Orleans that same month impeded the South's ability to use the Mississippi River, with New Orleans falling to riverine forces of Admiral David Farragut, of War of 1812 fame. Grant's brilliant siege of Vicksburg, Mississippi, the next winter, spring, and early summer would complete the process in the West. Union victories in 1863 in Mississippi and eastern Tennessee further fragmented Confederate territory and logistics lines. Railroads and rivers were increasingly unavailable to the South, even as the naval blockade of Confederate ports also impeded trade between the Confederacy and key European markets.

As for Lincoln's other two possible goals, they were often pursued simultaneously, largely because threatening Richmond tended to induce Confederate armies to try to block the Union advances—and fight. Thus, taking Richmond became almost synonymous with defeating Lee's armies. By the spring of 1865, those two goals were achieved within two weeks of each other.

That said, Lincoln did not have field commanders early in the war who shared his view about the proper intensity of how such a Union strategy should be implemented. As noted, George McClellan in particular was seen by Lincoln as having a case of the "slows," leading Lincoln at one point to ask McClellan that if the general saw no immediate use for his forces, perhaps the commander in chief might borrow them? Not until Ulysses S. Grant achieved great success in July 1863 at Vicksburg, and then again in Chattanooga that fall, would Lincoln find his general. Then, by early 1864, the Union had a field commander who also viewed Confederate forces—Lee's, as well as those in other theaters—as the main focus of his own strategy. Grant went after those outnumbered forces with a vengeance. He understood clearly his overall numerical advantage and the difficulty of Lee's position in protecting Richmond while replenishing the Army of Northern Virginia's outnumbered and beleaguered forces. Grant took advantage of the beefed-up Union Army and logistics system that Quartermaster General Montgomery Meigs and others had built up from mid-1861 onward.[57] Thus, Grant and Meade were relentless in the campaign of 1864–65, even when Union forces experienced tactical frustrations and defeats. The Battles of the Wilderness, Spotsylvania, Cold Harbor, Petersburg, and elsewhere in Virginia could be generally viewed as individual Union tactical defeats that, when stitched together as an integrated whole, nonetheless amounted to a successful campaign. They led to strategic success by pinning down and wearing down what was left of Confederate forces.

General William Sherman supported a similar strategy in the South, but the goal of taking Atlanta demanded somewhat different tactics. In threatening Atlanta in the summer of 1864, he largely avoided direct attack against entrenched Confederate units and waited for his moment to squeeze the Confederacy into abandoning the city more than seeking a showdown battle.[58] Later, he chose to break free from his dependence on the railroad, destroying a large swath of Georgia and then the Carolinas while living off the land.[59] He was highly innovative. Yet in some ways his March to the Sea was a throwback to earlier campaigns such as Scott's in Mexico and Gates's at Saratoga before the days of the railroad.

Union strategy coalesced in late 1864 and 1865, achieving virtually all the component goals in short succession—seriously attriting the main Confederate armies, claiming the Confederate capital (as well as its biggest city in Georgia), demoralizing Confederate citizens while inspiring Northerners with the sacking of Atlanta and Sherman's March to the Sea, breaking the Confederate economy into pieces and squeezing each one by land and sea, and finally cornering Lee at Appomattox.

FROM OCCUPATION DUTY TO CUSTER'S LAST STAND TO WOUNDED KNEE

Once the Civil War was over, a massive military downsizing naturally followed. About 98 percent of all U.S. fighting forces were demobilized. By 1869, the U.S. Army numbered only about 25,000 soldiers, a level it would hover around until 1898.[60] But defense strategy was far from winding down; the remainder of the century would witness several major operations and developments. In broad brush, they included the Union occupation of the South during Reconstruction, the ongoing battles against Native Americans farther and farther west, the buildup of naval capability, and finally, to close out the century, the Spanish-American War, with follow-on operations in the Philippines stretching into the early twentieth century.

The occupation of the South after the Civil War was a unique experience in the nation's history. But it had at least one lasting legacy of note that endures until the present: the passage in 1878 of the Posse Comitatus Act, which severely restricts the ability of federal troops to be used for domestic purposes. That law has shaped much of how the United States has responded to most domestic disturbances since, with National Guard units often being the preferred alternative to active-duty U.S. Army forces, given their ability to operate under state control.[61] Otherwise, what was most notable about the occupation was its short-lived nature, modest resourcing, and even more modest effectiveness. The number of federal troops in the former Confederacy dropped quickly, from 87,000 in 1866 to just 20,000 in 1867 (and then to 6,000 by 1876 just before the operation ended). Modern counterinsurgency theory would suggest that any comprehensive effort at protecting a population would require at least 200,000 troops for the population of nearly 10 million then living in the Southern states. The mission's main purpose was to enforce equal rights as promised in the Thirteenth, Fourteenth, and Fifteenth Amendments to the U.S. Constitution; it generally failed to achieve these goals.[62]

Meanwhile, however, the nation's westward push continued. First, to review again the backdrop: starting in 1830, building on an earlier idea from Secretary of War John Calhoun in 1825 under President John Quincy Adams, the Jackson administration pressured Native American tribes to accept land west of the Mississippi. That region featured a great swath of land from Texas up to Canada. Along the east-west dimension, it extended from the western borders of today's Minnesota, Iowa, Missouri, Arkansas, and Louisiana all the way over to the Rockies.[63] But after the passage in 1862 of the Homestead Act, which promised free land to pioneers, settlers were no longer quite so content to leave those lands to the various tribes. At a minimum, they wanted to build railroads through them, move wagons through them (en route to the Oregon Territory and California and other areas west of the Rockies), shoot buffalo within them, and sometimes prospect for precious metals on or near these parts of what was seen as the Great American Desert. Eventually, they also began to figure out how to farm or ranch in parts of the central American territory themselves. By the end of the Civil War, only modern Oklahoma was still unorganized territory. Oregon and California and Nevada were states, as was Kansas. New territories in Arizona, Colorado, Nebraska, Dakota, Montana, and Idaho had been delineated.[64] Native Americans were increasingly pushed onto limited tracts of land or reservations within these spaces. Sometimes, they resisted.

Some of the famous Union generals of the Civil War, such as Philip Sheridan and George Armstrong Custer, were the key military leaders of the time for the United States. They employed some of Sheridan's and Sherman's Civil War methods of destroying the food, livestock, and winter encampments of the tribes if they would not submit to forced relocation. They also often used Native scouts, sometimes from rival tribes, to aid in their pursuits.[65] That set of tactics tended to work, destroying some tribes while forcing others to surrender and relocate to reservations.[66] Soon, rather than controlling nearly all of the center third of the country as had been the case, Native Americans were on a checkerboard of specific reservations. By the mid-1880s, there were some 187 reservations in the United States that included 181,000 square miles of land and nearly a quarter-million Native Americans (the land area of the continental United States is just over 3 million square miles).[67]

There was little formal doctrine, or regularized training, to guide these operations against Native Americans. For example, the Army manual *Instructions for the Government of Armies,* of 1863, was notable less for any decisive guidance than for the fact that it had something for everyone, including discussion of brass-knuckles tactics, on the one hand, as well as efforts to win hearts and minds and stabilize governance after battles were over, on the other. Military leaders learned from each other, passed along ideas orally, developed and trusted their instincts, built up an assertive martial culture that prized initiative and daring, and generally figured things out on their own.[68] There was no formal strategy or clearly defined enemy or even acknowledgment of an ongoing state of hostilities against Native Americans. Indeed, most campaigns ended with peace accords promising future friendship that were soon ignored, generally by settlers, when Americans' ambitions and their local numbers grew in subsequent years.[69]

One battle from this period stands out as an exception, in that it was a major win for Native Americans against U.S. forces. General Custer, the swashbuckling Civil War hero known for his energy and courage and at times recklessness, was charged with subduing Lakota and Cheyenne warriors led by Sitting Bull in today's Montana in the early months of 1876. The underlying rationale was familiar: American gold prospectors were moving into land previously promised to Native Americans, and when they met occasional resistance, the U.S. government decided to assert itself in their defense. What would follow was a disastrous outing for the American forces. A total of some 670 U.S. soldiers in the Seventh Cavalry regiment set out in pursuit. After a number of preliminary battles, a showdown occurred at the Little Bighorn River on June 25, 1876. Custer divided his forces into pieces that were too small to defend themselves and too far separated to help each other, hoping he could take Native women and children hostages and use them to force surrender by the male warriors. His plan failed disastrously; within his own battalion, all 200-plus soldiers were killed, including the general himself. He had underestimated Sitting Bull and his warriors—in their numbers, their courage, their weaponry (many were armed with repeating rifles), and their fighting skill. Later that year, President Grant publicly stated that Custer had sacrificed his battalion unnecessarily.[70] Yet he was emblematic of the boldness, and aggressiveness, of the war for the West.

Perhaps Custer's Last Stand has no particularly important role in a history of defense strategy, as it constituted a single notable tactical disaster (just ten days before America's centennial) more than a major development or seminal event. However, in another way it did mark a turning point in the "winning of the West," because after the defeat of Custer, the U.S. government resolved to retaliate—and ultimately succeeded in the effort, coming close to concluding the long struggle against Native Americans by 1890. As author Nathaniel Philbrick wrote in his seminal work on the battle, "While the Sioux and Cheyenne were the victors that day, the battle marked the beginning of their own Last Stand. The shock and outrage surrounding Custer's stunning defeat allowed the Grant administration to push through measures that the U.S. Congress would not have funded just a few weeks before. The Army redoubled its efforts and built several forts on what had previously been considered Native land."[71]

Soon major tribal leaders would have no choice but to live on reservations. In late 1890, Sitting Bull, resisting such displacement himself, would be shot to death on Standing Rock Reservation by Native American police working for the U.S. government. They had been instructed to arrest him in part because he was seen as too supportive of a religious movement called the Ghost Dance that envisioned a return of the dead and a peaceful reclaiming of North American lands by Native Americans.[72] The arrest was intended to be peaceful, until a melee broke out involving Sitting Bull's supporters. A number of those followers would be massacred by Custer's old regiment at Wounded Knee, South Dakota, a few days later. This tragic episode in many ways marked the end of the centuries-long struggles between the United States government and Native American tribes.

GREAT POWER RUMBLINGS AND THE SPANISH-AMERICAN WAR

As the West was being won, and the United States was becoming a modern industrial power that already rivaled any in Europe, American strategists began to think bigger thoughts about the world beyond. Eventually, defense strategy—and military resources—would follow.

In Washington, at West Point, and elsewhere, some army strategists were taking note of lessons not only from the Civil War but from ongoing fighting in Europe: the Crimean War in the 1850s, Germany's birth as a nation and military wins in the late 1860s and early 1870s, and other trends. Key participants in the debates about future warfare included generals with Civil War credentials as well as other leaders and strategists—to include Ulysses S. Grant, William Tecumseh Sherman, Philip Sheridan, John Schofield, Nelson Miles, Emory Upton, Arthur L. Wagner, John Bigelow, Clinton B. Sears, and John P. Wisser. Weaponry was becoming impressively more accurate, lethal, and rapid-fire in character, and these changes could not be ignored. Nor could the size and scale of the armies, and the battles, that were starting to manifest themselves in Europe (as they had in the American Civil War). Ultimately, however, American strategists collectively did no better than their European counterparts in correctly predicting what these trends would foretell about the nature of fighting in World War I, since no particular consensus formed about whether technological, industrial, and political trends pointed to a so-called revolution in military affairs. No such revolution was pursued by the U.S. Army, as historian Brian Linn has persuasively argued.[73]

Perhaps the lack of urgency resulted from a combination of the relatively easy wins the U.S. Army achieved against disparate Native American tribes, combined with the relative ease with which it closed out the century with the third declared war of its history.

That conflict, the Spanish-American War of 1898, was quick but consequential. Its impetus was the goal of liberating Cuba from Spanish misrule. But American ambitions quickly grew during the war. Seizure of the Philippines, Puerto Rico, and Guam from Spain, as well as the acquisition of Hawaii, became goals as well.[74] Subduing indigenous resistance in the Philippines became a bit of a millstone for the United States thereafter, however, and that effort lasted several years in contrast with just several weeks of fighting against the Spanish.

Cuba had resisted Spanish rule for decades, and America had long resented Spain's nearby presence as well.[75] After the Civil War, the United States found renewed interest in Latin America and the Caribbean. Although its own territorial ambitions were modest, it clearly wanted to be first among great power equals in shaping events in Latin America and the Caribbean. By contrast, it did have ambitions to the north and west, as it turned out. Having acquired Alaska by purchase from Russia in 1867 (the so-called Seward's folly, but really an act of genius by the American secretary of state), it would soon develop an interest in Hawaii as well as Guam and the Philippines.[76]

Throughout the last third of the nineteenth century, the United States had tried to throw its diplomatic weight around over crises and disputes from Chile, Peru, Venezuela, Brazil, and Nicaragua to Cuba and the Dominican Republic. And it would interject a few gunships and Marines, too; as Max Boot wrote, "A familiar pattern developed: A revolution takes place; violence breaks out; American merchants and diplomats feel threatened; U.S. warships appear offshore; landing parties patrol the city for several days; then they sail away."[77] Through the 1860s and 1870s and into the 1880s, the United States was not militarily muscular enough to do much more than that, even had it wanted to.[78]

Four vignettes illustrate much of the growing ambition—but also an ambition constrained by political ambivalence and relative military weakness—that characterized the United States for roughly a quarter century after the Civil War. First, in Korea, as America was trying to promote the same kind of open-door trading policies that it championed for Japan and China in this era, a U.S. ship was set afire and its crew executed in 1866. After various investigations and entreaties, the United States responded by sending raiding parties to attack forts along the Han River, killing 200 or more Koreans, but then returned to its traditional practice of negotiating for trading access rather than fighting for it. Second, when Chile was at war with Peru in 1881, the United States supported Peru but could not stand up to Chile militarily. America's wooden-hulled ships in the area, constituting the Navy's South America squadron, were no match for the Chilean navy, and effectively stood down. Third, now unified under Otto von Bismarck, Germany sought greater influence and control in the South Pacific. It colonized several archipelagos, including today's Marshall and Mariana Islands, and considered claiming Samoa as well. The United States considered putting up military resistance to ensure the island's independence. But in 1890 the chancellor decided it wasn't worth a fight so far from home over stakes of limited importance to Germany—and by then a typhoon had destroyed much of the German as well as American naval capability that had been brought to bear during the minicrisis. Again, the tension petered out. Ultimately the United States would annex Samoa, but it would not do so by driving another great power from the island.

Last, in regard to the closer-by Hawaiian Islands, the United States of course ultimately did annex them as well. But it took zig-zagging steps to do so over a number of years, taking a long time to decide how to pursue its ambitions. The United States deployed a Marine presence ashore and otherwise supported a coup in 1893 against independence-minded Queen Liliuokalani in the hopes of seeing her replaced with a local government willing to have Hawaii annexed by the United States. But later, once Grover Cleveland had replaced Benjamin Harrison as president, the United States changed its mind about annexing Hawaii and even toyed with the thought of trying to engineer putting the queen back on the throne. After yet another change of presidents, however, the American approach metamorphosed one more time. With President William McKinley in office, the United States annexed Hawaii in 1898 as part of a broader course of events in what proved to be a fateful year.[79]

Numerous structural factors gave rise to the Spanish-American War; the U.S. decision to use force was not born solely out of humanitarian concern for indigenous peoples. By 1890, the United States had become more populous than any European country save Russia; it produced more iron and steel than any other country on earth; it was displacing Britain as the world's greatest industrial power overall; and it was entering the ranks of the world's major naval powers, still well behind Britain and somewhat behind France in aggregate tonnage but roughly equaling Italy and exceeding all other global powers. It had not only ended its Civil War and paid off the corresponding debts but had bought Alaska from Russia, completed transcontinental telegraph and railroad lines, benefited from the creation of Canada and with that the lowering of any British threat to U.S. security in North America, and set its eyes on Asian markets.[80] The United States was starting to feel its oats.[81] Under President Cleveland it still showed a certain restraint; under McKinley and Roosevelt, it showed much less.

In terms of American military power, the transformation had really gotten going in the 1880s, including with the establishment of the Naval War College in Newport, Rhode Island, under the leadership of Commodore Stephen Luce in 1884. (Other notable military institutions of higher learning and study created in this era included the U.S. Naval Institute in 1873 and the Army's School of Application for Infantry and Cavalry at Fort Leavenworth, Kansas, in 1881. The Naval Academy at Annapolis, Maryland, had been established earlier, in 1845, to complement the U.S. Military Academy at West Point, which, as earlier noted, dated back to 1802.)[82]

The intellectual movement in favor of American naval power accelerated in the 1890s with the works of Alfred Thayer Mahan, who strongly believed that a modern world power required a major navy as a means of protecting and furthering control of the oceans as well as commerce. His other big ideas included an emphasis on the battleship and the great victory at sea, the importance of concentration of forces in battle, and diligent attention to logistics and resupply lines as well as base access. He was something of a romantic, not only for naval power in general but for eras gone by, including the age of sail. It was toward the end of that era during which he began his own career, after graduating from the U.S. Naval Academy in 1859. Although he served at sea during the Civil War, patrolling Confederate coastlines, most of his Navy career subsequently was on land, and most of it was uneventful—until a decision to accept an invitation from Commodore Luce (whom he soon succeeded) to teach at the Naval War College in Newport, Rhode Island. There his ideas would blossom—ideas, he acknowledged, that told a story of an ideal of naval power as much as they hewed precisely to the technical facts at hand.[83]

Mahan's first major work, published in 1890, *The Influence of Sea Power upon History, 1660–1783,* benefited from an upsurge in American strategic interest in naval power. It also gave further impetus and boost to that fledgling movement. Some consider it the most influential work of nonfiction by any American author of the nineteenth century.[84] There were other key champions such as Luce, President Benjamin Harrison's secretary of the navy Benjamin Tracy, Grover Cleveland's secretary of the navy Hilary Herbert, and then Theodore Roosevelt, first as assistant secretary of the navy himself and then of course later as president. Together, these personalities catalyzed a modest naval buildup centered on well-armored and well-gunned battleships with considerable size and range, envisioning the need to win a big naval showdown battle so as to dominate the seas and thus sea lines of communication. America's Gilded Age industrial revolution was making possible ample production of the kind of steel-hulled and coal-powered ships that naval technology of the day by now featured. Intensifying competition with European powers for access to key treasures in the Pacific such as Samoa and the Hawaiian Islands, as well as a desire for assured access to markets in Japan and mainland Asia, was creating a strategic rationale for a more expansive definition of the nation's naval interests. It squared well with what Mahan was arguing.

After a half dozen years of fledgling efforts, proper war games began to be conducted at the Naval War College by 1894. These had the net effect of reaffirming and strengthening the emerging consensus in support of a growing long-range American fleet.[85] In that day, a war game was defined as "an exercise in the art of war, either land or sea, worked out upon maps or tables with apparatus designed and constructed to simulate, as nearly as possible, real conditions." There were three types of games from the early days: duels of one ship against another, tactical games pitting a battle group against another, and strategic games looking at a broader theater in the context of a larger war.[86] Tactical games of the day were played with several model ships on a side (each typically of the same type), operating and fighting as squadrons. The game sometimes began with charts but generally wound up on a checkerboard painted onto the floor of a dedicated room at Newport. The games had umpires as well as clear rules for maneuvering and firing to guide the players. Effort was made to relate the performance of the simulated ships and weapons to the actual naval capabilities of the day or to those expected in the near future.[87] Usually one of the contestants was the United States Navy; the other might be the "pacing challenge" of Great Britain, or perhaps Spain, or another country or a generic opponent.[88]

As a result of all this intellectual and strategic ferment, American shipbuilding programs in the latter nineteenth century accelerated. The United States had built up a large navy for the Civil War, but most of that was oriented toward coastal operations and so was dismantled after the war.[89] A bit later, in 1880, the United States found itself in fourth place among all world powers in aggregate fleet tonnage (behind Britain, France, and Russia) and sustained that position through 1900, doubling the total weight of its navy along the way. Notably, the large battleships *Indiana, Massachusetts,* and *Oregon* would be funded in 1890—a consequential year for naval policy and U.S. foreign policy in general. All would be commissioned by 1896, well before the Spanish-American War.[90] They were armored vessels with displacements of about 10,000 tons, speeds of about sixteen knots, a unit cost of about $6 million, and weaponry featuring four thirteen-inch rifled guns as well as eight eight-inch cannons apiece.[91] (The United States would move into third place among the world's navies, behind Britain and Germany, by the outbreak of World War I.) Sometimes the advocates of such programs had a particular potential adversary in mind, such as Britain or Germany or Spain or even Chile, but the overall pro-navy movement in the United States reflected a more general sense of what it took to be a great power during the time of the Industrial Revolution. And America increasingly wanted to be such a power, if not in terms of imperial ambitions or big land armies, then at least in its naval aspirations.[92]

Mahanian thinking had limitations. It failed to anticipate the future need to project ground forces over large maritime distances, for example. It also underappreciated what fledgling technologies such as the torpedo and submarine could do to reshape naval warfare.[93] Again, Mahan was more historian than futurist. But this school of thought did much to move the United States into the realm of modern great power military competition and modern naval surface warfare.

With these changes underway and McKinley in office, the stage was now set for the United States to do something about the Cuba issue. To pressure and possibly coerce Spain, the United States deployed a warship, the U.S.S. *Maine,* to Cuban waters in early 1898. An explosion on the ship on February, probably an accident though not perceived as such at the time, set the United States on the path to open conflict against Spain.[94] Congress officially declared war in late April; it also appropriated additional funds for a military buildup.[95] The Army quickly grew from 25,000 to 200,000 soldiers over the ensuing months.[96] And American military leaders prepared to implement a war strategy involving Mahanian concepts of naval showdowns and big victories, combined with battles on land that involved panache and bravado more than sophistication or mass.

The first fighting of the short war occurred not near Cuba but in faraway Manila Bay on May 1, when Commodore George Dewey led a force that quickly destroyed the local Spanish armada. Soon, the United States would annex Hawaii, both to counter growing Japanese influence there and to have a way station for reaching the Philippines as well as other parts of Asia. America's war aims and accompanying defense (read, offense) strategies had quickly expanded to include territorial expansion in faraway places, based on pent-up forces that had been developing in U.S. strategic culture and domestic politics for some time by now.[97]

By late April 1898, U.S. warships had already sailed toward Cuba. Their plan was to establish a blockade, sever undersea telegraph cables out of Cuba, and prepare to block or fight Spanish naval reinforcements. By June and early July, American ground forces were collaborating with Cuban revolutionaries to conduct attacks on Cuban territory. U.S. forces included Theodore Roosevelt's volunteers, the fabled Rough Riders, as well as the famed African American "buffalo soldiers" of the Ninth and Tenth U.S. Cavalry Regiments. They prevailed in battles in and around Santiago on the island's east side, including the Battle of San Juan Hill on July 1.[98] Spanish ships in the city's harbor were therefore no longer safe; when they sought to flee to the open sea, U.S. naval forces under Admiral William T. Sampson destroyed them on July 3.[99] The fighting against Spain soon moved to Puerto Rico. Between late July and August 9, American forces achieved a rapid success against the Spanish units on the island.

Back on the other side of the world, the United States then won Manila from the Spanish on August 13. All fighting against Spain was over by mid-August, less than four months after America's declaration of war. And in the process, America had become an accidental imperialist. In taking the Philippines, the United States was modifying a war plan concocted earlier at the Naval War College for the purpose not of running that country but rather of harassing Spain as part of a broader war.[100] Yet like the dog that caught the car, the United States was now in control of the massive and faraway Philippine archipelago.

This string of victories for the United States set the conditions for the signing of a peace treaty according to which Spain also ceded Puerto Rico and Guam to the United States and granted Cuba independence (after what would be a short period of U.S. occupation). To smooth things over slightly, the United States paid Spain $20 million for the newly acquired territories. The Treaty of Paris would be signed on December 10, 1898, with ratification in the two countries following in the new year.[101]

There would, however, be another war. The U.S. decision to replace Spain as imperial owner of the Philippines catalyzed a resistance that lasted officially until 1902 (with occasional skirmishes for years to come). It produced a significant counterinsurgency operation by the United States. More than 125,000 U.S. troops wound up serving there, with a peak strength of nearly 70,000 at one point. The American tactics involved efforts to track and fight the elusive guerrillas, led by Emilio Aguinaldo, who would avail themselves of jungle and mountains to evade the occupiers. U.S. forces placed a premium on intelligence gathering, on finding tribes and groups that would collaborate with them, and on trying to isolate the guerrillas from their areas of support and sustenance. Some of this built on the ideas, and experience, gained in fighting Native Americans in previous years by some of the same Americans who led U.S. forces in the Philippines. At times, the tactics were brutal, including forced displacements of some civilians, torture during interrogations, and occasional scorched-earth operations.

Even though American forces were ultimately victorious, largely subduing the resistance, the experience was difficult. It lasted much longer than the Spanish-American War that had been its proximate cause. Over the course of the war, more than 4,000 U.S. soldiers would die from combat and disease; tens of thousands of Filipinos perished as well.[102] The United States would not try its hand at such large-scale colonial rule again.[103]

The verdict on this war is mixed. Despite many errors and some heavy-handed tactics at times, the United States employed a relatively light touch politically in administering the Philippines. It was also far less brutal than many powers had been, and would be, in their own colonies. Overall, the United

States wound up with a decent longer-term relationship with its former colony.[104] The Philippines would become independent in 1946, once the Japanese occupation of the islands was defeated by a much different type and scale of American military power.

CONCLUSION

As the nineteenth century ended and the twentieth began, the United States found itself in a period of strategic transformation. The struggle against the Filipino insurrection from 1899 to 1902 and the American role in a multinational suppression of the Boxer Uprising in China in 1900 (motivated largely by the desire to free Western hostages who were in peril) demonstrated that the United States was prepared to flex its growing muscles in faraway places.[105] Yet the operations of this period also revealed the limits of American imperial desire. In the former case, its first real big foray into the ways of colonialism also wound up as its last. And with the nation stretching from sea to shining sea, the Civil War over, and the "West won," American armies (and militias) would no longer have to contend with major operations on home soil. This set up a period of grand strategy that would—with the huge exception of World War I—prove a relatively quiet time until about 1940. As we shall see, however, defense strategy in these early decades of the twentieth century was never quite as calm and quiet and retreating as the nation's overall grand strategy; there were plenty of small interventions, lots of military innovations, and a building up of the nation's latent defense industrial base that would quickly position the United States as a world superpower once it chose to accept that burden.

The nineteenth century itself had not been quiet in any sense. To think of it as a period of strategic withdrawal or isolationism would be a major mistake. The United States had fought a war of choice against its former colonial master (after also fighting a quasi-war against its former Revolutionary War ally, France, at the end of the eighteenth century). Then it used its armies to seize large swaths of land from its southern neighbor all the while keeping a jaundiced eye on Britain in the north until territorial issues there were resolved (roughly by midcentury). It fought a terrible civil war on its own soil that threatened to tear the country in two. As it became a major industrial power in the last third of the century, it started to want to turn that capability into military power, especially with its fledgling modern navy. It used that navy, and other military assets, to push Spain fully out of North America and to take several Pacific islands as well as the Philippines while keeping a vigilant eye on the activities of other countries in the Asia-Pacific region, especially in China.[106] Throughout the century until 1890, it waged war against Native American tribes, constantly trying to squeeze them into smaller and smaller land tracts, given the inexorable westward push of the nation's population.

The grand strategy was expansionism. The defense strategy of the period—the combination of military budgets, forces, operations, ideas, and innovations that the United States pursued through its Department of War and Department of the Navy—was really an offense strategy. It had various incarnations, but it was about offense throughout. Even in the Civil War, which might be called defensive in some broader sense, the military strategy was about defeating the Confederacy, mostly on Confederate soil. The Union used power projection and a strategy of offense to win the war and restore the union.

With the exception of the Civil War, the United States of America employed militarily efficient strategies for achieving its desired goals throughout the first half of its history, particularly the nineteenth century. Its military forces were about 1 percent as large in manpower terms as they are today, even as the country's population of that era grew into the many tens of millions. With military spending that was consistently under 1 percent of gross domestic product, the nation roughly quintupled its size—largely through force of arms in one way or another.

The nineteenth century was a remarkable time in U.S. history. Through diplomacy and cunning, but especially through military force, Americans had just finished creating one of the largest, and soon the most powerful, country on the face of the earth.

CHAPTER IV

From Quasi-Isolationism to Hegemony, 1901–1945

The period of 1912–20 was among the most complex in the country's history in the making of defense policy. It revealed a nation that was starting to feel its oats and beginning to recognize that Europe's (and Asia's) long-standing patterns of war fighting were far from over but still feeling very ambivalent about its own desired role in addressing those conflicts. The interplay among different political forces before, during, and after World War I—and indeed, the internal debates within the minds of both Theodore Roosevelt and Woodrow Wilson—showed that the United States was beginning to feel a certain responsibility for keeping the peace globally, but along a zig-zagged path. America tried not to intervene in World War I, then quickly changed its policy and went all in, then just as quickly defeated Wilson's big idea for trying to keep the peace after World War I and adopted isolationism (at least in regard to Europe and Asia) as almost never before. It would take a second world war to convince Americans more or less for good—or, at least, until today—that the United States was indeed the world's indispensable power, to borrow Madeleine Albright's memorable phrase.

In the presidential election of 1912, Roosevelt, who had been out of power for four years (but was not term limited since the Twenty-Second Amendment to the Constitution was not ratified until 1951) ran as an independent. That decision essentially handed the presidential election to Woodrow Wilson because the three-man field contained one Republican (the incumbent, William Howard Taft), Roosevelt—a former Republican running as an independent—and Wilson, a Democrat. After this period, knowing full well that he had effectively gotten Wilson elected, Roosevelt came to despise the former New Jersey governor and Princeton University president. His own role in helping Wilson win the presidency seemed to intensify Roosevelt's antipathy toward the nation's twenty-eighth president.

When World War I broke out in Europe, Wilson promised to keep the United States out, in part because of his contempt for all the belligerents, including the colonial powers of Britain and France (Wilson was a racist in American politics but still didn't like colonialism). He persisted in this attitude even as Americans died in the Atlantic Ocean at the hands of German U-boat operators. Roosevelt's anger mounted. When Wilson still refused to enter the war after the sinking of the ocean liner R.M.S. Lusitania *in 1915, it made Roosevelt contemptuous of a man he now viewed as a coward. "What a dreadful creature Wilson is!," Roosevelt wrote a friend in April 1916.*[1] *Such words were not atypical of what the former president often said about his successor once-removed.*

Wilson ran for reelection on a peace platform and won—then promptly changed his mind and took the country into war by the following spring. Within eighteen months, 4 million Americans would be at arms, and the war would be won. One might have expected Roosevelt to be happy since he had been calling for such intervention long before Wilson committed to it. Alas, that was not to be. Roosevelt died on January 6, 1919, angry and frustrated despite all he had achieved in his life.

At about the same time, hoping to be sure such a conflict could never happen again, Wilson spent more than four months in Paris (yes, even while president). There, he negotiated the terms of the Treaty of Versailles as well as the League of Nations, a body that was designed to prevent future war by coming down hard collectively on any member of the league that demonstrated likely hostile intent. Indeed, the League of Nations was woven into the peace treaty, so that their ratification fates would be united in the U.S. Senate and elsewhere.[2]

But the Republicans, heavily influenced by the spirit and substance of Roosevelt's earlier attacks on Wilson, fought the League of Nations tooth and nail and, under Majority Leader Henry Cabot Lodge, defeated its ratification in the Senate in March 1920 (by a 49–35 vote). This happened even though the league was originally a Republican idea, with support from Roosevelt himself.[3] *The United States would ultimately not become a member, and the League of Nations would prove toothless once tested in the 1930s. Without American power as part of the bedrock of the framework, it would not succeed. Wilson soon followed Roosevelt down the path of bad health, suffering a debilitating stroke after weeks of hard travel while campaigning for the Treaty of Versailles on October 2, 1919. (He would die in early 1924, three years after leaving office.) As a nation, the United States returned to relative isolationism.*

There was a silver lining in all of this history. Even if the nation's political leaders often did a poor job with grand strategy, as well as defense budgets and overall preparations, there were key innovators within the military services both before World War I and before World War II. Many of the big ideas and new capabilities that helped turn bad starts in both conflicts into victorious outcomes were conceptualized, prototyped, and tested by the tiny peacetime defense establishments that the United States maintained before the wars. For World War I, the preceding innovations and insights largely concerned how to mobilize a military fast. For World War II, the innovations were much more sweeping and covered the gamut from carrier warfare to amphibious assault to strategic bombing to long-range logistics required by a country that was far away from where it would fight. Military innovators did a much better job than political leaders in the first half of the twentieth century. Defense strategy was much better than the overall grand strategy within which it operated. Had it not been so, the outcomes of the wars might not have been the same.

As America turned the corner into the twentieth century, even with the Philippines still under U.S. control, the era of expansionism was effectively over. Fights against Mexicans, Spaniards, and Native Americans to dramatically increase the size of the United States were done. The country had reached the same borders that demarcate its territory today, even if the formal process of turning certain territories into states was not yet quite complete. America (mostly) turned inward, focused its energies on increasing its prosperity, and gradually turned into the world's preeminent manufacturing and economic superpower.

But this era was also strategically dizzying. A forty-year period dominated most of the time by isolationism—or at least regionalism, given that the United States did stay active in nearby parts of Latin America as well as the Philippines—was interrupted by the two largest military efforts in the nation's entire 250-year history. By the end of the years 1901–45, America was sitting alone atop the world as the dominant power and yet was realizing that this status did not allow it to rest on its laurels, lay down its arms, or disengage from the world. It was surely the most transformational period of grand strategy and defense policy in the nation's history.

In 1943, the famed writer Walter Lippmann began his classic monograph *U.S. Foreign Policy: Shield of the Republic* with the following lament: "As the climax of the war finds the people of the United States approaching a national election, we must face the fact that for nearly fifty years the nation has not had a settled and generally accepted foreign policy."[4] At the broad levels of grand strategy and foreign policy, Lippmann was surely right.

Yet at the level of defense strategy, there was a steadier stream of progress. The benefits of that progress were severely constrained by the politics and grand strategies of the day, but they nonetheless left the country far better prepared for the world wars than it might otherwise have been. America may have mostly stayed home except in 1917–18 and 1941–45, but it intervened in Latin America even during other years in this era, even constructing a Roosevelt Corollary to the Monroe Doctrine in an attempt to wrap its operations with a certain legitimacy. It may have had very small armies before each world war, but it was beginning to have more of a navy. It also began to institutionalize training and innovation, as well as to strengthen the connections between the historically small regular army with the nation's various guard structures. The nation may have laid down most of its arms and again dismantled the preponderance of its armed forces after 1918 (while failing to ratify the Treaty of Versailles and thus also the League of Nations), but its Naval War College began to explore the concepts of aircraft carrier warfare and amphibious assault that would prove crucial in World War II, while the nation also improved its submarines and other key naval technology. Meanwhile, even though it was not viewed as defense strategy per se, the rocketlike growth of American industry provided what would become the foundations of the world's top military arsenal by the 1940s.

The United States may not have been quite ready to commit to participation in World War II until December 7, 1941. Yet by March 1941, it was beginning a massive expansion of its defense industrial capacities under the Lend-Lease program to provide weaponry to Britain and the Soviet Union, and of course ultimately to America's own armed forces as well. This program foreshadowed in some ways the creation of the U.S. alliance system after World War II, in the sense that the United States began to see its own security as inextricably linked with that of other nations. As Walter Lippmann cogently argued in 1943, that had never been the case before, and the United States needed to transform that aspect of its grand strategic outlook.[5] Doing so constituted a huge change in foreign policy behavior for a country that had generally been unilateralist in its employment of military power throughout its history—with the notable exceptions of the Revolutionary War (when it had little choice but to accept French help) and World War I (when it fought with Britain, France, Canada, and Italy for eighteen months but was quick to disentangle itself from foreign encumbrances thereafter).[6]

DEFENSE STRATEGY IN A YOUNG CENTURY: THE ROOSEVELT AND TAFT YEARS

Despite all the machismo and energy surrounding Theodore Roosevelt, of Rough Rider fame in the Spanish-American War, with all the bravado and confidence that made him prone to offer exhortations such as the one that gives this book its title, his presidency wound up relatively quiet on the military front. He was active diplomatically much more than militarily, with the caveat that throughout the early decades of the twentieth century the United States was quite active with its armed forces to its immediate south (plus ongoing if reduced action in the Philippines).

Roosevelt tried to pursue his philosophy of "speak softly and carry a big stick." That was a phrase he, as vice president, had coined when speaking to an audience at the Minnesota State Fair on September 3, 1901, two weeks before William McKinley would be assassinated and Roosevelt would become president. Roosevelt began to professionalize the U.S. Army in his time in the White House.[7] He undertook as much of a naval buildup as Congress would let him. Partly shifting American naval and other military sights away from Britain and Europe (even as Germany rose and the European powers increasingly built up their armed forces), Roosevelt also initiated the planning for a possible war against Japan, denoted by the color orange by war planners. War Plan Orange would become the foundation for U.S. strategy in the Pacific until 1941.[8] During this period, the Joint Army and Navy Board, though denying fortifications for basing in the Philippines in 1909, did approve reinforcement of Pearl Harbor in 1908.[9]

The U.S. Army numbered only in the tens of thousands of soldiers throughout the first decade and a half of the new century, in contrast to the several or many hundreds of thousands for the major European powers. But the Navy would grow faster. It had taken pride in winning the Battle of Manila Bay in 1898 against Spain—its first naval victory against a foreign fleet since the Battle of Lake Erie in 1813![10] Its fleet of seven battleships at the turn of the century was decidedly outnumbered by Britain (with fifty battleships), France (twenty-eight), Germany (twenty-one) and Italy (fifteen), though in aggregate fleet tonnage it surpassed Italy and Germany at that time.[11] As president, Roosevelt persuaded Congress to appropriate funds for ten battleships in his first term and then four big dreadnoughts of the type European powers were starting to build in his second term. President Taft later built another six. By 1914, the U.S. Navy was the world's third largest by aggregate ship tonnage. Still, in that first decade and a half of the twentieth century, Germany and Britain built up their fleets even faster than did the United States. At the outbreak of World War I, the U.S. Navy, with about 1 million tons of total tonnage, trailed the German fleet's 1.3 million tons and Britain's 2.7 million tons.[12]

The United States at the turn of the century was still responsible for two countries, Cuba and the Philippines, that it had seized in 1898. With Cuba, it would effect a transition quickly and transfer authority in 1902 to a newly elected Cuban government—after Congress in 1901 passed the Platt Amendment, by which the United States gave itself certain supervisory rights in Cuba (in 1903, America would establish the Guantánamo Bay naval base there).[13] In the Philippines, conflict lasted longer. Through much of 1899, the United States military conducted extensive conventional operations and pursuits against the main forces of revolutionary leader President Emilio Aguinaldo. These attacks were not known for their sophistication; they tended to be direct, aggressive, and successful. For the next two years, and to an extent even after the capture of Aguinaldo in 1901 and even after the United States claimed the war to be over in 1902, Filipino forces turned into insurgents.[14] By 1902, there had been some 4,200 American fatalities and five times that number among Filipino combatants; thereafter, the violence declined, even if it did not cease. Max Boot credits the United States with relatively sound use of counterinsurgency methods, to include fighting hard when necessary but also garrisoning in the countryside to gain intelligence and discourage recruiting by insurgents (even with a U.S. troop presence that averaged only 24,000 personnel in country), treating prisoners reasonably humanely, treating friendly and collaborative Filipino civilians well, undertaking development projects, and more generally creating economic incentives for cooperation.[15] The Philippines gained considerable autonomy from the United States in 1907 and full independence, after the Japanese occupation, in 1946.

In neither Cuba nor the Philippines did America discover much of a taste for colonialism. Although there was never a strong domestic U.S. reaction against either war, there was no real constituency for similar action elsewhere.[16]

That is not to say that all was quiet elsewhere early in the twentieth century. But excepting the Philippines operations, most of the military action carried out by the United States was small in scale and nearby in location. To be specific, there were interventions in Panama (1903), Cuba (1906–9), and Nicaragua (1909–12). Later, the United States also got involved in Haiti, the Dominican Republic, and Mexico. These generally fell under a philosophy or foreign policy dictum that became known as the Roosevelt Corollary to the Monroe Doctrine, after TR gave a speech to Congress outlining its general philosophy in late 1904.[17] By this unofficial policy, the United States would insist on a certain stability and good governance in the Western Hemisphere, according to itself the right to intervene militarily when such conditions did not obtain—while warning European powers, including Great Britain, to stay out.[18]

Strikingly, the United States eventually applied this philosophy even to the large neighboring country of Mexico during the Wilson presidency. In 1914, it engaged in a showdown with Mexican forces in Veracruz and then pushed the already teetering Mexican president, Victoriano Huerta, out of office. Wilson also sent U.S. forces into Mexico in March 1916 in an unsuccessful, almost year-long pursuit of the revolutionary leader Pancho Villa, who had just raided New Mexico. These operations involved around 7,000 and 10,000 U.S. troops, respectively (with 112,000 guardsmen and 48,000 regular soldiers also mobilized along the U.S.-Mexico border in 1916).[19] The National Defense Act of 1916 authorized placing guardsmen under federal control and gave the president the power to send them abroad if necessary, but only if the guard units were not broken up and integrated into regular army formations.[20]

Some of the logic of the Roosevelt Corollary and related ideas was intended to keep the highly imperialistic European powers of the day from feeling a temptation to meddle. Some was due to America's traditional and sometimes sanctimonious view of its "white man's burden" to help other countries advance.[21] Much of the net effect was to turn the Caribbean into an "American lake" by 1917 or so. As Max Boot wrote, "The Stars and Stripes now flew over the Panama Canal Zone, Puerto Rico, Haiti, the Dominican Republic, and the Virgin Islands, while the rest of the Central American and Caribbean states were firmly under Uncle Sam's thumb, with the exception of a few islands safe in the hands of America's allies, Britain and France."[22]

America's activities in Asia also grew in this period. Strategist and Asia specialist Michael Green, echoing Henry Kissinger, considers Roosevelt one of the greatest American presidents in terms of grand strategy. That is because, dating back to his days as assistant secretary of the Navy in the first McKinley term and then as president, he saw Asia policy and grand strategy in a coherent whole. By promoting the acquisitions of Hawaii and the Philippines as well as Guam, Wake, and Samoa, ultimately fortifying some of them, and expanding the U.S. Navy by as much as Congress would allow him, he created a stronger overall position in Asia. By mediating an end to the Russo-Japanese War of 1904–5, he not only won a Nobel Peace Prize but also created a dual policy of both deterrence and reassurance of Japan, the key rising power of the day. (Forebodingly, however, that peace accord gave Korea as well as parts of Manchuria to Japan.)[23] Roosevelt's accomplishments, according to Green, would not be sustained by successors. But he may nonetheless have laid some of the hard-headed realist groundwork for a more effective U.S. policy toward Asia decades hence.[24]

Roosevelt was also decisive in the matter of the creation of the Panama Canal. This was in fact a decision of consequence for defense strategy; it would allow the otherwise distant Atlantic and Pacific fleets to reinforce each other (and in theory swing from the defense of Cuba to that of the Philippines or Hawaii or American interests in China). This reality squared nicely with the popularity of Alfred Thayer Mahan's almost mystical concept of a "fleet in being" that would constitute the decisive measure of naval power. Thus, Roosevelt's strategic and military legacy should also include an appreciation for his role in the geopolitics of the canal—to be specific, the support for a secessionist Panama as it broke away from Colombia and invited the United States to help it build that canal and then protect it militarily in the years that followed.[25]

Not all the military action was in the Department of the Navy. Important innovations happened in this period in the Army and the Department of War as well. Indeed, in many ways, it was during the early decades of the twentieth century that the United States first truly professionalized its ground forces, as well as the rest of its armed forces. As noted, yes, there had been well-trained and smart leaders before, not least Lee and Grant (to say nothing of Washington). Yes, West Point and then Annapolis had been up and running for decades during the nineteenth century; also, the U.S. Naval Institute had been created in 1873, the School of Application for Infantry and Cavalry at Fort Leavenworth in 1881, and the Naval War College in 1884.[26] But it was really in the period from 1900 through the 1930s that these earlier efforts and some big new ones led to institutionalization of the notion of an American profession of arms. Even if it did not yet endorse a strong, well-resourced, standing military in peacetime, the country created enough support for core military expertise to develop such leaders as John Pershing, Dwight Eisenhower, George Marshall, Omar Bradley, and Hap Arnold in the Army and Chester Nimitz, William Leahy, and Ernest King in the Navy. That would make all the difference in the end.

Pershing deserves a special word, as he was the oldest of this distinguished group, a generation ahead of the others, and therefore a senior leader of the Army in the World War I era. He displayed impressive personal strength when his family was killed in a house fire in August 1915 back in San Francisco even as he commanded U.S. Army troops in Texas, where his unit had been transferred due to the unrest in Mexico that would lead to the raiding and border fighting of 1916–17. Yet he soldiered on. He wound up leading troops into Mexico the next year in response to a raid Mexicans carried out in New Mexico.

This was done in the absence of any usable U.S. Army plan for how to fight or conduct military operations within Mexico—Pershing and his team had to design their campaign on the spot in real time.[27] The restrictive rules of engagement that Wilson imposed on him for conducting the raiding were frustrating to the general, but he understood civilian control of the military, kept his mouth shut, and later recognized that Wilson had probably been right, given the undesirability of winding up in an all-out war with Mexico as possible American intervention in World War I brewed. Pershing would then find his true fame in the World War I history described below. He received the rarely bestowed honorific title of "general of the armies" as a reward and remained an important source of military advice until his death in 1948. He remains venerated in the Army today; as one symbolic but significant example, "Pershing's Own," a group he created as Army chief in 1922, remains among the Army's most celebrated marching bands. More important, he was a key mentor and role model to the World War II generation of outstanding Army officers.[28]

Under President Roosevelt, Secretary of War Elihu Root created a standing general staff as well as the Army War College. Military education promoted new patterns of education such as Civil War battlefield circulation tours, with role-playing for young officers as they sought to understand (or improve on) the decisions made decades before in these same locations. Root excelled in his career as an institution builder; he would also restructure the State Department when, in Roosevelt's second term, he became secretary of state. Despite his isolationist tendencies, Root strengthened the Department of War and the U.S. Army considerably—and mediated various disputes between foreign countries, including that of France and Germany over Morocco in 1907, winning the Nobel Peace Prize for his efforts in the year 1912.[29]

Some of the other changes in American defense strategy and policy early in the 1900s included more realistic training. Officers learned how to operate and fire artillery, both the field and coastal defense varieties.[30] Others were more institutional: under the Dick Act of 1903, the federal government provided equipment to guard units but insisted on certain training standards, including collaboration with active-duty forces. By the summer of 1910, for example, almost 47,000 guardsmen together with more than 25,000 regular army soldiers trained together.[31] By 1907, the Army had created an Aeronautical Division, first focused on balloons but soon including airplanes. And by the year 1916 it had established a flight school near San Diego.[32]

Although the Army remained small throughout this period, it did triple in manpower between late-nineteenth-century norms and the early years of the

1910s. Its plans for war may often have been fantastical, positing for example a British or German invasion of North America, but it did begin the war-planning process in a more formal way. And although many of its top thinkers had a hard time understanding what mechanization and other new technologies would do to change warfare, a debate had at last begun.[33]

AMERICAN MILITARY STRATEGY IN WORLD WAR I

The key point to understand about American military strategy in World War I is that the nation had studiously avoided having any such strategy up until the moment when it entered the conflict. In terms of strategy, therefore, it was not nearly as interesting a war as World War II or even the Civil War.

To see why, recall the political sequence of events. In 1914, when war broke out in Europe, President Wilson consistently favored neutrality. Two years later he campaigned for reelection with a similar message. Then, six months after that, he was asking Congress for a declaration of war.[34] This case supports Elizabeth Saunders's contention, based on subsequent cases, that American policy-making elites often are more hawkish than publics in decisions on the use of force.[35] It also is a cautionary note about how often Americans do not know their own minds when it comes to decisions on matters of war and peace and how swells of sentiment can profoundly change a debate.

Wilson was, as noted, at first simply disgusted with the war. It took the sheen off a century that had begun with remarkable discoveries and inventions and seemed to augur an age of globalization, prosperity, good governance, travel and communications, and international harmony. The guns of August 1914 changed all that; it soon became apparent that those who expected the boys to be home "by the time the leaves fell" were badly wrong. By year's end, hundreds of thousands were dead in the ranks of each of the major militaries participating in the fight. Whatever blame Wilson assigned the initiators of this war—Austria-Hungary for its July 28 attack on Serbia to punish it for the June 28 assassination in Sarajevo of the Austria-Hungarian heir to the throne, as well as Germany for its Schlieffen Plan attack on Belgium, Luxembourg, and France on the Western Front together with German support for Austria in the east—he considered all parties at fault. Ambitious Russia, as well as imperialistic Britain and France, shared plenty of guilt for the conflict in Wilson's mind. America's ethnic diversity, with plenty of German Americans and Irish Americans and other interested parties, provided one more reason why, for the sake of domestic harmony, it would make much more sense to stay out of the war. The sheer carnage that ensued made participation in the fighting even less appealing. As each of the first three years of the war came to their successive closes, the losses only piled up, even as the prospects for victory for any of the parties seemed as elusive as ever.

American attitudes did begin to shift, albeit gradually at first. An initial milestone was the sinking of the luxury British passenger liner *Lusitania* by a German U-boat on May 7, 1915. Some 1,200 individuals died, including 128 Americans. The U-boat was part of an "unrestricted submarine warfare" against shipping in the Atlantic.[36] Yet in his presidential campaign against Republican Charles Evans Hughes in 1916, Wilson promised to keep the United States out of the conflict and to ensure a "peace with dignity." Some prominent voices, such as former president Theodore Roosevelt, former secretary of state and senator Elihu Root, and former secretary of war (as well as future secretary of state and war) Henry Stimson, favored sterner measures. But Wilson found electoral success in rejecting such advice.[37]

Yet at the same time, Wilson was starting to recognize another possibility. By late 1915, Wilson had already directed the secretary of war and the secretary of the Navy to develop plans for expansion of their forces; as one indication of how much things would need to change, the U.S. Army of 1914 had about 98,000 soldiers (while Britain had 250,000, and Germany and France each more than 500,000).[38] Wilson proposed a major preparedness initiative in December 1915 in his annual speech to Congress, with ideas for major expansions of both the Army and the Navy. Parts of this plan met strong antiwar resistance, but other parts gained support, especially the naval elements.[39] In 1916, Congress began a defense buildup, passing the National Defense Act and the "Big Navy Act." The latter funded ten huge dreadnought battleships, six very large battle cruisers, and a slew of smaller ships and submarines. The composition of this buildup reflected the Mahanian thinking so prevalent in the United States (and beyond) at the time: naval forces should prepare for the great battle at sea, with the ultimate goal of achieving maritime dominance and thus freedom of maneuver. Alas, this view of naval warfare would not prepare the United States so well for what proved the real concern in World War I: getting supplies and troops safely across the Atlantic Ocean in the face of German submarines. Thus, much of the shipbuilding plan would have to be redirected to antisubmarine-capable destroyers once the United States entered the war.[40]

Wilson did run for reelection on a peace platform, but as noted he was already well into a hedging strategy by November 1916. His views would harden considerably over the following six months, as would those of the nation more broadly.

In early 1917, the U.S. military had a strength of around a quarter million active-duty troops, including roughly equal numbers of soldiers and sailors (with some 11,000 Marines, too). These totals were still very modest by the standards of the overseas armies that were already fighting the war, but they were growing.[41] Then, in May 1917, the Selective Service Act became the law of the land, and serious mobilization commenced.[42] That followed a declaration of war by the U.S. Congress, at Wilson's request, the previous month.

There were two main reasons for Wilson's, and America's, change of heart. First, early in the year, Germany tried to lure Mexico into alliance, with the hope that it would attack the United States so as to distract America. However, British intelligence intercepted the "Zimmermann telegram" in January 1917; by March 1, its contents were widely known throughout America. Mexico did not attack the United States, but for Germany, the damage was done.

Second was the resumption of unrestricted U-boat warfare on February 1, 1917, after an eight-month period when Germany had thought better of the idea. (During that latter period, it tried to warn ships from neutral countries before attacking, additionally pledging to try to save their crews if they were in peril.) Germany now had a much larger submarine fleet, totaling almost 150 vessels, and was much more effective than before in its attacks. Monthly loss rates for Allied shipping to Britain, which mostly needed food, and France and Italy, which needed coal, increased from less than 100,000 tons in 1915 and 1916 to 520,000 tons in February 1917, 565,000 tons in March, and 860,000 tons in April. The German admiralty believed that the Axis powers could win the war if such loss rates continued for just a few months. U-boat losses were averaging only about three a month, so trendlines were very promising for Germany and foreboding for the Entente powers.[43] The bad news for Britain, France, and Italy did not stop there. Entente offensives were failing on the Western Front, and Russia was weakening from within on the Eastern Front; indeed, Russia would be largely out of the war by the late fall of 1917 (and formally out in March 1918).

The indiscriminate U-boat attacks proved to be the last straw for the United States, as ships were sunk in March with considerable loss of American life.[44] With the U.S. declaration of war against Germany in April (and another to follow in December against Austria-Hungary), the race was now on. Could the Central Powers prevail before America's entry into the war on the Western Front turned the tide in the Entente's favor? Could American and English antisubmarine warfare capabilities ensure that those supplies could cross the Atlantic? And could German society remain cohesive in the face of a more concerted Entente effort, now fully aided by the Americans, to prevent Germany from getting supplies by sea? As it turned out, the blockade against Germany would be central to the war's outcome.[45]

The U.S. strategic task ahead was simple enough—build up big armies, then join in the fight in Europe as soon as possible and with maximum numbers. There was little thought of tactical or operational cleverness, of a big new concept of warfare or unexpected maneuver or what British strategist B. H. Liddell Hart would later call "the indirect approach."[46] Nor was there widespread appreciation of the horrors of modern weaponry and war, the kinds of tactics needed to cope with artillery and machine guns on the battlefield, or the type of training needed to become proficient in such tactics. Rather, the purpose was to apply force against force.[47] That mobilization task was daunting, and the achievement of such a rapid buildup must count as a major success for strategy even if American forces did not make many notable innovations on the battlefield.[48] U.S. military forces would grow enormously and very fast. From a starting point of fewer than 300,000 uniformed personnel in early 1917, they would manage somehow to exceed 4 million in 1918. Of that total, 300,000 American troops would be in Europe by March 1918, 1.3 million by August, and some 2 million by war's end (most of them Army soldiers, plus about 25,000 Marines at peak).[49] U.S. military spending as a percentage of gross domestic product would rise from roughly 1 percent in 1914 to almost 14 percent by war's end.[50]

To get all those people to Europe, as noted, the U-boat challenge needed to be countered. Some of the necessary progress involved technical and tactical innovation. In that sense, at least, there was innovation and cleverness to American defense strategy. The key elements of submarine and antisubmarine warfare, to include the airplane and the rudiments of sonar and depth charges, were all either very new or relatively novel.[51] Thus, the pace of progress in technology as well as tactics was fast in this period. Initial American hesitancy to devote its modest-sized navy to operations in open ocean waters, rather than keeping ships near U.S. coastlines, had to be overcome. The Allied forces also needed to realize that shipping vessels should traverse the ocean in convoys to reduce the odds of U-boats finding targets randomly on the open ocean. Sending transport ships in convoys also made it more realistic to protect each of them with an armed escort vessel. The American naval shipbuilding industry redirected its efforts toward producing destroyers and smaller escorts as fast as possible for this purpose (after the Navy's previous preference for battleships). Many shipbuilding programs were only getting fully going when the war ended, but the increase in scale and redirection of purpose was impressive nonetheless and important for the outcome of the war.[52]

The tables began to turn as a result of all these changes. Even though Germany continued to build and launch new submarines at least as fast as existing subs were destroyed, the improved Allied methods succeeded in their central task. Shipping losses in August 1917 declined to just over 500,000 tons, and December losses to 400,000. By the spring of 1918, monthly loss rates for Allied shipping dropped below 300,000 tons of aggregate ship weight.[53] By this last year of the war, more than 90 percent of Allied shipping was sailing in convoys, often with fifteen or more ships per group. Their average loss rate dropped to just 0.5 percent.[54] As a distinguished naval historian wrote, "Safely transporting the AEF [American Expeditionary Forces] to France was the Navy's major accomplishment in World War I."[55]

Weaponry, or at least American-produced weaponry, would have to wait.[56] France wound up supplying more than three-fourths of the heavy equipment used by American forces in the remainder of the conflict.[57] In this sense, World War I was almost the flip version of what would happen later in World War II, when the United States became the "arsenal of democracy" (as well as of much Soviet power) before it built up its own forces.

Yet for all this progress in rapid American mobilization, momentum actually shifted to Germany before it changed again in the Entente's favor. Russia's departure from the war gave the Central Powers a much easier task and an ability to focus on the Western Front in 1918. In the spring, Germany undertook a massive offensive in France. With an edge in total strength estimated roughly as 192 divisions to the allies' 178, Germany made real headway even against trench lines that had been prepared and strengthened for months or years. In many areas, Germany was able to move roughly halfway to Paris from where its forces had begun the year, often winding up within just a few dozen miles of the French capital. Germany even got close enough to use its new Paris gun (often confused with the Big Bertha) to target the French capital directly.

These German successes were not due only to an improved ratio of forces.[58] German forces assaulted in several sectors at once, so British and French forces could not concentrate their defenses or their reserves in just one place. Germany also empowered small elite infantry formations, including storm battalions, armed with light machine guns, to bypass Allied resistance and, where possible, to penetrate more deeply into enemy rear positions. Germany also did a more effective job of ranging artillery, by calibrating weapons in advance of attacks. Thus, the initial rounds stood a much better chance of doing significant damage to front-line defenses.[59] So as to make their storm battalions effective and take full advantage of surprise, German forces made their preparatory artillery attacks intense but relatively short. As the movements proceeded, artillery then shifted to attacking second-tier Allied defenses even as attacking troops reached the front-line positions. These rolling attacks, when combined with greater accuracy and quick exploitation of the ensuing damage and confusion, led to more significant breakthroughs than the Western Front had seen in years. Improved aircraft and other sensors also made greater contributions than before, helping identify and target enemy troop and artillery concentrations.[60]

The tide soon started to turn, however. German progress, even if impressive, came at a high cost—and it was not a cost Germany could sustain for long, four years into this terrible conflict. As historian Michael Neiberg wrote, "As long as German casualties remained roughly equivalent to Allied casualties, they only represented attrition on a larger and more mobile scale. Given that Germany could not replace its manpower losses as quickly as could the Allies, the German offensives were actually bringing Germany closer to defeat, not victory."[61] The Allies were also making some smarter decisions. Notably, as American forces arrived on the battlefield, the Entente allies agreed to unity of command in early April 1918. Field Marshal Ferdinand Foch, chief of staff of the French military for roughly a year at that point, was designated as supreme Allied commander for the duration of the war. Administrative bodies including the Supreme War Council, the Allied Maritime Transport Council, and the Inter-Allied Food and Munitions Councils helped ensure close cooperation.[62]

The natural ebbs and flows of battle also made a difference. As German forces moved forward, their logistics lines lengthened and became more vulnerable. Then Germany tried to split British and French forces from each other in a drive toward the coast.[63] But German advantages were not great enough to make the prospects of success very good. In the Second Battle of the Marne, beginning on July 15 and lasting until August 9, 1918, Germany had an advantage of no more than 10 percent in overall strength. Allied forces also benefited from intelligence breakthroughs that gave them knowledge of German positions and plans. They also had more tanks than before and were putting them to better tactical use.[64]

In a sense, American strategy in 1918 became subordinate to, and derivative of, French strategy, given Field Marshall Foch's command position. American forces were first positioned to help stymie German advances near Belleau Wood, around fifty miles northeast of Paris, making up the right side of the overall Allied position (with French forces in the center protecting Paris and British forces on the left, closer to the English Channel). There, over the course of June, Army and Marine Corps forces fought successfully, with the battle subsequently finding its way into a core part of Marine Corps history.[65] The German threat to Paris was countered for the time being.[66] U.S. Army and Marine Corps forces also managed to deny Germany access to key transportation arteries.[67] Foch anticipated that German forces would next approach the Marne River near the city of Rheims. That would leave their flanks exposed if Allied forces could prepare a counterattack in time. Foch's prognostication and preparations proved wise; the Second Battle of the Marne, in mid-July, would go the Allies' way.[68]

Throughout the year, U.S. troops continued to arrive. They were formed into their own army, the American Expeditionary Forces, under General John Pershing, and took up positions in the southern sector on the Allies' right side as they faced the enemy. With the U-boat threat now mitigated, around 2 million U.S. troopers would make their way to Europe (typically with only a few months' training each).[69]

The next big American contribution came in September. With Colonel Billy Mitchell's airpower backing them up, American and French soldiers won a big battle near the Saint-Mihiel salient.[70] Then, controversially, rather than continuing forward to sever German logistics lines, U.S. forces repositioned to attack German forces in the Argonne Forest, with the objective of seizing the communications hub at Sedan.[71] As the fall unfolded, in October and November, American forces continued onward through the Argonne Forest and toward the Meuse River. Throughout all this fighting, U.S. forces suffered big losses against the often well-dug-in German formations.

But whatever the wisdom of undertaking a direct frontal assault, the Allies now had numbers, with British, French, American, Canadian, Australian, and Italian forces at their beck and call. Despite their misjudgments, they were establishing momentum at the campaign level.[72] The Spanish flu also hit the famished and feeble German troops particularly hard.[73]

The end was now near. The combined effects of these military dynamics, combined with economic hardship resulting in large part from the naval blockade and political discontent back home, led ultimately to the collapse of the German government, the abdication of the kaiser, and the collapse of the German military by November 1918. Germany's armed forces now had to worry about internal revolt back home, and the Bolshevik threat, as much as the Allied threat in France. The Austro-Hungarian and Ottoman Empires were rapidly crumbling, too.

Thus, American defense strategy in World War I largely amounted to this: build up huge forces and get them across the ocean as fast as possible, then learn from the battle-tested French and British as much, and as fast, as possible about industrial-scale combined-arms warfare in the twentieth century on a battlefield filled with trenches and other fortifications. Then plow directly into German positions, using mass (and fresh troops) as the decisive advantages.[74] This strategy was clearly successful, even if not elegant or brilliant in the annals of warfare.

The experience would have a powerful legacy. It probably did much to shape World War II strategy—aptly caricatured by Russell Weigley in his depiction of an "American Way of War," with an emphasis on overwhelming mass and firepower.[75]

GRAND STRATEGY AND DEFENSE STRATEGY AT THE CLOSE OF WORLD WAR I

With the fighting over, after Woodrow Wilson spent more than a third of a year overseas (127 days) negotiating the Treaty of Versailles and the League of Nations, America seemed poised to embrace internationalism and ratify the legal documents that Wilson had brought home after so much painstaking work. Initially, the nation seemed to have a grand strategy of engagement abroad, to be implemented through the concept of collective self-defense. The idea was in some ways even more sweeping than what would follow World War II, since all major nations were to be part of the system, ensuring one another's safety through preventive action if and when necessary. America was not yet (again) isolationist. That tendency would, however, reappear in short order, culminating in the defeat of the League of Nations idea in the U.S. Senate in early 1920 and then the election of Warren Harding later that same year.[76]

It took time to negotiate these ideas in Paris because, even if Berlin was in no position to resist, Paris and London and Washington wanted somewhat different things. The initial terms, later formalized and toughened in June 1919 at Versailles, imposed only relatively modest territorial changes on Germany compared with what might have been expected.[77] But they placed strict limitations on German military capabilities, backed up by Allied occupation forces in part of the country. Most of all, and against Wilson's wishes, they imposed enormous reparations obligations on Germany to average 3.4 percent of GDP each year from 1918 through 1931.[78] The United States did have some responsibility for the reparations burden, however; Washington refused to forgive the war debts of its allies, meaning that Paris and London needed to look for funding somewhere, and Germany was the obvious place. These conditions set the stage for the economic woes of the Weimar Republic and ultimately the rise of Adolf Hitler.[79]

So one part of American grand strategy was to keep Germany weak, militarily and economically, thereby lessening the risk of future war. It also would make possible, in theory, for U.S. defense strategy to return to a form of minimalism. Yet minimalism did not equate to complete withdrawal, as Wilson saw it.

The other part of grand strategy was to be the League of Nations. It was Wilson's vision for how the world's powers could collaborate to check the aggressiveness of any future state that showed early signs of militarism. Alas, negotiated without much Republican involvement in the United States and injected into a very partisan political atmosphere, it never gained Republican support. There were constitutional problems with the league as well. It was seen by many, correctly, as committing the United States in advance to conflicts it might prefer to avoid while giving the president more or less sole decision-making power in the process, once Congress ratified the league—and thereby ratified away its own proper constitutionally grounded role in any future decision on the use of force.[80]

The overall grand strategy struggled to be one part visionary and reconciliatory, one part punitive and exclusionary.[81] That was perhaps oxymoronic. Another set of contradictions surrounded how Japan was treated at this juncture: Tokyo was allowed to keep previously German possessions that it had seized in China, as well as the Mariana and Caroline and Marshall Islands. Perhaps the hope was that the ideational power of the League of Nations combined with American and European commerce could incentivize Japan to deescalate its aggressiveness.

Also poorly thought through was America's fruitless (but mercifully modest) military intervention in northern Russia and Siberia at the end of World War I and lasting until 1920. It was intended somehow to put pressure on the new Bolshevik regime as it consolidated power internally, perhaps bringing about its downfall or at least its dilution as the exclusive power within Russia. The mission failed.[82]

In any case, oxymoronic or not, the League of Nations was voted down by the Senate. Lacking an American backstop, the league was left mostly toothless.[83] Defense strategy never even had to wrestle very hard with the question of what type of U.S. military, with what kind of mobilization potential, would be needed to give a league credibility. Possible American participation in any future enforcement operation had been dismissed as a possibility.

To be fair, even if the United States had joined, the methods of enforcement for a stable world order would have been unclear and almost surely contentious. The military concept backstopping the League of Nations was to have "armies and navies large enough for self-defense but no more," as Patricia O'Toole wrote in her biography of Wilson. Yet those armies and navies would also have to be strong enough to reverse any noncompliance with the core principles of the new world order, on a timely basis in a potentially distant battlespace.[84] That is easier said than done. Yes, if Britain and France had together maintained offensive combat power that could have reentered the German Rhineland should Germany choose to attack its eastern neighbors or remilitarize that Rhineland itself, they could likely have prevailed during the period of German weakness.[85] But that would have taken a very preventive and forward-leaning kind of strategic thinking that, while laudable, would have been challenging for those two countries to provide on their own absent American participation. And once German rearmament did begin, the opportunity was steadily lost. Alas, in military matters, it is very hard to construct stable balances of power or ensure that a defensive-minded coalition will be able to impose its will on any aggressor regardless of scenario. Even a three-to-one advantage in firepower for the league, notionally speaking, would not have been enough to guarantee victory—and certainly not on any particular timetable in any location whatsoever.[86] The League of Nations was a dream too far.

DEFENSE STRATEGY DURING THE GREAT ISOLATIONISM (WITH A TWIST)

With the United States out of the League of Nations and Warren Harding in the White House, the process of American withdrawal from the world would only accelerate. That trend had numerous manifestations in defense strategy.

Not everything was about withdrawal. The United States, at least for a time, kept up its tendency to intervene in Central America and the Caribbean. Limited ongoing operations continued for years in Haiti (1915–34) and the Dominican Republic (1916–24); the United States again intervened in Panama from 1918 to 1920; and the United States also intervened in Nicaragua from 1926 through 1933. As Antulio Echevarria pithily put it, "From an operational standpoint, these interventions fell into two broad categories: a swift, Patton-like show of force intended to preempt a counterrevolution (as in Panama) or to stabilize a political crisis (as in Cuba) or counterguerrilla missions designed to put down rebels or bandits who had already gained control of certain areas (as in Nicaragua, Haiti, and the Dominican Republic)."[87]

But in terms of the major muscles of defense strategy, the United States was indeed generally disengaging from Eurasia. First up was the Washington Naval Treaty of 1922. It was an agreement among the then-friendly powers to limit their respective fleets as a way to minimize military capabilities, promote arms control, and discourage future rivalry. Although a treaty, it was in many ways imposed by the United States, given the nation's relative power and influence at the time (and the fact that it led to American disarmament increased its appeal to rivals). It created the tonnage ratios of 5/5/3/1.7/1.7 in large ships (battle cruisers, battleships, and aircraft carriers) for the United States, Britain, Japan, Italy, and France. Other types of ships were unconstrained in number but required to remain less than 10,000 tons. But the treaty lacked an undergirding strategic logic for these numbers.

America's willingness to negotiate such a treaty also revealed a general disinterest in maintaining the strong global position that it had established by the end of World War I. Under the terms of the treaty, fifteen U.S. battleships and battle cruisers in the process of being built were scrapped; only three ships authorized in the Big Navy Act of 1916 would be completed.[88] America's economy was twelve times the size of Japan's in this period, and its shipbuilding capacity was severalfold larger than Japan's as well. However, as the 1920s unfolded, Japan outbuilt the United States five to one. It wound up with a larger navy than America's, in both ship count and aggregate ship tonnage, by the time of the Manchurian crisis in 1931.[89] Indeed, by 1941, Japan would have parity in the Pacific with all other naval powers combined.[90]

Things deteriorated in regard to the U.S. role in European security policy even faster. The same Republicans who had defeated the League of Nations in the Senate, including Henry Cabot Lodge and William Borah, did not relish keeping even a few thousand American troops in Europe to ensure that Germany complied with its Versailles obligations (not to militarize the Rhineland region west of the Rhine River in Germany or to exceed caps on the overall size of its armed forces). Through Senate action in 1923, they demanded that the United States pull all its troops out of Europe, and they succeeded in achieving their goal. Defense strategy and capability were coming into alignment with the grand strategy of isolationism.[91]

The results of this U.S. disarmament, disengagement, and isolationism (at least toward Europe and Asia) would soon prove tragic. Both Adolf Hitler and Franklin Delano Roosevelt reached power in 1933. Hitler at first did his best to preach a message of peace and solidarity, while FDR continued with the isolationist rhetoric of his predecessors. So strong was the American consensus in favor of disengagement that Neutrality Acts banning U.S. arms sales, and ultimately even loans, to belligerents at war (regardless of who attacked whom) were passed starting in 1935. A modest naval buildup was engineered by Roosevelt, but otherwise the nation's armed forces remained small, with the Army well under its very modest authorized strength of 280,000 and the Marine Corps smaller in 1939 than in 1922.[92] Indeed, even the Navy did not grow much. As historian Robert Love put it, "The decade of the Great Depression witnessed the renewal of American naval power, though at a pace so uneven and unguided that the Navy was clearly not prepared on the eve of World War II to deal with a two-ocean conflict."[93]

The (Theodore) Roosevelt Corollary to the Monroe Doctrine was replaced, in effect, by the (Franklin Delano) Roosevelt Good Neighbor Policy of disengagement in places closer to home as well. Arms manufacturers were belittled, and blamed for World War I, in much of the public policy discourse. FDR ran for reelection in 1936 on a platform of keeping the United States out of war—even after Hitler had occupied the Rhineland that spring in violation of the terms of Versailles. The Neutrality Acts remained in effect for several years, therefore, denying Britain and France the prospect of American material assistance in the event of war. Even in mid-1939, after Germany took Austria and Czechoslovakia, Congress refused to repeal the arms embargo resulting from the Neutrality Acts.[94]

It would take the German takeover of Norway, the Low Countries, and France in the spring of 1940 to shock America out of its self-indulgent stupor. Then, huge defense budget increases and plans for naval buildups ensued. So did the passage of the Lend-Lease Act to provide enormous amounts of assistance to Britain and the Soviet Union in March 1941.[95] Roosevelt also increasingly involved the U.S. Navy in antisubmarine warfare efforts against U-boats. The sleeping giant was awakening, and with its massive industrial capacity and engineering brilliance, it would be able to make up for lost time fast.

Still, until December 7, 1941, the sleeping giant remained a bit drowsy, half awake and still half asleep. The Selective Service and Training Act was passed in 1940 and created a draft for military-age men. But when reauthorization was required the following year, the vote to keep military conscription was very close (this was still before Pearl Harbor, of course). Much of the serious defense preparation focused on naval power and strategic bombing capability; George Marshall was among the few even in 1941 who thought that the United States might actually need to prepare for major ground fighting in Europe.[96]

THE SILVER LINING OF THE INTERWAR YEARS: MILITARY INNOVATION AND AMERICA'S TECHNOLOGICAL-INDUSTRIAL COMING OF AGE

Fortunately, some very good things happened in the 1920s and 1930s at the level of military innovation and entrepreneurship. Even as American grand strategy in the 1920s and 1930s remained built on the weak foundation of ostrichlike isolationism, defense strategy evolved. The United States was also completing its ascent to the number-one position in terms of global technological and manufacturing prowess. That was not defense strategy per se—certainly not explicit, conscious defense strategy—but its ramifications for the nation's armed forces would be enormous. The country's political and strategic leadership underperformed in the 1920s and 1930s, but its scientists, technologists, leaders of industry, and innovators within the military services did not. Grand strategy in this period was poor; defense strategy, or at least part of it, was much better.

In the interwar years, very good planning and strategic analysis were done at the Naval War College and an organization called the Navy General Board about how new technologies might be employed, tactically and across extended military campaigns. This work produced a much clearer vision about how Japan might be fought. The so-called War Plan Orange went through various iterations. The core scenario always involved a Japanese attack against U.S. interests in the western Pacific that would drive the U.S. Navy back toward its coasts (or at least Hawaii) before it could recover and rearm and, after pushing back westward, ultimately fight Japan near its own shores.[97] Big questions were explored, such as whether the United States would need to withdraw from the Philippines and Guam in the event of future war against Japan and hunker down in Hawaii temporarily so as to protect the West Coast from attack until a more general return to the Pacific could be resourced.[98]

Under the leadership of Admiral William Moffett and others, the United States Navy made major progress in thinking about the proper uses of aircraft carriers.[99] Much was done through war-gaming in how carriers might be used in future war against Japan in service of a broader defense strategy and its supporting campaigns. After having been introduced in the 1880s when Alfred Thayer Mahan was the president of the Naval War College by William McCarty Little, war-gaming had by now become a fine art at Newport. There were accurate representations of the weaponry and speed and maneuverability and survivability of ships, a dedicated facility with an ornate floorspace divided into grids, detailed rules for running games, various role players and referees or directors and judges—a whole community dedicated to developing new concepts of warfare and to educating naval officers about how to fight. Indeed, looking back on this period in 1960, Admiral Chester Nimitz said in a lecture at the Naval War College, "The war with Japan had been re-enacted in the game rooms here by so many people and in so many different ways that nothing that happened during the war was a surprise—absolutely nothing except the Kamikaze tactics toward the end of the war; we had not visualized those."[100]

War games, whether used to guide modernization decisions or to train practitioners, hardly provide a guarantee of prescience about the future. They depend on reasonably accurate data about weapons effectiveness and other key technological inputs; they also are limited by the fact that they are generally conducted in comfortable, safe situations without the stresses and dangers of actual combat. Even some proponents of war games, such as Peter Perla, warn about a "garbage in, garbage out" risk inherent in such simulations, as well as in computer models of combat. Thus, to be compelling, war games need to be repeated many times under different assumptions and with different players—and their results also need to be treated with a certain skepticism. It is partly because the Naval War College has established such traditions of skepticism and caution in how it undertakes war games and seeks to understand their results, dating back to the late nineteenth century and reinforced throughout the twentieth (and continuing into the twenty-first to date), that it has become such a bastion for this particular type of military analysis and military training.[101]

The results of these and other intellectual exercises and technological experiments were impressive. The Navy ultimately developed catapults and arrester systems, along with other key enabling technologies, including long-range military logistics systems, and built several carriers before 1941.[102] Change came slowly in some ways. But enough change had occurred by the outset of World War II that within a couple years, the nation would start to wield the maritime forces necessary for ultimate victory.[103]

The Army Air Corps—renamed as such and given greater bureaucratic clout and budgetary prioritization within the Army by the Air Corps Act of 1926—also made important decisions in the interwar years.[104] In the 1930s, it developed and started to build the B-17 and B-24 bombers. The bombers were equipped with the Norden bombsight that helped calculate bomb release points as a function of air and wind speed; these were not enough to make World War II bombing precise in any meaningful sense of the term, but the bombers' improved engines gave them the range to wreak havoc on Germany from the summer of 1942 onward. (As discussed more below, when good escort fighters became available the following year, the American as well as British raids became devastating to German cities and industries—as well as the people who lived and worked in them.)[105]

That said, the interwar theories of how to use strategic airpower did not prove as prescient as those for naval combat. To be specific, the British in particular focused on bombing of cities to shock and scare populations and polities into rapid surrender. These ideas were espoused by the Italian theorist Giulio

Douhet and American general Billy Mitchell and were in effect attempted by Germany with its blitz on England in the summer of 1940.[106] They did not succeed in their core goals. Yet at the level of technological development, airpower was moving fast. Key inventions and improvements in radar, radio, engines, and aerodynamics were ongoing. Inventions and improvements in these and other areas made airpower increasingly effective against economically and militarily important targets as World War II went on—even if it never attained the silver-bullet effects promised by its advocates.

The Marine Corps also carried out a great deal of innovation in the interwar years. It would make great strides in understanding and preparing for amphibious assault as a result. Refusing to be discouraged by the unsuccessful British-led Entente experience at Gallipoli in 1915, the U.S. Marine Corps pursued tactical and technological innovations that would ultimately produce many great Marine Corps (and Army) successes in the Pacific in World War II. Some of the ideas that were war-gamed as well as field-tested included use of smokescreens at various points in operations, daytime as well as nighttime landings, assaults with varying degrees of troop concentration or dispersal, different types of close-air support from aircraft, and varying types of preparatory bombardment. Technologies such as landing craft were also improved over time.[107]

There were mistakes, and limitations, to the progress. Some technologies, such as amphibious ships, and tactics, such as the proper use of preparatory bombardment as well as close-air support, would have to be improved in real time during World War II. But on balance, even if it was not always finding the right answers, the Corps was asking the right questions. It understood that methods of modern amphibious assault were a work in progress, as reflected in the name of its signature and constantly evolving doctrine of the 1930s, *The Tentative Manual for Landing Operations.* It was also doing the right experiments, often at large scale in the Caribbean or in California, even as soon as the early to mid-1920s, but especially in the Fleet Landing Exercises of the mid- to late 1930s. The long-standing and legendary commandant from the 1920s, Major General John Lejeune, as well as General Ben Fuller and several others, deserve great credit for driving the amphibious innovation debate in the interwar years. They conceptualized the Fleet Marine Force as the crucial organizing construct for the future Marine Corps. They saw amphibious operations as very much the future of the Corps when many would have relegated the Marine Corps to port and coastal defense roles—or to functioning effectively as a second American army for traditional ground combat, as had been the case in World War I.[108]

Again, for many of the technological inventions that supported and enabled these new war-fighting concepts, the nation's strong scientific and engineering foundations contributed importantly to defense strategy and policy. Not only military aircraft and ground vehicles but specialized systems such as amphibious tractors benefited from innovations made first in civilian and commercial sectors.[109] Improvements in computational power also would produce advanced code-breaking equipment and algorithms.

Less prescient was the Navy's thinking before World War II about the submarine threat. It was also slow to figure out the antisubmarine warfare mission once the war began and made major headway on the challenge only in 1943 after lots and lots of shipping found its way to the bottom of the Atlantic. Needing to relearn some of the lessons of World War I, the Navy did not initially appreciate the importance of convoys, of convoy escort warships, of long-range antisubmarine aircraft, or of high-frequency radar and search lights to find enemy submarines when they surfaced. The Navy would improve during World War II—aided enormously by scientists and engineers who developed key technologies such as long-range aircraft and better sensors over the course of the war.[110]

The Army was adrift in the interwar years in its thinking about land warfare. It was dominated by infantry and cavalry branches that resisted new technologies and, even more, new concepts for employing them. Many thought leaders, perhaps overlearning from World War I, emphasized preparation for static, trench-based defensive concepts, such as how to better concentrate artillery fire, rather than development of new concepts of maneuver warfare. Horses continued to have their powerful advocates. Some, including George Patton, wedded to a martial mystique of combat, remained proponents of not only the horse but even the bayonet as the ultimate determinant of battlefield victory.[111] Debates centered on dueling memos more than the results of serious field exercises or experiments; new types of innovative units were formed and tested only reluctantly and slowly. Major General John Herr, Army chief of cavalry starting in March 1938, said even as late as October of that year that he was "unwilling to give up a single horse or man from the horse cavalry" to form any mechanized units.[112] On the whole, the Army failed to integrate the tank into combined-arms warfare, prioritizing "tank destroyers" over actual tanks, at the behest of Lieutenant General Lesley McNair among others. As a result, American tanks went into World War II inferior to German tanks, generally unable to execute kills against the latter. Airpower advocates remained fixated on strategic bombing rather than paying much attention to close-air support for ground troops.

The Army wound up having to learn combined-arms warfare largely by improvising in the field in World War II, and by imitating German methods, because of its intellectual bankruptcy on the subject through the 1930s.[113]

Fortunately, despite it all, some good things were happening within the Army. Its school system, including the improved and expanded Command and General Staff School (now College) at Fort Leavenworth in Kansas as well as the Army Industrial College, created a generation of leaders who would shine in the 1940s.[114] For example, Dwight Eisenhower and others foresaw the importance of the economic and industrial base on which the country's military would be based. In the words of Brian Linn, "If a military institution's wartime success is the ultimate vindication for its peacetime preparation, the interwar period was clearly a high point in the history of military thought."[115] Great leaders were emerging; and even if great new concepts of combat were slow to develop, at least bad ideas were not gaining consensus support.[116] Moreover, even from the mid-1930s, the distinct possibility of a two-front world war was being studied and analyzed at the Army War College, among other places. Academically, at least, the Army was getting ready.[117]

Even though exercises were not doing a great job figuring out new concepts of warfare, they did help the Army think about geography and campaigning in ways that proved useful in World War II as well. For most of the period from 1920 until 1940, the U.S. Army had fewer than 150,000 soldiers, even though the 1920 amendment to the National Defense Act of 1916 had authorized almost twice that number.[118] But around a quarter of all U.S. soldiers that the Army did have were generally based outside the continental United States, mostly in Hawaii and the Philippines and the Panama Canal Zone, as well as Puerto Rico, Alaska, and China.[119] In addition to routine drilling and patrolling, soldiers would sometimes conduct complex and difficult maneuvers. For example, in the Philippines, soldiers would simulate operations expected under the Orange War Plan, and in the Panama Canal Zone, they would sometimes try to fend off a mock attack by U.S. Navy ships. In Hawaii, they would try to repulse a would-be amphibious assault by mock Japanese forces.[120]

Actual preparations for war were not always good, and some would prove badly inadequate once war broke out. As D. Clayton James wrote about the American interest in and colonization of the Philippines in this time, "Like the United States Congress, which wanted neither to abandon the archipelago nor to provide funds for its adequate defense, the planners of the War and Navy departments could not solve the dilemma of Philippine strategic security."[121] That was symptomatic of a broader confusion about how far west America's military infrastructure could be defended in the opening weeks and months of any future war. Again, however, at least some of the right questions were being asked, even if the attempts at answers were often wanting.

DEFENSE STRATEGY IN WORLD WAR II

World War II was one of the three most important wars in U.S. history. The Revolution was literally existential; the Civil War threatened to cut the country in two. But had World War II ended the wrong way, hostile powers could have been in control of much or even most of Eurasia, with the potential ability to consolidate that giant landmass's resources and industrial base under hostile control—and with the possibility of also perhaps getting the nuclear bomb before the United States did, or at least nearly as soon. Hitler was also America's most brutal and ruthless enemy in history—Britain in the Revolutionary War and the Confederacy in the Civil War were not, by contrast, run by genocidal maniacs—so there is no telling what he might have done if ever in a position to threaten the United States directly. These concerns would have been particularly acute if Germany had not attacked the Soviet Union and the Molotov-Ribbentrop Pact had remained in place. Perhaps it would have been implausible to have Hitler and Stalin coexisting in Eurasia indefinitely, like two scorpions in a bottle. But Eurasia is a big bottle, and by all appearances, Stalin was prepared to live and let live with Hitler, so that potential axis of evil had half of its parties committed to the idea in principle. In any case, my larger point is that the outcome of World War II was not preordained, especially not in the early going. Until the end of 1942 or beginning of 1943, it was moreover not yet clear that the Allies were headed in the direction of ultimate victory. What grand strategy, and defense strategies, achieved that crucial result in the end?

Much of the answer had to do with the sheer scale of effort. World War II wound up far and away the nation's most expensive conflict, with the largest number of Americans at arms, in all 250 years of U.S. history to date. It was the second most deadly in terms of American lives lost, exceeded only by the Civil War (largely because of how many died of disease and infection in that earlier conflict). The U.S. military budget shot up to more than 35 percent of GDP by 1944, as the nation engaged in an all-out effort.

The simplest way to describe U.S. grand strategy in World War II is that the Allies sought the unconditional, unqualified military defeat of the Axis powers. The simplest way to describe the U.S. defense strategy that supported this grand strategy is that it sought to marshal the scientific, industrial, demographic, and thus military potential of the nation to mount direct attacks on the German and Japanese homelands, with Germany the higher immediate priority.

These strategies took time to come together and then took more time to be translated into specific plans of action and military campaigns. Before December 1941, broader U.S. grand strategy was not quite so alarmist. It did begin to shift increasingly toward a more hawkish approach to world affairs after the fall of France in the spring of 1940.[122] Indeed, after spending less than 2 percent of GDP on its military in fiscal year 1940, the United States spent more than 5 percent in fiscal year 1941, ending on June 30, 1941, and then 17 percent in 1942 (the figures would exceed 30 percent each of the next three years).[123]

In January 1941, presidential envoy and close confidant Harry Hopkins privately assured Winston Churchill and a small group with him, quoting from the Book of Ruth in the Bible, that "wither thou goest, I will go; and where thou lodgest, I will lodge; thy people shall be my people, and thy God my God . . . Even unto the end."[124] In March 1941, America became the "arsenal of democracy," creating the Lend-Lease program to provide enormous amounts of supplies to the Soviet Union and Britain. Yet the United States was not yet all in. Lend-Lease was a noble effort—but it was undertaken partly in the hope that by playing such a role, the United States could itself stay out of the war. It was not at all clear to the main parties that the United States would become a belligerent.[125] Roosevelt may have been leaning in that direction fairly strongly by early 1941, but much of the rest of the country was not. And even if Roosevelt was increasingly inclined to think that war against Germany was likely, or necessary, he was not looking to fight Japan at the same time. Popular lore to the contrary, the Pearl Harbor attack appears to have been a most unwelcome surprise for FDR.[126]

By the time Japan attacked the United States on December 7, 1941, World War II was already more than two years old (or four, if one includes Japanese attacks on central China). Hitler had absorbed Austria in March 1938. He then took the Sudetenland part of Czechoslovakia the following fall after the infamous Munich conference with leaders of Britain and France. He invaded Poland in September 1939, took the Low Countries and Norway and France in the spring of 1940, then pivoted southeast for the Balkans campaign of spring 1941. Then, fatefully, he attacked the Soviet Union in late June of that same year. By December he was on the figurative gates of Saint Petersburg and Moscow, though his overstretched and exhausted and badly winterized forces would never take either. Stalin had seized parts of the near abroad himself, in Poland and the Baltic states (after having fought Finland to more or less a draw, with only modest gains for the Soviet Union, over the winter of 1939–40). Japan was by now controlling much of coastal China and chunks of Southeast Asia, too. Italy's conquests were, and would remain, much more modest, concentrated on parts of North Africa and the Balkans.

All of this trouble concerned American policy makers greatly—but not enough as to think the United States should necessarily join the fray directly. As noted, a bill to extend the draft for another year, after an earlier law had established the draft the year before, squeaked by Congress—with the House passing it by only a single vote in August 1941.[127]

Once ambushed by Japan at Pearl Harbor, however, staying out of the war was no longer possible. Japan had badly misread the United States on that matter. Then Hitler let his hatred, and twisted sense of loyalty to the Japanese government under Tojo Hideki, lead him to an ill-advised decision to declare war against the United States himself. As Americans started to learn more about what was being done by the Nazis in much of Europe, and by the Tojo government in China, the war became not only a strategic necessity but a moral crusade as well.[128]

So after December 7, 1941, U.S. grand strategy had become simple but hugely ambitious—the comprehensive defeat of the Hitler and Tojo and Mussolini governments, working in alliance with the United Kingdom and the Soviet Union. Demand for unconditional surrender would follow soon enough, at the conference in Casablanca, Morocco, between Roosevelt and Churchill in January 1943, but was almost inevitable by the early days after Pearl Harbor. Coexistence with such monstrous and expansionist regimes, even from the distant perches of North America, seemed unwise at best, and perhaps simply impossible.

America's manufacturing capacities by this point in history were enormous. The United States had about 2.5 times the industrial output of Germany just before the war; once it put its mind to military manufacturing, it would wind up outproducing Germany in value of weaponry by roughly 3:1 by 1943, and by more still in the two years to come. Thus, even before it had really ramped up military production, it was clear that the United States could arm itself for multiple axes of simultaneous attack while also doing much to help arm its allies (though the Soviets were themselves equaling Germany in war production toward the end of the war, and the British were in the same rough league).[129] At its simplest level, American grand strategy was to pour it on everywhere, as fast as it could, working with key allies that themselves represented two of the other top economies and industrial bases in the world. Churchill recognized that with America in the war, "we had won after all," long before the Allies actually did achieve victory or even a clear change in battlefield momentum.[130] It was not just that America was substantially larger than the other, enemy powers and that its territory provided effective sanctuary for industrial activity. The United States was also at the peak of its manufacturing capabilities, with unbelievable ability to undertake assembly-line production of massive numbers of vehicles, aircraft, and ships in a way not seen ever before (or, to a large extent, since). President Roosevelt was smart enough to staff the War Production Board, which oversaw armaments production, with captains of industry who knew what they were doing. The resource base was too lopsided for Germany and Japan to have much of a chance by that point, especially given that Hitler had also attacked (but failed to defeat quickly) the Soviet Union.[131]

America's scientists, innovators, and entrepreneurs were crucial in World War II as well. Never before or since has the nation developed so many new technologies, along with associated tactics and operational concepts, in real time during war. The development of the atomic bomb is of course near the top of the list. But huge breakthroughs were made in the quality and capabilities of numerous technologies, from radar to amphibious tractors to much better airplanes with longer range, greater speed, and greater payloads. These technologies were woven into new operational concepts, such as employing the P-51 Mustang with drop tanks to protect bombers raiding Germany starting in late 1943 and later in bombing Japan from the Mariana Islands with the newly developed B-29 aircraft and its 1,600-mile tactical radius.[132] As such, the heavy investment in science and technology, as well as experimentation to improve tactics and operational concepts with new military systems, should be identified as itself a central element of American and Allied strategy. This was not, to paraphrase Secretary of Defense Donald Rumsfeld in talking about the Iraq invasion, a war that the United States fought with "the army you have." The Army, and all the services, were much different, much bigger, and much better in 1945 than in 1941.[133]

Fleshing out the grand strategy of unconditional surrender and defense strategy of direct attacks on enemy homelands took considerable time, effort, and creativity. How would ends, ways, and means be balanced in this situation? There were about half a dozen major decisions about key campaigns that had to be made. They concerned whether and when to land forces in France (and how to approach Germany once safely ashore), where else to challenge Germany in the meantime, from which directions to approach Japan, how to finish the job with Japan, and how to conduct conventional as well as nuclear bombing of both enemy nations and their militaries.

Recognizing Germany's size, power, and potential, as well as the acute danger it posed to Britain and the Soviet Union, Washington quickly promulgated a "Europe-first" strategy.[134] It did so in conjunction with the United Kingdom, at the Arcadia Conference in January 1942 (following a similar declaration in early 1941 at the so-called ABC-1 Conference, with Canada joining as well). U.S. planners had done enough analysis to predict, more or less accurately, that some 9 million Army and Marine Corps personnel would likely be needed to win the war—plus millions more in the Navy—and realized that it would take time to mobilize and equip them.[135] So no all-out two-front war would be immediately feasible.

That Arcadia gathering, largely through the persuasive efforts of General George Marshall, also established the combined chiefs of staff system that would permit close military consultations between Britain and the United States throughout the war.[136] With Eisenhower in charge of the combined effort in Europe by 1944, the tradition of American military leadership in coalition operations would be firmly established as well. That tradition had some antecedents in World War I, where General Pershing had separate tactical control of American units.[137] But the tradition of American leadership in European security affairs really dates to World War II and the creation of the position of supreme commander, Allied Expeditionary Forces.

In fact, however, the Europe-first strategy was not as comprehensive in its effects as many believe. According to Russell Weigley's count, there were as of December 31, 1943, some 1.88 million American forces deployed against Japan in the broader Pacific theater to 1.81 million against Germany in the European theater. Admiral Ernest King and General Douglas MacArthur were among the key proponents of prioritizing the Pacific theater. The initial logic was partly to ensure that sea lines to Australia would remain open (hence all the fighting in the region around the Solomon Islands); a key additional argument was also to prevent Japan from having too much time to develop and harden its system of island fortifications that would create a defensive ring difficult to penetrate later on.[138] The Pacific-first logic for the U.S. Navy continued throughout the war. The distinguished Scottish historian Phillips O'Brien wrote, "It is impossible to say that the United States ever fought a clear policy of Germany-first. The US army and air force definitely did in 1943 and 1944, when they deployed somewhere between 70 percent and 80 percent of their force against Germany. However, with the navy doing the exact opposite, albeit more so, and having access to about 40 percent of American overall war construction, the United States as a whole fought relatively similar equipment wars against both Germany and

Japan."[139] Indeed, when the Allies invaded mainland Italy in early 1944 at Anzio, the lack of carriers in the European theater meant they were limited in their plausible landing zones by where land-based airpower could provide cover.[140] The Pacific-oriented carrier fleet would grow fast; for example, the large-deck Pacific carrier force increased from two ships to twelve between 1943 and 1945, and the overall Pacific carrier fleet including smaller vessels jumped from five to thirty-eight during that two-year period.[141]

That Pacific-first approach for the Navy was not set completely in stone. For example, had the Battle of the Atlantic continued to go badly beyond 1942 and early 1943, there could have been a much stronger case to pull naval forces out of the Pacific to protect convoys. As Winston Churchill once said, "The only thing that ever really frightened me during the war was the U-boat peril." Britain needed the weapons, food, and other supplies that only ships could deliver to its people and its armed forces.[142] Thankfully, momentum shifted (though only gradually, and not until early 1943) as a result of better techniques and technologies for antisubmarine warfare, including major organizational reform to promote faster learning and sharing of best practices on how to convoy, where to steam ships, how to protect ships, and how to track and attack U-boats.[143] Crucially, faster construction rates for transport ships were also achieved.

Even with a Europe-first overall strategy for the U.S. Army (and Army Air Corps) in particular, there was still the big question of how soon to try to put ground forces into Europe. U.S. military leadership wanted to drive to Berlin as soon as possible. Having witnessed successful Nazi attacks, they now tended to think that offensive warfare had become more powerful and effective than had been believed during and after World War I.[144] So they favored gaining a foothold in France as promptly as possible and using it to overrun German positions and then close on the capital. But it would take time to prepare the necessary combat capacity. Initially, American officials favored a date of perhaps the spring of 1943, as discussed at the Arcadia Conference in January 1942. They developed the idea further that year, with Bolero the code name for the preparation of the invasion and Roundup the actual plan to cross the Channel. The British did not favor such an approach. Perhaps they were wary of being part of it themselves, given the enormous challenge of such an operation relatively soon in the war; they also definitely wanted *some* kind of American effort in (or near) Europe as soon as possible, as did the Soviets, rather than waiting a year or more for the main effort.

What resulted was the American and British invasion of North Africa, and later Italy, starting in late 1942. The U.S. joint chiefs thought that the idea was a serious distraction and poor use of resources. But they were overruled by President Roosevelt, as the British effectively won the intra-alliance debates on the topic. In British eyes, and ultimately Roosevelt's, the invasion of North Africa in late 1942, Operation Torch, made sense as part of a campaign of increasingly difficult and large-scale operations. So would Operation Husky in Sicily in July 1943 and then the invasion of mainland Italy starting in September. By this way of thinking, the Allies were simply not ready to invade northern Europe in 1942 or 1943, given their own limited experience and the vast array of German forces that would meet them there. Bigger and more experienced American forces would be needed first.[145] That would require time to build the bigger forces, and smaller-scale operations to gain experience.

The United States also needed a better army. When it entered the conflict, the U.S. Army was not truly ready for World War II. It did not have good enough air defense and antitank and antimine weaponry. Coordination between ground troops and airpower was poor. All these things would begin to be better understood, and corrected, in the unforgiving crucible of combat starting in North Africa.[146]

Operation Torch had the added attraction of putting pressure on the German war machine, which had itself seized control of parts of northern Africa in 1941. There, German forces were somewhat exposed and vulnerable—and since Hitler hated to give up anything he had conquered, he could probably be induced to try to defend his positions in a place where geography did not favor the Third Reich. By doing so, moreover, he would be somewhat distracted from his main immediate objective of defeating the Soviet Union. Had Germany succeeded in that latter effort, the implications would have been catastrophic, freeing up more than 200 Nazi divisions to fight the Brits and Americans and Canadians and Free French. Attacking in North Africa would honor the Europe-first principle without being reckless or ignoring the Pacific.[147] Operation Torch, with landings in Morocco and Algeria in November 1942, was the result of this logic.

At the Casablanca Conference in January 1943, Roosevelt went along with the idea to authorize the invasion of Sicily followed by that of Italy proper in 1943. The appeal of keeping momentum going, regaining control of the Mediterranean and Suez Canal, and driving Italy out of the war—and avoiding a premature attempted crossing of the Channel—carried the day.[148] Meanwhile, America's massive industrial production would have a few more months, working with Allies, to prepare for June 1944. By the time the Allies did attempt the invasion of France, they would be ready—and Germany would be reeling from years of not only two-front ground warfare but also intensive aerial attack.

Bombing Germany and Japan was important for ending the war, beyond any doubt. That was true even though the aspirations of airpower proponents at the outset of the war had been completely discredited. Any early hopes that a Guilio Douhet–inspired air campaign would quickly win the war outright were dashed as the Germans fought on—just as the Brits had fought on despite the blitz. That early Italian theorist of air warfare as well as his influential American follower, General Billy Mitchell, turned out to be far too optimistic about what bombing could achieve in psychological and political terms. Yet by June 1944, a combination of damage to German aircraft production, and even more to fuel production, as well as greater Allied fighter ranges and numbers in the region around northern France did accord the Allies dominance of the skies during Operation Overlord and subsequent operations. Strategic bombing also placed a cap on German military production by 1944 and redirected much of that production to address the bombing threat, even if it never brought the German economy to its knees as initially hoped. Aerial attacks continued and expanded to hit railroad networks in Germany and France hard. These attacks, as well as air attacks against marshalling yards and bridges and tunnels, were considered crucial by Eisenhower and others for preventing Germany from reinforcing its troops at the point of attack in Operation Overlord beginning in June 1944 (even if using aircraft this way was initially greeted with skepticism by airpower's main proponents of strategic bombing, such as General Carl "Tooey" Spaatz, commander of U.S. strategic air forces, and Air Chief Marshal Sir Arthur Harris, commander in chief of Britain's Bomber Command).[149] Because Roosevelt had insisted on prioritizing production of aircraft over other types of weaponry, Allied air forces were amply stocked with lots of planes and firepower.[150]

The scope and scale of D-Day was truly mind-boggling. The defensive perimeter set up around the invasion corridor included more than 100 warships to protect troop ships crossing the English Channel. Several thousand additional ships transported some 150,000 soldiers, 2,000 tanks, and another 12,000 vehicles. More than 10,000 aircraft patrolled the skies, transported troops, and pounded German positions.[151] Airborne troops were used to protect flanks of the amphibious operation and for other specific objectives. Two mobile harbors known as Mulberries were towed across the Channel to help establish a high-capacity logistics line to provide supplies and reinforcements. Special vehicles known as Hobart's Funnies, many based on a Sherman tank chassis, were used to breech antitank ditches and minefields.[152] None of this made Operation Overlord easy; it was constant tough slogging and bogged down at times in the ensuing efforts to move through northern French farmland with its stone houses and bocage hedgerows. But Allied advantages in mass were considerable—and just kept growing.[153]

In the Allied approach to Germany after D-Day and the campaigning in northern France, two specific issues reached a high threshold of importance and consumed Eisenhower as well as his subordinates in late 1944. One was the debate over whether to concentrate even more Allied firepower in the northern sector of approach to Germany, under the command of British field marshal Bernard "Monty" Montgomery—who very much believed that he should lead the main effort. However, the supreme commander of Allied forces in Europe, Eisenhower, favored a less concentrated approach since it would create more problems for German defenses and avoid undue dependence on a single logistics line for the Allies. Ike gave in a little, but only modestly prioritized Montgomery's approach from the northern sector over Omar Bradley's from the center and south.[154] In addition to being Montgomery's superior officer, Ike had also watched the failure of Montgomery's latest big idea: to use airborne troops to try to secure a string of bridges in Holland so that a quick and easy way behind German lines could be found in the northern sector. That idea had led to disaster in September, making Eisenhower suspicious not only of Monty but also of quick-win concepts in general. The supreme commander would revert to a more conservative approach to defeating the Reich thereafter.[155]

Progress was not steady in the ensuing march on Germany. Notably, intelligence oversights and questionable decision-making opened up the Allies to a German counterattack through the Ardennes Forest. The Battle of the Bulge was the result, in December 1944. But fortunately, superior Allied numbers and dominant airpower in the west, complemented by the Red Army's approach toward Berlin from the east, carried the day.[156]

Another high-level question in American military strategy in World War II, at the intersection between military strategy and campaign analysis, was how to attack Japan. Early on, at least three ideas presented themselves (once a northern approach by way of the Aleutian Islands was ruled out as impractical, largely due to prevalent weather conditions).[157] One was through an island-hopping campaign in the central Pacific. A second was via Australia, the Coral Sea and Solomon Islands, and then the Philippines. A final option was through Burma and southwestern China. Despite the efforts of General Joseph Stilwell and other Americans, the latter idea never proved realistic, even as a location where sustained bombing of Japan could originate. That was largely because Chinese nationalist leader Chiang Kai-shek had priorities that differed from America's, and fickle personal qualities as well, making effective collaboration difficult. Daunting geography also played its role.[158]

Thus, it came down to this: Should the main American approach to Japan be via the central Pacific or the Australia-Solomons-Philippines route? Should Admiral Nimitz lead the way or General MacArthur? Resolving this dispute would have been a severe test of any chain of command, given the personalities and equities involved. And as it turned out, the United States did not resolve the chain of command issue. Rather, a loosely coordinated joint chiefs of staff divvied up oversight: Marshall and the Army for MacArthur, King and the Navy for Nimitz. (This system was integrated into formal alliance command structures at the Trident Conference in Washington in May 1943 and then reconfirmed that December at the Cairo Conference.)[159] Fortunately for the United States, given its commanding industrial and materiel advantages over Japan, it did not have to choose. Both efforts were well resourced, allowing American forces to converge on Okinawa from two separate axes in the spring of 1945.[160]

The United States was also fortunate in that its aircraft carriers survived the Pearl Harbor attacks, and then a combination of intelligence breakthroughs and tactical military cleverness allowed it to turn the momentum of battle fairly fast in the Pacific. The Battle of Midway, just six months after Pearl Harbor, was the key early case in point. The three American aircraft carriers involved in the battle were greatly aided by excellent U.S. cryptography through the Ultra cryptanalysis program that picked up and decoded early indicators of the Japanese plan to lure American forces into trying to protect Midway Island, where they would be ambushed by the Japanese carrier task force. Instead, the naval ambush was reversed.[161]

Thus, the stars were aligned for the United States to approach Japan from two general corridors. By having two general directions of advance, the enemy was kept guessing about whether one might become the main effort. Approaching via the Solomon Islands and then the Philippines had an additional logic of keeping open sea lines to Australia when they might have otherwise been imperiled early in the war. It sought to establish stepping stones or "strong points" to facilitate the eventual attack on Japan.[162] The two approaches used somewhat different mixes of weapons and tactics. Because so many new technologies were being developed, built, and deployed in World War II and so many new operational and tactical concepts were being developed, it made sense to pursue different approaches, at least at first, to see if one wound up working much better than the other. In particular, the improvements in carrier airpower that occurred throughout the war made it possible to bypass some Japanese positions in the central Pacific island-hopping campaign, at least by late 1943 and 1944, when the carrier fleet had become quite large.[163] It would no longer be necessary to make small steps across the Pacific (so as to keep gaining islands that could provide land-based air cover for ensuing forward movements). Many islands and Japanese positions could simply be bypassed, as it turned out.[164]

Things were a bit different on the southward approach. Part of this was due to geography. Part of it was due to MacArthur, who, having once promised the Filipino people that he would return, insisted for moral and strategic grounds on retaking the Philippines next. Debate continues even now as to whether that was the right move and whether all the fighting that then occurred between U.S. and Japanese forces in the Philippines (with huge costs to the Indigenous Filipino population) was really necessary.[165]

With the taking of the Mariana Islands (Saipan, Guam, Tinian) complete by mid-August 1944 or so, the other prong of the U.S.-led advance toward Japan had broken through Japan's security perimeter. Now, with a combination of land-based airpower, carrier airpower, and submarines, the United States could apply an increasingly intense squeeze on the home islands; the squeeze would produce huge shortages of fuel and metals. Japanese forces in the Philippines were not in a position to relieve this pressure and thus could have been bypassed with little effect; those joint chiefs who questioned the need to liberate the Philippines directly were probably correct. Indeed, had American forces not been partly tied down in the Philippines in late 1944 and early 1945, more American power may have been available to invade Iwo Jima and Okinawa in 1945—perhaps even sooner than they were ultimately taken.[166]

There were of course also debates about whether to invade Japan. The experiences on Okinawa and elsewhere suggest that land invasion would have been terribly deadly for both sides. In fact, the U.S. joint chiefs predicted more than 1 million American casualties in any battle to take Japan's main islands, with a quarter million of those killed. That would have increased U.S. losses in World War II by more than 50 percent. Japanese losses would likely have been even greater.[167] Such estimates should always be viewed warily, but they were based on recent precedent and were probably not far off.[168] In any case, estimates of losses were high enough in some cases that some American military leaders, notably Admiral Nimitz, felt growing concerns and doubts about the wisdom of any ground invasion—preferring to continue the economic strangulation and aerial bombardment strategies.[169] With the exception of Army leaders and notably MacArthur, most American military leaders favored trying a bombing and strangulation strategy and employing nuclear weapons. With luck, such efforts could accelerate Japan's surrender without a ground invasion; in any case, they should at least be attempted. If they failed, the United States might then invade the southern island of Kyushu in late 1945 and then if necessary the main island of Honshu in 1946.[170]

From the summer of 1944 onward, American submarines and aircraft together had dramatic effects on Japan. While faster, smaller Japanese ships could outrun the submarines, they could not outrun the aircraft.[171] Japanese merchant shipping tonnage plummeted by almost half in the final year of the war; oil tanker tonnage was reduced by two-thirds over that same time. Strategic bombing battered industry and killed hundreds of thousands. Inventories of aviation fuel in Japan were down to just 25 percent of 1942 levels by war's end. Metal production, and with it the building of aircraft and ships and vehicles, was cut by roughly half over the course of just 1944.[172] Japan appeared headed for collapse. Yet American strategists, warily watching the Soviet Union move into Manchuria and Korea, decided that the war with Japan needed to be ended fast before Moscow gained even more dominance on the Asian landmass. The arguments in favor of dropping the atomic bomb in Hiroshima and Nagasaki on August 6 and 9, 1945, therefore proved too powerful to resist. Japanese surrender would follow the next month.

CONCLUSION

World War II boggles the mind. And the scale and scope of the United States effort, along with those of the Soviet Union and Great Britain and others, does as well. Moreover, American strategy had been consistent throughout. Grand strategy demanded unconditional surrender from more or less the start of the war. U.S. defense strategy, with perhaps a slight Europe emphasis but only a slight one, poured it on as strongly as possible against both main enemies. Decisions on the timing and emphasis accorded different campaigns were constantly assessed and reassessed, but the overall approach was right from the start and never had to be changed.

It was a crowning moment. Surely, the Allies had earned a rest after defeating the greatest axis of evil in human history—an axis of evil the depravity of which remains hard to fathom.

Alas, there were already harbingers of Cold War everywhere. It would take a few years for the scale of the new challenge to become fully apparent, but there was barely any respite after the victories in World War II. This would be a Cold War with lots of hot spots, crises, and conflicts around the world as well. It would also be a period of permanent, institutionalized, large-scale American military power stationed at home and abroad and constantly active around the world. The U.S. military would draw down substantially, to be sure. It would drop just below 1.5 million active-duty personnel, and would consume only about 4 percent of GDP, by 1948—before ramping back up.[173] But the disengagement would not resemble what had happened after World War I. American isolationism and disengagement appeared to be gone for good. Grand strategy, and defense strategy, would never be like what they had been before.

CHAPTER V

The Cold War

The Cold War period is sometimes remembered nostalgically today by those of a certain age. For some of us, it is the time when we grew up, and we miss our youth. We might even remember fondly a time when cell phones and the Internet and even email didn't yet exist and when technology in general seemed already quite powerful yet less overbearing.

But for some strategists, the Cold War is remembered with a certain favorable glow. They talk of the stability and predictability of bipolarity in the global order. My view is that this attitude is nonsense. Perhaps in some ways the era of the Cold War was simpler than today's world. But it was much more dangerous, especially in the early decades, even in light of the dangers of today's world.

This reality can, to my mind, be well illustrated by thinking back on the political career of Dwight David Eisenhower. He was the calm, cool, collected planner and leader of the D-Day landings as well as the subsequent Allied victory in Europe. He later became NATO's first supreme Allied commander before returning to the United States to run for president.

Once president, however, even Ike had his hands full and wound up revealing many of the acute stresses and strains of the day. Much of this could be seen in his attitudes toward nuclear weapons and toward Vietnam.

What seemed to many like madness when Douglas MacArthur proposed it—threatening nuclear weapons use against China over the Korean War—was a strategy that Ike adopted early in his presidency to try to force a peace deal. The fact that his gambit seems to have worked does not make it innocuous, nor does it answer the question of what he would have done if Beijing had not agreed to compromise terms soon thereafter.[1]

Eisenhower threatened China again with nuclear weapons in regard to crises over Taiwan. In fact, the crises were not really even over Taiwan's main island per se but the small offshore islands of Quemoy and Matsu, tiny in comparison to the main island and also far closer to China. Yet Eisenhower was willing to wield America's nuclear monopoly against China over those two islands. After all, he had talked about nukes as being like any other weapon, adopted a broad strategy called the New Look that heightened their role in defense strategy, and hired a secretary of state who talked openly of the possibility of American "massive retaliation" with nuclear weapons in the event of war.[2] *(Americans often forget these particular nuclear crises of the early Cold War years; it is doubtful that the Chinese have forgotten, however.)*

There was also Iran. There, a nationalist named Mohammad Mosaddegh had come to power as prime minister and undone Britain's highly favorable oil concession contract. Winston Churchill favored instigating a coup right away; Harry Truman did not, but he would soon be replaced by Eisenhower, who would give his blessing. Anticommunism provided much of the rationale, whatever its relevance to actual circumstances on the ground.[3]

Then there was Vietnam. Eisenhower did not start the Vietnam War, and in an earlier stage, he chose not to reinforce the French position there during his first term as president. But he later encouraged John Kennedy and Lyndon Johnson to do whatever they needed to win it.[4]

I do not mean to challenge the historical greatness of Eisenhower, a man whom on balance I greatly admire. But if the early decades of the Cold War could lead him to such rather extreme ideas, then it was not really a Norman Rockwell time of bliss in America or in geopolitics.

American defense strategy in this period became ambitious: limiting communist encroachment wherever possible while building a system of alliances and the standing military forces to back them up, including with big and permanent forward-stationed overseas capabilities. Defense strategy had to be adjusted frequently as a function of what proved feasible, affordable, and reasonable. Wars were lost or stalemated in Korea and Vietnam; forward positions were successfully defended in Berlin and most of the Middle East; the Soviets were (mostly) kept out of Cuba; defense budgets were generally large but not astronomical. There were numerous successes and numerous failures—and a great deal of effort and anxiety. The endeavor was ultimately successful after forty-plus years, but it was never easy. In fact, it was often very scary.

With the arrival of fall 1945, World War II was over. A weary nation could finally mourn its lost youth who perished abroad, redirect its energies, and try to move beyond the most cataclysmic event in the history of humanity.

At a philosophical level, Americans knew they could not again detach themselves from the world. Two world wars had proven the futility of deliberately underpreparing and looking the other way in the hope that ignoring a problem would make it go away.

And at the level of defense strategy and preparedness, the United States would never again let down its guard. Defense spending shrank briefly to just 4 percent of GDP in 1948 before ticking back up again, but even that was a much higher level of spending than the nation had previously sustained after war. Not only did the nation's military become truly institutionalized as a large standing organization, but a remarkable constellation of defense industries took up a permanent place among the nation's largest private corporations, featuring some of the country's very best people and technology.[5]

During the Cold War, U.S. defense strategy and planning became formalized—and unrelenting. Not only the creation of the Department of Defense in 1947 but also the ongoing growth of a defense planning "ecosystem" to include numerous think tanks such as the RAND Corporation and offices such as Program Analysis and Evaluation (now Cost Assessment and Program Evaluation) as well as the Office of Net Assessment in the Pentagon made the business of strategy an ongoing and perpetual one involving many thousands of players. Annapolis, West Point, Newport, and a few other jewels of the nation that dominated strategy in earlier eras now had lots of company; more universities got into the act as well, joining the growing community of think tanks and research organizations and Pentagon support agencies.[6] It was also the period when documents described as National Security Council papers, presidential decision memoranda, national security strategies, national defense strategies, quadrennial defense reviews, and other formal publications became commonplace. I cite (and reference and discuss) such documents frequently in this chapter and the next. But again, I am at least as interested in how the United States actually behaved, how it budgeted for its armed forces and deployed and employed them, than in what it promised or said it would do through such documents. The documents, in addition to indicating actual plans and priorities, also often had political, diplomatic, public relations, and hortatory purposes and should not be seen as the be-all and end-all of actual United States strategy.

The U.S. grand strategy of the Cold War is usually described by the single word *containment*. That is, the United States sought to check communist expansionism, especially by a potentially united and coordinated Moscow-Beijing axis that possessed visions of global takeover. But containment meant different things to different people. It was more a slogan than a strategy. Deciding where and how to resist communist expansionism was generally much more difficult than articulating the big idea in the abstract, as John Lewis Gaddis memorably documented in his famous book *Strategies of Containment.*[7] Applying the general concept to various regions of the world and various crises and conflicts, determining where to take risk and where not to, deciding when to fight and when not to: these were the truly hard calls.[8] (Less matters of core U.S. defense strategy, but still quite important for broader national security policy, were decisions on how much to help American allies and security partners build up their own armed forces through security assistance. On this matter, the United States achieved some notable successes, such as South Korea and Colombia, and some partial successes, as for example in the Philippines and perhaps Egypt and Jordan, to go along with numerous failures.)[9]

Indeed, U.S. grand strategy from 1945 to 1989 cannot be summarized simply by the concept of containment, no matter the definition of that term. It would be incomplete to describe grand strategy in this period as simply a negative one of pushing back against a specific, if acute and profound, threat. For one thing, there was also an element of attempted rollback—of overturning regimes friendly to Moscow and Beijing. This was pursued through the support of dissidents, the encouragement of coup attempts, the arming of insurgents, and the stoking of unrest in countries that had come under communist influence. Professor Lindsey A. O'Rourke documents dozens of such attempts during the Cold War, especially during its first two decades (but with renewed emphasis during the Reagan years as well). Most were pursued with limited resources and limited effect and are better categorized as part of broader U.S. national security policy rather than defense strategy or military policy. But they were important just the same.[10]

Even more significantly, as scholars John Ikenberry and Stephen Wertheim and others have documented, the initial ideas that would shape Cold War U.S. grand strategy were developed even before Soviet and Chinese dangers were fully recognized.[11] The machinery of the United Nations, the commitment to a rules-based and largely cooperative global economic order, and the idea of occupying and essentially remaking both Japan and Germany into modern democracies while helping reconstruct war-torn regions in general were all concepts that originated in the years 1943–45. The joint chiefs, as military analyst and historian Stacie Pettyjohn has shown, were developing plans during that time for a network of air bases and access points that would remain in Atlantic and Pacific regions even after the war was over.[12] None of these ideas or policies follow automatically simply by articulating the general concept of containment.[13]

The grand strategy of the Cold War was not simply containment, however understood. Rather, it was containment plus promotion and protection of a democratic, market-based, interconnected, and peaceful community of nations. Or, in shorthand, perhaps this: containment plus internationalism, engagement, and interventionism. That is admittedly still a mouthful. Hence the appeal of the bumper-sticker term *containment*. But reality was more complex. Robert Kagan's evocative phrase, "the world America made," conveys the idea of what was being promoted better than this simple word.[14]

Strategists and leaders of the early years of this era—those who were present at the creation, as Secretary of State Dean Acheson put it—were certainly unafraid "to dare mighty things."[15] They sought to change the basic course of human history. They had seen the devastation of world war and massive killing of civilians and the Holocaust. They had also seen all these things ended by the successful employment of American and Allied power. They probably understood the stakes in international politics more profoundly and viscerally than most of us do today, and certainly much better than had their predecessors during the earlier years of the great isolationism. Once the Soviets blockaded West Berlin in 1948, China fell to communists in 1949, and North Korea invaded South Korea in 1950, the stakes were even more stark.

American defense strategy designed to support this grand strategy of containment plus internationalism, engagement, and interventionism was built on several foundations. One was a general philosophy of preparedness—substantial defense budgets combined with large and ready military forces—and a willingness to fight. Another was an emphasis on state-of-the-art technology, emphasizing nuclear weapons and long-range delivery systems but also advanced conventional weapons. A third was a network of active military alliances backstopped by the permanent presence of American armed forces along the Eurasian littoral, together with a readiness to use these forces to signal resolve.[16]

The United States struggled militarily on the battlefield during much of the Cold War. Its record of wartime defense strategy in this period was mediocre. The United States fought to a draw in Korea and lost in Vietnam. But the strategic deterrence record was excellent. No American treaty allies that hosted substantial numbers of U.S. forces were ever seriously attacked by a communist adversary during the Cold War (or since then).[17]

As Henry Kissinger pointed out, rules of international behavior themselves achieve little; they have often been violated in various postwar security arrangements through history, perhaps most notably of all after World War I. Kissinger compellingly wrote that "the test of Wilsonianism has never been whether the world has managed to enshrine peace through sufficiently detailed rules with a broad enough base of signatories. The essential question has been what to do when these rules were violated or, more challengingly, manipulated to ends contrary to their spirit."[18] By establishing alliances undergirded by forward-stationed American military personnel, that essential question was largely answered during the Cold War, and answered successfully.

Defense strategy often had to be rethought during the Cold War when theory and plans confronted reality. Decisions about which interests were "vital" and which were not sometimes had to be reconsidered. No simple Huntingtonian framework, whereby civilians decided on where to fight and let military leaders decide how to win (no matter what the eventual cost), was realistic in such a world. Too much was sometimes asked of the nation's general deterrent and defense capabilities.[19] Articulating a grand strategy of containment plus internationalism, engagement, and interventionism could not provide the needed answers about when and where to be willing to fight.[20] The United States initially decided that Western Europe and Japan were most important. It then added Korea and parts of the Middle East to the list of core interests.[21] In some cases, like Vietnam, and before that Korea, and Iran, it was the fact (or fear) of communist aggression that made a given country or region feel like a crucial interest of the United States, more than the inherent importance of the country at issue. Domino theories foretold even worse things to come, should the initial assaults by communist expansionists not be firmly resisted. As such, the United States chose to employ large, though not exhaustive, amounts of military firepower to defend some of these interests. But when doing so became impractical, adjustments were made. The nation realized that having all such countries in safe, noncommunist hands was not vital for the United States, a country that by virtue of its size and geography is blessed with many advantages in maintaining its own security and power.

There were also many places where neither superpower introduced main combat forces but where they competed in quieter ways through covert operations, training and security assistance, political and economic interactions, and other instruments of national policy. These zones of competition centered on Central America and the Caribbean, South and Southeast Asia, the Horn of Africa, Central Africa, and the broader Middle East.[22] But this chapter, and book, focus primarily on U.S. defense strategy—what the country did with its own armed forces—more than on a more sweeping consideration of U.S. national security policy. The rest of this chapter follows a loosely chronological flow, but with key themes also central to the narrative.

THE IRON CURTAIN DESCENDS AND THE COLD WAR ARRIVES

The pace of events in the late 1940s and into 1950 was dizzying. Maybe the United States hoped that it could simply recover, and move on, from the experience of World War II. Presumably most expected as much. They would be disappointed.

The fact that Soviet armies did not leave those countries in eastern Europe that they had "liberated" at the end of World War II was an early warning sign.[23] Already an Iron Curtain was descending on that region, as Churchill warned in 1946.[24] Communist threats to Greece and Turkey, and Europe more generally, led first to the Truman Doctrine and associated aid packages of 1947, then to the Marshall Plan of 1948.[25] The Soviet blockade of Berlin in 1948 ended all real doubt as to what the West was facing. (Interestingly, the joint chiefs of staff in the United States opposed Truman's proposed airlift, thinking it impractical; thankfully, they were overruled by the president.)[26] All of that led to the creation of the North Atlantic Treaty Organization by its twelve founding members in April 1949, with the U.S. Senate ratifying the treaty in July. Then, in August, the Soviet Union detonated its first nuclear device; in October, the Chinese communists declared victory in their country's civil war. The politics of defense in the United States were now changing fast, as a "Who lost China?" debate punctuated the growing sense of alarm and anxiety. The "Vandenburg moment" of bipartisan harmony in American defense politics was gone, and as usual in America's democracy, politics no longer stopped at the water's edge.[27] North Korea then invaded South Korea on June 25, 1950. The National Security Council paper NSC-68, initially controversial when released in April that year, would quickly gain widespread support. Decisions to undertake a massive U.S. defense buildup, base American forces in western Europe, and later to approve the rearmament of Germany would follow in relatively short order.

But first, back to the late 1940s. Defense strategy in the first few years after World War II emphasized maintaining the occupations of Germany and Japan even as overall U.S. military capabilities were dramatically downsized. Planning for an integrated effort had begun with the creation in 1944 of a State-War-

Navy Coordinating Committee under Secretary of State Edward Stettinius (a former General Motors executive and leader of the Lend-Lease program who had just replaced Cordell Hull at Foggy Bottom), Secretary of War Henry Stimson, and the successor to the recently deceased Frank Knox, Secretary of the Navy James Forrestal. This effective construct paved the way for the creation of the National Security Council in 1947 and had a huge and effective impact on how the occupations were planned and conducted.[28]

The United States together with allies would ultimately station several hundred thousand troops in Japan after the conclusion of World War II.[29] American troops in Germany maintaining one of the four occupation sectors totaled far fewer—more like 35,000. These forces had considerable capability and were initially, of course, ready for localized or even larger-scale resistance. But as time went by, those worries receded, and so did the size and combat prowess of the occupying armies. Both Japan and Germany were thoroughly defeated polities that did not generate prolonged resistance (or, for that matter, even very much crime) after their respective surrenders.[30]

In terms of doctrine and innovation, the late 1940s were a time of downsizing and drift. Some leaders wanted to hold onto the glory of the big win in World War II, and the kind of combined-arms maneuver warfare that characterized it, with a focus on a future big win against the Soviets in Europe. Others were wondering if land power should support airpower, rather than the other way around. This debate became an interservice matter with the creation of the Air Force in 1947, as well as the decision at a military summit in Key West the following year to accord responsibility for close-air support to the Air Force (rather than the Army) and for strategic air warfare to the Air Force as well (rather than being shared with the Navy).[31] The nuclear versus conventional debate was also beginning, as the nation wrestled with competing ideas on which type of weaponry should form the backbone of American capability for the Cold War. But mostly, the nation carried out a massive downsizing of its military, from about 12 million uniformed personnel to 1.5 million, and from 37 percent of GDP in 1944 to 4 percent by 1948.[32]

Key West as well as ensuing efforts at streamlining and clarifying core defense functions did not solve all the military's problems or end its often intense and even personal bureaucratic and institutional fights. This was a particularly serious challenge, given that President Truman and his second secretary of defense, Louis Johnson, maintained downward pressure on the defense budget (Truman's, and the nation's, first secretary of defense, James Forrestal, was fired in March 1949; he would commit suicide within two months).[33]

The Navy's frustration with Truman, and especially his secretary of defense, Louis Johnson, led to the so-called Revolt of the Admirals—a series of public disagreements in late summer 1949. It culminated when the nation's first chairman of the joint chiefs, five-star General Omar Bradley, publicly rebuked Navy leadership as having a "crybaby attitude" and the administration then sacked the chief of naval operations, Admiral Louis Denfeld.[34] The National Defense Act of 1949 had created that position of chairman, as well as that of deputy secretary of defense (and three assistant secretaries), and had strengthened the role of the defense secretary to "exercise direction, authority, and control" over the military services.[35] But forces and budgets languished.[36] Defense spending in 1949 and 1950 was greater than in 1948, but the real buildup would have to await fiscal year 1951, after the North Korean invasion of South Korea.[37]

DEFENSE STRATEGY IN THE KOREAN WAR

What key strategies did the United States employ militarily in the Korean War, attempting to link ends with ways and means, that shaped the military campaigns of that three-year conflict? Almost all of the interesting strategy was in the first year—except perhaps for Eisenhower's nuclear threats near the end.

To recap: North Korea invaded a badly prepared South Korea on June 25, 1950. The nearest American forces were in Japan and not organized or equipped as combat units. As a result, the early weeks of the war were a story of rapid North Korean gains. Then the United States and South Korea and other allies, acting under a U.N. mandate, stabilized the Pusan Perimeter in southeastern Korea in August of that same year. In mid-September, momentum swung dramatically in the coalition's favor with the famous Inchon landing on the country's west coast. Due to the advantages of surprise and location, with North Korean supply lines exposed and its forces unprepared to regroup, the landing led to the liberation of Seoul shortly thereafter. Then, fatefully, General MacArthur decided—and his civilian and military leadership in Washington agreed—to send coalition forces northward into North Korean territory in an effort to reunify the peninsula. This seemed to succeed for a time, with MacArthur promising the troops they would spend Christmas at home. That is, it succeeded until a massive Chinese intervention, in the works since October but unleashed in full fury only after Thanksgiving, drove American and Korean and other forces southward, racing for their lives. Army forces fared badly as a rule; Marine Corps units near the Chosin Reservoir in the country's more inland regions did better and managed a more successful tactical and operational retreat. Seoul again fell to the invading communist powers.

MacArthur then increasingly wanted to threaten or employ nuclear weapons and take the war directly into China. He publicly disagreed with his commander in chief on those subjects and ultimately wound up being fired for insubordination in April 1951. At that point, Matthew Ridgway replaced MacArthur in overall command in Korea. Through the general adoption of sound infantry tactics, Ridgway managed to claw back the capital city of Seoul and some land north of it by the summer of 1951. Then the war settled into something resembling stalemate, as the United States and allies chose to keep their main strategic and military attention on Europe rather than consider escalation of one type or another in Korea. An armistice was finally negotiated, but only after Eisenhower won the presidency and took office in early 1953. His apparent willingness to consider nuclear escalation helped break a logjam on terms for the armistice, and hostilities ceased.

What can be said of American strategy in this war? The United States went from complete unpreparedness and even strategic indifference to near disaster to tactical and operational brilliance to extreme sloppiness and overconfidence—all in the year 1950. It also sensed that, in many ways, it was fighting "the wrong war, at the wrong place, at the wrong time, and with the wrong enemy," as General Omar Bradley, chairman of the joint chiefs, famously put it. He might have added, with the wrong field commander for the war's first ten months as well. Maybe it is easier to begin by saying what strategy was not. In stark contrast to the experiences of the world wars, it was not steady or consistent. It was not all-out; this was a limited war, in the choice of weaponry as well as in the scale of effort. It did not usher in big new kinds or styles of combat, though the jet made its debut in Korea and the helicopter came into its own. It did seek the destruction of North Korean forces and the reunification of the peninsula under Seoul's rule, but without much of a plan for stabilizing the peninsula after the presumed military success (foreshadowing mistakes the United States would again make in Iraq in 2003).

Russell Weigley offers a compelling assessment of MacArthur's series of decisions during the war—a combination of brilliance with near incompetence with ultimate insubordination: "So far in the war the Korean peninsula, surrounded by water on three sides, had proved enough like the Pacific islands that MacArthur had grown accustomed to conquering that his World War II methods had in general served admirably all over again—cutting off the enemy from assistance by sea through naval blockade, using naval gunfire and carrier air power to supplement decisively land-based air power and the fire power of ground troops, employing the amphibious envelopment as a strategic trump card."[38]

But there the analogies would end, especially by the time of the Chinese intervention. The differences between fighting Japanese forces on Pacific islands versus fighting North Korean and Chinese soldiers in Korea proved stark. The nature of the fighting was different in Korea, given the close proximity of forces to each other and the complex terrain. In Korea, machine guns, other automatic weapons, hand grenades, mortars, man-portable satchel charges, and mines were often the weapons of choice. Much of the fighting occurred at night; much of it also occurred in cold weather.

The United States attempted to make maximal use of its advantages in airpower, both land-based and carrier-based, but with limited success. It built hundreds of B-47 aircraft as well as many other types in the war (and would ultimately have more than 1,000 B-47s).[39] Napalm was often used against cities, as was a great deal of explosive ordnance.[40] According to bomb damage assessments, eighteen of twenty-two North Korean cities suffered 50 percent or more destruction during the war.[41] Power plants and irrigation dams were struck as well. In addition to the strikes on logistics and transport routes, roughly 100,000 U.S. sorties were flown as close-air support, generally against enemy infantry.[42]

Airpower did have its benefits, of course. At times, Chinese rail capacity was reduced by 90 percent or more. But communist forces proved tenacious and skilled at repairing rail lines and roads and at using human porters for logistics. Their supply needs were also modest; a typical Chinese division required only about forty tons of supplies a day, meaning that the Chinese forces in Korea, which included around sixty divisions, needed some 2,400 tons daily. The net effect was that Chinese forces faced major logistical constraints only if they moved too far south on the peninsula.[43] Ridgway would take advantage of that fact when U.S. and Republic of Korea forces under his command liberated Seoul for the second time in mid-1951.

Targets in China were not bombed, despite MacArthur's pleadings. There were, however, many incursions by U.S. aircraft into Chinese airspace in pursuit of Chinese and Russian aircraft.[44]

Ultimately, MacArthur was not the decisive commander in Korea, unconditional surrender was not the endgame, and America had to find a strategy different from what Russell Weigley called a war of enemy *annihilation.* A U.S. grand strategy that placed primary emphasis on Europe and viewed the Soviet Union as the main enemy led to a strategy for Korea of trying to restore the status quo ante and ending the fighting. Weigley was right that, once South Korean and coalition forces had survived the initial North Korean onslaught, American strategy initially leaned toward the preferred all-out, annihilationist, maximalist objective of unconditional surrender and comprehensive territorial conquest. But if that is where American instincts and preferences lay early in the war, they would have to change considerably. In the end, the American way of war in Korea was *not* about all-out victory or enemy annihilation, just as America's objectives had wound up limited in most wars of the nineteenth century and just as they would be in future wars of the post-1945 era.

THE CREATION AND EVOLUTION OF NATO

As all the events of the late 1940s and the early 1950s sank into the American strategic consciousness, the basic nature of containment strategy transformed. It became much more centered on hard power and military force than at the outset. And perhaps the world's greatest alliance of all time, the North Atlantic Treaty Organization, went from a notional idea to a formal institution to a powerful standing military force with forward-stationed combat power all along the inter-German border. The United States went from a country that had had only one ally, France, for 150 years to the center of what would soon become the most extensive and durable network of alliances in human history.[45]

That turn of events was frustrating to the man who coined the term *containment* in the first place. George Kennan opposed the creation of NATO and the stationing of American combat forces in Europe, after also having opposed any emphasis on the Korean peninsula as a key zone of competition between East and West and after also implying that China's fate, and certainly Taiwan's, were themselves of secondary importance for the broad competition. Kennan was disciplined in his thinking about where American vital interests lay; by contrast, the Cold War American consensus that formed in 1950, as codified in NSC-68, tended to view all parts of the world as important, especially when they came under communist attack. It is striking just how many of the key recommendations of the supposed father of Cold War American grand strategy were rejected by his peers.[46] The disagreements began almost immediately after Kennan coined the term *containment* in 1947 and deepened with time.[47]

The big decisions that had to be made in this period came at leaders at a nonstop pace. They began with Europe, regarding Greece and Turkey, then Berlin, then Germany and western Europe in general. As noted, NATO was formed in 1949.[48] In Asia, the U.S.-Japan, U.S.-Philippines, U.S.-Australia, U.S.–New Zealand, and U.S.–Republic of Korea alliances were created in 1951, 1951, 1951, 1951, and 1953, respectively.[49] The United States and Taiwan also signed a treaty in 1954.[50] The Southeast Asia Treaty Organization was temporarily an element of this network as well, from 1954 through 1977.[51] In addition to creating alliances, between 1950 and 1955 the United States established a military presence in nineteen new countries, mostly in East Asia, North Africa and the Middle East, and Europe.[52]

Ensuring that Western Europe would not fall to communism was the essence of the Truman Doctrine. However, the *defense strategy* of figuring out how to make military instruments of policy help achieve that end needed to be worked out—and indeed were a work in progress throughout the Cold War. Over four decades, key elements of an evolving defense strategy included creating NATO, giving it military teeth as the United States and NATO put standing forces in Germany, agreeing that Germany itself should rearm, and backing up conventional deterrence with nuclear deterrence in the 1950s and 1960s and 1970s (permutations ranged from Eisenhower's New Look to Kennedy's Flexible Response to various other schemes). That approach was called the "first offset," given American nuclear advantages of the early Cold War years. Later, there would be a "second offset," or Follow-on Forces Attack concept, that centered on high-technology conventional weapons in the late 1970s and 1980s.

In September 1950, a year after NATO was created, the United States decided to send four to six divisions to Europe on an indefinite basis. Congress funded the proposal the following year. This was a revolution in American foreign and defense policy, coming as it did in peacetime. Never before in its history had the United States made such a commitment in a foreign land as a preventative measure. Part and parcel of the same policy was the decision to bring a rearmed Germany into NATO—a very difficult decision for those who had only a few years ago been the victims of Nazi aggression.[53] At the Lisbon NATO summit in February 1952, the Allies agreed that they should seek to build combined forces including ninety-six divisions, half of them on active duty, by the end of the year—up from the twenty-five or so they could muster at that point.[54] The worry that the Soviet Union fielded as many as 175 divisions made this goal, while hugely ambitious, seem the smallest that would be reasonable—both as a plausible defense capability and as a demonstration of American and Western commitment.[55] That goal would soon be recognized to be entirely unrealistic, however. By 1957, even with West Germany now in the alliance and rearming, NATO was aiming to have just thirty combat-ready divisions in its center. Even that goal would prove hard to reach.[56]

Eventually, by the 1970s, NATO would realize the situation was not, and perhaps never had been, so dire. It assessed that the Soviet Union had just thirty-one divisions in Eastern Europe, plus another sixty in the western parts of the Soviet Union.[57] By the early 1980s, it would have also adopted a number of measures to try to compensate for its perceived huge shortfall in necessary forces, to include the Follow-on Forces Attack and AirLand Battle concepts.

In 1950, the United States had one division in Europe. By 1953, it had five—and so it would continuously, even through the Vietnam War, until the number dipped to four in the early 1970s.[58] Prioritizing the European theater in doctrine and force planning, the Army adopted a much more nuclear-centric type of division in 1956, then shifted again to a greater emphasis on armor and heavy divisions in the early 1960s. After the Berlin crisis of 1961, it added more than 40,000 soldiers to Europe. In 1968, due to the demands of Vietnam and other factors, it sent about 28,000 soldiers from Europe back to the United States. But that did not change the number of divisions in Europe at either time.[59] As one snapshot, as of the mid-1970s, the United States had about 200,000 soldiers in Europe, a typical number for the Cold War decades.[60]

The overall size of the U.S. Army as measured in active-duty divisions tended to range from about thirteen to nineteen for decades after the Korean War. Specifically, after having numbered eighty-nine divisions in 1945, and then dropping to ten in early 1950, the number shot up to twenty by 1953—but then dropped back down to fourteen by 1960. Vietnam drove the number temporarily higher again—up to nineteen divisions by 1968—before it dropped to thirteen in 1972, then grew modestly up to sixteen by the mid- to late 1970s (and then stayed in the ballpark of eighteen through the 1980s). The totals did not vary greatly as the United States changed war-fighting paradigms or force-sizing frameworks. Whether it was adopting a New Look or a 2½-war planning requirement (as discussed below) or a 1½-war planning requirement, force size varied less than one might have expected. Army force structure has probably been determined less by what war-fighting requirements might have dictated at any given moment and more by what was affordable as well as what seemed "fair" in burden-sharing terms relative to the NATO allies. Shortfalls would be addressed largely through nuclear doctrine, and eventually high technology, not through big peacetime personnel buildups designed to close a theoretical gap between requirements and current capabilities.

The respective Marine Corps figures for these same years varied less over these Cold War decades. There were two Marine divisions in 1950, three through 1964, four by 1968, and then three again in the 1970s—the same number as today and the minimum number of Marine divisions the nation is supposed to sustain, according to U.S. Code.[61]

As it built up forces, NATO developed a forward defense along the 500-mile eastern border of West Germany. Its positions included Belgian, British, Dutch, and German forces in what was called the Northern Army Group. American as well as German forces were farther south, in the Central Army Group.[62]

Beyond its standing forces based in Germany, the United States also stationed equipment in Europe for rapid reinforcement over the next two decades, so that personnel could fly over from the United States and quickly marry up with weaponry to form more combat units. Equipment was prepositioned in Europe for two divisions in the early 1960s and for another four in the late 1970s.[63] This policy was premised on the hope, of course, that the warehouses holding the equipment would not be destroyed early in a war and that logistics lines from major western European ports to Germany could be protected as well.[64]

The United States also built up powerful airpower in Europe. By the mid-1970s, it would station around eight wings of fighter aircraft in Europe, or some 500 combat aircraft, mostly in Germany and the United Kingdom. The rest of NATO had 2,200 planes; the United States was also expected to deploy another 1,400 in the event of war. Thus, in short order, NATO could muster a bit more than 4,000 tactical combat aircraft, in contrast to some 5,500 for the Warsaw Pact—but with NATO's planes consistently of a higher quality.[65]

NUCLEAR STRATEGY IN THE AGE OF AMERICAN ADVANTAGE: IKE AND THE NEW LOOK, JFK AND JOHNSON AND FLEXIBLE RESPONSE

Four shelves of my own library are dedicated to nuclear-related books. I doubt that is unusual among students and scholars of my generation or the generation before. However, much of this can be distilled into simpler and much more concise terms when placing nuclear doctrine in a broader study of U.S. defense strategy such as this one. To quote Lawrence Freedman, in the preface to his seminal book on the subject, *The Evolution of Nuclear Strategy:* "The use of the word 'evolution' in the title of this book is somewhat misleading for it suggests progress along a learning curve, implying a higher level of present understanding than thirty, twenty, or even ten years ago. This was the assumption with which I began. Now, having completed the study, I believe it to be false. What is impressive is the cyclical character of the debates. Much of what is offered today as a profound and new insight was said yesterday; and usually in a more concise and literate manner."[66]

One can summarize the history of the Cold War nuclear balance as moving through four distinct phases: American monopoly, American predominance, American superiority, and superpower parity. Much early nuclear theory and doctrine amounted to an effort to find maximal benefit from nuclear weapons when the United States enjoyed a nuclear advantage of some magnitude. Much theory and doctrine in the second half of the Cold War, by contrast, amounted to an effort to retain some way of making nuclear threats plausible and nuclear deterrence useful beyond the immediate purpose of deterring Soviet nuclear use, even after that edge was gone and even as nuclear arms control became a central focus of policy. Throughout, nuclear weapons were not in fact used against any adversary even though the United States spent more than a quarter of the Cold War in actual combat.

To be fair, there was considerable learning about nuclear weapons over the first fifteen years or so of the Atomic Age. It took that long for a wide variety of weapons, and various types of delivery vehicles, to be developed, tested, produced, deployed—and understood for their physical as well as likely psychological and strategic effects. By the early 1960s, there was a general sense that any type of nuclear exchange would be highly deadly and dangerous; delusions of controllable and survivable war were, on balance, probably less widely entertained by then.

Nonetheless, the United States in particular sought even through the 1970s and 1980s to make nuclear threats credible in order to compensate for its geographic and conventional military disadvantages vis-à-vis the Soviet Union. The chief concern was always about the protection of Europe, though other regions of the world and other interests were part of the extended deterrence calculus as well.

One can identify three big nuclear doctrines or strategies through the 1960s: NSC-68 in the Truman years, NSC-162 and the New Look of the Eisenhower years, and finally Flexible Response in the Kennedy and Johnson years. Despite their differences, there were many similarities across these strategies as well. Proponents of each concept wanted nuclear weapons to be potentially available for a wide range of hypothetical purposes, preferably for deterrence but if necessary for war fighting.

Still, there were important distinctions. During the early years after NSC-68 was issued in 1950, the American arsenal was growing fast, from roughly 300 weapons in 1950 to more than 800 by 1952—and onward and upward from there, with thermonuclear weapons also an increasing part of the calculus.[67] But controversy reigned over whether it was legitimate to threaten nuclear strikes in the Korean War and whether to threaten them against China. Nuclear weapons, which had been in war plans since at least 1948, had not been the decisive instrument in the favorable resolution of the Berlin Crisis of 1948–49. Nor did they seem adequate in and of themselves to underwrite the defense of western Europe—hence the debate over the formation of NATO and, soon, the permanent stationing of U.S. forces in western Europe together with the remilitarization of West Germany. Yes, nuclear weapons would have *some* role in those missions and those geographies. But it was increasingly recognized that they would not provide a panacea or silver bullet to most of the nation's security challenges.[68]

Eisenhower sought to increase the importance of nuclear weapons with his New Look. During his eight years in office, the United States developed a thermonuclear arsenal with weapons now ranging into the hundreds of kilotons and even megatons range; it strengthened Strategic Air Command and formed the defensive North American Air Defense command with Canada; it replaced many of its medium-range bombers with intercontinental-range bombers in what would amount to a fundamental change in its force structure; it started to develop intercontinental ballistic missiles (ICBMs).[69] Eisenhower spoke of using nuclear arms like any other weapon, and he rattled the nuclear saber in regard to Korea, Taiwan, and Berlin. His secretary of state John Foster Dulles talked of "massive retaliation" at one point to remind any who might have forgotten about the U.S. advantage in thermonuclear weaponry.[70] Eisenhower believed that defense budgets needed to be capped and that Soviet leaders would not risk nuclear war to pursue expansionist policies. Both convictions led him to emphasize nuclear weapons in U.S. defense strategy.[71]

This nuclear "offset" of the need for big conventional forces could go only so far. Conventional forces were still needed for many cases where a nuclear response would be entirely inappropriate given the stakes at hand. Bernard Brodie, who early in the nuclear age had argued that the bomb made much about traditional military organizations and warfare obsolete, wrote in 1959 that a "basic principle of action for the United States is to provide a real and substantial capability for coping with limited and local aggression by local application of force. This is to avoid our finding ourselves some day in a dilemma where we must either accept defeat on a local issue of great importance, or else resort to a kind of force which may be intrinsically inappropriate and which may critically increase the risk of total war."[72]

Although they may have been preferable to conventional forces of Soviet size, nuclear weapons were not and are not cheap, as the nation learned well through the 1950s. Including all aspects of expenditure within the Department of Defense and the Department of Energy and including defensive capabilities as well as offensive systems and dedicated intelligence capabilities, expenses associated with the nuclear mission are estimated to have totaled more than $100 billion a year during the Cold War (in 2025 dollars).[73] But the New Look approach of Eisenhower helped him gradually reduce U.S. defense expenditures as a fraction of GDP down from about 14 percent to 10 percent and allowed the armed forces to be scaled back from about 3.5 million active-duty troops to 2.5 million.

By the end of the Eisenhower administration, the United States constructed its first Single Integrated Operational Plan (SIOP)—the comprehensive target set and weapons allocation plan that would be used against it. That first SIOP, finished in 1960 but called SIOP-62, reportedly would have used about 3,500 warheads to attack a total of 2,600 sites. The targets included Soviet offensive nuclear forces, strategic and territorial air and missile defense units and equipment, conventional combat units, key logistics nodes and other support capabilities for those combat units, command and control and communications assets, and general economic and industrial facilities (especially those most relevant to military capabilities). That first SIOP left about 1,500 locations within the National Strategic Target Data Base untargeted. Future SIOPs would be more extensive and more comprehensive.[74] By 1965, there were about 7,000 sites in the SIOP; by 1970, there were more than 8,000; by 1975, and then through much of the 1980s, there were upward of 14,000.[75] Then there were the theater and tactical weapons. In Europe, the United States had deployed 7,000 shorter-range nuclear warheads by the early 1960s, deliverable by missiles and aircraft and other means against Warsaw Pact targets.[76]

The Eisenhower period was best known for the so-called massive retaliation concept. But in fact, the strategy of the day is better described as asymmetric response. As noted, the Eisenhower administration itself liked to talk of a New Look.[77] The president was convinced that Truman's approach to defense strategy and to war fighting, including a prolonged war in Korea, was on the verge of overextending the country. As such, Ike used nuclear threats to force a negotiated compromise to end the Korean War, just as he would use such threats, along with conventional military superiority in air and maritime domains, to persuade the Chinese to stop shelling Quemoy and Matsu a couple years later.[78] Congress provided its blessing in 1955 for these presidential threats to Beijing, along with funding for the nuclear buildup. During the Eisenhower presidency, notably, the U.S. nuclear arsenal increased in size from about 1,000 warheads to 20,000 (roughly 7,000 strategic and the rest tactical or theater-range).[79]

The concept of Flexible Response developed under Kennedy and Johnson and their Secretary of Defense Robert McNamara was intended to be a big change from Ike's policy, but in reality it was more of a refinement. Yes, there were changes. The Army's Pentomic divisions with their nuclear-tipped artillery went by the wayside, for example.[80] But the basic idea that the United States would consider using nuclear weapons across a wide range of contingencies, and that it would certainly consider using them first, remained intact. SIOP-63, finished in 1962, allowed for more flexibility when executing a planned strategic nuclear attack operation. China could be spared, for example, as could Soviet leadership or Soviet conventional forces.[81]

The Flexible Response doctrine included considerable focus on Europe. The Thor and Jupiter missiles that had been deployed to Turkey, Italy, and Britain in the late 1950s were withdrawn as ICBMs came of age. But NATO allies, watching the Soviet Union develop a survivable strategic arsenal, increasingly worried that the United States might not really trade Boston for Bonn—that is, that America might not really use nuclear weapons in response to a Soviet attack on Europe if that meant likely Soviet retaliation against the United States. Various ideas were considered in the 1960s for NATO multilateral nuclear forces until the plans were deemed unwieldy and impractical. Instead, NATO set up a Nuclear Planning Group in 1966 to include the allies more fully in debates on how to think about nuclear weapons in defense and deterrence. (By this point, Britain and France already had their own independent nuclear deterrents, Britain having tested in 1952 and France in 1960.) Washington seemed to be listening to the allies when developing Flexible Response, which became NATO doctrine in 1967 to complement the U.S. doctrine of the same nickname. It seemed to avoid the Boston-for-Bonn paradox by creating possibilities for more limited uses of nuclear force on the battlefield, sparing cities at least at first.[82] It also was designed to make the Soviet Union worry that military forces from several NATO nations, facing a "use them or lose them" dilemma if attacking Soviet forces approached storage sites where U.S. nuclear weapons were stored, would in fact choose to employ the weapons rather than let them be confiscated or destroyed.

McNamara sought to impose some constraints on the growth in the arsenal—with belated and limited success, at best. He adopted the notion of "assured destruction" of Soviet society as a more reasonable (if still apocalyptic) basis for force planning than unconstrained counterforce. McNamara argued that once the United States had the ability to kill 20 to 25 percent of the Soviet population while demolishing 50 percent of its industry, it would have reached a level of sufficiency in its nuclear capabilities. This objective was estimated to require about 400 one-megaton bombs; Pentagon analysts further argued that even if additional weapons were added to the inventory above that level, the "curve of destructiveness" pitting estimated damage against American megatonnage would begin to flatten out.[83] Even though McNamara made progress with this conceptual debate, the actual U.S. nuclear arsenal continued to grow.

Although Kennedy also did achieve the first big arms control accords with the Limited Test Ban Treaty in 1963, it was during the 1960s that the U.S. nuclear inventory would reach its peak strength of some 30,000 warheads! This was also the period of the most frequent sustained nuclear testing in U.S. history. From 1962 until 1970, the United States typically tested forty to fifty nuclear weapons a year, albeit all underground. Alas, it was also in this period when the Soviet nuclear machine was fully engaged in high gear (with the corresponding period of maximum nuclear testing beginning around 1970 and continuing into the early 1980s), meaning that by roughly the halfway point of the Cold War, something akin to superpower nuclear parity would exist, with absolutely mammoth nuclear arsenals on both sides.[84] Perhaps more positively, the growing realization that mutual vulnerability was a fact of life (even if mutually assured destruction, or MAD, was never a formal policy, doctrine, or objective) helped turn attention to improving the survivability of command and control and communications systems. The imperative here was to persuade an adversary that it could not defeat the United States through "decapitation." Various efforts to make command posts and communications systems redundant and survivable were undertaken. For example, a fleet of Looking Glass command aircraft was built, and one was kept continuously aloft at all times from February 3, 1961, through July 24, 1990.[85]

The early decades of the nuclear age and Cold War produced quite a literature on nuclear doctrine. Bernard Brodie wrote of how the purpose of militaries must now be to prevent wars rather than win them. Theorists such as Herman Kahn at RAND wrote of rungs of escalation on a metaphorical ladder of conflict, admonishing the United States to have superiority at each rung. Kahn also became much of the basis for Stanley Kubrick's film *Dr. Strangelove* with his taxonomy of various "tragic but distinguishable" postwar states with varying numbers of millions or tens of millions dead.[86] Thomas Schelling wrote of the "threat that leaves something to chance," arguing that even seemingly irrational threats could have a certain rationality because once the superpowers ginned up their strategic and military machines in times of crisis or war, the outcomes of such situations could not be fully controlled or forecast. The reasons could be political, psychological, organizational, or technical. With this mental model in mind, a definition of *brinkmanship* emerges—it is not a form of crisis behavior where one walks up to a sharp cliff but instead one where the actor starts down a slippery and curved slope, unsure where the point of no return may be. Thus, even if not airtight or foolproof, the willingness to begin the process of taking risk (for example, during an incident such as the Cuban Missile Crisis or the decision to station U.S. tactical warheads in Europe) should have a deterrent effect all its own.[87] So went the logic.

In these and other ways, the American defense establishment sought to make sense of the post-1945 world—and continued to seek clever ways to extract deterrent capability from America's huge investment in nuclear weapons.[88] Author Francis Gavin is compelling in arguing that these and other nuclear strategists, including Bernard Brodie with his book *The Absolute Weapon* (1946), did not drive nuclear modernization and doctrine so much as provide what Eric Edelman calls "a vocabulary and grammar" for how to talk and think about nuclear weapons and their possible use.[89]

CRISES OVER BERLIN, TAIWAN, AND CUBA

All Cold War presidents faced crises short of war of one type or another. Certainly Truman had to handle a major challenge when the Soviets blockaded Berlin in the spring of 1948, and Eisenhower faced Taiwan crises as well as his own Berlin showdown. Kennedy then had to navigate crises over Berlin and Cuba himself (to say nothing of lesser but still significant problems such as the Sino-Indian War of 1962).[90] In figuring out how to handle such acute situations, none of these presidents benefited much from the fact that containment was widely accepted as a core element of U.S. grand strategy. Containment as a big idea did not say how important it was that Berlin, Taiwan, Cuba, or any other specific city or country be successfully protected, any more than it clearly indicated if it was essential to fight and win wars in Korea and Vietnam. To be sure, grand strategies in general are big ideas, often expressed theoretically and abstractly. But for a country like the United States that perceived a global threat from communist expansionism, the dilemma was even greater than for most great powers. What kind of interest was worth defending, and with what degree of effort?

Although they did not turn into hot combat as did Korea and Vietnam, each of these crises was relevant to the general subject of defense strategy. That is because perceptions of the balance of military forces, and plausible military options available to each side, helped determine their resolution. In addition, their outcomes influenced future defense priorities and strategies of both superpowers, as they sought to learn from what had happened and ensure the best possible outcomes in any future crises by redressing any weaknesses that had been revealed. For example, the recurrence of crises near Taiwan in the 1950s heightened in planners' minds the importance of a continuous U.S. naval presence in the western Pacific. Soviet threats to Greece and Turkey in the late 1940s led to the establishment of the Sixth Fleet in 1950. Later, British military disengagement from the broader Middle East, combined ultimately with the fall of the shah of Iran and Soviet invasion of Afghanistan in 1979, underscored the importance of the Persian Gulf in force planning as well, leading to the creation of the Rapid Deployment Force and then Central Command.[91]

Truman decided that holding onto West Berlin was crucial for broader grand strategy. So he took the gamble that defense capabilities of the day would be up to the job even when his military leadership, including the formidable Army chief of staff Omar Bradley, disagreed.[92] He was prepared to use America's still-strong fleet of aircraft as "candy bombers" for many months in order to keep West Berlin afloat. Had U.S. defense capabilities not been up to the task, the cordon for America's containment strategy might have had to be pulled back to the inter-German border—or Truman might have had to threaten escalation with nuclear weapons in an effort to get the Soviets to back down. By succeeding with the airlift, Truman found a way for the defense capabilities of the day to sustain the grand strategy goals he preferred; defense capabilities were up to the job. It took much of the summer and fall to string together enough of an airlift capacity to keep Berliners going. The task was daunting; Berlin was believed to need 15,000 tons of supplies a day, whereas General Curtis LeMay calculated that the available fleet of seventy C-47 aircraft (each with three tons' payload) could provide only roughly 225 tons a day! That meant less than 100,000 tons of supplies over a year. However, by accessing the country's global fleet of C-54 aircraft and other transport planes, the operation was ultimately able to provide some 2.3 million tons over roughly a year (the blockade lasted slightly less than a year, but the airlift continued through the summer to help build up supplies). Only half of what had initially been thought necessary, that amount proved adequate to help Berlin survive the attempted strangulation.[93]

Similarly, Eisenhower decided that keeping not only Taiwan but small islands within eyesight of the Chinese coast free from control by the PRC (People's Republic of China) was essential. He used a combination of conventional operations—helping Taiwan supply the islands—with some degree of nuclear brinkmanship to persuade Mao to back down. It is hard to believe that Ike saw the tiny offshore islands as themselves inherently important. But he availed himself of the defense capabilities of the day to face down Beijing lest it develop greater confidence, and ambitions, after potentially conquering Quemoy and Matsu. Like Truman with the airlift, Eisenhower did so over the objection of the joint chiefs.[94] Again, defense strategy and U.S. military capabilities proved up to the task of underwriting an ambitious and expansive interpretation of what containment strategy required.

Eisenhower also had his own Berlin crisis, in 1958–59, when Soviet premier Nikita Khrushchev issued an ultimatum that Western access to West Berlin would be cut off within six months. American nuclear superiority faced off against Soviet conventional superiority, Berlin of course being well within East Germany. Various vague U.S. nuclear threats proved adequate at least to push the crisis off for a while.[95]

That meant that Kennedy would have his own Berlin crisis, too. Testing a green American president, hoping that Soviet strategic modernization programs of recent years had improved the nuclear balance enough that the Americans might have even less credibility—and confidence—in wielding their nuclear superiority in any Berlin showdown, Khrushchev revived the ultimatum concept and effectively pledged to cut off Western access to West Berlin within six months. The Soviet motivation was also to stymie an exodus of East Berliners to West Berlin that had picked up speed dramatically in recent months. That would be the one part of Khrushchev's problem that he was able to solve, with the construction of a wall between the two Berlins. But he would not be able to achieve the other, more fundamental goal and wrest West Berlin away. The crisis came to an end by October 1961.[96] Kennedy has been criticized for his performance at a summit in Vienna earlier that year, at which he purportedly showed weakness to Khrushchev, and also for allowing the Berlin Wall to go up thereafter.[97] But that seems an unfair assessment. Given the risks of general war, preserving access to, and therefore the freedom of, West Berlin—while also reducing the odds of yet another Berlin crisis in the future—seems a reasonably good outcome.[98] Yes, Western powers lost their access to East Berlin, a net setback.[99] But the Soviet bloc had already lost millions of East Germans fleeing to the West, in preceding years.

In Cuba, Khrushchev sought to redress a strategic nuclear balance that was still in America's favor. He also wanted to protect a communist revolution that had just been threatened by the infamous Bay of Pigs operation. (In that operation, Cuban counterrevolutionaries landed on the coast of Cuba in April 1961, expecting to be met with great local enthusiasm followed by battlefield success, benefiting as well from American attacks on the Cuban air force over the preceding days—only to be soundly defeated by Castro's forces.)[100] Khrushchev's plan was hatched over the spring and summer of 1962. Missiles as well as various types of Soviet combat units began to arrive in Cuba late summer; in October, they were identified by U-2 aircraft.[101]

Moscow sent more than 150 nuclear warheads for missiles that could reach the United States as well as for aircraft and tactical delivery systems that could be used against any invading Americans on Cuba proper.[102] The discovery of the construction of missile launch sites by U.S. intelligence led in October 1962 to perhaps the most dangerous confrontation of the Cold War. Ultimately, the Soviet Union would withdraw the missiles—in the face of an American naval blockade—in exchange for a U.S. promise not to invade Cuba (and a secret promise to pull American missiles out of Turkey within a short time). Kennedy was counseled by much of his military leadership and some hawkish civilian advisers to bomb the missile sites and/or invade the island. Other key advisers, notably McNamara and U.N. Ambassador Adlai Stevenson, considered even the quarantine and blockade option too risky and argued that the United States could live with the missiles in Cuba.[103] We now know that the bombing option might at a minimum have led to the localized use of nuclear weapons by Soviet field commanders, perhaps at America's Guantánamo Bay military base.

Kennedy appears to have made a brilliant choice, in the face of bad advice from most of his confidants. His advisers may have overestimated the capacity of U.S. airpower and ground power in any air strike, underestimated the degree to which the Soviet Union already had usable nuclear weaponry on Cuban soil, and generally failed to foresee how the blockade option (combined with flexible diplomacy) might succeed.[104] Or perhaps Kennedy was just lucky. But what JFK and most of his advisers agreed on, except McNamara and Stevenson, was that defense capabilities and strategy *must* serve the goal of keeping North America free of Soviet weapons. Wherever the line was drawn on the applicability of a containment grand strategy, whether America's defense perimeter against communist expansionism included Berlin and Korea and Vietnam and Quemoy and Matsu, it would definitely have to keep the Soviet military machine far from the United States. That the crisis ended favorably for the United States also reaffirmed the perceived relevance of the overall nuclear balance between the two sides, further ensuring that a vigorous nuclear arms competition would continue.[105]

The resolutions of these three crises stood in contrast to what happened earlier in Korea and what would happen later in Vietnam. In those actual conflicts, the United States had to settle for much less than it preferred (and of course in Vietnam it simply lost). In these cases, the defense capabilities and defense strategies of the day were not up to the job of backstopping a maximalist definition of containment. Thus, the grand strategy's objectives, and geographic boundaries, had to be reassessed. The hard calls were not at the level of grand strategy so much as one level down in granularity, at the level of defense strategy.

A final crisis that should appear on anyone's short list of acute Cold War moments of danger was the U.S.-Soviet showdown during the Yom Kippur War of 1973. As Moscow contemplated direct military intervention to help Egypt salvage its position and its forces on the Sinai Peninsula, after a successful Israeli counterattack, Henry Kissinger placed U.S. nuclear forces on high alert to warn Moscow against doing so. Kissinger took that action even at a time when the American nuclear advantage over the Soviet Union had effectively evaporated. Then, realizing that they needed a way to wind down the war without raising risks even further, the superpowers worked with the United Nations to give themselves a certain amount of diplomatic cover and maneuvering room. Kissinger and Richard Nixon persuaded Israel to end the offensive; ultimately, Israel would also give back the Sinai to Egypt.[106]

MCNAMARA AND THE MODERN PENTAGON

Reorganization and reform of the Department of Defense took place throughout the Cold War. The big bang moment was the very creation of the department—along with the Air Force, Central Intelligence Agency, and National Security Council—in 1947. But in many ways, the most important changes occurred under Robert McNamara in the early to mid-60s, with the strengthening of the office of the secretary of defense and creation of a structured defense budget process. As discussed below, that reform process continued under Melvin Laird in the early 1970s as military conscription was ended and the modern all-volunteer force was created. In many ways, it culminated with the Reagan administration's defense buildup of the 1980s, which provided the resources needed to make these reforms and reorganizations effective, as well as the Goldwater-Nichols Act of 1986. But it was McNamara who got the whole reform thing going.

A tragic figure in regard to Vietnam, McNamara was pathbreaking and innovative in running the Pentagon, and he also had the longest run as secretary of defense of anyone in U.S. history. He narrowly exceeded the tenures of Donald Rumsfeld, with his aggregate time over two periods of service, and Caspar Weinberger during the Reagan years.

I knew both McNamara and Rumsfeld, and I liked them both. Rumsfeld I watched in action, and interacted with, both in his two years of rock star–like fame after 9/11 and in his subsequent years of difficulty. McNamara I knew only in the 1990s, well after his government service but around the time of the publication of his remarkably thoughtful book *In Retrospect.* Both are almost Shakespearean figures in their falls from grace after strong starts at the Pentagon. Both were charismatic and charming; both had a confidence verging on overconfidence (though in his later years of life, I did not see that as much in an older McNamara). Both were unlucky, in terms of how their skill sets (and weaknesses) intersected with the big problems of the day that they were asked to solve, most of all Vietnam and Iraq. They both displayed the can-do attitude that makes Americans, and America, great—but also the boldness and assertiveness that can get us into trouble. Both dared to do mighty things; both fell tragically short on what history will likely most remember each man for. Their careers are thus stark reminders of this book's central argument: that Americans are far more assertive in their defense strategies and military operations than we tend to appreciate about our history or ourselves, and that this assertiveness can have a downside even if on balance it has been a net positive for the role the United States has played in world history to date.

Of course, there was more to the McNamara legacy than Vietnam (and, as discussed in the next chapter, more to Rumsfeld's than Iraq). Although the biggest pieces of legislation affecting the composition and functioning of the Department of Defense were passed in 1947, 1949, 1958, and 1986, rather than the 1960s, it was McNamara who arguably made greatest use of new legislative authorities and created the strong system of civilian control of the military that has since characterized American defense policy.

One key element of McNamara's strengthening of the Office of the Secretary of Defense (OSD) was the introduction and widespread employment of the PPBE process—that is, the planning, programming, budgeting, and execution process or system (initially, it was just PPBS, with the execution phase explicitly added several decades later and the letter "S" referring to "System"). With this approach, McNamara's teams of largely civilian analysts grouped different proposed modernization efforts into conceptual and strategic categories that allowed weapons systems from different services that purported to achieve similar goals to be weighed against each other. Previously, the services had largely been free to build their own budgets, with considerable redundancy as the inevitable result. Later, under Secretary Melvin Laird in the Nixon administration, part of the PPBE process was in effect outsourced back to the individual military services and departments—but with the proviso that civilians at OSD would always have the prerogative to review proposals to ensure consistency with the secretary's initial broad guidance.[107]

Among other benefits, this PPBE process probably put some brakes on a nuclear weapons planning system that otherwise might have lurched completely out of control. It also required planners to take a multiyear approach to weapons and force planning that was more consistent with the time horizons over which new capabilities are introduced and maintained. It brought greater emphasis, and sometimes more resources, to such unsexy budget categories as transportation that the services tended to deemphasize.[108] And it put some checks on the frequent tendencies of the services to "gold plate" new weapons with the latest technologies rather than think in cost-conscious terms about which new technologies really were crucial (and likely to be truly available within the time horizons of given weapons programs).[109] All that said, PPBE did not—could not—definitively solve all the problems that make defense planning and budgeting difficult and inefficient, given the uncertainties of developing new technology, the hazards of trying to predict the future security environment, and the inherent challenges of running a multi-million-person organization.[110]

Sadly, for all the good he may have done with management of the Department of Defense, it is Vietnam for which McNamara will be forever remembered most of all.

STRATEGY IN VIETNAM

Vietnam was probably the worst war performance of the United States in its history. Many brave Americans served there, to be sure, and most had no say over how it was fought. But leadership, civilian and military, dropped the ball. So did the broader American political debate that managed to turn such a peripheral conflict into a matter of perceived strategic life or death. The resulting costs were not only very high in direct terms. They also led to a "No More Vietnams" mentality that persuaded the U.S. Army, and military writ large, not to prepare for future counterinsurgency missions—out of a hope that if the military was not prepared to conduct such missions, it would not be asked to conduct them. That mindset, and that legacy, came back to haunt the country in Iraq and Afghanistan.[111] Along with U.S. experiences in the attempted Iran hostage rescue of 1980, the tragic intervention in Lebanon in 1983, and the Black Hawk Down episode in 1993, the legacy of Vietnam provided grist for America's enemies such as Osama bin Laden who thought they detected a paper-tiger quality in the modern American polity.

There was one silver lining to the long, hard, ultimately unsuccessful slog that fits within the broad argument of this book and the broad sweep of U.S. military history: by fighting so doggedly in such a remote place, where the stakes for American security seemed modest at most, the United States demonstrated its assertiveness and resoluteness. Global deterrence was likely reinforced to some extent by the very fact of the fight itself, despite the poor outcome. Just as in Afghanistan decades later, there likely was some broader deterrent benefit that came from trying so hard. That said, I wish we had never sent U.S. combat forces to Southeast Asia, and I certainly wish we had not fought the war the way we did.

The basic decision to intervene was widely supported—and badly done. Not only was Congress kept on the margins of all major decisions, especially at the outset; not only did the country fail to carry out a sober and open strategic debate about the stakes in Vietnam and the realistic prospects for any intervention. But the country's strategic community, including at least three straight presidents dating back to Eisenhower, failed to assess the true importance of Vietnam in global context. As Henry Kissinger compellingly argued, they conflated all worldwide interests into a single anticommunist dogma, failing to apply realpolitik strategic prioritization. Was it not strange, he argued, that taking an even broader brush, American policy makers tolerated the fall of China to communism in 1949 yet decided they could not allow the far smaller and more remote Vietnam to fall in the 1960s? It was one thing to see Vietnam as having a certain importance and attempting to help it in modest and indirect ways; it was something else altogether to send a total of several million GIs to its defense, with more than 55,000 losing their lives there.[112]

The essence of American strategy in Vietnam was to pound North Vietnam and thus the Viet Cong into submission one way or another. Hence the various bombing campaigns against North Vietnamese cities. Hence the concerted efforts to interrupt supply lines, most notably the Ho Chi Minh Trail, from North Vietnam into the South. Hence also the unrelenting attacks, largely from artillery and aircraft, against suspected Viet Cong positions in the South. The United States sometimes tried more canonical counterinsurgency warfare, but not frequently or consistently. Rather, it resorted to the massive application of firepower.

The war did not usually involve major movements of large armies. It was spread out in time and space, as is generally the case with insurgency and counterinsurgency warfare. That said, there were numerous important efforts centered on geography—the Tet Offensive in 1968 by North Vietnam against many large South Vietnamese cities, U.S. efforts to establish a barrier along the Fourteenth Parallel dividing the two Vietnams, various American bombing campaigns in specific parts of North Vietnam and Cambodia, South Vietnamese attacks supported by the United States into Cambodia and Laos, and North Vietnam's major assault across the demilitarized zone in March 1972 as well as its successful assaults a couple of years later after the U.S. departure.

Once president, John F. Kennedy expanded the existing American advisory mission, which had involved some 3,000 Americans in early 1961. The mission would grow to 16,000 by the end of Kennedy's life in 1963. No ground-combat troops were sent during Kennedy's presidency—but some of the American "advisers" were American pilots who conducted bombing raids.

During these early years, a "strategic hamlet" program relocated many South Vietnamese peasants to communities where they could be separated and protected from the insurgents. In theory, at least, it hinted at proper counterinsurgency strategy. But the heavy-handed way it was implemented caused resentment among the South Vietnamese civilian populations. Indeed, resentment at the South Vietnamese government, according to prisoner-of-war interviews and other information, was a key motivator for the resistance movement throughout much of the war—probably more than any ideological devotion to communism.[113] Cronyism and incompetence were rampant throughout the South Vietnamese armed forces as well.[114]

In early August 1964, American ships, sailing inside the twelve-mile territorial water limits of North Vietnam, wound up in an engagement with North Vietnamese vessels. No American casualties resulted, though the North Vietnamese did suffer some losses. Seeking to force the issue, the United States sent vessels back into the same waters the next day. Confusion reigned about what then happened, due to weather conditions, boat traffic, and human nervousness. The United States, probably wrongly, concluded that its ships had been fired on. That led Congress to pass the Gulf of Tonkin Resolution on August 7, giving President Johnson the right to carry out assertive actions in the name of self-defense against North Vietnam. It was sweeping in scope and undefined in duration. It preceded any decision to place American ground forces on Vietnamese soil or even any serious consideration of that option. Regrettably, it would wind up as the only authorization Congress ever considered for the Vietnam War, even as circumstances and the U.S. level of combat involvement escalated dramatically in the years to come.[115]

After Viet Cong guerrillas attacked American installations at Pleiku in the central highlands of South Vietnam on February 7, 1965, President Johnson then authorized a short bombing reprisal known as Flaming Dart. It was followed soon by Operation Rolling Thunder, a graduated and sustained bombing campaign of North Vietnam by the United States that would last three years. To protect the Danang airfield, two battalions of American Marines (a couple thousand personnel in all) then came ashore on March 8. Things would escalate fast from there.[116] By December, U.S. troop totals in South Vietnam would total 200,000. A year later, they would number 400,000. By the end of 1968, there would be some 540,000 Americans in uniform fighting in defense of the Republic of Vietnam.[117] In addition to soldiers and Marines, these figures included up to forty-four Air Force tactical fighter squadrons and three to four aircraft carrier battle groups.[118] There might have been 600,000 or more if General William Westmoreland had had his way, but by that point civilian leadership had soured on the idea of reinforcing failure.[119]

In addition to the bombing campaigns, the U.S. strategy for the war centered on search-and-destroy tactics involving the massive use of firepower. Algorithms for sizing necessary U.S. forces were based largely on the estimated size of the enemy. It was assumed that at least ten counterinsurgents were needed per individual insurgent. A major problem with that methodology was that a modest increase in the estimated size of the enemy, however imprecise, implied a "requirement" for a tenfold-larger increase in combined U.S. and Republic of Vietnam forces.[120] Such was the funny math on which force sizing decisions were largely made; by contrast, modern U.S. counterinsurgency doctrine bases the size of necessary counterinsurgent forces primarily on the size of the civilian population to be protected.[121]

Asserting that the enemy was moving into phase three of a classic Maoist guerrilla war, which resembles traditional force-on-force combat more than the hit-and-run tactics of phase two, American leaders later claimed that a 3:1 ratio of friendly forces over the enemy might suffice. That became a necessary adjustment when U.S. intelligence estimates of the size of the enemy grew to more than 250,000 by 1968.[122] The South Vietnamese government fielded hundreds of thousands of troops, so by changing the algorithm, American military leaders could claim—or at least hope—that they were near adequate force ratios (while typically still asking Washington for more). Alas, the South Vietnamese forces were generally mediocre—and the logic of the force-sizing calculations was dubious at best, especially given the poor tactics employed by the South Vietnamese together with the Americans.[123]

There were more flawed assumptions. The United States believed that the North Vietnamese did not have capacity to replace more than some 60,000 casualties a year. That was wrong.[124] So, too, was any doubt about Hanoi's dedication to the war effort and its willingness to endure great sacrifices in pursuit of its maximalist goals.[125] Also incorrect was the notion that the Viet Cong could be strangled in place by cutting off their supplies. In fact, the Viet Cong needed only some fifteen tons of supplies a day to arrive from North Vietnam, given how much of their food, weaponry, and ammunition they could obtain locally.[126]

In 1966, in an attempt to cut off the Viet Cong, the United States came up with the idea of a "McNamara Line" of electronic fencing, sensors, land mines, and other barriers along the inter-Vietnam border and then through Laos to Thailand. President Johnson approved it in 1967. But this plan was later abandoned as requiring too much effort for its likely useful effects.[127]

The air war had two major components. One part was directed against Viet Cong positions, supply lines, supplies, and logistics assets in the South, including the Ho Chi Minh Trail. Those attacks were also directed at times against South Vietnamese citizens believed to be aiding and abetting the rebels.[128]

Then there was the campaign against North Vietnam. Target sets in the North were authorized in a progressive fashion. The pace of aerial attacks increased with time, from about 25,000 attack sorties in 1965 to 108,000 in 1967, as the tonnage of bombs increased from 63,000 to 226,000.[129] Alas, enemy strength over that period grew at least as fast.[130] The Tet Offensive, launched on January 31, 1968, and continuing through February, demonstrated its resilience; the offensive involved attacks on more than 100 South Vietnamese cities with 70,000 to 85,000 troops. Although a military failure, it proved a major strategic success, discouraging the American public as well as the Johnson administration about the prospects for victory in the war.[131]

Initially, most bombing targets within North Vietnam were transportation or military assets. As time went on, a wider range of industrial targets was included, too. It was hoped that such a gradualist strategy might induce the enemy to negotiate. In theory, the desire to avoid future attacks would persuade Ho Chi Minh and the rest of the North Vietnamese leadership to accept a deal.[132] Some Americans, including Air Force chief general Curtis LeMay, favored a more intense bombing operation, and over time, they came closer to winning internal debates.[133]

The weaknesses of the Republic of Vietnam government were doubly troubling because it was that government, and its security forces, that had primary responsibility for what was probably the most important part of the fight: the population protection mission. In Vietnam, this meant a major focus on securing the densely populated coastal regions. South Vietnamese forces were not, however, up to the job.

In some northern regions of South Vietnam, the United States tried to help. Specifically, the U.S. Marine Corps formed Combined Action Program (CAP) platoon teams of about fifteen Marines. The basic concept derived largely from the service's famous *Small Wars Manual* (1940) and was informed by some of the better practices the United States had employed earlier in the Philippines as well as Latin America.[134] CAPs showed the capacity to improve security with roughly half the casualty rate of other U.S. forces, using more of a clear-and-hold approach rather than a search-and-destroy tactic and emphasizing the gathering of good intelligence as well as the protection of the population.[135] By extrapolation, if applied nationwide, this approach might have secured most Vietnamese hamlets with fewer than 200,000 American personnel.[136] That said, the CAP concept was probably never attempted systematically enough to warrant confident assertions about its nationwide potential in Vietnam.[137] And the overall commander, General Westmoreland, was unwilling to divert American troops to such missions, instead staying with his search-and-destroy philosophy. The joint chiefs were of mixed views, but the chairman, Earl Wheeler (himself former Army chief), sided with Westmoreland.[138]

Once in office, Richard M. Nixon looked for a new strategy. He attempted both to escalate and deescalate the war. If nothing else, when combined with his opening to China, he hoped to produce a "decent interval" between eventual American withdrawal and any collapse of the South Vietnamese government so that America's broader position in the region would remain acceptable. In that sense, Nixon hoped that even a failed defense strategy in Vietnam could help salvage a more important global U.S. grand strategy. He carried out a downsizing of U.S. forces and a "Vietnamization" of the war on the ground, though with occasional escalation in the air and in neighboring Cambodia (where Prince Norodom Sihanouk gave his tacit blessing to the effort, before being overthrown in a coup).[139]

The ground fight changed in this period not only because of Vietnamization but because of a change in command. General Creighton Abrams took a much different approach than had Westmoreland, rejecting tactics that emphasized search-and-destroy operations, enemy attrition, and body counts, as well as the pursuit of a so-called crossover point at which the enemy's rate of attrition would exceed its capacity for regeneration. Instead, taking a page out of the Marine Corps playbook, Abrams shifted to a greater emphasis on clear-and-hold operations—even while seeking to attack and weaken the enemy directly when the opportunity presented.[140] Relatedly, the Civil Operations and Rural Development Support program, started in 1967 under Robert Komer, was taken over and strengthened by William Colby in late 1968. Much greater efforts were placed on fostering collaboration across different U.S. government agencies and building trust with South Vietnamese president Nguyen Van Thieu so that he would be more inclined to replace poor leaders of the security forces, and poor local political leaders, when appropriate.[141]

Yet, as noted, escalation also took place. A secret bombing mission in Cambodia was undertaken; the bombing would last fifteen months. A major offensive was also conducted in Cambodia, by American as well as South Vietnamese ground troops.[142] The combined efforts achieved some impressive results, in terms of supplies seized and logistics lines interrupted. But they did not fundamentally shift overall battlefield momentum.[143]

By the end of 1970, Congress, angered by Nixon's secret campaigns, banned any further American ground combat beyond South Vietnam's borders. Thus the battle of Lam Son 719 in February and March 1971, a major effort that sought to sever Viet Cong supply lines in Laos, could only employ South Vietnamese ground forces (along with lots of American airpower, including helicopter transport). South Vietnamese forces took heavy losses and failed to achieve their main objectives.[144]

By some measures, the Vietnam War went better in this period, at least for a while.[145] By 1972, even after most U.S. forces had been withdrawn, the Saigon government purportedly "controlled" (at least by day) some 75 percent of the country's territory, corresponding to regions where 85 percent of its population lived.[146] North Vietnam tried an "Easter offensive" in the spring of 1972, but U.S. air power combined with South Vietnamese ground capabilities fended off the assault.

Nixon did not authorize major bombing campaigns against North Vietnam in earlier years of his presidency. But by 1972, hoping to coerce the North Vietnamese into serious negotiations, he escalated that part of the war as well. The ensuing Linebacker operations against targets in North Vietnam were intensive.[147] Yet their coercive leverage against a battle-toughened North Vietnamese government was still severely limited, especially in light of America's disengagement on the ground and its clear intention to get out of the war altogether.

The Vietnam experience provided some of the perspective and historical knowledge that would lead a group of military leaders to develop much better tactics and concepts of operations for counterinsurgency and stabilization during the surge in Iraq in 2007 and 2008. But its good ideas and innovative leaders proved too little, too late. The initial U.S. emphasis on search-and-destroy operations, "prophylactic" uses of firepower on the ground and from the air, maximization of Viet Cong body counts, isolation of enemy forces through massive bombing of logistics lines, and pursuit of an elusive "crossover point" in enemy manpower—while trying to strengthen a badly flawed partner nation enough that it could take over more of the fight itself—together amounted to a failed defense strategy. Nixon's secret war in Cambodia as well as the Watergate scandal further eroded Congress's willingness even to sustain large-scale security assistance to South Vietnam thereafter, putting the finishing touches on its ultimate defeat. Thankfully, U.S. grand strategy was doing better.

THE NIXON DOCTRINE AND MILITARY RETRENCHMENT: FROM 2½ WARS TO 1½

With the nation's defeat in Vietnam, defense reform took its next big steps. Along with the opening to China, Richard Nixon engineered a big cutback in the military, ended the draft, promised to avoid land wars in Asia (more or less), and resolved to rely primarily on local allies for the defense of "the perimeter" in the global struggle against communist expansionism. Overall, this period of defense reform would not go that well at first; the 1970s in general were a period of frustration and relative weakness for the United States. But the foundations were nonetheless established for a much more successful 1980s. And the strategic patience that presidents, secretaries of defense, and other leaders would demonstrate proved to be more effective than the assertiveness of much of the two previous Cold War decades. At least the United States stayed out of new wars, while maintaining deterrence in key regions.

The size of the American armed forces between the late 1960s and early 1970s declined from 3.5 million to 2 million. (Again, they had numbered about 2.5 million at the end of the Eisenhower presidency, before Vietnam.) The Army was cut almost in half, winding up below 800,000 active-duty soldiers by the early 1970s—the smallest it had been since 1950.[148] Inflation-adjusted budgets would, by the mid-1970s, hover some 30 percent below the late 1960s average and more than 10 percent below even the latter Eisenhower and Kennedy years.[149] The effect of declining budgets on military compensation made it that much harder to recruit a strong all-volunteer military in the aftermath of Vietnam. Fortunately, the military as an institution remained widely respected by the American public even after Vietnam, with nearly 75 percent favorability in

1974 according to one poll. But, understandably, its leadership was not so respected, with a positive score of only 33 percent in 1974 and 24 percent in 1975.[150]

Melvin Laird was Richard Nixon's first secretary of defense. He inherited the reins of the Pentagon at a time of military cutbacks and partial American retrenchment on the world stage—at the same time that the Soviet Union was to some extent feeling its oats. That made for a dangerous combination. Laird's attempted solution to this crunch in force size and budgets, in a policy sustained by his successors to this day, included greater reliance on the reserve components—the Army National Guard and Army Reserve, the Air Force National Guard and Air Force Reserve, the Navy Reserve, the Marine Corps Reserve, and the Individual Ready Reserve (as well as capabilities within the Coast Guard and Merchant Marine). The active Army would be made up with a higher percentage of combat units than before; the Army Reserve in particular would take primary responsibility for many support functions. Other innovations were attempted as well, such as Army Chief General Creighton Abrams's concept of a roundout division, with two active-duty combat brigades and one guard brigade. Under the Abrams Doctrine, the Army sought to increase its active-duty combat divisions from thirteen to sixteen. These changes meant that only the total force would be able to conduct sustained large-scale operations; reservists would be necessary early in any substantial combat force deployment. Congress supported the thrust of these changes with a law in 1976 allowing the president to call up 50,000 reservists for up to ninety days without congressional authorization (by the time of Operation Desert Storm, the law had been revised to allow presidential call-ups of up to 200,000 reservists for up to 180 days).[151]

Some interpreted a political purpose in this new force-design architecture. By requiring a future president to have to mobilize reservists, and therefore disrupt the lives of many older Americans who were established and well known within their communities, presidents might have a harder time taking the country to war. A stronger and more compelling case for interfering with citizens' lives would, so the narrative went, have to be made than was ever the case in Vietnam, when almost all draftees were young.[152] But even though it makes for a good story, this was not the key logic behind the idea at the time.[153] In fact, Abrams' more important motivation was to maintain a viable American military defense capability and deterrent with a smaller defense budget and smaller active-duty armed forces than the country had previously possessed.[154]

Due to the total-force policy, by the late 1980s, the Army National Guard provided 36 percent of the Army's combat divisions. It also provided almost half of its maintenance companies and combat engineer units. The Army Reserve provided all the Army's railroad units, nearly all of its civil affairs units, and the majority of its supply and service units.[155] The Air Force also built in major dependencies on its own guard and reserve components.

Nixon also set somewhat more modest goals for what the reduced American armed forces should be expected to accomplish. His so-called Guam Doctrine placed greater importance on regional allies such as Japan and led to further U.S. troop cutbacks in the region. In 1960, the United States had had some 75,000 military personnel in Japan and more than 50,000 in South Korea. Those numbers would grow to almost 90,000 and more than 60,000, respectively, by 1964, but by the end of the Gerald Ford presidency, they were down to 45,000 and 40,000.[156] In terms of combat-force structure, the presence in Japan included two-thirds of a Marine Corps division and associated airpower, as well as Air Force tactical airlift. The presence in South Korea included one Army infantry division, down from two before the Guam Doctrine was implemented, and three Air Force fighting squadrons, among other assets (including nuclear weapons).[157] The cuts to U.S. capability in Korea also reflected an appreciation that South Korea's relative military strength was growing—even as its politics remained, at that time, autocratic. (For that latter reason, President Jimmy Carter would even consider pulling U.S. ground troops off the peninsula altogether, before thinking better of it.)[158]

At the level of strategy and force planning, the Nixon Doctrine led to a scaling back from a "2½-war" framework for sizing American combat forces to "1½-wars."[159] This transformation would be achieved through greater reliance on allies, the strategic good sense to avoid future Vietnams, and a recognition of the importance of strengthening the economy at home rather than overinsuring against worst cases abroad.

The opening to China early in the Nixon years helped undergird this shift, by reducing the odds of direct confrontation against China. Along with the Soviet Union, China had been one of the two big countries that previous presidents had thought the United States might need to fight—hence their 2½-wars paradigm. That opening did not entirely end worries about conflict against China, of course. Although the United States did break off the security agreement between itself and Taiwan in 1978, the Taiwan Relations Act of 1979 walked that decision partially back. The United States would retain some degree of responsibility for Taiwan's defense, depending on circumstances. With that law, plus the "Third Communique" with Beijing and "Six Assurances" that Washington offered Taipei, the United States created the concept of "strategic ambiguity" or dual deterrence. Washington was trying to deter China from attacking Taiwan, but also to deter Taiwan from pursuing independence, with one and the same policy and one and the same set of policy instruments.[160]

It is worth noting that Carter had created a precedent for a president unilaterally ending a previous treaty arrangement, without any role for the Senate in doing so. He also established the precedent of preparing to end U.S. military presence in Korea without a role for Congress, though he later decided against such a dramatic change. Other presidents have also withdrawn from treaties subsequently, including George W. Bush with the Anti-Ballistic Missile (ABM) Treaty and Donald Trump with the Intermediate-Range Nuclear Forces (INF) Treaty.

The 1970s also witnessed at least two hugely important developments in the broader Middle East, one of which helped stabilize the region and one of which very much did the opposite.

First, Israel's position improved through the decade. Secretary of State Henry Kissinger had helped set up this outcome with his deft diplomacy during the Yom Kippur War in 1973. With Nixon reeling from the Watergate scandal, Kissinger effectively took charge and employed a carrot-and-stick approach to end the fighting. Acting in Nixon's name, he put U.S. military forces worldwide on DEFCON-3 to discourage Soviet conventional intervention at a time when Israel appeared on the verge of decisively defeating Egypt's Third Army on the Sinai Peninsula. That condition is essentially a heightened state of peacetime alert, not an actual preparation for war. As such, and because of the general recognition of U.S.-Soviet nuclear parity at the time, most observers question the seriousness with which the U.S. threat was made or perceived. But it was hard to ignore altogether. Meanwhile, Kissinger ensured that Arab forces survived the war with most of their force structure and most of their pride; Egypt would also get the Sinai Peninsula back as part of the Camp David Accords, which established peace between Israel and Egypt under Jimmy Carter several years later.[161]

However, on the other side of the Middle East, the fall of the shah of Iran in 1979, combined with the Soviet invasion of Afghanistan later that same year, created a major dilemma for the United States. Now, oil supplies on which so much of the world had come to depend seemed at risk, and there were neither British nor pro-Western Iranians in place to protect them. Part of the American response was, working with Pakistan, to provide covert and overt military assistance to the Afghan resistance, or mujahideen.[162] In regard to its own armed forces, the United States, without increasing the size of its military, created a

Rapid Deployment Force (RDF) in 1980 (the precursor to CENTCOM, itself formed in 1983) as a means of response. Yet that RDF would have had to borrow forces from other regions or commands to have any capability at its disposal. Such "borrowing" is largely the norm for a U.S. military that always has more potential missions than force structure. Nonetheless, the United States had in effect added one huge new set of responsibilities for its defense strategy to underwrite without providing additional or dedicated means of doing so. Former secretary of defense James Schlesinger noted that the RDF was neither rapid nor deployable nor, for that matter, really a force.[163] Brookings Institution scholar William Kaufmann estimated that to make the RDF more rapidly deployable would have required an investment approaching $100 billion (in 2025 dollars) in strategic lift, including 130 large airlifters and twenty large ships, as well as prepositioned equipment and improvements to regional basing.[164] One might have added more aircraft carriers to the list.[165] Eventually, during the Reagan years buildup, some of these resources would be forthcoming, and the creation of Transportation Command in 1987 helped, too. Spending on mobility forces, having been relatively neglected since Vietnam, roughly tripled in the 1980s. Fast sealift, featuring ferrylike ships that ground vehicles could drive on and off, grew to have the capacity to move several divisions of armored forces at once; airlift grew toward 50 million ton-miles per day of capacity.[166]

So over the 1970s, some American global responsibilities became easier to maintain but others became harder. The shift from 2½ wars to 1½, as the worst-case scenario on which American military forces would be sized, could not change these basic strategic facts. As such, all the theorizing over how many wars the United States could fight at a time sometimes resembled debates over how many angels can dance on the head of a pin. As noted earlier, the number of divisions in the active-duty U.S. Army reached twenty-three during both the Korean War and the height of the Vietnam War but otherwise ranged from sixteen to nineteen during most of the Cold War—seventeen in 1960, sixteen in 1972, and nineteen by the mid- to late 1970s, even as the war-fighting construct changed fundamentally.[167] The degree to which the Army's eight to nine reserve divisions might be counted on for a simultaneous war was debated and changed, partly to accord with whatever strategy was current at the time. But the active-duty force did not change greatly even as simultaneous wars against both the Soviet Union and China were first considered plausible and then discounted. The Vietnam War itself fit uncomfortably within this framework—too big to be a "half war," clearly, but also not a conflict against the Soviet Union or China.

Secretary of Defense Laird explained the change using the 2½- and 1½-war lexicon in 1970, accepting the framing that had been introduced during the McNamara era. But by 1972, the same Melvin Laird was expressing discomfort with the whole idea of sizing and posturing U.S. forces based on war-fighting expectations rather than the (related but distinct) requirements of global deterrence.[168] We will again see evidence in the twenty-first century about the limited impact that formal war-fighting requirements and force-structure paradigms actually have on the size and shape of the American armed forces.

NUCLEAR STRATEGY IN THE ERA OF PARITY, ARMS CONTROL, DÉTENTE . . . AND CONFRONTATION

By the last two decades of the Cold War, both superpowers had achieved overkill, in massive amounts, and in rough equivalence with each other. These facts helped produce a movement toward arms control. But they hardly ended the nuclear competition or the pursuit of a theory of victory in nuclear war, however farfetched at times. Achieving the nuclear victory, or at least making Moscow perceive that the United States had some kind of usable nuclear advantage, was a greater concern for the United States, given its alliance network and geographic position. It must be remembered that MAD was never really a doctrine of either side so much as a nod to reality—but a begrudging nod at that.

Thus, in the 1970s, the Soviet Union pursued a massive nuclear buildup to be sure it would effectively equal the United States by most metrics of nuclear capability—and exceed it in some. The United States led the way on development of multiple independently targetable reentry vehicles (MIRVs)—technologies allowing several warheads from the same intercontinental ballistic missile or submarine-launched ballistic missile (SLBM) to be separately targeted. But the Soviet Union caught up and, with its SS-18 "Satan" ICBM, managed to deploy ten warheads on a single long-range missile. Thus was born a decade-long obsession with the "throw-weight" gap favoring the Soviet Union and its large rockets.[169] The United States led the way on accuracy, but again the Soviet Union was not far behind. As missile silos became more vulnerable, each side attempted to deploy mobile ICBMs on its own territory—with greater success on the Soviet side.

Both sides pursued missile defense technologies even as both recognized that they were likely to be of limited effectiveness and utility. The exception was the Reagan administration, starting in 1983, with the announcement of the

Strategic Defense Initiative (SDI, but better known colloquially as Star Wars) that sought to render nuclear weapons "impotent and obsolete."

The United States definitely led the way on development and deployment of stealth aircraft. But in some ways this development did little more than counter and partially checkmate the huge growth in Soviet air defenses that took place during the Cold War.

Various permutations on formal nuclear doctrine were developed in this period to try to make deterrence more effective and the possible use of nuclear weapons for less than existential purposes more plausible. It is probably fair to say that the era of big-name theorists—Bernard Brodie, Thomas Schelling, Henry Kissinger, William Kaufmann, Herman Kahn—was mostly over by this point (even if there were still a few, such as Robert Jervis and Harold Brown, who came up with big ideas). Yet the conversation had not ended. For example, under Secretary of Defense James Schlesinger in the Nixon administration, a Schlesinger Doctrine, otherwise known as National Security Decision Memorandum 242 (or NSDM-242), sought ways to emphasize counterforce targeting (against the other side's weapons, and most likely its nuclear weapons) rather than countercity or countervalue targeting. To resort to the latter was recognized as suicidal in the MAD era. By contrast, with counterforce targeting, it was hoped that both sides might together find a way to terminate any nuclear exchange short of all-out war, perhaps with one side somehow even "winning."[170] Accordingly, in 1976, a new "SIOP-5" allowed for preplanned and coordinated attacks against smaller target sets that might include fewer than 100 sites.[171]

The Reagan administration sought to profit from new technologies (notably, more accurate MIRV'ed ICBMs, especially the MX "Peacekeeper") to make a counterforce strategy seem less irrational than it might have otherwise. But it struggled to deploy the MX in a way that would enhance the survivability of the American arsenal, only belatedly and reluctantly putting the missile in limited numbers in the very Minuteman-era silos that had been deemed sitting ducks. (By contrast, SLBMs were becoming more accurate, with the D5 or Trident II missile, over this period, and the submarines that carried them were still widely considered to be very survivable).[172] Reagan also deployed new Pershing intermediate-range ballistic missiles and ground-launched nuclear-tipped cruise missiles to Europe, largely as an antidote to Soviet deployments of weapons such as the SS-20 intermediate-range ballistic missile. These developments were politically very controversial at the time, partly because they seemed to confirm the death of détente and arms control, partly because it was increasingly appreciated how all-out nuclear war might threaten the survival of the human race (by causing a complete breakdown in the modern global economy on which virtually all people depended, and/or a "nuclear winter" that would snuff out all life on earth).[173]

By the 1980s, the size of the SIOP, and the National Strategic Target Data Base, had grown enormously. At the end of the Cold War, the database contained some 21,000 separate aimpoints—about 11,000 associated with nuclear forces, 5,000 for command and control and communications and intelligence, 2,000 for other military targets, and a bit more than 3,000 for industry as well as the economy. The SIOP contained 8,000 targets. The category-by-category allocation within the SIOP was estimated to have included 4,000 aimpoints associated with Soviet nuclear forces, 2,000 with command, control, communications, and intelligence, 1,000 with other military targets, and about 1,000 for economic and industrial assets.[174] That would be in a first strike. For a retaliatory or second strike, according to calculations by Joshua Epstein, the United States might have had some 4,000 warheads available—unless it had put forces on alert in advance of the Soviet attack, putting more submarines to sea and bombers on alert, in which case it might still have had 7,500 warheads available even after absorbing an all-out first strike.[175]

Then there were the substrategic weapons. To give a global snapshot of America's roughly 11,000 tactical nuclear weapons in 1983, there were just over 3,000 such warheads in the United States, almost 6,000 in Europe (with nearly 4,000 for U.S. forces and nearly 2,000 under dual-key arrangements with allies), almost 1,500 at sea, and about 350 in Asia-Pacific countries.[176]

Despite the intense acrimony and suspicion within the superpower relationship, particularly from 1979 through 1985 or so, the United States and Soviet Union did not have a showdown as in Berlin and Cuba in years past. However, in the very tense year of 1983 (during which Reagan had announced the Strategic Defense Initiative on March 23 and the Soviets had shot down Korean Air Lines flight KAL 007 on September 1), miscalculation and malfunction created serious dangers—first in a software glitch in a Soviet early warning system, then in a temporary Soviet misinterpretation of a NATO "Able Archer" training exercise that was mistaken as a preparation for actual attack.[177] As such, the risk of accidental or mistaken use of weapons was increasingly appreciated. Strategic nuclear weapons might not have been on hair-trigger alert literally, but they were still on high alert, and that carried dangers. Some came to believe that if there was any path to "winning" a nuclear war, it would happen through a decapitation strike against adversary command-and-control rather than the wholesale demolition of the other side's force. Hence, Presidential Directive 59

(PD-59) under Carter sought not only to add further options for limited (and protracted) nuclear war to the American nuclear portfolio but also to streamline, and harden, U.S. command-and-control systems and processes partly in the hope of convincing Soviet leaders that those U.S. systems could survive indefinitely in a protracted nuclear war (thereby denying Moscow any plausible theory of victory).[178] Collectively, these Carter administration innovations were sometimes described as the countervailing strategy—though they were more evolutionary than revolutionary.[179]

Even as these nuclear modernization efforts continued, a superpower nuclear arms control process started in the Johnson administration and continued in fits and starts with every American president thereafter. The talks and associated accords never went nearly as far as advocates wished. But with the possible exception of the dubiously constructed SALT I Treaty, they probably did help cap the intensity of the superpower arms competition while substantially improving communications between the superpowers.

The Strategic Arms Limitation Talks began in 1967, under President Johnson, and reached their first major agreements in 1972 under President Nixon. SALT I, as the treaty limiting long-range offensive arms was known, froze total numbers of ICBMs and SLBMs and nuclear-weapons submarines for each side. That locked in a Soviet numerical advantage in each of those categories, but since the United States was preparing to deploy multiple independently targetable reentry vehicles (MIRVs) by then, it did not worry too much about launcher numbers: it could put several warheads on each missile. This logic was later seen as flawed, but it carried the day at the time. The Anti-Ballistic Missile Treaty of 1972 was also negotiated in this period. Once a protocol was added in 1974, the treaty limited each side to one missile-defense site (at either the national capital or an ICBM field). The United States did not ultimately avail itself of either option, whereas the Soviet Union built a system around Moscow.[180]

SALT I was noteworthy, and successful, in establishing joint consultations around strategic arms as well as standing mechanisms for discussing issues or problems that arose. It involved a sustained period of summitry as well and contributed to the increasingly vogue concept of "peaceful coexistence." However, by failing to ban or limit MIRVs, it amounted in many ways to whack-a-mole. Limitations of one type simply allowed maximal effort to be redirected to areas where limitations did not apply. In addition, the approach of freezing launchers on both sides, by locking in Soviet advantages in these categories, began to create a sour taste in the mouths of some American critics of détente and arms control.[181] These critics would only grow in number and conviction as the decade unfolded. Conventional arms control in this era was faring even worse under the so-called Mutual and Balanced Force Reductions talks and giving arms control a tainted reputation in the process.[182]

The post-SALT nuclear numbers ultimately spoke for themselves. While the total number of U.S. nuclear weapons (counting shorter-range systems as well) had already peaked in the late 1960s and begun a steady decline thereafter, Soviet aggregate numbers kept growing fast even after the 1972 accords were signed.[183] Long-range or strategic warheads increased on both sides after 1972—dramatically so for the Soviet Union.[184]

FROM THE HOLLOW FORCE TO THE REAGAN BUILDUP AND GOLDWATER-NICHOLS REORGANIZATION

The last fifteen years of the Cold War were, on balance, less eventful than the twenty-five that preceded them. But they were still fraught with dangers and tension—and they began with the United States in a collectively sour mood, unsure of its prospects for successful global leadership. That was nothing completely new, of course; there had been the great uncertainties of the McCarthy period, the Sputnik scare in the late 1950s when the Soviets seemed to take the lead in the Space Race, and the great social and political cleavages of the Vietnam period. Again, it is hard to look back at Cold War history and find too many Norman Rockwell moments of national bliss. But what happened in the 1970s lasted longer, leaving the country unsure of itself from roughly 1973 until the early years of the Reagan presidency. In addition to defeat in Vietnam, as well as Watergate and presidential resignation, the nation had to contend with upheaval in the Middle East, stagflation, the Soviet invasion of Afghanistan, the overthrow of the shah of Iran, the failed hostage-rescue effort in Iran soon thereafter, the terrible tragedy of the Lebanon intervention in 1983, and very tense periods in the U.S.-Soviet relationship to include the nuclear scares discussed above.

Fortunately, a sense of "morning in America" began to be felt by the mid-1980s. Key developments on the defense reform, reorganization, and rearmament front were by now underway; they would create a much stronger American military by decade's end. This transformation started with a major infusion of resources that began under Carter but had its greatest manifestation by far under Ronald Reagan. Whatever the wisdom of previous changes in defense strategy and policy—going from a 2½-war planning framework to 1½, shifting to an all-volunteer military, creating a "total force" with its synergistic blend of active-duty troops as well as guard and reserve personnel—there was still the matter of the quality of the American military. In the late 1970s, General Shy Meyer spoke of a "hollow force"; only four of the ten U.S. Army divisions needed to reinforce positions in Europe in the event of war were considered at strength and promptly deployable. Drug use was rampant, with as many as half of all sailors under age twenty believed to indulge on any given day, for example.[185] Attrition was high across the force; discipline was poor. The professionalism that we now routinely associate with the all-volunteer American armed forces was not yet rooted in the culture of the U.S. military. It was a vastly different time.

Reagan and Weinberger changed much of that radically. A great deal originated with reforms and ideas dating to the 1970s, but the Reagan administration funded them and implemented them.[186] The annual Department of Defense budget overall grew by a third in real terms in the first term; by the end of Reagan's eight-year presidency, overall levels of national defense spending, or "outlays," were up 50 percent relative to 1980.[187]

The positive results were widespread. Military pay shot upward far faster than the rate of inflation, and the Montgomery GI Bill improved educational benefits for those who had served.[188] Partly as a result, the quality of military recruits improved greatly; for example, in the mid-1970s, only 55 percent of recruits had at least a high school degree, whereas that figure had grown to 85 percent by the early 1980s.[189] Resources for training were dramatically increased—by roughly a third per soldier in the Army.[190] National training centers for the Army and other services came into their own. Not only did combat readiness improve as a result, but the rate of fatalities in training accidents went down by a third.[191]

Key modernization programs across all the services moved into advanced stages, benefiting from research and development programs in precision-strike weapons, cruise missiles, and stealth that had been championed by Secretary of Defense Harold Brown and Under Secretary of Defense for Research and Engineering William Perry during the Carter administration.[192] That set up the Reagan team for big procurement initiatives (to include the "big five" in the Army—the Abrams tank, Bradley fighting vehicle, Apache helicopter, Black Hawk helicopter, and Patriot missile, as well as the F-14, F-15, F-16, F-18, B-1, and B-2 aircraft, among many other systems across the services).[193] Army, Marine Corps, Air Force, and Navy munitions stockpiles went up by 20 percent, almost 50 percent, 50 percent, and 250 percent, respectively, by 1986 (though they were still considered too low relative to expected wartime usage).[194] Once all was said and done over the decade 1980–90, so-called mission-capable rates for key equipment had increased dramatically. Notably, overall Air Force aircraft rates improved from 66 to 85 percent, Navy and Marine Corps aircraft from 59 to 70 percent, Marine Corps ground equipment from roughly 85 to 90 percent, Army ground equipment from 88 percent to 91 percent, and Navy surface ship readiness from about 58 to 66 percent.[195]

The Reagan buildup was not so much an increase in the size or global posture or global activity of the American armed forces as it was an increase in their proper resourcing and therefore their per-unit combat readiness and strength. That said, there were certain areas of specific growth. The Army reserve components grew by almost 200,000 soldiers, or more than a third, even as the regular Army held basically steady in size.[196]

The Navy pursued a vision of more than 600 ships—to include fifteen large-deck aircraft carriers, four battleships, 137 battlegroup escorts (for example, destroyers), about 100 frigates, some 100 attack submarines, some seventy-five amphibious assault ships, thirty-nine mine-warfare vessels, sixty-nine replenishment ships and twenty-seven material support ships as well as thirty-three fleet support ships, and perhaps thirty-five ballistic-missile submarines. This was to support its well-branded Maritime Strategy.[197] This strategy went beyond what had become standard Cold War methodologies for sizing and shaping the U.S. Navy. Previously, the Navy had focused chiefly on protecting sea lanes to Europe and Japan as well as the Persian Gulf, on projecting power with aircraft carrier battle groups and amphibious ships, and on hunting down Soviet attack submarines as well as ballistic-missile submarines. The Maritime Strategy kept all of those priorities and then added some. It would have countenanced, among other things, attacks against far northern positions in the Soviet Union (notably, around the Kola Peninsula) in times of war. Critics worried that such attacks could blur the conventional-nuclear threshold or otherwise increase the risks of escalation in any conflict, but Secretary of the Navy John Lehman largely carried the day.[198]

The Navy did grow substantially, but not quite as much as hoped—by about 15 percent, from about 480 ships at decade's start to some 550 ships in 1990.[199] That did not reverse, by ship count, the earlier decline; the Navy had had about 850 ships in 1970.[200] But given the quality, and size, of the vessels procured in the Reagan years, the Navy had indeed become much stronger. Among the goals of the naval buildup: to be able to maintain the Navy's apparent operational requirement for sixty submarines watching the barriers between Greenland, Iceland, and the United Kingdom while also conducting intelligence missions and tracking Soviet submarines; maintaining up to four aircraft carrier battle groups on forward station at a time (since on average a naval vessel based in the United States is able to be on station only about 25 percent of the time, given the demands of crew rest and home leave, training and maintenance, as well as ocean transit); and being able to transport up to a full Marine Expeditionary Force (including a full division) at a time.[201]

It would be a mistake in looking back at this period to think that the 1980s quickly became a halcyon period of fulsome defense resources and general stability. It is worth remembering that, stunningly, there were more than twice as many tanks in the broad European theater toward the end of the Cold War than in 1944 at the height of World War II![202] And through Ronald Reagan's first term, it sometimes felt as if they, or even more deadly weapons, might wind up being used. Even once Mikhail Gorbachev came to power in the Soviet Union in 1985, things stayed tense for some time—and the United States continued to worry that its military position globally was fragile.[203] In 1987, the supreme Allied commander in Europe, General Bernard Rodgers, said of the unfavorable NATO–Warsaw Pact military balance that "every year . . . the gap continues to widen."[204] That was a debatable point; between 1980 and 1985, for example, NATO had added almost 4,000 tanks and 600 combat aircraft to its weapons holdings in Europe, whereas the respective Warsaw Pact totals were 400 and zero. But the Warsaw Pact retained a 2.5:1 edge in tanks and almost a 2:1 advantage in combat aircraft.[205] By that point, it also retained an estimated capacity to field 121 ground-combat divisions in a European war, once all of its forces were mobilized and deployed, by contrast with NATO's 72.

Yet it is also worth remembering the adage that there are lies, damn lies, and statistics. Other metrics told a different story. Even without accounting for weapons quality, each alliance had about forty divisions either in one of the Germanys or immediately contiguous to them. Moreover, U.S. divisions contained almost 60 percent more soldiers than did Soviet divisions, largely because of the superior logistics capacities of American units, suggesting that they should have been seen as substantially more capable on a unit-by-unit basis. And Western estimates of how fast the Soviet Union could mobilize and deploy reserves probably gave the Warsaw Pact more credit than it deserved, as was the norm historically.[206] Soviet-based divisions were generally small, undermanned, far from the battlefield, and reliant on rail lines of a different gauge from those in Eastern Europe.[207] A number of independent analyses that gave NATO credit for its technology, airpower, logistics capabilities, and defensive fortifications as well as other preparations came to much more nuanced and hopeful assessments of the state of the conventional military balance in Europe.[208] They also noted how a prepared and dense defense might succeed in countering an enemy attack even if outnumbered.[209]

Whatever the real situation, perceptions took time to shift. And geopolitics took time to improve, even after Gorbachev came to power. It was only in late 1987 that the INF Treaty was signed between Washington and Moscow, banning ballistic and cruise missiles with ranges between 500 and 5,500 kilometers (about 300 and 3,400 miles, respectively); it was only in 1988–89 that Soviet forces withdrew from Afghanistan. Even after that time, and even as *glasnost* (opening up) and *perestroika* (restructuring of the economy) took hold, many worried about possible reversals of the Soviet reforms.

Of course, Moscow could find plenty to worry about, too—its own defeat in Afghanistan; NATO's AirLand Battle doctrine backed up by new precision technologies that it would have to contend with in any European fight; America's many strong allies.[210] Moscow also understood its need for economic reforms.[211] Collectively, many things were working in the West's favor, even if it was taking time for that reality to sink in.

Moreover, the Reagan period's ample military resources and positive, patriotic spirit were not enough to achieve all that was required by way of defense reform. The military was still not well organized for joint operations or efficient command and control. Ironically, or perhaps predictably, the Reagan administration's top leaders were not the first to push the need for reform. They saw it undercutting the case for more resources as the Reagan defense budget buildup plateaued; they also may have felt that it disrespected the progress they had made with the military buildup to date. Caspar Weinberger hoped that a combination of dramatically increased resources and improved patriotic sentiment across the country, together with his Weinberger Doctrine, announced in November 1984, which sought to provide key constraints on future uses of force, would largely solve the problems the administration had inherited. Weinberger proposed that force be used only as a last resort and when the vital interests of the country were at stake—and then that it be used overwhelmingly and decisively, for a clear purpose, with good prospects of sustained public support.[212]

But by the time Reagan had been inaugurated for a second term, the pressures for change within parts of the military and with key members of the House and Senate had coalesced into what would prove a winning coalition for major change. That turned out to be a very good thing for the country in the end, but most of the Pentagon and the White House did not see it that way.

What followed was remarkable: the Goldwater-Nichols Defense Reorganization Act of 1986. Far from a sure thing at the outset, as noted, it was opposed by the long-standing secretary of defense Caspar Weinberger, the secretary of the navy John Lehman, and most of the joint chiefs of staff. Specifically, Chief of Staff of the Army General John Wickham, Chief of Naval Operations Admiral James D. Watkins, and Marine Corps Commandant General P. X. Kelley were adamantly opposed. (Air Force Chief of Staff General Charles Gabriel and Joint Chiefs Chairman Admiral William Crowe were less dogmatic but ambivalent themselves.)[213] Former chairman General David Jones and former Army chief Shy Meyer were strong supporters of reform, however.[214]

But it was the Senate and House that provided the main firepower—and that again showed how important, indeed essential, the legislative branch has been historically in American defense strategy and policy. Several key members of Congress, including the bill's namesake sponsors, Senator Barry Goldwater of Arizona and Congressman William Nichols of Alabama, as well as Senator Sam Nunn of Georgia, and dedicated congressional staff including Archie Barrett and Jim Locher, were the bill's most important proponents.[215]

The reform effort was motivated by a number of debacles that, despite the growing sense that America's all-volunteer armed forces were clearly getting better by the mid-1980s, still weighed heavily on policymakers' minds. The Reagan defense buildup, with its improved military pay, greater resources for training and maintenance, and big weapons modernization programs, could not fix everything that was wrong with the Department of Defense.

Two tragedies revealed huge problems with command and control. One was the failed Iran hostage rescue mission under President Carter in April 1980. It was a clear demonstration of what can happen absent multiservice jointness in training and command. It involved two separate tactical commanders for different phases of the operation, as well as Navy helicopters with Marine Corps pilots flying off aircraft carriers, plus big and separate roles for the Air Force and the Army.[216] Rehearsals were not done to scale; even simple things such as providing pilots with access to current meteorological conditions were not achieved.[217]

The second travesty was the bombing of U.S. Marine Corps barracks in Beirut, Lebanon, in October 1983 under President Reagan. American and other foreign troops had been deployed there as "peacekeepers" (there being, however, no real peace to keep), in the face of opposition by the Secretary of Defense. But their tactics, techniques, and procedures were atrocious. They were not even allowed to load their weapons with live ammunition.[218] Despite the deadly bombing of the U.S. embassy earlier that year in Beirut, few efforts were made to provide force protection at the barracks.

The list of problems was not confined to those two cases. Even the successful invasion of tiny Granada during that same month of October 1983 revealed American military weaknesses, such as the inability of members of different services to communicate with each other in real time. Indeed, a local phone booth became the backup plan for interservice coordination in one storied example of things gone amok.[219]

Goldwater-Nichols attempted to fix these problems. It strengthened the regional combatant commands so that they reported directly to the secretary of defense, without interference by the joint chiefs of staff. It also enhanced the role of the chairman of the joint chiefs, as well as his or her control over the joint staff, by clarifying that the chairman was the main military adviser to the president and National Security Council rather than a mouthpiece for the chiefs as a group. Goldwater-Nichols also created a framework for other reforms, including the creation of Special Operations Command and Transportation Command in 1987.[220]

CONCLUSION

By the end of the 1980s, and the end of the Cold War, a metamorphosis had occurred in U.S. defense strategy. This would soon be manifested in the presidency of George H. W. Bush, first in the Operation Just Cause overthrow of Manuel Noriega in Panama in late 1989, but especially in Operation Desert Storm, the war that evicted Iraqi leader Saddam Hussein's forces from Kuwait in early 1991. The American military had been transformed.[221] To be sure, Just Cause and Desert Storm were the types of wars that played to American strengths. To be sure, as good as the American armed forces were (and would remain, even as they downsized) by the end of the Cold War, they would still encounter major challenges in the years ahead. Black Hawk Down happened just two and a half years after Desert Storm; America's inability to end the war in Bosnia would persist into 1995. The Iran-Contra affair, by which the Reagan administration illegally sold weapons to Iran to generate cash for the Nicaraguan rebels, cast a pall over an otherwise strong Reagan administration security-policy legacy. It would be a mistake to push the positive hype too far.

But remarkable things had happened by the end of the Cold War in U.S. defense strategy—most of all, its role in backstopping a successful outcome to that Cold War that took place without the firing of superpower shots at each other. The greatest success of the American armed forces over this forty-plus-year period was not the battlefield victories it delivered but the World War III that it prevented.

CHAPTER VI

The Post–Cold War World

I wish Ken Adelman had been right.

When Phil Gordon and I wrote an op-ed in late 2001 warning that any invasion of Iraq would be difficult and protracted, my friend Ken Adelman decided to challenge us. Close to Secretary of Defense Donald Rumsfeld and a member of the Defense Policy Board, Ken—a bright and affable figure who had run the Arms Control and Disarmament Agency under President Reagan—was probably reflecting much of the Pentagon's own thinking at the time. What resulted was the well-known "cakewalk" op-ed, also in the Washington Post *in January 2002, in which Ken disagreed (amicably, but firmly) with Phil and me, predicting that any invasion of Iraq would go fast. If Desert Storm had turned out to be a romp a decade before, Ken reasoned, any war, even an invasion, would be easier now—after a decade of tough sanctions on Iraq and further high-tech modernization of the American armed forces. It would be a cakewalk.*

If only Ken had been right. I hoped he would be.

In fact, to be fair, he appeared to be right at first. The initial invasion, with a much smaller force than the Department of Defense would have preferred under previous leadership, and less than half the personnel used in Operation Desert Storm, did very well. No long preparatory bombardment was employed this time. Iraqi forces often fought from urban positions, yet they did no better than Saddam's exposed units had performed in the Kuwaiti and southern Iraqi desert in 1991. Within twenty-five days, Operation Thunder Run had seized Baghdad, Saddam had fled, and the Iraqi military had been routed. In fact, it crumbled away. U.S. and coalition forces solidified control of the capital and much of the country. Adelman again took to the pages of the Washington Post, *allowing himself a bit of a victory lap as he boasted of his prescience and, more important, of the outstanding performance of the U.S. military under Rumsfeld's leadership. Proponents of a high-tech, precision-strike revolution in military affairs also seemed vindicated. America's unipolar moment seemed real.*

But then all hell broke loose. Iraq started down a slippery slope toward first resistance, then insurgency, then terrorism, then sectarian-based civil war. The result almost a decade later, once U.S. troops were finally (if only temporarily) gone from the country, was 4,500 American dead, at least 200,000 Iraqi dead, and a country increasingly under the sway of Iran—with something called ISIS looming on the horizon. Another decade later and ISIS would be (mostly) gone, but Iran and its minions would not be, casualty tolls would be even higher, and Iraq's path toward becoming a more functional and prosperous state would remain a slow and zigzag one at best.

Iraq is today a better place than it was with Saddam and his sons and his fellow Baathist elite. But the price of the war was far too high—and the damage to that region of the world and its people as well as America's reputation far too great—to consider the U.S. policy itself a success.

More than anything, Iraq should be a warning to us today. We Americans often seek to do mighty and good things in this world but often fail, whether because we do not understand how others see us (as much more assertive and self-promoting than we like to believe about ourselves) or because we perform difficult strategic tasks less well than we should. Iraq also teaches much about modern warfare. Many things have changed. Today's technologies are incredible; America's cutting-edge innovators and outstanding defense industry give the nation tremendous advantages vis-à-vis potential adversaries. At the same time, many types of combat remain extremely difficult, not so different than warfare of the past. Modern sensors can only find targets when those targets have distinct signatures; precision-strike weapons can only hit targets that we can identify; innovative opponents can intersperse themselves in cities and civilian populations, hide underground or within buildings where they are hard to spot, and find clever ways to use even relatively simple technology against us.

The U.S. experience in Iraq is sobering and humbling at many levels—just as Afghanistan proved to be as well. The paradox of American power is that, since 1945, the nation has developed and implemented the most successful grand strategy in the history of civilization (at least since that of the Roman Empire, anyway, and more global than Rome's)—even as it has continued to struggle on the battlefield. U.S. defense strategy has been successful at keeping the great power peace through deterrence; it has on balance been less successful in combat. And like most peoples and leaders through history, Americans have made their fair share of mistakes in assuming that war would prove easier and more controllable than often proved to be the case.

When the Berlin Wall fell on November 9, 1989, and the Soviet Union dissolved at the end of 1991, the United States did not discard its grand strategy altogether. Containment of communism was no longer a driving imperative. But trying to preserve, and expand, a community of like-minded nations committed to democracy, human rights, open economic interaction, and the peaceful resolution of disputes remained central priorities. The key elements of defense strategy designed to serve this grand strategy remained largely the same as well—multiple alliances with key industrial and military powers in Eurasia, together with forward-positioned and highly active American military forces designed to undergird those alliances.[1] To be sure, the size and cost of American military forces declined, as did the size and scale of their overseas presence, particularly in western Europe. But the basic idea of maintaining highly combat-capable and globally engaged American military power did not. The general notion of maintaining some form of a two-war capability remained central to force planning and deterrence strategy as well, but now the focus would shift to so-called rogue states such as Iraq and North Korea (and, as it would turn out, Afghanistan). American grand strategists kept an eye on developments in Russia and China throughout, but without great urgency or priority.

Much of this approach seems sound in its core logic. Yet America waged major wars in Iraq and Afghanistan over this period with very mediocre overall results. This happened at a time when its strategic position, by the standards of great powers in history, was excellent. Did it really need to work so hard, fight so long, and expend so much in the way of blood and treasure to sustain the general contours of this world order? Why were its wars in Iraq and Afghanistan, using the world's best military against technologically unsophisticated enemies, so difficult? Yes, they contained elements of military and strategic brilliance—as with Operation Desert Storm in 1991, the overthrows of the Taliban and Saddam Hussein in 2001 and 2003, the counterterrorism campaigns against al Qaeda in Iraq and Pakistan, and the surge in Iraq. But overall outcomes were mixed at best in Iraq, and poor in Afghanistan. Why was the United States not militarily ready for the kinds of counterinsurgency operations that proved necessary in Iraq and Afghanistan, even after having learned many lessons from Vietnam only a generation before?

There is another key question: Has the United States been too messianic at times, provoking counterreactions from other great powers in ways that were foreseeable and avoidable? Most notably, has the general approach to NATO expansion, especially with the decision to promise membership to Ukraine and Georgia back in 2008 yet with no timetable for honoring that promise and no interim security guarantee, been mistaken?[2] One need not blame the United States and the West for the Ukraine war—and I most emphatically do not, at any moral level—to question the strategic wisdom of taking such a path. Russia's reaction to this and other developments, while not justifiable, was nonetheless largely predictable (and predicted).

As in earlier chapters, this chapter begins with an overview of grand strategy: the big idea about how America sought to protect itself and promote its power over the period in question. The remainder of the chapter then traces, in rough chronological order, the evolution of defense strategy over this period—that is, the combination of national security budgets, military forces, overseas deployments, alliance relationships, war-fighting strategies, and military modernization concepts. That defense strategy went through two main phases between 1989 and roughly 2015. The first phase included the dozen years "between the wars," in Jim Goldgeier and Derek Chollet's phrase—or what some others called the age of chaos, though at this juncture a quarter of the way into the twenty-first century, that age of chaos appears a bit more like a halcyon period of calm.[3] The second phase was dominated by the "war on terror" and, in military terms, by U.S. and allied operations in Iraq and Afghanistan. In analyzing the histories of those latter wars, I tell the story here through the present time for the sake of simplicity and flow, even though the rest of the chapter ends chronologically with the year 2014.

BEYOND CONTAINMENT

If Cold War American grand strategy was a combination of containment of the communist threat combined with protection and promotion of a liberal, democratic, peaceful, market-based global order, then the second half of that framework remains relevant to this day. It remains more or less intact as of early 2025, despite the different foreign policy priorities under President Donald Trump, even if at considerable risk. But just as containment, as a general concept, could never tell us just how much effort to put into the defense of each country that Moscow and later Beijing might set their sights on, or explain which tools of American foreign policy should be applied at any given time and place, so the protection and promotion framework still leaves many questions unanswered. Which interests are worth defending with the lives of American troops? Which if any alliances, and other close security partnerships, should be expanded or created from whole cloth in service of the more ambitious part of this grand strategy—the "promotion" plank?

It is worth unpacking all the adjectives in the framing of "liberal, democratic, peaceful, market-based global order." The term *liberal* in particular is confusing to some. It does not of course mean the same thing as in American domestic politics today. Ronald Reagan was a conservative at home but a liberal abroad because he wanted to promote the values that are central to the American Bill of Rights—individual freedoms, the notion of inalienable rights, checks on government power that go beyond the simple idea of majority rule. It is this kind of world order that the United States, always more evangelical than it tends to realize, has typically pursued. The United States, a dangerous nation in Robert Kagan's apt phrase, has in fact often gone abroad in search of dragons (and dictators) to slay. Sometimes it has done so out of naked national interest; more often, it has done so out of conviction that it was doing the right thing for Americans as well as humankind in general. Democracy promotion has in modern times been seen as a way of reinforcing a peaceful global order, given the empirical reality that solid democracies do not tend to fight each other. But America's frequent interest in promoting democracy as well as individual human rights as core elements of foreign policy predated that finding of modern political science by scholars such as Michael Doyle and drew its original motivation more from ethics and from political philosophy.[4]

During the George H. W. Bush administration, several important policy decisions were made at the level of broad national security strategy. When the Berlin Wall fell, Bush and his top team of impressive strategists—Brent Scowcroft as national security adviser, James Baker as secretary of state, Dick Cheney as secretary of defense, Colin Powell as (newly minted) chairman of the joint chiefs of staff, and other notables—figured out their priorities quickly. First, they sought the dissolution of the Warsaw Pact and the removal of the Iron Curtain from Europe. Next, they realized it would be important to achieve the peaceful reunification of Germany and its inclusion within NATO and reached out extensively to Soviet premier Mikhail Gorbachev to make such an outcome tolerable to him as well as the rest of the Russian security community. Baker privately assured Gorbachev that NATO would not expand eastward from the borders of Germany, showing more realpolitik and restraint than would subsequent presidents.[5]

Third, when Saddam invaded Kuwait in August 1990, Bush determined within days that such blatant interstate aggression could not be tolerated in the post–Cold War world. Even if Kuwait was neither an ally nor a democracy, aggression against such a peaceful (and oil-producing) state contiguous to Saudi Arabia was not consistent with Bush's vision of a "new world order." Fourth, however, Bush also decided *not* to intervene in civil wars in the Balkans, despite their geographic proximity to key European allies of the United States, on the grounds, as Baker put it, that "we don't have a dog in that fight."[6] That was a blunt, Texas-style way of saying that primarily humanitarian concerns should not drive high-end decisions on the use of military force.

Fifth, when the Soviet Union dissolved in 1991, the United States sought to calm the situation and not exploit Russia's vulnerability for its own designs. Sixth, while far from happy with the Tiananmen Square crackdown in Beijing, Bush again chose to maintain a pragmatic posture toward China, sustaining the relationship with only relatively mild rebuke. Yet he did agree to a huge arms sale to Taiwan in 1992 that complicated efforts to stay on good terms with the PRC.[7]

The most consequential change going from George H. W. Bush to Bill Clinton at the level of grand strategy was probably the adoption of a policy of "engagement and enlargement" for NATO's eastward growth. Senate Majority Leader Bob Dole's quip that the slogan sounded like what was happening to his prostate notwithstanding, the Clinton national security strategy was significant. It underscored the promotion of democracy and the enlargement of a European "zone of peace," in Princeton professor Richard Ullman's elegant phrase.[8] When Poland, the Czech Republic, Slovakia, and Hungary joined the NATO alliance in 1999 (after being promised membership in 1996, during Clinton's reelection campaign), a process was set in motion that would yield great benefits for much of Europe yet also raise the risks of deteriorating relations with Moscow.[9]

Clinton also supported humanitarian military intervention more than Bush had. But he struggled in the implementation of that priority, especially during his first two years in office. First was the Black Hawk Down tragedy in Somalia in 1993. Bush had begun the operation as humanitarian relief when a lame duck; on Clinton's watch, as the security environment in Somalia deteriorated, the operation became more complex and suffered "mission creep." Black Hawk Down was followed by the nonintervention the next year in Rwanda's genocide, a failure to act for which Clinton would later express deep regret.[10]

As time went on, Clinton did better—helping bring peace to Bosnia in 1995 and helping NATO to win ugly, as Ivo Daalder and I put it, in Kosovo in 1999.[11] This period had become, in Charles Krauthammer's phrase, the "unipolar moment." In Madeleine Albright's framing, the United States had again shown itself to be the "indispensable nation" in world affairs.[12]

Many Americans, however, wondered why Europe could not handle more of its own problems and complained about burden sharing—foreshadowing what Donald Trump would do, with a more raw and caustic approach, a couple decades later. It is worth noting, however, that at the end of the 1990s, NATO's European nations were actually spending 77 percent as much of their GDP on defense as was the United States (2.3 percent versus 3 percent). In relative terms, that was a marked improvement from the situation in the mid-1980s, when NATO's European members spent about 3.5 percent of GDP on defense and the United States about 6 percent.[13] Like the first Bush, Clinton continued to try to handle Saddam Hussein with a version of containment strategy; he later developed a "dual containment" approach that applied as well to Iran. Clinton was somewhat tougher on China than Bush had been when he responded to China's intimidation tactics against Taipei by sending U.S. carriers into the Taiwan Strait in 1995 and sending two near the strait in 1996.[14] But like Bush he tried to maintain a positive and workable relationship with Beijing as he pushed for China's World Trade Organization membership. Meanwhile, with its gradual development of nuclear weapons, North Korea was becoming a more serious problem for American grand strategy and defense strategy again.

In the late 1990s, a global debate crystallized over whether the international community had a "responsibility to protect"—often known by the acronym R2P—when extreme civil conflict or genocide threatened innocents.[15] The terrible experiences of intervention in Lebanon in the early 1980s and Somalia in the early 1990s were by this point at least partly counterbalanced, in the policy debate, by the tragedy of the nonintervention in Rwanda in 1994 and the somewhat successful Balkans interventions of the mid- to late 1990s. Thus the policy atmosphere was open to new initiatives. Like the NATO expansion debate, this did not lead to any major change in U.S. defense posture or strategy per se; the details of military planning were not significantly affected. But the idea gained considerable prominence—that is, up until the moment when the 9/11 attacks changed the global strategic conversation dramatically, and then when the U.S.-led invasion of Iraq, ostensibly done in part for humanitarian motives, changed the optics about what the responsibility to protect really meant. The idea lost much of its earlier luster, since many viewed the concept in more cynical terms—as a rallying cry for misguided interventions as much as a genuine call to protect innocents.[16]

Grand strategy took a major turn under President George W. Bush after the 9/11 attacks. That day shook America to the core. Many of the problems of the 1990s, such as civil war in the Balkans and Central and West Africa, now seemed minor, at least in broad national security terms. More attacks, perhaps even of an even more catastrophic variety, seemed entirely plausible. While airplanes remained an obvious worry, as did truck bombs against tunnels or skyscrapers or chemical plants, other scenarios took hold of the popular imagination as well. The anthrax scares in the fall of 2001 on Capitol Hill and at major media centers seemed to portend a world of much greater biological weapons risks. Reports of al Qaeda's interest in obtaining a nuclear weapon led to Vice President Dick Cheney's purported One Percent doctrine, whereby if there was even a 1 percent chance of al Qaeda having the bomb, the United States needed to take the threat completely seriously and act as if the danger were 100 percent likely.[17] Otherwise, Lower Manhattan or another urban center could be lost in an instant, with casualties perhaps 100 times greater than on 9/11 itself. However illogical it may seem at one level, this concept gives a window into the thinking of Vice President Cheney and perhaps others in the administration. Grand strategy shifted toward protecting the homeland, going after threats abroad, and establishing a greater respect for American power to deter would-be attackers of all stripes. Thus followed not only the broader war on terror, as it was called, but the invasions of Afghanistan and Iraq, both discussed in more detail below.[18]

Any lingering hopes of an "end to history," as Francis Fukuyama had put it, or of a new world order and age of peace, were dashed.[19] U.S. national security policy became both more defensive, in terms of protecting the territory of the United States and its allies with much greater vigor than had been thought necessary in the recent past, and more offensive, as the nation sought to root out possible future threats and dissuade potential future adversaries from believing that the United States was somehow a paper tiger. The Bush administration's National Security Strategy of 2002 hit on many evergreen themes such as the importance of alliances and international engagement—but forebodingly also warned of the potential need for the United States to preempt possible future threats before they could cause the kind of death and destruction experienced on 9/11, or even worse. That strategy thus foreshadowed, and sought to justify, the U.S.-led invasion of Iraq the following year.[20]

Preemption had of course always been an option for American policy makers, and it had a basis in international law under the principle of anticipatory self-defense. But as applied to Iraq, the U.S. attack in March 2003 was more akin to preventive war than preemption, since no imminent Iraqi attack against the United States had been specified at the time of the invasion. As such, with the National Security Strategy of 2002 and its application to Saddam Hussein, the United States made clear that it placed higher priority on national security than international law. It would arrogate to itself the right to determine when national security considerations overrode the desirability of gaining international consensus and approval for military action. (Indeed, the United States had already demonstrated its willingness to make such decisions without formal international legal backing on numerous previous occasions, most recently in the Kosovo War in 1999, but at least in the case of Kosovo it had formal NATO blessing and participation.) Many saw hubris in Bush's grand strategy, but it was probably motivated by fear as much as arrogance. The United States had determined, in the aftermath of an attack on its homeland that killed almost 3,000 people by a group that aspired to even more deadly aggression, that it needed to find and destroy monsters abroad (disagreeing with John Adams's admonition two centuries before) rather than let those monsters strike the American homeland or other core interests yet again.[21]

George W. Bush ultimately sought to wrap much of his realpolitik grand strategy in a more noble and visionary garment. His Freedom Agenda, most prominent in his second term with Secretary of State Condoleezza Rice as America's top diplomat, prioritized the protection and extension of Western-style democracy and respect for human rights. Hence the fateful NATO Bucharest Summit of April 2008, where both Georgia and Ukraine were promised eventual alliance membership (though, again, with no date certain and no interim security guarantee). That half-pregnant policy outcome was the result of compromise within the alliance, Bush having to concede his goal of early membership in the face of German and French skepticism.[22]

Under President Barack Obama, some things about U.S. grand strategy changed again, but many did not. Obama certainly sought to position the United States in a more multilateral posture in its international security dealings and also sought to wind down the wars in Iraq and Afghanistan—though in Afghanistan, only after dramatically ramping up the scale of the U.S. effort roughly threefold. He also sought to repair damaged relations with the Islamic world. His Cairo speech of June 2009 reflected the same desire for a fresh start in U.S. grand strategy, and radical break with the past, that his speech two months earlier on nuclear weapons had attempted. As his presidency unfolded, he also sought to shift geostrategic emphasis more toward the Asia-Pacific region in what was called a "pivot" or "rebalance."[23]

Obama did carry out big reductions in the overall U.S. military presence in the broader Central Command area, stretching from Egypt to Afghanistan. But he struggled to move assets or priorities to the broader Pacific region and failed to complement his modest military shifts toward that theater with a commensurate economic reprioritization. In addition, by the end of his presidency, the resurgence of extremism in the Middle East, this time in the form of ISIS, the general failure of the Arab Spring, and growing assertiveness by both Russia and China, suggested that America's overall geostrategic burden would not decline in Europe, East Asia, or the Middle East. There were severe limitations to what even Barack Obama's amazing biography, intellect, and rhetorical skills could do to heal the deep wounds on the international political and security landscape. It was proving difficult to rebalance away from anywhere—be it the Middle East or Europe—to free up more assets for East Asia. And it was also proving difficult to aspire to a more peaceful world, where counterterrorism efforts could again be relegated more or less to police activities and where great power relations would stabilize in a context of mutual respect and restraint. Meanwhile, on most of the underlying pillars of American security strategy, notably alliances and forward-positioned U.S. military assets, Obama was cautious and careful, not changing very much.[24]

Through the period of the war on terror and through the mid-2010s, the United States often was able to apply sanctions against North Korea and Iran with the support of Moscow and Beijing. In the case of Iran, the sanctions helped produce the Joint Comprehensive Plan of Action of 2015, however controversial it has subsequently been. Strong U.N. sanctions were also placed on North Korea even as late as 2017 after North Korean nuclear and ICBM tests that year. Alas, these days of great power strategic cooperation on at least some issues would not last.

With this sketch of overall grand strategy in mind, let us now turn to a review of the key defense strategies of the quarter century after the fall of the Berlin Wall.

MILITARY STRATEGY IN OPERATION DESERT STORM

Rarely in American military history has a conflict been so tailor-made for the American armed forces of the day. When Saddam Hussein, angry with rich Arab neighbors for their unwillingness to help him recover financially from the recent long and bloody Iran-Iraq War, seized Kuwait on August 2, 1990, he surprised U.S. strategists and planners. But the American armed forces were ready.

They had been preparing for a decade for almost exactly the same kind of military challenge that Saddam presented. NATO had been adopting AirLand Battle doctrine, and the associated Follow-on Forces Attack concept, along with relevant weaponry and sensors. Central Command had been developing infrastructure for a decade with Arab partners, most notably Saudi Arabia.[25] Transportation Command had been expanding airlift and sealift capacity. The timing was exquisite, like an Olympic athlete preparing for four years for the big games along a carefully developed schedule—except that, in this case, the U.S. armed forces did not taper off like an Olympian just before the big race. They trained intensively in the months leading up to the invasion, including once deployed in Saudi Arabia and nearby locales. Compared with Soviet and Warsaw Pact forces, Saddam just presented a smaller, less competent version of that same kind of military, wielding similar weaponry and preferring similar tactics. Yes, the geography was different from that in Europe. But trading the cloudy skies, uneven terrain, and densely populated regions of central Europe for the relatively clear skies, flat terrain, high temperatures, and occasional sandstorms of the Middle East proved a good bargain for American and allied planners—especially since they could choose to have the war during the winter.

Parts of the U.S. military had also had a good warm-up for Desert Storm about a year before. American forces carried out an impressive operation to overthrow the illegitimate government of Manuel Noriega in Panama in late 1989. The United States benefited from a standing head start; it already had combat forces stationed permanently in Panama at the time of the invasion. But the ability to handle urban combat effectively and track down an individual hiding within a significant city while limiting the scale and duration of the violence was nonetheless impressive. It validated several core elements of American military preparation and strategy that had improved over the 1980s, to include well-trained special forces, the regional command structures of the Department of Defense, investments in transport and logistics, and improvements in precision-strike weaponry.

Thus, the United States was ready for Saddam—perhaps even more than it thought it was. American and allied military strategy intended to devastate Iraqi forces in and near Kuwait so they would have to evacuate the country and so that Saddam would have to accept terms of surrender that would prevent him from mounting similar future attacks. The U.S.-led coalition included a dozen countries together wielding 1,800 combat aircraft, 1,000 additional support aircraft (for refueling, transport, electronic warfare, command and control, and reconnaissance), and around 200 naval vessels (127 of them American, of which six were aircraft carriers) in the Persian Gulf and Red Sea. All in all, the coalition fielded some 660,000 personnel.[26]

The war began on January 17, 1991, local time, and continued for 40 days and nights, with coalition aircraft pounding military and civilian infrastructure most relevant to deploying and sustaining Iraqi forces in the field. Target sets included air defense radars, missile batteries, runways, aircraft, command and control sites, major logistics depots, marshaling yards, bridges and other transportation chokepoints, and suspected weapons of mass destruction sites (even though many of these were not known at the time and were ultimately uncovered only by investigators and inspectors).[27] The attacks were carried out by cruise missiles, stealth jets, nonstealth jets, attack helicopters, and other aircraft. Drones were already available in this war but were used for limited purposes such as drawing the attention of Iraqi air defenses, which when activated could be identified and attacked by high-speed antiradiation missiles among other ordnance. Television viewers watched laser-guided bombs land within feet of their intended targets.[28] The "CNN effect" captivated audiences. It meant that many would be highly impressed with the capabilities of American and allied armed forces. But it also would mean that public opinion would be shocked by vivid scenes of violence, ultimately increasing the pressure on President Bush to end the war perhaps earlier than he should have.[29]

Iraq fired Scud missiles at Saudi oil facilities and at Israel. Its goals were to increase the economic pain associated with the war to the point where the international coalition might crack, in the first instance, or to provoke an Israeli counterattack that would turn Arab opinion against Israel and its American friend, in the second.[30] Either way, Saddam hoped to force a premature end to the conflict by indirect means. The first Scud attacks against Israel were conducted on January 18, 1991, and they continued throughout the war. In the end, forty missiles would be fired at Israel and forty-six against Saudi and Gulf targets. Coalition forces had great trouble finding Scud launchers in western Iraq, despite devoting dozens of daily aircraft sorties in the "great Scud hunt" in the war's opening ten days. The coalition continued these operations throughout the war, but at a somewhat reduced pace thereafter; they also employed special forces in the effort. Alas, it was to little avail. Iraqi "shoot and scoot" tactics, with missiles launched from unpredictable locations, as well as an effective use of decoys, hampered the anti-Scud efforts. After the war, U.S. intelligence could not confirm any kills against the mobile missile launchers or their communications networks. Fortunately, the coalition efforts did complicate and slow the pace of the Scud attacks.[31]

Saddam's gambit of trying to draw Israel into the war almost worked. But American diplomacy, the deployment of Patriot missile defense systems to Israel (however imperfectly they functioned), promises from Joint Chiefs Chairman Colin Powell and others that the United States would devote more assets to searching for Scud launchers, and the generally low level of casualties from exploding or impacting weapons persuaded Jerusalem to stay out of the conflict.[32] Sadly, on February 25, a lucky Scud shot—almost surely aimed elsewhere—hit a U.S. troop barracks in Saudi Arabia, killing twenty-eight Americans. That was the largest U.S. loss of life from any single event during the conflict.[33]

Saddam's forces in and near Kuwait were still hunkered down through all of this. Therefore, in the second part of the air war, mostly during the month of February, coalition aircraft shifted their emphasis to attacks against the deployed Iraqi army. They continued to conduct roughly eight hundred or more strike sorties a day.[34] It was during this part of the war that the practice of "tank plinking" saw its heyday. In tactics developed during the war, infrared sensors on combat aircraft were used to locate and target Iraqi vehicles hidden against the desert floor. Because the vehicles retained the day's heat (and the night's cool) longer than the desert sand, this tactic was often particularly effective in the evening (or morning) hours.[35]

Originally, U.S. intelligence thought that Iraq had more than half a million military personnel in and near Kuwait. It turned out, however, that it probably had closer to 350,000 troops in the broader Kuwait theater at the start of hostilities. Most of Iraq's fifty or so divisions there were badly understrength, throwing off the estimates of intelligence analysts; Iraqi desertions further reduced the numbers.[36] After forty days of pounding from the air, there may have been 200,000 to 220,000 Iraqi troops in the Kuwaiti theater when the ground war began.

Over the course of the conflict, almost fifteen thousand precision-guided air-to-ground munitions were employed by the coalition. About half were dropped on Iraqi forces in the Kuwaiti theater. The precision ordnance included laser-guided bombs and Maverick air-to-surface missiles guided by either infrared or electro-optical systems. Even though such precision weapons became the signature ordnance of the war, they constituted less than 10 percent of munitions consumed in the conflict.[37] Coalition aircraft wound up flying about 120,000 sorties.[38] They operated out of some twenty-three bases in the region, with eleven in Saudi Arabia. As noted, a half dozen U.S. aircraft carriers were employed as well.[39]

Not everything was perfect, of course. There were some shortages and bottlenecks in certain capabilities—electronic-warfare and jamming aircraft, night-vision capabilities and infrared targeting pods for attack aircraft, global positioning system receivers for aircraft and vehicles (GPS being a relatively new technology then).[40] But the capabilities of the U.S.-led coalition, combined with the high combat readiness of American military equipment coming out of the Reagan buildup—with so-called mission-capable rates for major equipment often in the range of 85 to 90 percent or even more—were more than enough to do the Iraqis in, quickly and decisively.[41]

Coalition analysts could not agree on how much Iraqi equipment was destroyed by the air war. The CIA thought losses to be around 1,000 major pieces of equipment; Central Command's estimates were several times as high. Whatever the losses, they came out of an estimated total of 10,000 to 11,000 such weapons in theater at the start of the war (tanks, armored personnel carriers, and large-bore artillery).[42] The original coalition goal of destroying 50 percent of Iraqi equipment throughout the theater before ground operations began was ultimately recognized to be unnecessary, given the disarray in Iraqi military cohesion after weeks of bombing, together with the dominance of the airspace and information space enjoyed by the coalition.[43]

Then the 100-hour ground war was launched on February 24. There was no semblance of World War I trench warfare. Most American and British forces, profiting from their dominance of the air and space that left Iraqi forces largely blind at the theater level, went around the Iraqi positions along the Kuwait border in a "great left hook." By contrast, U.S. Marines, rather than simply fixing Iraqi forces as had been expected, went straight through the Iraqi positions en route to Kuwait City. They carried out combined-arms warfare with alacrity, employing heavy preparatory fires with artillery and aircraft, then armored bulldozers and explosive line charges to penetrate fortifications, and then exploitation of initial holes created in Iraqi lines.[44] Kuwait City was quickly liberated, with the help of Arab members of the coalition.[45]

Notably, what was *not* attempted was an amphibious assault on Kuwait City. This decision reflected the realities of modern warfare. Planners decided that Americans' mine-hunting capacity in shallow waters, including its dolphin force (made up of the actual mammals), was inadequate for the task. Amphibious ships simply carried out a feint instead.[46]

Saddam had kept eight Iraqi Republican Guard divisions north of Kuwait in Iraqi territory as a strategic reserve. But they had to face, among other things, the JSTARS—joint surveillance and targeting radar system aircraft—capable of spotting moving metal objects at any time of day in any weather.[47] JSTARS had helped thwart an earlier attack by Iraqi forces into the Saudi town of Al Khafji between January 29 and January 31.[48] Still, during the ground war, Saddam managed to move some units into positions in the western and southern parts of the theater where they could at least slow the movement of coalition forces, allowing other Iraqi units to escape northward toward Basra.[49]

On balance, Iraqi forces fought poorly in the war. Given their earlier performance against Iran the previous decade, this should have come as no surprise.[50] The mistakes were myriad. They failed to post advance guards ahead of their dug-in positions and failed to remove dirt from the vicinity of those positions, giving themselves away.[51] Iraqi forces were generally poor at maneuver options or at tactical improvisation. Saddam had cashiered his competent generals after the war with Iran to ensure political control of the military, and that came back to haunt him.[52]

Thus, the American-led victory over Iraq was far more lopsided than Israeli victories in previous wars against Syria, Jordan, and Egypt. In those wars, Israel generally achieved "exchange ratios" of 3:1 or 4:1 in its favor, in terms of casualties on each side; in Desert Storm, exchange ratios favored the coalition by more than 10:1.[53] To give another revealing metric, the Abrams tank main gun needed only about 1.2 rounds for each enemy tank it would destroy in the war.[54]

The coalition's overwhelming success proved a mixed blessing in some ways. Televised images of Iraqi casualties, such as American strikes against an Iraqi military convoy on the so-called highway of death, persuaded President Bush to agree to a ceasefire within 100 hours of the start of the ground war.[55] The terms of the ceasefire were controversial. Saddam was required to allow the verifiable disarmament of his weapons of mass destruction capabilities. But he had managed to retain much more of his Republican Guard than the original U.S. war plan intended, and those forces were not dissolved under the terms of the armistice. Up to a third of their armor in theater survived.[56] Saddam was allowed to keep and use his helicopters as he wished—including against internal opponents.[57]

Inspectors did soon arrive in Iraq. Ultimately, they would discover three separate nuclear weapons-related programs that had previously been unknown to the international community and therefore largely untargeted during the war. This revelation of the limitations of stand-off intelligence would prove to be one of the contributing factors, twelve years later, to the decision by the George W. Bush administration to overthrow Saddam Hussein's regime. And after a decade of occasional strikes at weapons sites (and radar sites) when they found targets worth hitting, the 1990s also revealed the associated limitations of airpower for dealing with a menace like Saddam.

During the ground war, around 80,000 Iraqi prisoners were taken.[58] Over the whole conflict, total Iraqi fatalities probably numbered in the low tens of thousands.[59] U.S. total losses were under 400; direct losses from hostile action were just under 150.[60] The quick conflict would prove much less lethal for all sides than would the U.S.-led invasion of Iraq and subsequent occupation a dozen years later. The defense strategy for Desert Storm—applying mass, precision, innovation, surprise, and maneuver by a well-trained force with strong centralized command and control for limited territorial objectives secured by a negotiated, conditional surrender of the enemy—proved to be an overdetermined success.

DEFENSE STRATEGY AND PLANNING IN THE 1990S

With the Berlin Wall down, Operation Desert Storm in the books, and the Soviet Union itself soon dissolving, the United States of the early 1990s was dealing with a cascade of good news. But it was good news that left defense planning unmoored. How should America's armed forces be sized, structured, postured around the world, modernized, and budgeted in an era without a Soviet threat—and now with even the Middle East in a seemingly somewhat more stable place?

Not everyone was immediately on board with the idea of refashioning and downsizing the American armed forces after 1989. Secretary Cheney, in the early months after the fall of the Berlin Wall, when asked when the peace dividend would show up in the defense budget, challenged the premise of the question and retorted that "the peace dividend is peace." In early 1990, with the Berlin Wall now just a heap of bricks, he submitted a budget for fiscal year 1991 calling for only about a 10 percent cut in defense spending—not yet quite convinced that Soviet reforms were durable, not quite ready to downsize a military that had just finished its Reagan-era buildup (again, a buildup more in weaponry and readiness, less so in force size).[61]

Of course, Saddam's invasion of Kuwait on August 2, 1990, ended these defense downsizing debates for a while. For the next half year, America was on pins and needles, fundamentally unsure of how hard the fight in the desert would be or how long and sanguinary it would prove. Nothing about its eventual overwhelming success was obvious at the time. Yet of course the forty-day war proved to be a huge U.S. victory. Operation Desert Storm was the culmination of a successful period of military recovery and buildup that began slowly under President Carter but really had its heyday and great success under President

Reagan. Secretary of Defense Dick Cheney, widely respected for his role in overseeing the victory, remarked that he called President Reagan to thank him for the fine fighting forces that Cheney as secretary had inherited from the previous administration.[62] The U.S. wartime performance had a few blemishes—the mediocre performance of early versions of the Patriot against Iraqi Scud missiles, inadequate communications to prevent friendly-fire incidents from accidentally killing American forces—but the dominance and excellence of American armed forces were clear for all to see.[63]

But in another sense, the American armed forces were now all dressed up with nowhere to go. Their size had contributed to the overwhelming U.S.-led victory against Saddam. Yet it hardly seemed appropriate in deficit-conscious America to retain a military of Cold War proportions to deal with Iraq-like threats in the future. Such challenges were not of a scale or apparent prevalence to warrant the expenditures. Chairman of the Joint Chiefs General Colin Powell said almost wistfully that he was running out of demons, with only Fidel Castro in Cuba and Kim Il-Sung in North Korea remaining as plausible American adversaries (at that moment, Saddam seemed to have been safely declawed, and Iran was still recovering from the debilitating Iran-Iraq War of the previous decade).[64] Hence a great debate began about downsizing the armed forces and realizing a peace dividend, measured not just in peace, as Cheney would have preferred, but in dollars as well.

Soon the American military would be about one-third smaller and one-third less expensive than had recently been the case. It would have a much smaller footprint in Europe, but still a substantial presence there; postures in the broader Middle East as well as East Asia would not change dramatically from before. Readiness would be largely sustained, even if it sometimes frayed in the years ahead; modernization strategies would be slowed quite a bit, with acquisition accounts providing a large chunk of the peace dividend as America took a bit of a "procurement holiday" (and expected the defense industry to figure out itself how to survive that holiday).[65]

Perhaps five central organizing principles gained wide acceptance in the American defense strategy debate of the 1990s. First, the United States would try to reduce the role of nuclear weapons in its overall defense strategy, largely through bilateral arms control with Russia and through unilateral reductions in its deployed tactical nuclear forces, while still being sure that it had a formidable, redundant, reliable arsenal. The notion of a triad of nuclear delivery systems—land-based missiles, submarine-based missiles, and bombers—continued to enjoy wide support. Major weapons laboratories at Los Alamos, Livermore, and

Sandia were retained as nuclear-weapons design and support laboratories, even as their other functions expanded. U.S. nuclear testing was soon suspended and would remain suspended (to this day) even though the Senate would fail to ratify the nuclear Comprehensive Test Ban Treaty (CTBT) later in the 1990s. This outcome was made possible by the fact that the other established nuclear powers agreed to moratoriums themselves (only India and Pakistan tested in the latter part of the 1990s, and only North Korea has tested in the twenty-first century). Thus, the CTBT became akin to the U.N. Convention on the Law of the Sea in that, even without formal American approval (or, in the CTBT's case, without China's or Russia's at this point either), its core provisions gained widespread acceptance as norms, if not binding international law.

Second, the United States determined that it still needed to continue to undergird American alliances around the world, not only with hypothetical combat power based at home but with an active and capable military presence abroad. As before, it was the steady presence of combat power that gave credibility to the American promise to help undergird stability in key regions of the Eurasian littoral. Potential adversaries knew that to attack U.S. interests or allies in these regions was therefore akin to attacking the United States itself, and they generally chose not to. Even though the U.S. military presence in Europe would be downsized by about two-thirds over the 1990s, it remained at nearly 100,000 personnel. This philosophy also led to a floor being placed on U.S. forces in the Pacific region only modestly below later Cold War levels (Assistant Secretary of Defense Joseph Nye committing the United States to keep 100,000 uniformed personnel in the region indefinitely), and to a U.S. Navy posture that could sustain simultaneous presence in the western Pacific, Mediterranean, and Persian Gulf.

Third, and relatedly, America's military would remain combat ready. There would be no more haggardly defense drawdowns after big buildups and wars; there would be no more Task Force Smiths, as in Korea in 1950. Individual units might decline in number, but every effort would be made to sustain their near-term preparedness for battle. Force structures would not be hollow; personnel would be well compensated, preserving the great improvements in the quality of the force from the Reagan years; training and maintenance standards would be upheld. For the most part, these bipartisan objectives would be sustained through the 1990s.

Fourth, the United States needed the capacity to fight at least a single major regional war effectively—assuming some allied help, yes, but not necessarily too much—and preferably two. That first regional war should be assumed to be difficult, requiring substantial hedging and margins for error in estimating necessary force requirements. The vision of how it might unfold was unfortunately shaped too much by the (relatively happy) Desert Storm experience. There was to be a clear sequence: an initial buildup and then a larger buildup in response to a crisis; selective military operations to shape and structure the battlefield; then a big, decisive operation producing a clear and victorious outcome; finally, some follow-on operations but otherwise a relatively rapid builddown. These were defined as the four phases of war, with Phase Three the main act. (Sometimes, Phase Zero was described as the peacetime "shaping" of a region or theater through various military preparations, further development of alliance relationships, military exercises, and so forth.)[66] As such (and to be fair to each service!), the requisite force structure for a future major-theater war was assumed to be a slimmed-down version of what had been deployed to the desert in 1990–91. Specifically, the United States would itself deploy four to five Army divisions (typically with three brigades per division), four to five Marine expeditionary brigades, ten Air Force fighter wings, 100 Air Force heavy bombers, four to five aircraft carrier battle groups, special operations forces, and possibly National Guard enhanced readiness brigades.[67]

Fifth, the procurement holiday notwithstanding, the U.S. military would take advantage of what many were calling a "revolution in military affairs" to upgrade its forces technologically. Much of this was related to the Internet and dot-com revolutions happening in the civilian economy. Since the United States led the world in these domains, and since even a U.S. defense industry on holiday still dramatically outproduced anyone else in the world, this so-called RMA was assumed to be mostly good for the United States, at least by most scholars and strategists. At times, the debate about what technology could do was breathless, with some advocates talking about making the oceans transparent or building ground vehicles that could go 120 miles per hour by the year 2010 or reducing the cost of space launch by 90 percent.[68] At other times, it stayed more specific and practical. For example, a group of RAND scholars described "the new calculus" of modern war that placed a higher premium on airpower and stand-off weaponry relative to earlier eras of warfare.[69]

There should perhaps have been a sixth piece to this defense strategy debate: greater discussion about the wisdom of expanding formal alliance commitments to a large number of newly democratic states, especially in Europe. On that issue, there was arguably too much consensus; perhaps politics should not have stopped at the water's edge. That policy, which by this writing in 2025 has led to a doubling in the membership of NATO since the Cold War ended, was treated more as an element of democracy promotion than one of defense policy. Yet it hugely increased American security commitments in Europe and contributed to a dynamic that has produced a far worse relationship between Russia and the West than had been expected in the 1990s. One need not sympathize with anything about Vladimir Putin's worldview to view NATO expansion as a much more fraught decision than it was treated in the 1990s and early 2000s, and one with much greater implications for America's hard-power obligations than was recognized. What Russia later did was not justifiable in any way, but it should have been foreseeable.

I was fortunate to have a small role in the force-sizing debate. As a graduate student in the late 1980s, I wrote a dissertation outlining a post–Cold War U.S. military for "overseas presence, crisis response, and a half war." Mercifully, thanks to welcome advice from my dear friend Dawn Jahn and others, I found a pithier title for the ensuing book, *The Art of War in an Age of Peace.* My proposal required no brilliance to devise; after all, the concept of a "half war" had been around since the 1950s, and the nation had already fought two of them by then, in Korea and Vietnam. The book version of the dissertation, published in 1992, could—like Secretary of Defense Dick Cheney's "base force" of 1992 and Secretary of Defense Les Aspin's "bottom-up review" of 1993—also draw on the Operation Desert Storm experience.

Over the early 1990s, the United States decided that a single half-war capability was insufficient. Policy makers in both parties would wind up deciding that it was better to aim for something akin to a two-war capability. The logic of this goal was largely to discourage opportunistic aggression by an aggressor in a second theater, should the United States (with allies) wind up in a conflict against another adversary in a first theater. Of course, the United States would wind up fighting two wars at once, in Afghanistan and Iraq. And it wound up not having enough combat power to fight two at full strength at the same time, despite its plans and preparations. The Afghanistan and Iraq Wars were much different in dynamics than Operation Desert Storm, but they were against foes of roughly the same size and strength as Iraq of 1991. The experience is thus sobering and humbling about the ability of planners to figure out the character and duration of a future war even when they prognosticate correctly about likely locations and enemies.

In my 1992 book, I wound up advocating for a U.S. military of 1.2 million active-duty troops. That was intended to provide the backbone for a "half war" (or "major regional contingency" or "major theater war," as such operations were called over the 1990s) at any one time, plus the capacity for smaller additional operations. That figure stood in contrast to the roughly 2.1 million active-duty military personnel making up the American armed forces at the end of the Cold War (that is, as of 1990). By contrast, the Base Force of the Bush administration envisioned 1.64 million active-duty military personnel as its end-state, with a two-war capability. The Bottom-Up Review of the Clinton administration kept the two-war framework but lowered the active-duty troop figure to 1.45 million. In the actual event, the Clinton administration would reduce the active-duty force to just under 1.4 million by 2000.[70]

At the end of the Cold War, U.S. military force structure included eighteen active Army divisions plus ten in the Reserve Component. It also featured three Marine Expeditionary Forces, fifteen active aircraft carriers, 546 major ships in the Navy, twenty-four active-duty Air Force fighter wings (each of about seventy-two aircraft) with twelve more wings in the Reserve Component, and 268 bombers.

The Bush administration Base Force and Clinton administration Bottom-Up Review Force featured force postures that were, as noted, roughly one-third smaller: twelve and ten active-duty Army divisions, respectively, six and five Reserve-Component Divisions, three Marine Expeditionary Forces each, twelve and eleven active-duty aircraft carriers, respectively, 430 and 346 major ships, fifteen and thirteen active-duty Air Force combat wings (plus eleven and seven in the respective Reserve Components), and 176 and 154 strategic bombers. Averaged across all these categories, the Bottom-Up Review force had 36 percent less force structure than the 1990 force.[71]

Two stories illustrate the nature of the debates of the day. First, when Les Aspin was Bill Clinton's first secretary of defense and before settling on a two-war structure for the armed forces himself, he considered a less-demanding way to size forces. It was called "win-hold-win" and imagined that, if two wars happened at once, the United States with allies could win the first outright while essentially holding the line and limiting enemy encroachments in the second. Then, with the first war over, it would swing forces to the other conflict and finish off the second enemy. Derided as "win-hold-oops" by critics, however, this framework was ultimately dropped; it was not seen as hedging sufficiently against the unpredictability of war and, moreover, might not have brought decisive combat power quickly enough to the Korean peninsula to limit damage to Seoul in a war there. So Aspin reverted back to the two-war paradigm—though he claimed the United States could fulfill its demands with a smaller force than the Bush administration had advocated. His successors under President Clinton, Bill Perry and Bill Cohen, stuck with the main elements of Aspin's plan.

Second, after becoming secretary of defense for the second time but before the 9/11 attacks, Donald Rumsfeld went through a similar thought process. He contemplated deemphasizing regional conflicts in favor of a more dynamic and modern way of war that would emphasize mobility, maneuver, and lethality. Although perhaps too optimistic about what a modern revolution in military affairs could really deliver, Rumsfeld was in some ways ahead of his time, as the debates of the late 2010s and 2020s would later often echo his ideas.[72] In any event, he wound up being a secretary of defense who actually fought two regional wars at once. Each was only about one-quarter to one-half the size (at maximum) of what had been envisioned based on the Desert Storm model but, alas, about ten times as long. While overlapping, they were not both equally large and intensive at the same time. The Iraq effort was most demanding on the force structure and personnel from 2003 through about 2010, peaking in 2008. The Afghanistan mission ramped way up in 2009 and then started to ramp down by 2011.[73]

One additional advantage to a two-war capability in the minds of some was that it could be used to justify a larger and more expensive post–Cold War American military than might have otherwise resulted in a deficit-conscious and casualty-averse time in U.S. politics. It could also therefore sustain a larger margin of superiority over a declining Russia and still-rising China than would otherwise be the case, solidifying America's claim to hegemonic leadership and setting up the possibility of a "second American century" as the year 2000 approached. Here, there was less agreement in the U.S. debate, as some valued this argument more than others. Notably, although it was intended to stay classified, the Defense Planning Guidance document of 1992, written with the supervision and guidance of Under Secretary of Defense for Policy Paul Wolfowitz, advocated maintaining dominant capabilities vis-à-vis Russia—particularly in regard to any war over the Baltic states, which had recently gained their freedom from Moscow when the Soviet Union broke up. The Baltic states were not yet candidates for NATO membership; indeed, neither were the states contiguous to it, notably Poland, meaning that any U.S.-led effort to defend Estonia, Latvia, or Lithuania would require long-distance power projection. Given the state of Russia's military in the early 1990s, this still seemed a doable task. But the contingency's inclusion on a short list of planning scenarios for post–Cold War American armed forces still foreshadowed, and revealed the beginnings of, a broader debate concerning how to think about U.S. power in what was largely a unipolar world. Specifically, the Defense Planning Guidance based much of its recommendations for force structure and defense budgeting on the following logic: "The third goal is to preclude any hostile power from dominating a region critical to our interests and also thereby to strengthen the barriers against the reemergence of a global threat to the interests of the U.S. and our allies. These regions include Europe, East Asia, the Middle East/Persian Gulf, and Latin America. Consolidated, nondemocratic control of the resources of such a critical region could generate a significant threat to our security."[74]

That was the theory. Then there was the practice. Although it is sometimes remembered today as a period of relative calm in world affairs, the decade of the 1990s rarely felt that way in real time. Talk of a possible end to history did not last long; more common was talk about an age of chaos that the end of the Cold War had purportedly unleashed.[75]

Under both the George H. W. Bush and Clinton administrations, the United States struggled to figure out a reasonable way to limit the bloodbath in the Balkans, and most specifically in Bosnia. Airpower was less conducive to ending the fighting in this kind of a civil war, with interspersed and largely urban populations. In a memorable exchange in 1993 that said a great deal about debates over the American way of war, Joint Chiefs Chairman Colin Powell and Clinton administration U.N. Ambassador Madeleine Albright sparred publicly over what should be done. Albright challenged Powell, in the aftermath of Operation Desert Storm, to find a way to use America's outstanding military to limit the carnage. Powell replied, with an argument similar to what he had written in *Foreign Affairs* the year before, with a criticism of civilians who want to do "a little surgical bombing or limited attack" with American power rather than define an achievable, specific set of military objectives that the nation could rally behind and sustain.[76] Then, tragically, days after Powell's tenure as chairman, what had been a benign humanitarian assistance operation in Somalia led to Black Hawk Down, in which eighteen GIs lost their lives in early October 1993 when a Somalian militia challenged them in pitched urban combat.[77] The U.S. presence in Somalia would soon end—and President Clinton would have little appetite for considering any other humanitarian-inspired military operations in Africa when the Rwandan genocide took place the following spring.

Not all was bleak. In both 1995 and 1999, the United States and NATO allies found more effective ways to use limited amounts of airpower in the Balkans. The first time was in Bosnia, where by 1995 the ethnic divisions had solidified enough that targets could be more easily identified and attacked from the air (Croat and Bosniak ground forces had also become more effective and better armed by then). That coerced Serbs into a negotiated peace deal that was then backed up with tens of thousands of NATO ground troops, with numbers declining but the presence remaining for years. (A similar dynamic would play out in Kosovo from 1999.)

The mixed track record of the 1990s continued in the broader Middle East. In 1998 in Operation Desert Fox, the United States conducted a four-day bombing campaign that destroyed a fair amount of Iraq's remaining infrastructure and equipment with which to make weapons of mass destruction. It did not know it at the time, however. Standoff reconnaissance methods, in the absence of personnel on the ground (since U.N. inspectors were kicked out afterward), could not confirm or deny the effects of the attacks.[78] And that same year, after the August bombings of U.S. embassies in Kenya and Tanzania by al-Qaeda operatives, America's reprisals with just uninhabitated cruise missiles probably did more to convince Osama bin Laden about the *limitations* of U.S. resolve, and the country's high aversion to casualties, than about any American resoluteness or military dominance.[79] By the time the cruise missiles showed up on their targets in Afghanistan, bin Laden was long since gone. The intelligence leading to the strikes was not wrong, just outdated, and the capabilities used to attack the targets in question were not defective, just insufficiently flexible to adapt to changing conditions on a fluid battlefield.

Then in 1999, the Clinton administration probably achieved its greatest battlefield success. In the early months of the year, the same Slobodan Milošević who had stoked Serbian aggression in Bosnia conducted pogroms against the ethnic Albanian population in Kosovo, a province of Serbia. NATO's response began with lackluster and ineffective pinprick attacks on Serbian irregular forces. Flying above 15,000 feet to keep aircraft safe from shoulder-launched air defenses, NATO pilots could not effectively identify or target those Serbian militias.[80] NATO did find a way to "win ugly," as mentioned earlier. It multiplied its aircraft in the region tenfold over a war lasting two and a half months, ultimately flying a total of some 40,000 combat sorties. It expanded its target set to include many facilities and assets in Belgrade, Serbia, and attacked that target set with a higher fraction of precision-guided munitions—about 30 percent—than had been available eight years before in Operation Desert Storm. By now, the GPS-guided, and inexpensive, Joint Direct Attack Munition was available. Finally, NATO also began to hint at the possibility of a ground invasion.[81] As the lights increasingly went out in Belgrade, Milošević finally relented, allowing autonomy for Kosovo as well as the deployment there of NATO peacekeepers. Some military strategists concluded that technology had finally progressed to the point where it was possible to win wars largely if not entirely from the air.[82]

Taking the whole decade together, many were persuaded that a revolution in military affairs was in the offing—that the new American way of war was no longer industrial-scale mass armies but high-tech standoff precision strikes, involving few risks to U.S. troops and only modest risks to civilian populations in targeted countries. Some of us, however, were more struck by several longstanding and enduring realities of war—including the facts that enemies are adaptable, guerrilla and terrorist fighters are hard to find within civilian populations, and battlefields are far from transparent. Even modern precision weapons cannot destroy targets they cannot find.[83]

Beyond the high-level debates about military revolutions and the future of warfare, at least four more specific debates were also brewing through the mid- to late 1990s that wound up having substantial ramifications in the years to come. They involved missile defense, protection of troops and the homeland against weapons of mass destruction, the weight and logistics footprint of the modern American military (the Army in particular), and the relevant importance of homeland defense.

The first key doctrinal development to address some of these new issues in a major way was probably the Quadrennial Defense Review of 1997. The concept of a QDR had been mandated by law the year before, as Congress found the previous two administrations' major strategic reviews—the Bush, Cheney, and Powell Base Force of 1992 and the Clinton, Aspin, and Powell Bottom-Up Review of 1993—to be useful documents for framing the debate about defense priorities. To be sure, such documents go only so far to guide future policy as new crises and opportunities arise on the world stage. But they do create a certain structure, shared vocabulary, and sense of priorities for the strategic debate, wherever it may go. In prior decades, there had been big documents from time to time—NSC-68 under Truman, NSC-162 under Eisenhower, PD-59 under Carter—as well as major studies such as the Gaither and Killian reports under Eisenhower that called for greater resources for U.S. strategic capabilities and big new ideas such as the New Look under Ike, Flexible Response under Kennedy and Johnson, and the so-called Guam Doctrine under Nixon. But all were ad hoc. Congress was looking for something more dependable and systematic.

Five QDRs would result—in 1997, 2001, 2006, 2010, and 2014. Then, the National Defense Authorization Act of 2017 replaced QDRs with a requirement for a somewhat loftier National Defense Strategy (of which there have been two, in 2018 and 2022, as of this writing, with the second Trump administration likely to do a third).[84]

The 1997 QDR, developed under the leadership of Secretary of Defense Bill Cohen, made its greatest contributions in addressing several vulnerabilities of the American military that could interfere with its ability to achieve Desert Storm–like outcomes in future war. Accordingly, it focused on such mundane matters as mine warfare and on scary subjects such as the possibility that weapons of mass destruction would be employed against deployed American forces in a future war. Its recommendations were modest in significance and cost, but useful, with advocacy of ideas including better protective gear against chemical and biological weapons for troops on the battlefield and new research and development ventures to improve the nation's ability to find and address mines at sea. They also placed continued emphasis on missile defense. (The Clinton administration had shifted its emphasis in missile defense from the Reagan and George H. W. Bush focus on long-range or strategic defenses to theater defenses but kept overall resources robust.) The Desert Storm experience had been sobering on this front. U.S. planners had worried a great deal that Saddam might employ biological or chemical weapons on the battlefield and did not feel confident in their ability to have American forces operate effectively in such an environment.

The 1997 QDR supported peacekeeping and humanitarian operations—by 1997, they had a slightly better reputation given their apparent relative success in Bosnia. But they continued to be viewed as "lesser included cases" within a combat force structure developed and sized fundamentally to handle two major theater wars (as the preferred vernacular now called such scenarios) at once.

In addition, the 1997 QDR, as well as an independent National Defense Panel set up to critique it, focused attention on the importance of saving money within the defense budget. That led to recommendations for more military base closures, after Base Realignment and Closure rounds in 1988, 1991, 1993, and 1995. It also prodded the Pentagon to adopt best commercial practices in industry, acquisition, and supply-chain management for the Department of Defense.[85] Thus began a process that was later partly regretted, as a desire to streamline industry reduced its resilience to supply-chain shocks as well as its surge-production capacity.

The revolution in military affairs debate continued through these years as well. The Kosovo War provided an additional impetus. During that war, United States European Command under Army General Wesley Clark had decided to reposition some eighteen Apache helicopters to Albania as preparation for possible aerial attack against Serbian irregulars. In the end, authorization was never given for those helicopters to be used in combat. But it took the Army most of

April just to get eighteen in position—even though the distance from Germany (where the Army keeps many Apaches) to Kosovo was only about 1,000 miles by air. The perceived need to build up fortified positions and protect them with artillery and air defense systems made the deployment very slow—and made the U.S. Army appear far too plodding and hidebound. Capping off the regretful situation, America's only fatalities in the war occurred when two Apache pilots tragically had a training accident as part of the whole operation. This experience led the Army, under a new chief of staff as of 1999, General Eric Shinseki, to commit itself to become much more agile and light. The result was a plan to build medium-weight Stryker brigades in the short term, then units centered on a Future Combat System (FCS) over the longer-term future, with twenty-ton vehicles eventually replacing the seventy-ton Abrams tank. It was a Muhammad Ali concept applied to ground warfare: "fly like a butterfly, sting like a bee" and depended on sensors and speed rather than heavy armor to elude enemy attack. Alas, this plan worked better on PowerPoint than in the real world of practical and available defense technologies; it was one of the most blatant examples of the so-called revolution in military affairs overpromising on what modern weapons could deliver.[86] The FCS would be canceled within roughly a decade.

There was other churn in the missile-defense debate as well. A congressionally mandated study under the leadership of Donald Rumsfeld argued in a report of July 1998 that, among other trends and dangers, North Korea could soon develop a direct threat to North America. Its argument felt precocious later that same year when North Korea sent a medium-range missile over Japan on September 1. The group reaffirmed the existing bipartisan commitment to theater-range missile defense but gave added impetus to the case for a national missile defense system that would protect the United States from long-range attack, be it from a so-called rogue actor or from Russia or China (perhaps due to an accidental or demonstration shot). Its impact was considerable. The Clinton administration developed a plan to deploy such strategic missile defenses, even if that would have required withdrawal from the existing ABM Treaty. The administration was saved from a difficult decision it probably did not want to have to make by the failure of the technology in repeated tests as the Clinton term in office ended. President George W. Bush, with a newly ensconced Donald Rumsfeld as secretary of defense, would however make such a decision by 2002.[87]

Then there was the Hart-Rudman Commission and its focus on other dangers to the homeland. It wound up sounding hauntingly and tragically precocious when the Twin Towers were brought down and the Pentagon attacked on September 11, 2001. The Report of the United States Commission on National Security in the 21st Century, as it was formally known, led by former senators Gary Hart and Warren Rudman, issued its final report in January 2001 calling for much greater attention to protection of the homeland, including from possible terrorist attack.[88] (Drug cartels, arguably even more dangerous then and now to the American civilian population, were not discussed as much in this or any other major defense debate—yet Plan Colombia, launched in 2000, would soon demonstrate how the United States could play at least an important support role by providing helicopters and other equipment to a Colombian military that made great progress against insurgents and drug cartels early in the twenty-first century.)[89]

Thus, at the dawn of a new century, America's defense debate was at a crossroads. Contradictions, or at least severe tensions, were rampant. The country with the world's greatest military was so casualty averse that it responded to deadly attacks on two of its embassies with only cruise missiles and was labeled a paper tiger by its new number-one nemesis, Osama bin Laden. The advent of precision-strike weapons and ubiquitous forms of reconnaissance made some see the promise of a revolution in military affairs and perhaps a new age of standoff if not even sanitary warfare. Yet U.S. troops struggled in traditional infantry and urban-combat environments, and American airpower had trouble reliably eliminating the weapons programs of a defeated dictator in the Middle East. Improving missile defense systems promised protection even as car bombs and exploding skiffs (as used against the U.S.S. *Cole* in Yemen in October 2000) and other tools of mass-casualty terrorism spread fear from Oklahoma City (where homegrown terrorism killed 168 in 1995) to Khobar Towers in Saudi Arabia to Kenya and Tanzania and beyond.

After 9/11, taking stock of all of the above, top officials in the Bush administration decided that something dramatic must be done to avenge the 9/11 attacks, show the world that the United States was no paper tiger, and shake up the Middle East. The results would be momentous.[90] And the defense strategy debates, and policy decisions, of previous years would leave the U.S. military well prepared for what was to come in many key domains—with its excellent training, very good special forces, formidable power-projection capabilities, remarkable intelligence assets, roughly right-sized force structure, and precision-strike capabilities. Alas, in other ways the preparation would not be so good, most of all in the post-Vietnam military's decisions not to prepare or train its troops for the complexities of counterinsurgency warfare.

MILITARY STRATEGY IN AFGHANISTAN FROM 2001

The 9/11 attacks, originating out of Afghanistan, not only caught the United States completely by surprise but caught it without any kind of meaningful military concept of operations for waging war in the land of the Hindu Kush. Yes, U.S. intelligence failed to connect the dots and failed to use sufficient imagination about how terrorists might strike the country. That was the case even after many warning signs in the 1990s, with at least a dozen major attacks against American interests by Islamist extremists, including embassy bombings in Africa in 1998 and an earlier attempt to bring down a World Trade Center tower in 1993. There were also failed attempts to use aircraft as guided bombs with plots originating from the Philippines and Algeria in 1994, the latter targeting France.[91] Al Qaeda had been around for years and had been attacking the United States with regularity since at least 1998. Yet there was no plan for how to pursue its headquarters or main sanctuary at the time the Twin Towers were destroyed.[92]

Thus, the resulting war effort, beginning as it did less than a month after 9/11, was largely an improvisation. In that light, its early success was remarkable. Alas, its follow-up operations were not, especially with the escape of al-Qaeda leadership over the border into Pakistan—and the absence of a good plan to stabilize the country and prevent the reemergence of the Taliban thereafter. By the time the United States built up proper capabilities for this type of mission and applied them to Afghanistan, the nation was growing weary of counterinsurgency and would lack the patience to sustain the operation even after it had been dramatically scaled back by the mid-2010s. There was, however, a silver lining; by the time the Taliban came back to power in Afghanistan, two decades after losing it, the movement's new leadership did not appear interested in picking a fight with the United States again.[93]

The American role in Afghanistan from 2001 through 2021 can be demarcated into five major phases with distinctive political-military strategies. In sequence, they might be called the overthrow, the light footprint, the surge, the support mission, and the hasty withdrawal. The last two extend beyond 2014, but are included in this chapter to keep the narrative smooth. The predicate to all of them was a demand by President George W. Bush, shortly after the 9/11 attacks, that the ruling Taliban government in Afghanistan surrender Osama bin Laden and other al-Qaeda leadership to the United States. When the Taliban refused, the stage was set not only for the American pursuit of al Qaeda but for the overthrow of the Taliban government as well.

Air attacks against Taliban positions began in early October. The United States also deployed special forces and CIA teams—a total of just several hundred American personnel—to work with the Tajik-dominated Northern Alliance of Afghanistan in its fight against the Taliban and its pursuit of al Qaeda. (The Northern Alliance had lost its top leader, Ahmad Shah Massoud, when al Qaeda assassinated him on September 9.) These Americans accompanied the Afghan resistance fighters, calling in precision strikes from U.S. aircraft against Taliban positions during key battles.[94] Several hundred Marines flew into southern Afghanistan to establish a foothold and initial logistics hub there as well. Just as with tank plinking during Operation Desert Storm, the effectiveness of these special forces teams working with Northern Alliance fighters was not foreseen. Without that success, it is not clear where the campaign would have gone next, as American planners were running out of fixed targets to hit from the air. The Taliban were probably not nearly as vulnerable to coercive bombardment as Serbian leader Slobodan Milošević had proven to be just two years before.

As Taliban forces dissolved and gave up their holds on the country's main cities, bin Laden and other al-Qaeda leadership took flight. They hoped for safety in Pakistan. So they began to move in that general direction, reaching the Tora Bora area near Jalalabad (and the Khyber Pass, at the Afghan-Pakistani border) by late November. But the United States had few forces on the ground anywhere in the area. Whether overconfident or casualty averse, Bush administration leaders chose not to establish an American military presence in the Tora Bora region. They might have considered creating a makeshift set of helicopter landing pads and refueling sites, for example (even though doing so in much friendlier terrain in Albania during the Kosovo War had taken weeks of effort, given standard operating procedures of the day). Instead, they chose to bomb mountain passes and to pay local militia commanders to watch ingress and egress points. Happy to do so by day but disinclined to stay out in the cold at night, the locals let bin Laden along with perhaps 1,000 cohorts slip away.[95]

The second phase of the Afghanistan War was the combination of a light footprint effort to stabilize the country combined with ongoing operations against remnants of al Qaeda still in the country. During this chapter of America's twenty-year Afghanistan saga, Washington was preoccupied with Iraq, as were some NATO allies. Chairman of the Joint Chiefs Admiral Mike Mullen put it well, a few years into the war: "In Afghanistan, we do what we can. In Iraq, we do what we must."[96] In this period, the CIA developed its capacities to conduct drone surveillance and targeting of al-Qaeda leadership over the border in Pakistan. (Later, the U.S. military's Navy SEALs carried out the raid to kill Osama bin Laden in Abbottabad, Pakistan, on May 2, 2011.)

American allies gradually built up their collective force strength in Afghanistan from about 5,000 troops in 2002 to 25,000 troops in 2007. These troops, making up the International Security Assistance Force, or ISAF, initially deployed only to Kabul, after Pentagon officials successfully lobbied against a larger force and broader geographic scope for their mission.[97] That restriction was gradually eased over time, as security conditions were seen to require it—something that should have been obvious from the start. Peacekeepers were first deployed outside of Kabul in 2005; they arrived in the south of the country in and around Kandahar in 2006.[98] By mid-2007, there were some 2,500 Canadian troops in Kandahar, as well as 6,000 Brits in the country, mostly in Helmand Province to Kandahar's immediate west. By the end of 2008, Canada had increased its troop total to 2,750 and the Brits to just over 8,000. There were also 1,700 Dutch and 1,000 Australian troops in the south. The United States also gradually increased its strength, more or less commensurately. It had had around 10,000 troops in Afghanistan in 2002 but increased that number to 25,000 in 2007.[99] Its primary emphasis throughout this period was on counterterrorism; its forces operated under separate command. Most U.S. efforts were directed toward Pashtun-majority regions in provinces near Pakistan, since it was Pashtuns who made up the preponderance of the Taliban movement (even if most Pashtuns were not Taliban). In 2003, General David Barno, commander of U.S. forces in Afghanistan, set up brigade-level headquarters in the country's east and south.[100]

Unfortunately, ISAF did not do a serious job in helping build Afghan security forces during this period. Training programs were short and skimpy and reached only a modest fraction of uniformed personnel; police and army leaders were not particularly well chosen, mentored, or supported in the field.[101] Although the accomplishments of the NATO mission in Afghanistan in this period were limited, many felt initially that they were adequate to the task. Schools were opening and basic health care services were spreading. Electricity production doubled over the first five years; the nation's GDP grew by half; Internet use was growing fast. Things seemed pretty good.[102] Alas, they were not.

Already, the Taliban were plotting their comeback. Angered by their exclusion from the new Afghan government formed in Bonn by the international community in early 2002, and benefiting from sanctuary in Pakistan, they developed a plan of action. By early 2006, they were undertaking offensives under their commander Dadullah, first in northern Helmand Province, later in southern Helmand and western Kandahar Provinces as well. They attacked police checkpoints and stations and set ambushes when they could anticipate the movements of government personnel.[103] Afghan political leadership was unable to unite the Pashtun tribes in these regions to fight the Taliban, which at this point remained generally unpopular and fielded perhaps only 7,000 to 10,000 fighters nationwide (with about 4,000 in Helmand and Kandahar).[104] American decision makers continued to reject the idea of reaching out to former Taliban to bring them into the political process in a way that might have taken some wind out of the insurgency.[105]

From 2005 to 2006, suicide bombings in Afghanistan quintupled. Detonations of improvised explosive devices and ambushes more than doubled. U.S. troop fatalities, having averaged about fifty a year from 2002 to 2004, topped 100 in 2007. Other foreign troop losses, after averaging around twenty a year in the period 2002–4, also topped 100 that year.[106] Several major clearing operations were attempted by U.S. and other NATO forces, including Operation Medusa and Operation Mountain Fury in southern provinces of the country starting in September 2006.[107] But the available resources were not up to the challenge.

Meanwhile the Taliban were regenerating fast and gaining revenue from opium production in the remote regions of the south that its followers increasingly controlled.[108] Counterinsurgent strategist David Kilcullen estimates that their numbers reached about 10,000 hard-core full-time fighters and roughly another 30,000 part-time fighters by 2008.[109] According to one estimate, they were able to carry out "heavy activity" in only five of the country's thirty-four provinces in 2006, but in two-thirds of them by 2008 and more than three-fourths by 2009.[110] At this time, the Afghan people remained generally hopeful for their future, but polls showed increasing worry about where the country was headed.[111]

As this period came to a close, U.S. and NATO leaders progressively realized they had a problem on their hands, one big enough that the gradual and modest increases until that point in deployed troops would not solve it. ISAF and American military commands were unified in 2007; U.S. Army General Dan McNeill arrived in Afghanistan to lead both.[112] American leaders, including President Bush as well as Senator John McCain and Senator Barack Obama, increasingly realized that much more would soon need to be done.

At the very end of the Bush presidency, a third main phase of the U.S.-led war effort began and continued more or less through President Obama's first term in office. Emboldened by the success of the surge in Iraq, and enabled by troop reductions in Iraq that freed up resources for possible use elsewhere, the United States decided to try a similar kind of counterinsurgency, or COIN, effort in Afghanistan. President Bush and Secretary of Defense Robert Gates initiated a force buildup in Afghanistan in 2008, encouraged by the fact that both major U.S. presidential candidates advocated doing so as well. However, available resources were not yet adequate; it would be left to President Obama to make a serious attempt at a successful COIN operation.

In both absolute and proportional terms, the surge in Afghanistan was larger than the surge in Iraq of 2007 had been. On Obama's watch, U.S. troops in Afghanistan would grow in two phases from roughly 30,000 to 100,000 through 2009–10 before coming back down almost as fast as they had been built up in late 2011 and 2012. By contrast, during the Iraq surge, U.S. uniformed personnel grew from roughly 140,000 to 170,000.

After his first buildup but before the second, Obama also chose a new commander for the mission, General Stanley McChrystal, in the spring of 2009. Gates instructed him to conduct a thorough review of the country's security conditions and to develop options about troop requirements for President Obama. McChrystal and team, including outside experts from think tanks and universities in Europe and the United States, assessed the overall situation as dire. McChrystal determined that about 20 percent of Afghanistan's 407 districts were key strategic terrain in greatest peril of being overrun by Taliban forces. Applying the precepts of the new *U.S. Army/Marine Corps Counterinsurgency Field Manual,* with its rule of thumb that there be twenty to twenty-five counterinsurgent personnel for every 1,000 civilians being protected in an indigenous population, he estimated overall force requirements for coalition and Afghan forces.[113] Ultimately three options were developed, with the largest based on the objective of trying to stabilize all the key strategic districts more or less at once. Unfortunately, the options were leaked to the media, complicating White House relations with McChrystal's command, elements of which were suspected by some to have been behind the leak (though the leak could well have originated in Washington, D.C., for all we know).[114]

After an autumn of numerous policy discussions in the Situation Room, Obama chose a variant of the middle option, though he scaled it back slightly from the proposed increase of 40,000 U.S. troops. Given increases that had taken place earlier in the year, that meant total U.S. troops in Afghanistan would reach 100,000 GIs. Allied nations agreed to increase their strength, too, but much more modestly, collectively exceeding 40,000 troops once all was said and done. So the foreign coalition would approach 150,000 troops in rough numbers. The new strategy also envisioned generating well-trained and well-equipped Afghan security forces numbering around 300,000 personnel in relatively short order—arguably an even more ambitious and challenging goal, since there were only about 150,000 Afghan security forces at the beginning of 2009, and most of those were poorly equipped and trained.[115] Obama's decision to choose "medium-option, light" meant that the concept of surging would have to be applied sequentially. McChrystal chose to focus first on Helmand, then Kandahar; the east of the country, also key strategic terrain, would have to wait. As it turned out, this region would never receive the requisite resources as contemporary COIN doctrine would have recommended.

In choosing the new strategy, Obama felt obliged to promote Afghan political reform as well. Believing that Afghan leaders needed to get serious about their own responsibilities, including a fight against rampant corruption, Obama coupled the promise to build up foreign troops with the promise to build down almost as soon.[116] After U.S. forces had surged into country in 2010, they would surge out starting by the summer of 2011—returning to the preexisting force levels of some 68,000 U.S. troops by late summer in 2012 and declining further soon thereafter. Given logistical realities, these time constraints meant that peak force levels would be in position for only a brief time. This approach was probably never very promising; among its other defects, the announced time horizon gave the Taliban motivation to try to wait out the surge.[117] McChrystal himself was not defeatist about this policy outcome, however, writing in his memoirs that "it gave us an opportunity. I strongly believed we could succeed, and committed myself completely."[118]

As part of the new strategy, ISAF established regional commands in the east, south, southwest, west, and north, as well as the capital city, and matched up its own regional forces (each under two-star command) with Afghan army units.[119] About half of the ISAF regional headquarters were run by Americans by this time; Germany held command in the north, Italy in the west, Britain for a time in Kandahar, and Turkey in Kabul.[120]

The campaign plan sought to achieve early victories in key sectors of the country. The theory of the case was that doing so would generate momentum that would convince other insurgents to flee or reconcile and convince Pakistan to stop aiding and abetting the Taliban—while also motivating President Hamid Karzai and other leaders to improve Afghan governance. Then the rapidly mobilized, trained, and equipped Afghan security forces would take increasing responsibility, preserving the territorial gains and newfound stability. On that entire campaign wish list, however, only the first goal was achieved, and only to a limited degree.

Just as had been the case in Iraq, American and allied casualties were heavy during the surge phase of the strategy. American fatalities totaled 499 in 2010 and

418 in 2011, comparable to the highest rates during the Iraq War on a per-troop basis. Other NATO and foreign losses were proportionate in magnitude.[121] Afghan security force fatalities now reached into the low thousands a year. As NATO drew down its own forces and attempted the handoff to Afghan units, losses among the Afghans only grew. Annual Afghan army and police fatality levels would reach perhaps 10,000 a year later that decade. It was hard to hold onto troops and police when they knew their lives would be at acute risk; turnover rates in the nation's security forces were very high, as was absenteeism. To be sure, the Taliban suffered high losses, too. U.S. and NATO command refused to provide public estimates, trying to avoid the body-count fixations of Vietnam. But Taliban losses were probably at least comparable to those of the government's security forces throughout the war. As for Afghan civilians, the United Nations consistently estimated their annual fatalities from war in the low thousands—though those figures were likely undercounts. Still, civilian fatalities in Afghanistan never reached the tragic totals of those in Iraq in the years after the overthrow of Saddam.[122] For those of us privileged enough to visit Afghanistan during these years (I went more than a dozen times as a researcher and election observer), there was an air of almost quasi-normalcy in most of the country most of the time—in dramatic contrast to the situation in Baghdad and many other major Iraqi cities, where Jersey walls and security gates dominated much of the urban landscape.

Various attempts were made to harness the local militias in the country (known in Afghanistan as *arbakai*) in support of foreign and Afghan forces. The idea sought to emulate the successful Sons of Iraq program, paying members of these groups to help monitor and protect their own home territories. Various new programs, such as the Afghan Local Police, as well as the Afghan Public Protection Program and the Local Defense Initiative, were hatched as a result. None worked very well. Loyalties were divided; corruption was rampant; overall performance was generally poor.[123]

The overall effectiveness of the surge was not very good, either. By spring of 2010, Obama was developing a negative sense of the progress—and of the mission's future prospects. Later that same year, now in command himself in Kabul, General David Petraeus advocated a slower drawdown to provide more time to clear the east. But Obama was unpersuaded, perhaps having lost much of his initial hopefulness about what could be realistically achieved in Afghanistan. His vice president, Joe Biden, was apparently even less hopeful. Once Petraeus returned to the United States in the summer of 2012, his successor, Marine Corps General John Allen, would have to attempt to sustain battlefield momentum while sending home many of his surge forces.[124]

On balance, while not an abject failure, the surge in Afghanistan did not achieve the fundamental transformation of the security environment seen in Iraq. There was no corresponding "awakening" movement to complement the work of official security forces; the Pakistan sanctuary for the insurgency remained a huge hindrance to progress; the Taliban remained resilient, and committed; Afghan forces remained of highly uneven quality, to put it mildly; the surge was set to a calendar rather than to conditions on the ground. (By contrast, in Iraq, though security forces had been sectarian and often corrupt and undisciplined before the surge, and would again become so after the U.S. departure of 2011, they improved greatly during the period 2007–11.) Increasingly, the trend for President Obama and his successors would be to adjust strategy to live with the likelihood of mediocre outcomes and to limit the U.S. commitment in order to prioritize more important strategic goals elsewhere. This was not unlike the realizations that had dawned on earlier generations of American policy makers regarding Korea and Vietnam.

As Allen completed his command and another Marine, future chairman of the joint chiefs General Joseph Dunford, took charge, a fourth chapter of the U.S. and NATO involvement in the war began. The troop drawdown continued on Dunford's watch. Accordingly, at the end of 2014, the ISAF mission was formally ended, replaced by Operation Resolute Support. NATO moved away from a direct ground-combat role—even as it continued to provide most of the coalition's airpower, much of coalition intelligence and communications, the bulk of the logistics, and many special forces capabilities. It also provided security force assistance teams, grouped together into security force assistance brigades, an innovation dating from Allen's tenure. The teams embedded within major Afghan combat formations to provide training, advice, and intelligence (and to call in rapid-reaction reinforcements as well as air support when needed). All of this would have taken about 15,000 U.S. troops, according to official estimates—but alas, that number would not be available for long. Total U.S. troop numbers in country would decline below 10,000 in 2015 and continue their downward trajectory thereafter.

As the security force assistance brigades were withdrawn, NATO consolidated its positions into a few large bases. From these locations, it conducted air operations, positioned intelligence platforms, staged occasional raids, and trained Afghan forces. By the spring of 2015, the U.S. military presence in Afghanistan was principally located at a half dozen main bases—at Bagram (near Kabul), Herat, Mazar-e-Sharif, Kandahar, Jalalabad, and Kabul itself, plus another five smaller bases. The U.S. troop total soon dropped below 10,000, under the command of General John Campbell, who would in turn be succeeded by General Mick Nicholson and then in the end Scotty Austin (all American Army four-star generals).[125]

Accordingly, from 2015 onward, embedded advisory teams did not operate below the corps level except with Afghan special forces. Indeed, they could not even maintain a consistent presence with the 203rd Corps in Paktika Province in the east or the 215th Corps in Helmand Province in the south.[126] President Obama also attempted to restrict the use of U.S. airpower to operations in which NATO forces were at risk or where al-Qaeda elements were suspected to populate enemy ranks. That policy bred a certain cynicism about America's commitment to its Afghan allies in some quarters. The restrictions were especially severe in 2015 and part of 2016, until it became clear that the Taliban were profiting from the new U.S. policy.[127]

It seemed likely that a new American president, Donald Trump, would carry out a big withdrawal of U.S. forces in Afghanistan (meaning that other foreign forces would have to leave, too, given their dependencies on the United States). But with Secretary of Defense Jim Mattis at the Pentagon and H. R. McMaster as national security adviser, Trump doubled down for a while. Heading a recommendation from his field commander General Mick Nicholson, Trump relaxed restrictions on airpower and added several thousand more U.S. troops temporarily. Under this modification to the strategy, Afghan special forces doubled in size; increased pressure was also placed on Pakistan to address the sanctuary issue. The plan slowed Taliban momentum but did not reverse the trendlines. Soon, like Obama before him, Trump grew deeply frustrated with the Afghan situation.[128]

Over the period 2015–20, the Afghan security environment gradually deteriorated. Modest additional amounts of territory went over to Taliban control or became contested each year.[129] The cities stayed in government hands, however, with only rare and temporary exceptions, as with the brief fall of Kunduz in the north before its recapture by U.S.-backed Afghan special forces in 2015. By decade's end, the security picture was decidedly mixed. The Afghan government fully controlled only an estimated 54 percent of the nation's 407 districts. Yet because it held the cities, it still controlled territory where some 63 percent of the population resided.[130] The Taliban controlled about a fifth of the country's districts; other areas were contested or in flux.[131]

Despite the expanding presence of ISIS-Khorasan, or ISIS-K, fighters within Afghanistan as the years went by, Trump instructed his negotiators to look for a way out of Afghanistan through negotiations with the Taliban. A deal was reached on February 29, 2020, that promised a U.S. and NATO withdrawal by the spring of the following year. That deal required the Taliban to avoid ties with al Qaeda—a seeming impossibility, given that the al-Qaeda-friendly Haqqani Network was part of Taliban leadership. But Trump as well as his successor, Joe Biden, would choose to overlook that blatant violation of the accord. Trump and Biden also ignored the Taliban's lack of seriousness about negotiating a political power-sharing accord with the Afghan government under President Ashraf Ghani. The Taliban do appear to have complied with their promises not to target foreign troops and not to allow territory they controlled to be used for plotting and preparing terrorist attacks against the United States.[132] Citing these factors, and declaring that the Afghanistan mission had largely achieved its counterterrorist purposes, Joe Biden decided in the spring of 2021 to remove U.S. (and thus all NATO and other foreign) forces by the summer.

After averaging ten to twenty fatalities a year over the previous half dozen years or so, U.S. forces did not suffer another fatality in Afghanistan until the tragic loss of thirteen personnel during the withdrawal operation in August 2021. Before that departure, the financial costs of the war, which in all totaled well over $1 trillion for the United States over the twenty-year time horizon, had been brought down to about $20 billion a year.[133] Troops were the main cost, but munitions expenditures were significant as well; annual totals for 2018 and 2019 each exceeded 7,000 weapons, levels not seen in Afghanistan since the height of the surge.[134]

The fifth phase of the war was quick, and tragic. By this point there was no meaningful U.S. strategy for success in Afghanistan, except to get out as quickly and safely as possible and hope for the best for the Afghan government. After the U.S. and NATO troop withdrawal, Afghan security forces and then the Afghan government collapsed. The process began locally and then quickly snowballed (not unlike how the Taliban fell in the fall of 2001). By mid-August 2021, the Taliban was in control of almost all the country. It was even guaranteeing security, albeit with only partial effectiveness, for the huge U.S. airlift operation that ultimately took more than 100,000 people out of the country. By early September, the Taliban had taken the last holdout of opposition forces in the Panjshir Valley as well—an area it had never controlled during its earlier stint in power. The Taliban then formed a transitional government made up primarily of hard-line elements, making its victory—and America's defeat—just as complete as when North Vietnam conquered South Vietnam in 1975.

Yet in one sense, perhaps not all was lost. The United States and allies had destroyed almost all the al-Qaeda and Taliban leadership such as it was in 2001.

They also demonstrated a willingness to fight a frustrating war in a faraway place for twenty years even when that war never seemed to be going particularly well. That showed a toughness and resoluteness very typical of the American strategic culture since the beginning of the Republic. Americans saw Afghanistan as a defeat, and it surely was. Yet others around the world probably also saw it as a demonstration of the stubbornness, and toughness, of U.S. strategic culture. The sacrifice was not in vain.[135]

MILITARY STRATEGY IN IRAQ FROM 2003

There was much to like in Donald Rumsfeld's war plan for invading Iraq and overthrowing Saddam in 2003. Unfortunately, there is much to criticize as well.

Rumsfeld's plan for a tactically clever and militarily nimble invasion of Iraq had considerable merit. And indeed, through early April 2003, when Saddam fled the capital and organized Iraqi resistance to U.S.-led forces evaporated, it was going well. Rumsfeld's vision for a twenty-first-century military revolution seemed largely correct for a moment. Within weeks, President George W. Bush would give TV audiences around the world his famous "mission accomplished" speech from the deck of an American aircraft carrier adorned with flags and graced by rows of proud American servicemen and servicewomen.

But Rumsfeld had committed the cardinal sin of the strategist: overconfidence. He had fallen in love with his own war plan to the point where he assumed not only that it *might* work but that it *would* work. He claimed a greater confidence and prescience about the future course of events in war than should any student of Carl von Clausewitz—with the Prussian general's metaphor about the fog of war and his reminder that while in war everything is simple, even the simple things are hard—or any student of military history in general. War is full of unexpected twists and turns. To quote another great, the elder German strategist Helmuth von Moltke, no military plan survives first contact with the enemy; the adversary always has a great say in how wars unfold and how they end. Sometimes, the enemy is not defeated even when it appears he has been; sometimes, as in Iraq, he comes back to life in a different (if related) guise. War is usually harder than predicted and almost always different than predicted. Backup plans, contingency capabilities, and mental as well as strategic flexibility are all essential. It is better to prepare for the possibility of a war being harder than expected rather than to assume it will go like clockwork. And when invading another people's country with the intention of even temporarily replacing its government, it is crucial to be humble about the kind of reception one might encounter. The United States ignored all these time-tested verities about war in invading Iraq in 2003; nor did it quickly recognize or recover from its mistakes. Fortunately, it did carry out one of the great military comebacks in its history with the surge of 2007—only to give away much of the headway a half-decade later—and then, to have to fight alongside a new Iraqi government in a whole different manner to deal with a new kind of threat within Iraq starting in 2014.[136]

The American experience in Iraq from 2003 over the next couple decades can be divided roughly into seven phases (and by my count, five clear and distinct military or political-military strategies). First, the shock and awe campaign and slender, sleek, bold invasion of early spring 2003. Then, the gradual descent into mayhem, lasting through 2006 or so. Then, the surge of 2007 into 2008. Next, the U.S. disengagement from Iraq over a three-year time horizon during the Obama administration, through the end of 2011. Then, the repolarization of Iraq under Prime Minister Nouri Maliki, leading to the rise of ISIS; technically, however, this was a period that did not involve the United States in any military sense (that was much of the problem, in fact), so I do not associate it with any clear American strategy. Then, the campaign against ISIS, though this time without a significant U.S. ground-combat presence, culminating in the overthrow of the caliphate in 2019. Finally, in a continuation of the previous strategy but on a lesser scale, continued vigilance against ISIS, and continued vigilance against Iran as well as its ambitions to dominate the Iraqi polity (though this phase appears destined to end soon after the publication of this book, given the agreement for a two-year drawdown reached by Baghdad and Washington in September 2024).

The war was launched in 2003 in the early morning hours of March 20 Iraqi time (still the evening of March 19 in the United States). The timing was influenced by the hope that Saddam might be killed in the war's opening raid, carried out by cruise missiles and F-117 stealth fighters, when coalition forces wrongly thought they knew his whereabouts at a place called Dora Farms in the outskirts of Baghdad.[137] Although Saddam survived, there was, more generally, a hope that a shock and awe attack that involved major air raids throughout Iraq in subsequent days, combined with an unexpectedly early ground invasion, would lead to the rapid collapse of Iraqi security forces. That was more successful. The air raids were aided by the fact that Iraqi air defenses were already in a shambles, after Operation Desert Storm as well as strikes in subsequent years (such as Operation Desert Fox, the four-day bombing campaign in 1998). In addition, a dozen years of U.S. conduct of no-fly-zone operations had produced considerable intelligence on the locations of remaining air defense capabilities and other Iraqi military assets.

About 250,000 U.S. troops were deployed to the broader region for the war effort, two-thirds of them ground forces. Allies provided another 50,000 coalition personnel. Perhaps 165,000 coalition ground forces wound up inside Iraq in the March–April invasion.[138] As powerful as this force was, the U.S. part was only about two-thirds of what had been anticipated in Operational Plan 1003 back in the late 1990s, should an invasion of Iraq ever be undertaken.[139] About 800 coalition fighters and bombers participated (compared with 1,800 in Operation Desert Storm), 90 percent of them American. They flew some 20,000 sorties in all; another 20,000 were flown by tankers as well as airlift and other support aircraft. Some 30,000 bombs were dropped; two-thirds were guided weapons. More than three-fourths of all targets were mobile land forces in various assigned "kill boxes."[140]

Baghdad was the main goal of invasion forces.[141] Most American units went up the main highways. They had to cope with sandstorms, semiregular forces known as Fedayeen Saddam wielding machine guns and rocket-propelled grenades and mortars, and elements of traditional Iraqi military units that sometimes employed tanks, artillery, rockets, and antiaircraft artillery. Nonetheless, the coalition made rapid progress. Its forces seized bridgeheads and other potential choke points quickly to facilitate their movement.[142]

In about two weeks, units reached the outskirts of Baghdad. On April 5, a battalion of the Second Brigade Combat Team of the Third Infantry Division conducted a Thunder Run reconnaissance in force through the main thoroughfares of the Iraqi capital to test defenses in the city. Having found that approach successful, coalition forces followed up with a brigade-sized operation on April 7 into the heart of Baghdad, seizing major governmental buildings quickly.[143] On April 10, Ken Adelman published his *Washington Post* op-ed mentioned at the start of this chapter.[144] Baghdad's main sites were all in U.S. hands. Tikrit, Saddam's hometown to the north, fell on April 14, and the invasion phase of the war was effectively over.[145] President Bush then celebrated the success with the made-for-TV speech on the aircraft carrier on May 1. Alas, by then, storm clouds were already gathering in Iraq, as wholesale looting of major government buildings, stores, factories, and anything else with valuables within created a sense of pandemonium and deprived the future government, whoever might lead it, of many of the resources and assets that would be needed to get the country moving forward.[146]

Then began the second main phase of the war—the great worsening. On May 22, Iraq was placed under a U.N. mandate by a U.S.-led occupation force, with the United Kingdom also formally an occupying power as specified under international law. U.S. Ambassador Paul "Jerry" Bremer became charged with running the country temporarily—and developing a twelve-month transition plan to hand power to a group known as the Iraqi Governing Council.[147] Elections would then ensue for an interim government and, ultimately (after a constitution was approved), a full-term government. Unfortunately, given the absence of proper planning, the United States and partners had to rush to develop an improvised economic and political stabilization plan in the summer and fall of 2003.[148]

The atmosphere in Iraq worsened, and violence began to build, after Bremer banned many former members of Saddam's Baathist Party, a largely Sunni organization, from positions of responsibility in the new government.[149] Bremer also formally disbanded the Iraqi army. Even though that policy was largely reversed a couple months later (at which point many former Iraqi soldiers did join the new army), the initial decision exacerbated Sunni angst and anger. It would be unfair to blame Bremer too much, however. He was given little warning to prepare for the job. Moreover, Iraq was such a broken and polarized and corrupt state by 2003, after so many years of abusive rule by Saddam and his henchmen, that sectarian divisions were bound to be serious, and straightforward solutions to its future politics were likely to prove elusive.[150]

Lest there be any doubt about the absence of a serious plan to stabilize the country, one need only consult the U.S. Army Third Infantry Division's after-action report, which reads: "Higher headquarters did not provide the Third Infantry Division (Mechanized) with a plan for Phase IV. As a result, Third Infantry Division transitioned into Phase IV in the absence of guidance." A broader Department of Defense report on the war similarly observed that "late formation of Department of Defense [Phase IV] organizations limited time available for the development of detailed plans and pre-deployment coordination."[151] What planning did occur focused on issues such as humanitarian relief for the internally displaced population and the possibility that Saddam's loyalists would set oil wells on fire.

By the summer of 2003, the combination of all these factors created a witches' brew of political grievances and ambitions that would produce disaster. The ensuing violence would first be described as the flailing final efforts of "dead enders" and "former regime elements." That led to a strategy of trying to find and arrest or kill them; a "deck of cards" with names and faces of fifty-plus key individuals was mass produced and widely circulated to aid in the search. Soon, however, it would become clear that a powerful insurgency was emerging. In mid-July, the new commander at Central Command, General John Abizaid, became the first American official to describe the resistance as a guerrilla-style insurgency, and others joined in his assessment in the months to come.[152] Terrible large-scale battles in Fallujah and Ramadi in the spring of 2004 ended any real hope that Iraq would soon become peaceful, and vividly displayed the risks for U.S. personnel. That was not the extent of it, however; a civil war was starting to rage, as extremist actors increasingly organized along sectarian lines.[153] The insurgency was countered with Bremer's plan to get coalition forces out of Iraq within a year, but by then it was too late for such a move to quell the violence, as the sectarian civil war was underway.

Not all was glum. In the north, under General Petraeus and Colonel H. R. McMaster, some early efforts at counterinsurgency strategy, building on historical models from Malaya to the Philippines, were attempted. Petraeus and McMaster, foreshadowing methods that they and others would employ later in the war, emphasized inclusive governance and economic opportunity, plus extensive patrolling and an emphasis on population security. But this kind of counterinsurgency was not all sweetness and light. Saddam's sons were ultimately tracked down and killed in Mosul in that same time frame. (Saddam himself was found and arrested in a region near his hometown of Tikrit in December, jailed for three years, and ultimately hanged at the end of 2006 after an Iraqi court found him guilty of multiple capital offenses.)

Fewer than 150 Americans died in the overthrow of Saddam's regime. But by the end of 2003, nearly 500 had died in the Iraq mission. At least 800 Americans a year would then perish in Iraq over the next four years before U.S. fatalities would start to decline, and dramatically at that, in 2008 and thereafter.[154]

In addition to hoping that a rapid end to the occupation and a series of elections could defuse the violence, the United States hoped that a much-improved—or at least better trained and equipped—Iraqi security force could stabilize the country. If the American train-and-equip program were sufficiently well resourced and rigorous, there might be the possibility of a handoff in security responsibilities by 2006 or so to complement the handoff of political control that had occurred in 2004. But making Iraqi soldiers and police better marksmen with more tactical skills could not change the fact that their leadership was often corrupt and incompetent. Making security forces stronger also had the effect of giving them more means to abuse the population as well as their political enemies—and therefore often worsened the sectarian divide and accelerated the civil war.[155]

The mastermind al-Qaeda terrorist Abu Musab al-Zarqawi was tracked by special forces under General Stanley McChrystal and killed by an airstrike in

June 2006. Much of the violence al Qaeda perpetrated in Iraq was against Iraqis, done with the intent of provoking retribution and thereby worsening the sectarian conflict. But even with Zarqawi's killing, the cycle of retaliatory violence had reached such a self-perpetuating and terrible level of intensity that his absence did little to improve the situation.[156]

In the course of 2006, President Bush asked his advisers for fresh thinking about political and military strategies for Iraq.[157] National security adviser Stephen Hadley, with the help of aides including Meghan O'Sullivan and William Luti, as well as outside advisers such as Frederick Kagan of the American Enterprise Institute and Kenneth Pollack of the Brookings Institution and Stephen Biddle of the Council on Foreign Relations, as well as retired General Jack Keane, tried to mine history for ideas.[158] Petraeus was asked to succeed General George Casey as the top coalition general in Iraq; he took the helm in February 2007, a month after Bush, with support of his new secretary of defense, Robert Gates, had announced the new strategy. It was not all about force levels by any stretch of the imagination. The new COIN strategy emphasized dispersal of foreign and Iraqi forces into many more small "combat outposts" and "joint security stations," patrolling on foot, seeking as a top priority to protect the civilian population, and gaining intelligence from that population about the identities and whereabouts of threatening actors. Unmanned aerial vehicles and aerostats were employed to improve the intelligence picture of the battlefield. Jersey walls were erected to complicate the job of car bombers, protecting buildings, markets, and other sites where people congregated.

Reconciliation with those actors who may have previously been violent adversaries, but were willing to turn over a new leaf, also became crucial—for example, in Sunni-dominant Anbar Province. Many tribal loyalists in Anbar joined an Awakening movement, patrolling their neighborhoods and keeping al-Qaeda fighters at bay. This concept was institutionalized in Anbar Province and elsewhere through the Sons of Iraq program, by which tribal fighters were paid government stipends to participate.[159] The new strategy included a "civilian surge" as well, with many more development specialists embedded with military forces, even in dangerous forward locations, to try to jumpstart economic activity. The overall philosophy was described as "clear, hold, build."[160]

General McChrystal continued the special-forces efforts to pursue high-value leadership targets.[161] McChrystal emphasized the creation of a "team of teams" that prioritized the sharing of information across bureaucratic barriers. That approach in the field built on the integration happening stateside as a result of the Intelligence Reform and Terrorism Prevention Act of 2004 and its creation of the Office of the Director of National Intelligence as well as the National Counterterrorism Center.[162] This improved intelligence in turn allowed for more effective and frequent raids. A virtuous cycle resulted: captured suspects were often interrogated on the helicopter flight back to a detention facility, and information they provided could be used in real time to allow prompt follow-on action against their associates.[163]

The surge added more than five brigades—about 30,000 soldiers and Marines, including support, all told—to the existing U.S. presence. U.S. troop tallies increased from 140,000 at the end of 2006 to 170,000 by the autumn of 2007. There were a comparable number of contractors working in direct support of U.S. forces, some American but most not.[164] Iraqi forces grew even faster, from roughly 323,000 in all at the start of 2007 to about 440,000 by year's end.[165] More importantly, for the first time, they started to get much better. American military leaders and Ambassador Ryan Crocker managed to persuade Iraqi prime minister Nouri al-Maliki to replace many sectarian, corrupt, or incompetent Iraqi military and police leaders.[166]

The surge also included conventional military operations to search and clear areas that had become sanctuaries for extremist groups. A three-phase campaign plan was initiated in 2007. It began with a strengthening of coalition positions within Baghdad. Starting in June, attacks were then launched against extremist strongholds, weapons caches, and truck-bomb factories in the Baghdad belts in what was called Phantom Thunder. Then, additional operations to deprive remaining al-Qaeda or militia elements of other sanctuaries were undertaken in Phantom Strike.[167] Key cities such as Fallujah and Ramadi, as well as Mosul, were also targeted.

The net effect of all of these changes was remarkable, amounting to one of the greatest turnarounds in U.S. military history. After a period of several months in which casualty levels worsened during the most trying clearing operations, violence levels began to drop dramatically. Civilian fatalities dropped by half, then by 75 percent, then in 2008 by more like 90 percent relative to the horrendous levels of 2004 through 2006.

To be sure, there were ups and downs. Prime Minister Maliki, in the spring of 2008, impulsively ordered a "charge of the knights" to retake the southern city of Basra from Shia militias without coordination with Petraeus and other American officials. Disaster almost ensued. But in the end the militias were weakened. And at least Maliki had shown that he was willing to employ Iraqi security forces against his fellow Shia when necessary, however reckless his approach.

Then the United States entered its next major phase of the war (the fourth out of seven proposed before): the Obama drawdown and departure. In fact, the drawdown had begun under Bush and was a logical consequence of the success of the surge, but Obama would speed it up—even if he went slower than initially promised on the campaign trail. Rather than get out in 2010, he took three years to leave (after formally ending the American-led combat mission in 2009). Regrettably, however, the United States wound up supporting Prime Minister Maliki's efforts to hold onto power after the Iraqi elections of early 2010. Washington did so even though Maliki had attempted, before the elections, to push many Sunni candidates off the ballots in an act of fairly brazen sectarianism. For Washington, it was easier to stick with the devil we knew than take a chance on a relative unknown. That was almost surely a mistake. The United States would have been much better served to support—or at least not oppose—the less-sectarian Shia leader Ayad Allawi, whose political party included many non-Shia as well. Allawi had actually outpolled Maliki and deserved first shot at forming a government.[168]

Compounding the mistakes, President Obama then chose to push the Iraqi government to decide whether it really still wanted American help or not. With a previous agreement governing the status of American forces in Iraq soon to expire, Obama insisted on a clear invitation from the Iraqi parliament for U.S. forces to stay and a new framework that would formally shield American troops from any possibility of trial within the Iraqi legal system. Obama could, for example, have accepted an extension of the previous status of forces agreement, but he chose not to. Alas, Iraq's parliament refused to grant the formal immunity by law, and American forces departed Iraq by the end of 2011.[169]

Catastrophe was the result. An unbound Maliki sought to arrest many Sunni politicians on trumped-up charges for corruption and such purported offenses, including a number known for having impeccable credentials. He deposed Vice President Tareq al-Hashemi and leveled terrorism charges against the well-regarded finance minister, Rafi al-Issawi, forcing Issawi to flee the capital for safer areas in Anbar Province. Political sectarianism was reinforced by economic and financial nepotism.[170] Maliki also reversed much of the progress made with his army and police during the surge, dismissing competent commanders and often replacing them with the very people whom Dave Petraeus, Ray Odierno, Lloyd Austin, Ryan Crocker, and others had worked so hard to have replaced several years before. The fledgling partially independent judiciary that had been starting to develop in Iraq was a casualty as well.[171]

That led to what scholar Will McCants calls the "ISIS apocalypse." The Islamic State in Iraq and Syria (or al-Sham) was also sometimes instead called ISIL, for the Islamic State in Iraq and the Levant. Either way, it was a group that had broken off from al Qaeda in Mesopotamia-Iraq due to personality and ideological disputes. It favored the near-term creation of a transnational caliphate and made great progress toward achieving that very goal through much of Syria and northern Iraq in 2014 in particular.[172] Videotaped beheadings, mass executions of prisoners (including soldiers who surrendered), and other atrocities were part of its modus operandi—to glorify its methods and thereby gain more recruits, as well as to terrify any groups or armies that might think about standing in its path. As it conquered territory, ISIS gained access to banks, oil fields, and populations from which it could earn more funds through extortion and kidnapping. Adept at social media, it drew followers from more than 100 countries around the world. One-fourth to one-third of both Syria and Iraq fell under its control, with nearly 10 million souls forced to live under its brutal governance.[173]

The United States was caught off guard by the rise of ISIS, but it reacted reasonably well. As ISIS threatened to take cities in Iraqi (and Syrian) Kurdistan as well as Baghdad, the United States settled on a strategy of providing American airpower to help fend off ISIS when the threat was acute. At the same time, by necessity, Washington chose to tolerate the role of Iranian-sponsored militias who also fought ISIS in what amounted to a virtual coalition among the Iraqi, Iranian, and American governments. Then, the United States sought successfully to help push Prime Minister Maliki out of power in Baghdad and began work with his successor, Haider al-Abadi, to rebuild the Iraqi army and police. Although ISIS units approached within some thirty miles of Baghdad, they were fended off in 2014. The rebuilding of Iraqi security forces took time, yet it would prove successful when supported by American intelligence and airpower and special forces.[174] With this strategy, the United States was able to limit its footprint on the ground to about 5,000 troops in Iraq and 2,000 in Syria. By 2018, the coalition was able to defeat the caliphate. As a coup de grâce, its leader, Abu Bakr al-Baghdadi, was found, targeted, and killed in October 2019 under President Trump.[175]

During the war, the United States used some 70,000 precision weapons—a hefty number—out of more than 115,000 munitions employed. Some 200,000 American military sorties were flown (including tanker and reconnaissance flights). But only some $20 billion was spent on the effort, far less than in Operation Desert Storm or Iraqi Freedom.[176]

FORMAL DEFENSE PLANNING DURING THE WAR ON TERROR

Beyond what happened in the big wars themselves, as well as the broader counterterrorism effort, much about U.S. defense planning, strategy, and budgeting stayed fairly steady from 2001 through 2014.

Of course, there was innovation. A great deal of effort went into improving the tools of counterterrorism, including a wide range of military, intelligence, economic, law enforcement, foreign assistance, and diplomatic instruments of statecraft.[177] But the basic priorities, forces, modernization agendas, postures, and purposes of the American armed forces were not fundamentally reconceptualized. Special forces and intelligence capabilities, along with uninhabited aerial vehicles and certain other specific weapons, were improved and expanded. But main combat forces remained largely as they had been before, albeit with much greater emphasis on training and operations in counterinsurgency than on classic maneuver warfare. The geographic focus of U.S. military operations focused on the broader Middle East, reinforcing a trend that had been underway for at least a decade or so already.[178]

In some ways, 9/11 led to bigger changes in other parts of the government. The Department of Homeland Security was created; many of its constituent agencies' combined budgets were tripled or quadrupled relative to previous expenditures. The Office of the Director of National Intelligence was also established, providing an overarching official to supervise the intelligence community and its eighteen different organizations; the National Counterterrorism Center was created as well. Watchlists and travel-ban lists and other means of tracking known terrorists were interlinked nationally and internationally, as were the bank accounts and other assets of suspected extremists, and the Department of the Treasury became much better at finding and seizing illicit assets. The New York Police Department devoted hundreds of officers to counterterrorism; other cities made more modest but noteworthy efforts as well. Iconic buildings and landmarks received greater perimeter defense; airport security was tightened substantially, as the Transportation Security Administration was created; inspections of containers at ports of entry became more frequent and sophisticated as well.[179]

The Defense Department's role in homeland security remained very much a support function, as the nation's traditions and laws would rightly suggest that it should. Northern Command was created in 2003 to improve the military element of any response to natural disasters as well as terrorist attacks and other violent threats to the homeland. But there was no flood of new resources to support its new role or purposes.

The size and relative composition of the military force structure barely budged. As the Iraq War settled into a slog, the Bush administration pushed numbers up modestly from the force of 1.4 million it had inherited from the Clinton administration. But the differences were very modest; the military grew to about 1.43 million active-duty personnel by 2009–10 before gentle reductions resumed. Active-duty Army end-strength, not counting full-time members of the reserve component, grew temporarily by as much as 85,000 soldiers during the Bush presidency, and the Marine Corps grew by 30,000 active-duty personnel. But Air Force and Navy totals continued to drop. By early in President Obama's second term, the increases in the Army and Marine Corps would be reversed as well. The military would plateau at a total size similar to today's force of 1.3 million active-duty personnel (not counting several tens of thousands of full-time uniformed members of the country's reserve components). That was actually modestly *smaller* than the Clinton-era force.[180]

The Quadrennial Defense Reviews of 2006, 2010, and 2014 made modest changes to formal doctrine and defense strategy, as did the Defense Planning Guidance document of 2012. Ironically, even as the nation did fight two wars at once in real time, its doctrinal commitment to a two-war framework for force design gradually faded. The QDR of 2001 had introduced the concept of 1-4-2-1, meaning the United States needed a military that could protect the homeland, maintain credible and functional presence in four separate overseas theaters, and fight two wars at once with one of them possibly a regime-change operation (and also be able to handle smaller military contingencies).[181] However, those two wars were no longer imagined as repeats of Desert Storm; semantics and analysis shifted from "threat-based planning" with its focus on specific potential adversaries and scenarios to a more general "capabilities-based planning."[182] Planners in the 1990s assumed that the Army and Marine Corps together might send fifteen to twenty brigades to a *single* conflict, meaning thirty to forty for two—essentially equal to the nation's total supply of active-duty force structure through this period. In fact, at the peak of the Iraq and Afghanistan overlapping efforts, the United States never sent more than twenty-two brigades to the two wars combined yet still found the demands on force structure excessive.[183] It was for this reason, in fact, that the service chiefs were generally unenthusiastic about the surge in Iraq, as they sought to protect readiness standards for other possible wars and avoid "breaking the force."[184] The Army National Guard became, in effect, an operational reserve for the active Army, as its combat brigades were needed to spell those in the active-duty force—whatever the theoretical or doctrinal preference might have been to keep the guard as a strategic reserve for other possible contingencies.[185]

By 2014, under Secretary of Defense Chuck Hagel at the Pentagon, and building on the Defense Planning Guidance issued by Secretary of Defense Leon Panetta in 2012, the United States determined that it would no longer size forces for large-scale counterinsurgency or stabilization missions. The immediate implications of this decision were modest, even for the Army, because Army force structure had not changed much since the 1990s whether the nation was explicitly preparing for stabilization missions or not. But with that document in 2012, the Pentagon signaled that any large cuts it might need to make to comply with the provisions of the Budget Control Act of 2011 for possible "sequestration" of discretionary budget accounts would likely come from the Army. That would reduce its capacity for large-scale and prolonged overseas operations of most any type, along with its capacity to engage in two substantial conflicts at once.[186] As it turned out, budgetary compromises were reached and large-scale defense budget cuts were averted, so the strategic objective of opting out of future big COIN and stabilization missions remained a theoretical debate more than a decision with major practical implications. As the Iraq and then Afghanistan missions wound down, fewer Army (and Marine) units were training intensively for these kinds of operations, so in that sense there was a change in strategy. But the change was not dramatic, and it was more backward-looking than futuristic; it essentially meant that the nation's ground-combat units would again train much as they had during the 1980s and the 1990s.[187]

In this period, the United States chose to develop and deploy a limited national missile defense system, mostly directed against the gradually forming if still hypothetical North Korean threat to North America. But it chose to deploy only some forty-four interceptors during the Bush and Obama administrations—and did not deploy any other long-range missile defense systems. It did continue to develop and improve tactical and theater-range systems, including the Patriot and Navy Theater Wide/Aegis and Army THAAD (terminal high altitude area defense) systems. As the Ukraine War, as well as the defense of Israel against a massive Iranian attack in April 2024 showed, these systems have become much more capable over the years, though far from airtight or perfect.[188]

The notion of an ongoing revolution in military affairs remained part of the strategic and military dialogues throughout this period. Various hortatory concepts, such as "net-centric warfare" and "Joint Vision 2010" as well as subsequent versions of the doctrine, were articulated. However, some of the earlier enthusiasm around the RMA vision was lost as the nation found it difficult even to win low-tech wars against relatively unsophisticated opponents. Moreover, as the period neared its end, the strategic community began to worry that the United States had created dependencies and vulnerabilities—on exquisite intelligence and communications systems involving satellites that the Taliban and Saddam could not threaten but that China or Russia might, on big bases and aircraft carriers that could be hit by precision missiles (conventional or nuclear), on software systems that were vulnerable to infiltration and sabotage, on logistics systems centered on highly vulnerable ports and airfields as well as big and easily detectable ships and planes.[189]

For all the RMA talk, however, the actual action concerning military modernization and innovation was relatively quiet throughout most of this period. Top leaders were busy fighting the wars right in front of them, rather than planning for possible future conflicts. As such, acquisition priorities for the military centered on technologies such as jammers, aerial drones, and mine-resistant ambush-protected vehicles (MRAPs) designed to absorb a land-mine hit while protecting the crew inside. Most MRAPs, however, were retired after the big wars were over. That was emblematic of the times; what innovation did take place was in many cases modest and even temporary.[190]

The Air Force tried to make bigger changes, in ways that foreshadowed much of what has been happening over the past ten years, with a focus on space as well as stealthier high-performance combat aircraft. Alas, it was taken to the woodshed by Secretary Gates in part for its focus on the future, since in his eyes it was not focused enough on the current fight. There were other reasons that Gates fired the secretary of the Air Force and its chief of staff, but the divergence in strategic priorities was part of the rationale.[191]

Other changes were notable more for their modesty, and temporary duration, than for lasting strategic significance. Of the Army's two brigades normally deployed in Korea until 2001 (the normal state of affairs ever since reductions in U.S. force structure in Korea in the 1970s), one was brought into the force rotation base for operations in Iraq and Afghanistan and never returned to Korea. But by that point, South Korea's army had certainly become one of the ten best in the world, so this change did not seem so risky. This change was a central feature of the Bush administration's Integrated Global Presence and Basing Strategy of 2004. Other chief elements included moving thousands of Marines from Okinawa, Japan, to Guam, establishing a number of Cooperative Security Locations in Africa, and slimming down America's overall military presence in Europe while reorienting some of America's remaining presence there away from Germany and, at least on a rotational basis, to some of NATO's newer members.[192] But the Defense Department was mostly reallocating troops by the hundreds here and thousands there—not the tens of thousands or more.

There were bigger changes in the Central Command–Middle East theater over the first decade and a half of the century—but most were temporary. Operation Desert Storm and the invasions of Afghanistan and Iraq led to development of major logistical and operational bases in the broader Persian Gulf region, most notably in Kuwait, Bahrain, and Qatar as well as Iraq and Afghanistan themselves. Big bases in Saudi Arabia were developed for a while, but U.S. forces mostly left after 2003. Small numbers of American troops also operated within Syria after that country's civil war began in 2011. Bases in Turkey and Djibouti, smaller numbers of troops in Jordan and the United Arab Emirates and Egypt, and limited U.S. presence in Somalia as well as Syria largely rounded out the regional picture. Complemented by naval assets in the Mediterranean, Gulf of Aden, Persian Gulf, and Indian Ocean, this constellation of capabilities made for a diverse and widespread overall U.S. military posture in the greater Central Command region.[193]

Many of these facilities helped in the conduct of counterterrorism operations throughout the broader Middle East during the war-on-terror period (and beyond). Some, plus others in Europe, also provided the launching points for U.S. and NATO attacks on Libya in 2011. Undertaken partly in a desire to uphold the "responsibility to protect" concept, they wound up also resulting in the overthrow and killing of Muammar Gaddafi there. Unfortunately, chaos ensued.[194]

CONCLUSION

The period from 1990 through 2014 was a busy quarter century in American national security policy. Two big wars were fought—three, if Operation Desert Storm is counted separately. A cataclysmic event in the history of the nation on September 11, 2001, changed the world for a while. Yet some aspects of U.S. defense strategy endured. Throughout the period, the United States was focused on so-called rogue states or regional enemies in its force planning; throughout, it tended to think of two overlapping regional wars as the correct scenario for sizing its forces, and it actually did fight two at once for nearly a decade. It also tried to profit from the dot-com revolutions and precision-strike revolutions, as some called them. Yet the changes in the U.S. military from Vietnam to Desert Storm were arguably more dramatic and important than those over the next quarter century or so. Moreover, U.S. military force structure and global posture were not that different at the end of this period than they had been at the beginning.

On the personnel side, however, one big thing had certainly changed by the conclusion of this period: the nation had fought major wars with women, at and near the front lines in substantial numbers. That said, women represent only about 18 percent of America's military today, and there remain serious gender issues within the armed forces as in all of society.[195]

Another noteworthy change: to reinforce civilian control of the military, Secretary Rumsfeld directed in 2002 that leaders of unified combatant command no longer be known as "commanders in chief" and instead be described as "combatant commanders."[196] This was a useful corrective. Also of interest was the fact that both Jim Mattis and Lloyd Austin required wavers from a law, included in the National Defense Authorization Act of 2008, requiring an individual to wait seven years after military retirement before serving as secretary of defense.[197] Yet both served admirably, with few arguing that their tenures led to any discernible weakening of civilian control of the military.

The United States continued to succeed in its grand strategy of protecting and promoting a democratic, peaceful, market-based, and rules-based international order over this quarter century. Over the twenty-five years, most of Europe cohered into a democratic and prosperous bloc, East Asia continued to grow, and the big countries of South Asia became more peaceful and prosperous. The Middle East continued to struggle, and Africa as well as Latin America made only gradual forward progress on overall economics and governance. But the world approached a milestone with fully half of its population reaching what economist Homi Kharas calculated as a middle-class level of well-being, and great power war continued to be avoided on planet Earth.[198]

Yet America's track record in actual combat remained mediocre. The period started with a quick win in Panama followed by Operation Desert Storm but was dominated by difficult wars in Iraq and Afghanistan. Its "peacetime" defense strategies did well at helping keep great power peace. They were less stellar in preparing the country for the wars it would wind up fighting.

CHAPTER VII

Defense Planning in the New Era of Great Power Rivalry

After a quarter century of what political columnist Charles Krauthammer called the unipolar moment, the United States was tired. Far from reveling in its supposedly exclusive claim to superpowerdom, America was spent by terrorism, wars in the Middle East, financial crises, and growing polarization at home. The middle-class dream seemed elusive to many; the post–World War II consensus in favor of internationalism was fraying. The election of Donald Trump to the presidency in 2016 would soon make these realities palpable, if there were still any real doubt.

But tougher things awaited, most of all Russia's revanchism and China's rise. The United States would no longer have the luxury of focusing only on smaller and weaker threats; meanwhile, rapid technological change made the future of warfare, especially against well-resourced and technologically formidable potential foes, highly uncertain.

Still, the nation retained considerable strengths. One of particular note was its strong tradition of civilian control of the military that made it relatively easy politically for first retired general James Mattis, then in a few years retired general Lloyd Austin (with retired colonel Mark Esper serving in between), to become civilian secretaries of defense and guide the Pentagon through a remarkably collaborative and bipartisan stretch of American military reinvention. Austin's team publicly stated how much the Biden administration's vision for defense reform and innovation owed its main ideas to Mattis (who had perhaps borrowed a few from Barack Obama's last secretary of defense, the physicist Ash Carter). In a period of remarkable turmoil at home and abroad, this American strategic community displayed cohesion, conviction, and at least some capacity for fresh thinking in the American Department of Defense.

By 2015, one can surely say, the post–Cold War era was over. That was not simply because the world was changing; after all, it had already changed fundamentally on September 11, 2001. What was different this time was that, just as during the Cold War and the world wars, great power rivalry would define the geopolitics of the day. That era continues. It surely will remain at least until Vladimir Putin and Putinism exit the Kremlin and the United States and China find a way to stabilize their superpower-to-superpower relationship.

DEFINING THE ERA AND ITS GRAND STRATEGY

The United States of the past decade has not been quite the same actor on the world stage as in previous decades. The legacy of the "forever wars," gnawing doubts about the future of the middle-class dream in America given economic and industrial trends, and growing concerns about a rising China as well as a reassertive Russia, led to considerable change in the politics of foreign policy. The election of Donald Trump as president not once but twice was but one notable manifestation of these trends; in fact, they have affected both parties.[1]

Although there were clearly enormous differences between the security strategies of the latter Obama as well as the Trump and Biden years, with Trump far more critical of alliances and trade agreements, elements of continuity have persisted. Obama, first-term Trump, and Biden all continued to attempt to focus more on the Asia-Pacific region; all struggled to do so. None wanted to prioritize the Middle East, yet all had to deal with the ISIS challenge while keeping vigilance and eyes on Iran. All three American leaders had to worry more about Russia than had any U.S. president since Ronald Reagan, even if it was only under Biden that the threat became acute, in the form of Russia's all-out attack on Ukraine in February 2022. All three had to face a more assertive, confident, and autocratic China, as the U.S. consensus in favor of engaging China that dated back to the Kissinger and Nixon opening of 1971–72 first wavered and then dissolved in bipartisan fashion. Trump's approach to Beijing represented the most dramatic change. But what is most striking, again, is the continuity—with Biden continuing the greater U.S. military emphasis on what was now called the Indo-Pacific and also keeping many of Trump's tariffs and technology-transfer restrictions.

Not all was the same, of course. Biden's emphasis on alliances and partnerships, particularly in the Indo-Pacific in the form of the Quad (with India, Japan, and Australia) and the AUKUS (Australia, United Kingdom, and United States) submarine and technology pact, as well as tightening and interlocking of relationships with Japan, Korea, and the Philippines, were distinctive. Biden also did much to repair the workings of the NATO alliance and wielded it successfully in pushing back against Russia's assault on Ukraine. But Biden's prioritization of China, and policy pushback against Beijing, followed what had become a strong decade-long tradition.[2] The growing collaborations with India had their bipartisan roots in policies dating back a quarter century.[3]

During the first Trump and Biden presidencies, the United States refined several economic instruments of national security policy to serve its evolving grand strategy—applying economic sanctions in a more targeted and effective way against not only Iran and North Korea but Russia, developing better export controls, maintaining more vigilant protection of American crown technological jewels, paying greater attention to building resilient supply chains, and making the country (gradually) more self-sufficient in key commodities and technologies.[4]

The grand strategy of this last decade of American foreign policy resembles in some ways that of the Cold War more than that of the 1990–2014 era. Now, even if containment is not the watchword for dealing with Russia and China, and even if we are not in another Cold War, geopolitics and great power relations have definitely taken a turn for the worse.[5]

The Biden administration tried to capture this new era's approach to China with various slogans and concepts. It began in March 2021, when in a major foreign policy speech Secretary of State Antony Blinken said, "Our relationship with China will be competitive when it should be, collaborative when it can be, and adversarial when it must be."[6] Blinken modified that slogan to "align, invest, and compete" the following year.[7] But since the latter slogan needs to be explained to be understood (aligning is what the United States does with its allies, in order to invest in the capabilities needed to compete all together against China), it seems unlikely to endure. The huge question now under Trump is whether U.S. grand strategy can still be described as a continuation of post-1945 foreign policy—promotion and protection of a democratic, peaceful, market-based, rules-based community of nations—combined with a new emphasis on great power rivalry.

Even though I have dated this era to roughly 2015, its actual beginning cannot be precisely specified. No single date such as December 7, September 11, or

November 9 (the day the Berlin Wall fell in 1989) heralded the arrival of the new era; there was no battle of Lexington or Concord or Manassas. Already in 2008, Russia had invaded Georgia, telegraphing that relations between Russia and the West were no longer going to be smooth. By this time, scholars such as Princeton University's Aaron Friedberg were warning about China's rise and the likelihood of a much tougher future relationship with the PRC. In 2010 and 2011, the Obama administration was talking about a pivot or rebalance to Asia, including decisions to reposition modestly some U.S. military assets. In 2012, presidential candidate Mitt Romney was presciently warning about the dangers of a Russia again run by Vladimir Putin (after Putin had spent four years as prime minister during the presidency of Dmitry Medvedev). By 2012 and 2013, Xi Jinping, with his greater ambitions, was establishing his hold on power in Beijing; in 2013, China provocatively declared an Air Defense Identification Zone in international waters in the East China Sea and made its decision to build military infrastructure on islands in the South China Sea.[8]

Yet it still seems reasonable to conclude that, as 2014 unfolded and surely by 2015, we were indeed in the new period. By the end of 2014, ISIS's march through Syria and Iraq had been halted, even if not yet rolled back. Meanwhile, Vladimir Putin, back in the Kremlin since 2012, initiated a series of military reforms and modernization projects that were well underway by 2014–15.[9] Russia stole Crimea from Ukraine in early 2014 and began to foment separatist violence in the Donbas region of eastern Ukraine, with Putin's lackeys shooting down a Malaysian passenger jet in the process in July.[10] That same year, the United States expressed concerns that Russia was violating the INF Treaty; arms control efforts in general, and certainly the aspirations of some for a "Global Zero" general nuclear abolition, were increasingly in serious doubt.[11] Russia would then intervene in Syria's civil war in support of President Bashar al-Assad in 2015. After having decided on the plan in late 2013, China made major progress between 2014 and 2017 on its main construction projects on seven separate land features in the South China Sea and increasingly prioritized aircraft carrier construction, with an eye toward power projection.[12]

DEFENSE STRATEGY IN THE ERA OF GREAT POWER RIVALRY

Chuck Hagel finished his stint running the Pentagon and was replaced in early 2015 by the technically and scientifically sophisticated Ash Carter, who as secretary of defense was more inclined to think about great power rivalry than had any of his twenty-first-century predecessors. General Joseph Dunford and General Paul Selva took over the chairman and vice chairman jobs at the Department of Defense. The team coined the phrase "4+1" to emphasize that going forward, the United States Department of Defense would not be riveted just on the threats of rogue states and terrorists but on five dangers: Russia, China, North Korea, Iran, and transnational violent extremists. There was also a growing awareness that conflict against one of the larger powers might not be confined to the region within which it began.[13]

Deputy Secretary of Defense Robert Work emphasized the idea that the United States should employ a "third offset strategy" to handle the new security environment—using technology and innovation to address the growing threats from powerful yet relatively less advanced rivals. At that point, in 2015, China had not yet quite caught up to the United States in many areas of science and technology to the extent that it has today. In this way, the United States could in theory mimic what it had done with its "first offset" of nuclear weapons superiority against huge Soviet armies in Europe in the early Cold War era and its "second offset" of precision-strike technologies with the AirLand Battle concept developed for Europe toward the end of the Cold War (and employed against Iraq in 1991). The third offset could be at least a partial response to China's (and Russia's) growing capabilities in antiaccess and area-denial weaponry—increasingly serious concerns for a country such as the United States that still depended on large, fixed bases and large, slow transport assets to project power globally.[14] A concept called AirSea Battle became popular with the Navy and Air Force. While framed as a global shift, it surely had its greatest catalyst in the rise of China. It emphasized early attacks on enemy offensive weapons and command, control, communications, and reconnaissance systems, as well as more use of dispersal and hardening and redundancy in American bases, logistics assets, and command and control systems, to achieve war-winning effects.[15]

The Army, in cahoots with the Air Force, would soon develop a broad concept called Multi-Domain Operations to address the complexities of the modern battlefield including cyberspace and outer space. A slightly tighter and more focused concept called Joint All-Domain Command and Control (later further modified by the term *Combined* at the beginning to underscore allied involvement as well) focused on the command, control, and communications challenges of modern warfare in a period when rivals could be expected to target American and allied operations in these realms.[16]

President Obama's rhetoric, and foreign policy instincts, meant that there was no dramatic restatement of American grand strategy from the White House in the final two years of his presidency.[17] Nonetheless, taken all together, these developments at the Department of Defense initiated a major change in U.S. defense strategy.

The full refinement, and full-throated articulation, of the changes in both American grand strategy and defense strategy would happen in the Trump administration, with the release of the H. R. McMaster–directed National Security Strategy of late 2017 as well as the Jim Mattis–directed National Defense Strategy of early 2018.[18] President Trump may not have fully engaged on this strategic shift, but he blessed much of what his national security adviser and secretary of defense wanted to do with these landmark national security documents.[19] They would have a major legacy, as it turned out—and their main ideas would survive into the Biden administration with much more continuity than one might have expected given the sharp political differences between Trump and Biden.

Mattis's National Defense Strategy of 2018 focused on the importance of taking on both Russia and China. He also emphasized the paramount priority that must be given to improving U.S. military lethality. Mattis did not propose an expansion of the force; the size and relative composition of the American armed forces have remained remarkably constant over the past thirty years (again, with only a limited and temporary buildup of the Army during the 2000s as the main exception to this generalization). As such, under the Mattis plan, the United States stated that it would seek the capacity to defeat either Russia or China but not both at the same time. The two-war paradigm that had dominated American defense planning for decades was largely gone. Mattis sought to improve military readiness but even more to hasten modernization across numerous areas of defense technology, many of them pertaining to offensive operations—such as hypersonic weapons, robotics, nuclear weapons, attack submarines, fighter jets, and stealth bombers. He called for annual real-dollar increases in defense spending of 3 to 5 percent a year to demonstrate American commitment to competing with Moscow and Beijing and resource the planned investments, saying that the nation "can afford survival." Defensive weapons such as missile defense systems were also emphasized; so were more resilient satellite constellations and computer networks.[20]

Four years later, the Pentagon under Lloyd Austin would retain almost all of these priorities. Its National Defense Strategy of 2022 would prioritize China, describing it as the "pacing challenge." Russia was recognized as the "acute threat," given its aggression against Ukraine. Austin also emphasized resilience and survivability, to go along with lethality; yet in programmatic terms, the same range of new systems was effectively still on the Pentagon's shopping list. The main difference in defense strategy between Trump and Biden, or Mattis and Austin, probably was in the realm of military resources—in addition, of course, to the fact that Biden had to address the greatest conflict on European soil since World War II, when Putin's Russia invaded Ukraine in February 2022, as discussed further below. In budgetary terms, during the Trump presidency real-dollar defense budgets increased about 3 percent a year, with the 115th and 116th Congresses; Biden as well as the 117th and 118th Congresses kept inflation-adjusted budgets more or less flat (though at that higher level achieved by Trump).[21] Some of the key architects of the Mattis National Defense Strategy have expressed concern that, with all the modernization priorities laid out in that plan and its successor, budgetary resources have not been adequate to the task, so in that sense, there is not complete continuity from the 2018 strategy to the 2022 plan to today.[22]

The composition of the budgets changed, too, relative to earlier eras. There has been more of an emphasis on developing new technology of late. During the Clinton years, funding for RDT&E (research, development, testing, and evaluation) was typically about $65 billion a year, out of a defense budget typically around $525 to $550 billion (in 2025 dollars). During the George W. Bush years the RDT&E budget rose to the ballpark of $115 billion, out of a far larger defense budget that ranged roughly from $800 billion to just under $1 trillion. The RDT&E figure came down to about $85 billion annually by the end of the Obama presidency, as overall defense budgets declined to about $800 billion. Then, with the Mattis and Austin National Defense Strategies, RDT&E shot up quickly to around $120 billion and then kept climbing, with typical levels in the Biden years around $140 billion, reflecting a greater emphasis on modernization and innovation. Indeed, the majority of the resources added to the defense budget between 2017 and 2024–25 are located within the RDT&E budget. (Put differently, during the Clinton budgets of FY 1994 through 2001, RDT&E averaged just over 12 percent of the defense budget; during the Bush years, the figure grew to almost 13 percent; during the Trump years it increased to almost 15 percent; by the end of Biden's presidency, it exceeded 16 percent of the Department of Defense budget.)[23]

There were a few other distinctions between the two administrations and their respective defense strategies, as well as their nuclear posture reviews and missile defense plans. (There were also reviews on Arctic strategy, Indo-Pacific strategy, industrial base strategy, cyber strategy, and other specific subjects done by one or both administrations that, while important in their own realms, do not necessarily reach a comparable level of enduring national security significance.) For example, Mattis and Trump proposed two new types of nuclear warheads; Austin decided that one was enough. Mattis and Trump suggested that there might be situations in which a sufficiently heinous nonnuclear attack against the United States or its allies might lead to an American nuclear response; without dismissing that possibility altogether, the Biden administration emphasized that the "foundational purpose" of American nuclear weapons was deterrence of others' use of nuclear weapons against the United States or its allies.[24] Whether such minor semantic differences add up to much, in the minds of adversaries or neutrals or friends or allies, is debatable. Austin and Biden, by contrast, had more success with allies—strengthening the so-called Quad, AUKUS, and U.S.-Korea-Japan collaborations in various modest but meaningful ways, for example in intelligence sharing, and also in reinvigorating the U.S.-Philippines alliance under its new president, Ferdinand Marcos Jr. Austin and Biden also negotiated provisional access to bases in the Philippines, Papua New Guinea, and Palau.[25]

The greatest Defense Department innovators over the past decade have probably been the Marines. While commandant of the Marine Corps, General David Berger (now retired) shook the defense establishment with several big changes. His goals, and those of his successor, General Eric Smith, have been to make the Marines more focused on China and the Pacific—and therefore more expeditionary, less dependent on centralized command, control, communications, and intelligence support, less dependent on large bases as well as big (and vulnerable) ships, and more lethal, especially in the realm of long-range missile strikes. They have eliminated tanks and deemphasized unguided artillery, diversified the footprint of Marines in the Asia-Pacific region in particular, and equipped new "littoral combat regiments" with antiship missiles as well as their own sensor and communications networks to reduce dependence on satellites. These ideas are tied together in the Marine Corps Expeditionary Advanced Base Operations concept; the Air Force has developed a related Agile Combat Employment concept.[26] The strategic goals include helping joint-force commanders better monitor, and attempt to deter, China from various "gray zone" microaggressions as well as from larger attacks in places such as Taiwan.[27]

Still, the Pentagon has a long ways to go in carrying out transformation. Ideas such as those that RAND scholar David Ochmanek has been promoting for years—including the use of uncrewed aircraft and submarines in the western Pacific that could threaten Chinese ships trying to cross the Taiwan Strait without requiring long runways or big aircraft carriers to do so—have been slow to see the light of day.[28] Drone technology and various types of robotic swarms, controlled by advanced algorithms including artificial intelligence, can also contribute to this and other defense requirements.[29] And even with new contingency access points in the region, the buildup of military facilities on Guam, and the gradual deployment of newer technologies, there has been limited net strengthening of the U.S. military posture in the Asia-Pacific region. As Robert Blackwill and Richard Fontaine sized up recent developments in 2024, "In the end, then—more than a decade after the 2011 announcement of a U.S. pivot to Asia—little meaningful shift of military resources to the Indo-Pacific had taken place."[30]

Another potential problem with current thinking on defense strategy: the emphasis on the Taiwan invasion scenario in U.S. defense planning toward China. To be sure, as noted above, that scenario must be addressed. But given its all-or-nothing nature, it would seem to represent a cosmic role of the dice for Beijing that PRC leaders may elect to avoid if at all possible. Crossing the Taiwan Strait requires the People's Liberation Army to protect big, vulnerable ships and airplanes. By contrast, using various gray-area methods of harassment against shipping, limited missile strikes against ships and ports, or submarine attacks as part of a blockade (whether airtight or "leaky") seems more consistent with Chinese military thinking—and more promising in light of the current balance of military technologies. I have argued that, were China to attempt a robust blockade of Taiwan with its submarine fleet, the United States with Japan and Taiwan would have considerable difficulty reopening safe shipping and air lanes into Taiwan. China might even win such an engagement. The United States and allies thus probably need a broader range of counters against this scenario, to include not only better military capabilities but a more robust preparation for waging economic war against China in the event of such a blockade.[31]

One more central element to America's defense strategy in the new era of great power rivalry concerns the U.S. defense industrial base. Since the Covid-19 outbreak of 2020 and the all-out Russian attack on Ukraine of 2022, problems with the defense supply chain—indeed, supply chains of many types—have been recognized as acute national vulnerabilities. This is especially concerning when China, now the world's top manufacturer, plays a disproportionately important role in producing many components and commodities that are needed in military systems (as well as in critical national infrastructure, medicines, and other goods without which many American lives could soon be in jeopardy). Gone is the insouciance with which defense officials, at the famous "last supper" of the early 1990s and on other occasions, used to tell the American defense industry essentially to take care of itself. Injections of cash into some parts of the defense industrial base, such as submarine-building shipyards, to shore up subcontractor supply lines and improve surge capacity, have begun. But much remains to be done.[32]

CRISIS MANAGEMENT IN THE BIDEN YEARS

Defense strategy includes formal documents, including those discussed above, as well as budgets and modernization plans. But of course, it also includes the ways force is used—and the ways force is threatened. Thus, as with other periods, we need to think about crisis management over the past decade to understand modern American defense strategy, with a particular eye on how the United States has handled challenges with China and Russia. Thankfully, no new major wars directly involving American armed forces in sustained combat began over the past decade (and other conflicts, in Iraq and Afghanistan, were discussed in the previous chapter).

First, though, it is worth making a brief observation about the Middle East: as much as American strategists may prefer to deemphasize that theater in defense planning, reality tends to intrude. U.S. defense planners may not have an interest in the Middle East, to paraphrase the old Bolshevik saw, but the Middle East tends to have an interest in us. Biden withdrew U.S., and therefore NATO, forces from Afghanistan. To date, while that has been a tragedy for Afghans, it may not be seriously jeopardizing the United States on the terrorism front. But it did help create a sense of American disinterest that rippled through the broader region and complicated any desire to make reductions in U.S. military posture elsewhere in the general vicinity of the Persian Gulf. Moreover, the heinous Hamas attack on Israel of October 7, 2023, followed by Israeli retaliation and the threat of a broader regional war with Hezbollah and Iran in particular, has led the United States to increase deployments in the region. Aircraft carriers have often been surged to the broader Persian Gulf area, sometimes two at a time. In October 2024, the Biden administration also sent a THAAD missile-defense system to Israel along with some 100 troops.[33] All in all, the Carter and Dunford "4+1" framework for force planning may be a more realistic way to think about the future security environment, and America's efforts to address it and shape it, than any presumption that the country can really focus only on great power rivalry.

The Russia-Ukraine war represented a turning point in modern combat in many ways. Drones for reconnaissance and for attack, commercial satellites providing Internet service to deployed forces, cell phone apps helping citizens provide targeting information to central authorities, intercepts of Russian troops' use of social media—all of these things have been employed to a degree never seen before. Yet the war has also validated old truths: mass still matters, prepared defenses still have big advantages, a country's political resolve and toughness are crucial, stamina in terms of manpower and military production still counts in long wars. In addition, when superpowers are involved in major wars, nuclear threats—albeit of uncertain seriousness and nature—are not off the table.[34] The net result of all of this has been a war that, while not quite a stalemate, has seen a very slowly moving front line since late 2022.[35]

When the full-scale Russian invasion of Ukraine began on February 24, 2022, President Biden decided that the United States should not directly enter into the conflict and thereby risk World War III. Biden did, however, help lead a Western response in the economic realm that has cut off most high-tech cooperation between the West and Russia (even if it has not substantially reduced Russian oil and gas export earnings or brought the economy to its knees). Biden also provided massive security and economic assistance, and unprecedented intelligence support, to Ukraine to help ensure its security as well as the survival of its government. The United States has committed total assistance to Ukraine of more than $100 billion since 2022 (with even more coming from the Europeans and Japan and Canada, though their aggregate assistance has focused a bit more on Ukraine's economy).[36] The overall effort has been impressive.[37]

By 2023, however, the United States sometimes seemed a day late and a penny short in providing weapons—even though its overall effort was extraordinary by historical standards of security assistance, exceeded only by the Lend-Lease program of World War II in size and scale. Washington begrudgingly agreed to provide tanks, to offer Ukraine longer-range surface-to-surface missiles, to agree to train Ukrainian pilots on F-16 aircraft, and to see F-16s shipped to Kyiv. The understandable concerns that Biden had in 2022 about avoiding escalation, and about focusing arms transfers on the most urgent threats to Ukraine, were not as understandable in 2023 or thereafter, as he himself seems to have concluded since he ultimately allowed most of these transfers. His hesitancy to agree to weapons shipments on multiple occasions, only to relent later, gave the administration's approach a somewhat sclerotic feel that contradicted its strong rhetorical support for the Ukrainian cause. Nevertheless, those who think that if Biden had only transferred the big weapons sooner, when Russia was still reeling from its initial mistakes of 2022, things would have gone much better for Ukraine may be unrealistic in their expectations of how quickly weapons can be absorbed and turned into decisive military capabilities.

Does Biden deserve any blame for the outbreak of the war? Biden's pullout from Afghanistan may have affected his credibility as a leader in the eyes of Russian president Vladimir Putin, who might have surmised that, like Afghanistan, Ukraine was a second-tier strategic concern of the United States in general and of Biden in particular. If Biden wouldn't sustain a modest U.S. commitment to Afghanistan, perhaps he wouldn't react strongly if Russia attacked its own neighbor—or so the Putin hypothesis might have gone. It is easy to exaggerate how much decisions in one theater by the United States or any other major power affect its image in entirely different regions; domino theories are usually exaggerated. That said, leaders do form images of the credibility and resoluteness of other leaders.[38]

Yet on balance, it is hard to pin too much blame for Putin's decision on Biden. It was a long time in the making. Of course, Putin's scheming against Ukraine went back at least to 2014, when Barack Obama was U.S. president; it was then that Russia stole Crimea and began to foster unrest in the Donbas region of eastern Ukraine. In the years before the all-out attack of 2022, Putin laid the propaganda backdrop that produced, among other things, his highly tendentious essay in the summer of 2021 arguing that Ukraine was not a real country.[39] Putin's acute disagreements with the United States—and his sense of U.S. wobbliness on its commitment to Ukraine—went back at least to the George W. Bush era and the Bucharest Summit of 2008, where NATO promised eventual membership to Ukraine without giving a date or interim security guarantee. Even before then, at the Munich Security Conference in 2007, Putin indicated that his patience with the West had largely dissipated. That is not to excuse Putin, but rather to take stock of the long series of events and decisions stretching back fifteen to twenty years that constitute the backdrop to the invasion in 2022. If U.S. defense strategy failed by leaving Ukraine in a strategic no-man's-land, it was a mistake made over at least two decades.

Discussing cases such as Afghanistan and Ukraine does go to underscore, yet again, that for post-1945 America, figuring out where to draw the (red) line has often been the greatest challenge in defense strategy. It is fine to say that grand strategy was one of containment, plus the protection and promotion of a democratic, peaceful, market-based, rules-based community of nations, with "containment" being replaced by "great power rivalry" in recent years in that formulation. But figuring out where to draw the line, and how rigorously to try to uphold that line, has always been the hard part. Defense strategy, with decisions on specific alliances, forward military commitments, and combat engagements—when and where to be willing to fight and for how long and with what means—has, I believe, always been more challenging than grand strategy. Or, to put it differently, defending core allies has been relatively straightforward for the United States since 1945, and quite successful. But deciding who is a core ally and core interest has been much more difficult—from South Korea to South Vietnam to Kuwait to Iraq and Afghanistan to Taiwan and Ukraine. The United States has been good at deterrence when it really tries to deter. It has been less successful when unsure of itself.

This discussion leads naturally to the enormously important question of Taiwan. Some argue that Taiwan has become the linchpin of America's security position in Asia; were it lost, so goes the theory, formal treaty alliances could then be put at risk, and the U.S. posture in the Pacific might crumble.[40] Even those of us who do not subscribe to such a view must worry about the possibility of direct U.S.-China war over the island, whether in response to an attempted PRC invasion or a blockade or something else. China's decision to build up its nuclear forces over the next decade, perhaps to a level approaching that of the United States, and to develop a launch on warning option for those forces, should remind all parties of the potential for escalation as well.[41] A U.S.-China war could be worse than World War II overall; indeed, it could threaten the future of the human race.

In this light, President Biden's frequent misstatements, if in fact they were mistakes, about how he would authorize a U.S. military response to any Chinese attack on Taiwan may have been good for deterrence.[42] They carried some risk of encouraging Taiwan's leaders to pursue independence, thinking that the United States would have Taiwan's back no matter what—and these risks are not to be ignored. But it is doubtful that most politicians in Taiwan think that Washington could come quickly and easily to their rescue with rapid victory assured, so this risk was likely manageable. Even though White House staffers always then walked back Biden's words and reaffirmed the long-standing policy of so-called strategic ambiguity about a possible U.S. military defense of Taiwan, the fact that Biden publicly stated his own view on four separate occasions signaled a certain conviction and sincerity on the matter. Yet the administration was careful not to take things to the next level and formally abandon strategic ambiguity (also known as dual deterrence, since the policy is designed simultaneously to deter China from attacking Taiwan and deter Taiwan from pushing for independence). The Biden administration ultimately concluded that abandoning strategic ambiguity in favor of "strategic clarity" could be a mistake for two reasons: it would likely inflame relations with Beijing, and it would promise a military protection of Taiwan that, depending on the scenario, the United States might not be capable of providing reliably. It could also embolden Taiwan, and its president, Lai Ching-te, to push things too far and too hard. President Trump's views and public statements on this same subject will be important for stability going forward.[43]

Secretary of Defense Lloyd Austin's concept of integrated deterrence, a phrase I had also coined with similar purpose in my book *The Senkaku Paradox* (2019), probably helped preserve stability, too. Especially when coupled with the West's strong collective response to the Ukraine invasion, it signaled to Beijing that whether or not America intervened militarily in a Taiwan scenario, it would work with allies to severely punish China economically in the event of a major Chinese assault against Taiwan. To be sure, such a process would necessarily be painstaking, gradual, and piecemeal—but it could also be sustained and expanded over time, just as in the West's current dealings with Russia.[44] Indeed, a distinctive characteristic of the current era and its return to great power rivalry has been the more central role of economics in grand strategy.[45] In the past decade, as worries have grown about China's ability to compete head-to-head with the United States in advanced technologies, some of the same kind of thinking that led to restrictions on technology transfer to the Soviet Union has resurfaced. The United States and allies are now seeking to reduce dependencies on China in certain commodities and component parts while beefing up their own high-tech industries including those for semiconductor production.[46] All of this is overdue, and in need of further implementation. In addition, although the United States has dispersed bases in the Indo-Pacific, most of the new facilities are more lily pads than they are serious operational nodes, with limited underground fuel and ammunition storage facilities or dedicated maintenance facilities, and little in the way of air and missile defenses. They, too, will require further development.[47]

There are also important vulnerabilities in American civilian infrastructure. The consequences could be serious, not only for the well-being of American citizens, of course, but also for the deployability and sustainability of U.S. military forces abroad. The armed forces depend on national infrastructure—trains, ports, airfields, electricity grids—to get from their U.S. bases to overseas theaters. Moreover, were many millions of civilians put at risk through attacks on infrastructure, perhaps to include water systems as well as electricity, whether done by cyber or kinetic means, American military forces might have to be tasked with helping their fellow citizens at home rather than fighting a war abroad. As such, Beijing might see a certain military logic in placing malware inside American infrastructure, prepositioned so as to be activated during crisis or war. China appears to have done precisely that, already, in recent years, through groups such as Volt Typhoon (there is also a Salt Typhoon, Raspberry Typhoon, Flax Typhoon, . . . the list goes on)—as the Federal Bureau of Investigation and other elements of the Department of Justice have determined. In the United States, the private sector controls most such infrastructure; cybersecurity and safety requirements on the private sector are often not rigorous or binding.[48]

There is no pressing reason to think that China will attack Taiwan by 2027. Xi has asked his military only to strive to have the capability to seize it by then, a much different proposition than actually deciding to attempt it. Nor is it clear that requesting such a capability will easily turn into the creation of such. Crossing the Taiwan Strait with a big amphibious operation remains a daunting task, especially in light of enduring (if possibly slipping) American advantages in antisubmarine and undersea warfare and in stealth bombers.[49] But deterrence can and should still be strengthened further beyond the steps taken by the Biden administration.

Nor has the North Korean problem gone away. In previous eras, the United States could, with the Republic of Korea, base war plans on the premise that in any large-scale conflict on the Korean peninsula, the logical outcome of such a war would be the forceful reunification of the two Koreas on Seoul's terms. Now, in light of North Korean nuclear weapons, that premise must be questioned. It is not clear that Combined Forces Command has done so; unclassified reports talk of early decapitation strikes against North Korean leadership in the event of war, as part of a new "5015" war plan that would supersede the earlier 5029 plan and try to preempt North Korea's ability to launch nuclear weapons southward (or eastward). But if such strikes fail to eliminate North Korean leadership (as the attempt to kill Saddam in March 2003 in the shock and awe attack failed)—and even if they succeeded—North Korea could remain a nuclear-armed angry nation fighting for the survival of what was left of its regime. There is little reason to think that such a regime would go quietly; if North Korea could credibly threaten nuclear attacks as a way of dissuading U.S.-ROK forces from entering its territory and pursuing its leadership, it might very well do so. As such, American defense strategy in the modern era may require further rethinking to deal with the problem of a nuclear-armed rogue state. The current U.S. claim that, should North Korea use nuclear weapons, its regime would not survive seems to ignore the possibility that a first North Korean nuclear shot could be a warning or very limited isolated strike. On this matter, U.S. defense strategy seems to have a major flaw.[50]

CONCLUSION . . . AND A PREDICTION: ONE WAR, TWO WARS, THREE WARS, FOUR WARS?

One big new defense debate began to brew in 2024: how to think about, and plan for, the possibility of more than one war happening at a time. This was a central conclusion of the landmark report of the 2024 independent commission on the national defense strategy, with solid logic and good reasoning behind it.[51] The next U.S. national defense strategy will likely rethink this important question. With a somewhat different approach than the rest of the book employs, in the next few pages I will hazard a conjecture as to where that debate might be going—or, at least, where I think it *should* be going.

Like the Trump National Defense Strategy as developed by Secretary of Defense Jim Mattis and further implemented by Secretary Mark Esper, the Biden National Defense Strategy under Secretary Lloyd Austin established the following key objectives for the American armed forces:

- Be able to fight, together with at least some allies, and defeat China or Russia (but not both at the same time), presumably in conflicts centered on the western Pacific region and eastern European region, respectively;
- Defend the American homeland while also maintaining a ready nuclear deterrent;
- Deter North Korea and Iran; and
- Maintain momentum against transnational violent extremist organizations as part of the so-called war on terror.

This list is thus similar to the "4+1" force-sizing framework used by General Joseph Dunford and others at the end of the Obama administration, with its focus on Russia, China, North Korea, Iran, and transnational violent extremism. But since that time nearly a decade ago, Russia and especially China have been elevated to "first among equals" in the threat pantheon. The list does not even include other possible tasks, such as massive disaster response and humanitarian relief.

At least, that's how things currently stand. Yet the assumption that it is enough to be able to fight and win one war at a time seems questionable in light of the growing strategic cooperation and coordination among Russia, North Korea,

Iran, and China. Simultaneous or overlapping crises, even conflicts, are hard to dismiss as a possibility. That is not to say that the nation will move from its current "1-war" force-sizing paradigm to a 1½-war or 2-war framework, as in previous eras. But the strategic talk on the street in Washington increasingly recognizes the importance of figuring out how to best deter several potential adversaries at once.

One possible framework for addressing multiple overlapping contingencies could be to limit damage and territorial loss in other theaters while focusing a main effort elsewhere—say, against China in defense of Taiwan. This logic might lead to the following kinds of modest additions to the force structure:

- In the Middle East, we need to have the kinds of defensive capabilities in place that were used to help shoot down 500-plus Iranian missiles and drones on April 13 and October 1, 2024. The United States has often used two aircraft carriers plus land-based assets in these tasks. Aircraft carrier battle groups are an expensive way to do this job; building a dedicated fleet that could always keep two in the region without being homeported there would literally require building eight more, given ship rotation demands. That would lead to a whopping average annual price tag, including procurement as well as operating and personnel costs, of around $50 billion. Moreover, the United States could not plausibly build that many added ships until the 2030s even if we went all-out. But adding the equivalent capability in dedicated land-based air and missile defense systems, to be kept in the Middle East under all circumstances, even in the event of war with China, would have an average annual cost of $5 billion to $10 billion depending on how it was done.[52]
- With North Korea, the goal of any "hold" strategy should be to help South Korea defend itself from air, missile, artillery, and drone attack on Seoul in particular while having enough U.S. airpower to go after the North Korean launchers and weapons depots (including any for nuclear weapons that we can identify) early in a war. Those would be the tasks that should not have to await the resolution of the postulated U.S.-China war. Fortunately, we already have nearly 30,000 U.S. troops in South Korea today and they have most of these capabilities. However, they might be required for the conflict against China that is assumed to be already underway. At a minimum, therefore, we would need the ability to bring additional airpower and air and missile defense systems to the peninsula in time of war over Taiwan, to avoid any perception

that the United States is incapable of also helping defeat North Korea's early spasms of attack. That could imply almost doubling our current footprint on the peninsula: say, four more squadrons of combat aircraft and four more Patriot or THAAD defense batteries. Estimated average annual cost: $10 billion, plus construction costs for additional airfields, fuel depots, aircraft shelters, and munitions stocks that South Korea could help fund.[53]

- With Russia, the simplest long-term solution might involve stationing real American combat power in NATO's most exposed eastern flank—the Baltic states. The idea would again be to discourage a rapid enemy assault, in this case perhaps against the eastern parts of Estonia and Latvia, where there are lots of Russian speakers whom Putin has claimed the right to "protect." Adding one Army brigade combat team (about 3,500 soldiers, plus again as many in support units) and a combat aviation brigade to the permanent U.S. Army force structure for this purpose would, in the steady state, cost about $5 billion a year, once bases were built. These would be modest but serious elements of American combat power.[54]

Altogether, assuming that we actually added these forces to the standing U.S. military (rather than trying to maintain additional commitments out of hide), the average annual costs of the new force posture would total by my estimates around $25 billion a year. Initial costs would be somewhat higher as equipment was purchased, but longer-term costs would average out in this range. The defense budget would then have to grow with inflation or slightly more in the following years to sustain this buildup.

Nuclear force planning could require rethinking as well. The bilateral U.S.-Russia arms control framework that has simplified aspects of nuclear planning for decades is under serious strain and probably obsolete. Beyond the matter of Russia's recent aggressiveness, history suggests that arms control in a multipolar strategic environment is complex, to say the least.[55] With China apparently headed for an arsenal with 1,500 warheads, many of them long-range and modern in character, and Russia already in the range of 5,000—and the two countries acting in greater strategic collusion than at any time since the 1960s—does it suffice that the United States have nuclear parity with Russia while ignoring China's capabilities? Before, the fact that France and the United Kingdom each brought a couple hundred warheads to the table for the Western alliance could be seen as balancing out whatever capability China possessed; that is no longer likely to be the case. Even if one is not particularly worried about target coverage at this point, given the huge numbers of nuclear weapons that still exist in the American arsenal, there is the matter of perception and the sense of strategic momentum that may develop in some capitals. It would be worrisome if a sense of combined superiority against U.S. forces, even if that superiority were militarily rather meaningless, emboldened Moscow or Beijing or both to take dangerous actions.

The United States may need to take some combination of measures to address this new set of strategic challenges. It has numerous options, including a modest strategic nuclear buildup, limited deployments of strategic defenses (perhaps some of them concentrated near key industrial and military assets), deployment of a certain number of conventionally armed hypersonic missiles, or greater forward stationing of tactical nuclear weapons on the territories of key allies. At least, such ideas seem likely to be raised in the near future. Their cost implications could likely range from the low billions into the low tens of billions a year, depending on the priciness of the proposed solution.[56]

Wrapping all of this together, as of this writing in early 2025, it appears the world is continuing to be more demanding on the United States and its defense strategies and military forces, not less so. That is not an argument for fatalism; many of the problems seem manageable, especially with the tools of deterrence that have been developed since the end of World War II. Again, in conclusion, it is worth underscoring the central success of American grand strategy and defense strategy since 1945 in preventing World War III by preserving the great power peace. The United States generally succeeds in dissuading other countries from attacking its core interests once it clearly indicates where those interests lie and demonstrates the resolve as well as the capacity to defend them. But it will all take work, and resources, in the years ahead.

CHAPTER VIII

America the Assertive

The United States is a strategically blessed nation. With generally friendly neighbors to the north and south, as well as oceans to east and west, it has an outstanding geography for purposes of national defense. As a result, to talk of defense strategy for the United States verges on the oxymoronic. Most of the time, its grand strategies and associated "defense" strategies have been highly assertive. Often, this has been for the good, not only of Americans, but of the world in general. Rarely, however, has the United States been peaceful or passive. The United States is no shrinking violet on the world stage and never has been. Nor is it simply a defender of the status quo; it promotes democracy, individual human rights, and market-based economies (for the most part), sometimes quietly but sometimes also with messianic zeal.[1]

Thus, there is an American way of grand strategy. It is to take advantage of the country's unparalleled geography and remarkable base of people and resources to build a powerful nation and then use that power to shape a world order to our liking. More specifically, America's grand strategies can be defined as *expansionism* for the first half of its existence, followed by quasi-*isolationism (or regionalism, perhaps more precisely) interrupted by intense interventionism* during the first forty-five years of the twentieth century, followed by *internationalism with sustained forward engagement and interventionism* since World War II. In the first and last of these long periods, the United States was highly assertive throughout. Only in the second were there times of genuine national restraint, and even that restraint was relative. Moreover, during that same period of 1900–1945, the United States developed an industrial base that would make it the arsenal of democracy once the country put its mind to it.

Since World War II, U.S. grand strategy has created the most stable, peaceful, and prosperous world order in human history (the Romans were impressive, but they created a stable order only in the broad Mediterranean and west European region, not across most of the planet). That world order has not Americanized the planet, solved the problems of civil war and poverty, or guaranteed permanent U.S. supremacy in economic and scientific terms. Dangerously, it has also been backstopped by an American nuclear deterrent that, were it ever used, could put the future of the species at risk. But the order, while imperfect and under duress, has nonetheless so far held in preserving great power peace and promoting global prosperity as well as democracy and human rights.[2]

The strong thread of assertiveness in American foreign policy throughout most of the nation's 250-year history is even more evident if one goes beyond grand strategy to examine the details of defense strategy. America's standing armies were generally small for the first half of the nation's history, but they were highly efficient at what they did—taking land from Native Americans and Mexicans and Spaniards while consolidating government control of a growing nation. Even if its fleets were generally small too, from the late nineteenth century onward the United States started to get into the great power naval game—first by thought and theory, with Alfred Thayer Mahan and others, and then with shipbuilding as well. Indeed, the United States had shown inklings of being interested in a major power navy as early as the 1790s, even if its progress toward building one remained inconsistent for another century.

Even as Woodrow Wilson tried to keep the nation out of World War I, he was sending American armies into Mexico, just as presidents before and after threw U.S. weight around frequently in the broader Caribbean and Central American regions. Theodore Roosevelt might have exaggerated somewhat when he talked about the virtues of speaking softly and carrying a big stick. He himself rarely spoke softly, and the U.S. military stick he wielded as president was not yet all that big. But one thing is true: he and other presidents of that era of so-called isolationism did wield what they had, at least in the nation's neighborhood. This country truly is, and always has been, America the assertive, America the ambitious. That is not a bad thing; it is mostly a good thing. But it is the reality, and the history, and the strategic character of the United States.

AN AMERICAN WAY OF WAR?

With all this history in mind, it is natural to step back and ask: Is there an American way of war? Are there certain ways the country tends to fight, or prefers to fight, when it goes into battle? Or are there certain ways it tends to be most successful when engaging in combat?

In broad brush, I would argue no. Nor, I believe, has there been any compelling trend toward an American way of war over the country's 250 years.[3] It has never been that simple. The prospects for war becoming more controllable and more predictable for the United States in the future are unpromising as well.

In attempting to discern an American way of war in the past, some have pointed to America's size and industrial capacity. For them, big armed forces wielding massive firepower typify "the American way of war."

Russell Weigley, writing in 1973, concluded that "the strategy of annihilation became characteristically the American way of war."[4] Perhaps that was true in the Civil War, World War I, and World War II. Other American wars, however, from the Revolution through the War of 1812, the U.S.-Mexico War, the Spanish-American War, the Korean War, and the war in Kosovo have employed more limited and specific types of force leading to negotiated outcomes that left adversaries still standing. Operation Desert Storm in 1991 employed a massive or "decisive" force to achieve a limited war objective.[5]

Even in World War I, it was not U.S. industry or technology that carried the day, so much as American manpower (and the effects that previous years of war with the Entente powers had had on Germany before the U.S. entry into the conflict). The United States tried to use superior firepower to pound enemies into submission in Korea and Vietnam, with mediocre results.

In yet other cases, such as the overthrow of the Taliban in 2001 and Saddam Hussein in 2003, the United States annihilated the enemy with regime change operations, but the methods of overthrow were quick and clever; they did not really amount to wars of annihilation.[6] Many of the nation's successes in the so-called war on terror, such as the killing of Osama bin Laden on May 2, 2011, in Abbottabad, Pakistan, were the result of painstaking intelligence work and highly effective employment of special forces or other niche military assets, not overwhelming force.

It is true that, overall, the United States has done less well in messy wars of counterinsurgency or stabilization. So even if there is no clear American way of war, there may be certain types of wars America should try to avoid.[7] Alas, historically, that often proves difficult to achieve. When the United States tries to avoid counterinsurgency and stabilization missions as a matter of principle, it often winds up failing—with its initial unwillingness to prepare for such missions hurting it badly. Naturally, most nations in history prefer rapid and decisive victory to the alternative, and most countries prefer to avoid messy and protracted wars resembling counterinsurgency or stabilization operations. Reality often gets a vote, however. Staying away from such missions is often more difficult than expected.

To some extent, an emphasis on technological excellence has become a defining aspect of American war fighting. The nation's science and manufacturing strengths contributed enormously to victory in World War II. Since the 1940s, the United States has also profited from three "offsets"—asymmetric American advantages based on technology. The first offset was the invention of the atomic bomb and creation of a nuclear arsenal. The second was the advent of precision weaponry and advanced targeting networks that made possible, among other innovations, the AirLand Battle concept of the late 1970s and 1980s. The third is ongoing. It involves a wider range of advanced capabilities to include modern missile defenses, hypersonic missiles, submarine technology, stealth aircraft, robotics, small satellites, artificial intelligence, and perhaps someday quantum computing.

But there are limitations on the degree to which technological preeminence can guarantee victory in modern war, as the modern U.S. track record in combat underscores emphatically. It is precisely in the modern, high-tech era during which the United States has struggled the most on the battlefield, compared with all other periods in its history. America suffered outright defeats in Vietnam and, later, Afghanistan.[8] Moreover, its modern victories have required more than fancy gadgetry. The success of the surge in Iraq, although facilitated by technology, was at least as much a tribute to traditional counterinsurgency tactics and methods, as well as strong leadership and team discipline, and a well-designed political-military strategy sensitive to the human realities of the country where it was undertaken.

This conclusion should come as no huge shock. As Carl Builder noted, of the major American military services, only the U.S. Air Force has really been built around the idea of technology (and now the Space Force has as well). Yes, other services have their fancy weapons, but their identities are formed differently. For the Navy, in Builder's telling, it is the spirit of independence that most defines the service and its sailors. For the Army, it is doing what the nation asks across a wide array of tasks. Tom Ricks explains that, for the Marine Corps, a culture of grittiness, old-fashioned martial skills, and teamwork is at the center of its identity.[9] Averaged across the military services, there is no single defining American way of war.

Is the American way of war perhaps that we are always completely surprised by our next conflict? In other words, is unpredictability itself our defining tradition? It is true that, often, the United States was surprised by the wars it wound up in, as for example with Korea, Iraq (the first time around), and Afghanistan in the modern era. Yet the United States chose to have a revolution, chose to fight the British in 1812 even after London had considerably softened the policy disputes between the two countries, chose civil war in 1861, and chose to undertake wars of expansionism against Mexico, Native Americans, and Spain. We hoped to stay out of both world wars but certainly had wrestled with the possibility of intervention for years before getting involved in either case. We watched the French lose Indochina in the 1950s only to conclude, gradually and reluctantly, that we must come to Vietnam's major military assistance in the 1960s. We chose to invade Iraq in 2003 after debating the idea for a decade. Former secretary of defense Bob Gates has said that the United States has a perfect record of predicting future war: since Vietnam, we always get it wrong.[10] His comment was probably intended as a pithy reminder that war is unpredictable, and in that sense, it is useful. But it is not really true.

Often, the United States has started slowly in its major wars, losing for a stretch and requiring a major revamping of strategy as well as a greater mobilization of effort to prevail. Even here, however, there are exceptions. In World War II, the United States was never really losing, at least not for long. Yes, its allies were losing for a time, and yes, the Battle of the Atlantic was not going well at first; the surrender and tragic death march on the Bataan Peninsula in the Philippines culminated in April 1942. But overall the country had reversed Japan's momentum in the Pacific within months, and in regard to Europe, it simply needed time to build up forces. In Vietnam, there never really was a turnaround for the better. Desert Storm went well from the start in 1991. The overthrow of the Taliban in 2001 and Saddam Hussein in 2003 proceeded with great dispatch—though things did not go so well in Afghanistan or Iraq thereafter. Indeed, this century the purported pattern seems to have reversed—we get off to a good start, then stumble later.

Are Americans good at studying war, learning its past lessons, anticipating its future and preparing accordingly? Reflecting on the full 250 years, I do not detect a clear answer to this question. Sometimes, this country has learned well or innovated well. That was true for the Revolution, for the U.S.-Mexico War, for many battles against Native Americans (acknowledging the moral dilemmas associated with these myriad conflicts), and for the Confederacy in the Civil War. It was also true in most of World War II, for Operation Desert Storm, and for the opening phases of the twenty-first-century wars against the Taliban in Afghanistan and Saddam Hussein's Iraq. Military leaders get much of the credit, uniformed and civilian; so do political leaders and scientists and innovators in industry.

But Union generals before Grant did not learn well. Neither, particularly, did the top American generals who fought World War I, or MacArthur in Korea, or Westmoreland and LeMay in Vietnam, or Army generals during the first four years of the occupation of Iraq after the overthrow of Saddam. Their civilian leaders share fully in these mistakes. Sometimes, civilians deserve the main blame for mistakes, as with micromanagers of the various bombing campaigns of the Vietnam War, or Donald Rumsfeld with the Iraq war plan in 2003, or NATO leadership with the "light footprint" approach to trying to stabilize Afghanistan after 2001.

America is an inventive and entrepreneurial society. These attributes have on balance helped it to prepare for war and usually to win in the end. This seems especially true when innovations were evolutionary rather than revolutionary, tapping into Americans' historical traits of pragmatism and persistence. These traits included, to mention just a few examples, the Newport planners who figured out how to use aircraft carriers more effectively at a specific operational level of warfare, the innovators in the use of radar and airpower and convoys for antisubmarine warfare in the Battle of the Atlantic in World War II, and the developers of AirLand Battle doctrine in the late 1970s and early 1980s. The list of course goes on: George Washington, in figuring out a counterpunch strategy for the rebels in the Revolutionary War; American logisticians including Robert E. Lee who figured out how to get up Mexican mountains in the 1840s; the "tank plinkers" of Operation Desert Storm; the Northern Alliance–supporting special forces in Afghanistan in 2001. Long-term vision and big ideas have a role in defense strategy, to be sure, but the actual progress is usually made step by patient step. Some of these successful innovations happened on the battlefield; many saw their big breakthroughs in the laboratory and test range; some started as visions at war colleges. All had an element of pragmatism.

By contrast, strategists have done less well when trying to predict, or reinvent, warfare more fundamentally. Billy Mitchell and Curtis LeMay were less successful and less prescient with their visions of dominant airpower, for example, including their ideas on strategic bombardment that guided the United States in World War II and Vietnam. So were big believers in a modern revolution in military affairs in more modern times, including those who wanted to remake the U.S. Army wholesale in the late 1990s and early 2000s. Earlier Army leaders who tried to build American ground forces around the Pentomic division also stumbled.

Has the United States tended to be overconfident that it could win the next war quickly and easily?[11] Patriots in New England in 1775 hoped that after taking a few lickings, Britain might pack up and go home rather than double down on defeating the rebels. Lincoln and most of his contemporaries hardly expected the Civil War would be such a saga. MacArthur thought the boys would be home for Christmas from Korea in 1950. Secretary Rumsfeld expected that a high-tech American-led coalition could rapidly subdue Iraq in 2003.

But the hope that the next war, with new technology and bold new ideas, would prove a cakewalk is probably more of a human attribute than a strictly American one.[12] Over the centuries, aggressors in particular have tended toward overconfidence—think of the Germans with their Schlieffen Plan in World War I, or Hitler and his attack on the Soviet Union in World War II (even if blitzkrieg against France went better than expected, the year before), or the German blitz against Britain in World War II. Or Putin in attacking Ukraine in 2022. The list goes on.

On balance, Clausewitz, with his warnings that war is usually very hard, is probably a more accurate explainer of the human condition than is Sun Tzu, with his exhortations to win quickly or better yet to win without even fighting. Such expressions are fine as far as they go, as a matter of preference. But they usually do not accurately predict the nature of combat.[13]

The closest approximation to an American way of war that I have read was probably that offered by Williamson Murray and Wayne Wei-Siang Hsieh. In their study of the American Civil War, they wrote the following: "The signature characteristic of American military might is its ability to project power across the globe with land, air, and sea forces."[14] That framing is rather general, but still insightful. It captures much about not only the Civil War and the world wars but even the U.S.-Mexico War and many aspects of the nation's post-1945 wars (though some of those conflicts have been unsuccessful, as previously discussed). However, it does not do as well with the nation's first and perhaps only existential war, the American Revolution, or the country's myriad battles against Native Americans, or the most important aspects of the surge in Iraq as well as the successful targeting of al Qaeda with drones and special forces. In addition, much of the success of U.S. deterrence since 1945 has depended on the permanent forward-stationing of American troops on allies' territory, since that forward presence has conveyed a conviction and credibility that hypothetical power projection capabilities themselves cannot.

So much for a grand theory of an American way of war. Now let us examine in more detail the historical track record as we seek more specific lessons for today. The most important finding from the following analysis may be that the United States would appear to be better at "waging peace" than at waging major war. In other words, its defense strategies during relative peacetime have been more effective on average—in terms of prevailing in more limited combat, deterring war, or being well prepared for the next big war should deterrence fail—than have its defense strategies in its eight biggest wars in its history—that is, the Revolution, the Civil War, World War I, World War II, Korea, Vietnam, Iraq, and Afghanistan.

THE CASE-BY-CASE TRACK RECORD

The above are big-picture impressions and observations. Looking one level closer, and more systematically, at the record of U.S. defense strategies in times of peace and war, are there other patterns we can observe, other lessons we can learn? To attempt to answer these questions, I have reviewed the material presented in this book's main chronological chapters and identified some twenty-five major wartime defense strategies and almost twenty peacetime defense strategies (with peacetime being a relative term) employed by the United States since 1775–76. For each, I have hazarded an assessment of how well they worked. Wartime strategies needed to produce victory or at least limit losses. Peacetime strategies needed to manage the crises and lesser conflicts of the day while deterring future great power war and preparing to fight such wars effectively should they occur anyway. I have also attempted to attribute each strategy to the individuals, military services or institutions, and political leaders most responsible for developing or sustaining that strategy. They are listed in tables 1 and 2.

I have not conducted rigorous regressions to look for causality in these datasets. There is too much subjectivity in my assessments of what should count as a major defense strategy, as well as in my assessments of the effectiveness of each strategy. Coding would be controversial. Moreover, not all cases should presumably be weighted equally. Some defense strategies, such as that of the Union in the Civil War, were much more important existentially for the country than others, such as, say, that employed in the Spanish-American War of 1898 or those in the wars involving Iraq since 1991. Some were more complex than others, as with those of World War II, for example. As such, my approach here is to propose a list of what should count as major defense strategies, offer an assessment of each, attempt to pinpoint the authorship of each, and then peruse the findings to search for any patterns. I propose five types of outcomes: failure, partial failure, mixed results, partial success, and total success.

What to make of this list? First, and most straightforwardly, the United States has a good overall record of defense strategies in war, but not an unblemished one. On the list of major wartime defense strategies, not counting that of the Confederacy, nine of the twenty-five examples were ultimately either failures or partial failures, 36 percent of the total (table 1). Yet of all the wars listed, fourteen by my count, the United States has only lost two outright—Vietnam and Afghanistan—or 14 percent. In both cases, the United States and allies were undertaking complex counterinsurgency operations in areas of secondary strategic importance to help prop up unpopular governments—daunting challenges under any circumstances. (American armed forces also fought more or less to a draw or stalemate in the War of 1812, Korea, and Iraq to date.) Thus the United States has often adjusted well in war, albeit often slowly and gradually.[15] It has developed new and usually better military strategies when initial approaches did not succeed. It has had the resource base, geography, strategic depth, and tenacity to stay in most of its wars long enough to turn them around even if they started badly. Perhaps these advantages help explain its poor starts in many wars; it has sensed that it could afford to start badly and work things out as it went. The danger in this apparent American proclivity to depend on military comebacks is that, for various reasons including the speed and lethality of modern weaponry, the country may not always get second and third chances in future conflicts.

An additional observation is that the United States has had a worse battlefield record in the past eighty years than it did in the first two-thirds of its history. Of the fourteen examples of distinctive wartime defense strategies since 1945 shown here, seven wound up as either failures or partial failures. And its only two resounding military defeats in major war in its history occurred over this period, in Vietnam and Afghanistan.

Ironically, this mediocre track record has taken place in a period when the American armed forces were generally considered the best in the world. The difficult types of wars fought since 1945, combined with the nation's unsteady approach to some of the conflicts at the level of political leadership and commitment, probably go far toward explaining why such a good military could struggle so frequently. The country's proclivity to define its core interests in quite faraway locations, where it has difficulty projecting power and difficulty working with partner or allied nations, may help explain the mediocre track record as well.

The other great irony in this history is that U.S. grand strategy has arguably flourished—helping keep the great power peace while promoting prosperity and democracy abroad—during the very period when the nation has struggled

TABLE 1. MAJOR U.S. DEFENSE STRATEGIES IN WARTIME

Key Years	Essence of the Strategy	Origins	Outcome
1775–76	Head-on fight against the British, especially in New York	Washington, others	Failure
1776–83	Counterpunch strategy, with French assistance	Washington, Greene	Success
1812–15	Head-on fight against the British on land and sea	War Department, Navy, Madison	Mixed
1846–47	Clausewitzian showdown battles versus Mexico	War Department, Navy, Scott, others	Success
1861–62	Cautious search for a showdown	McClellan	Failure
*1861–62	Confederate counterpunching	Lee, Jackson	Success
1863–65	Grind, Anaconda, March to the Sea	Scott, Grant, Meade, Sherman	Success
1783–1890	U.S. campaigns against Native Americans	Jackson, many others	(Tragic) success
1898	Force-on-force against the Spanish	Navy, War Department, Dewey, Roosevelt	Success
1898–1902	Counterinsurgency in the Philippines	McKinley	Mixed
1917–18	Breakthrough on the Western Front, WWI	Pershing, War Department	Success
1941–45	Maneuver, innovation, annihilation, WWII (carriers, amphibious vehicles, antisubmarine warfare, airpower, nuclear weapons)	Marshall, King, Eisenhower, Nimitz, MacArthur	Success
1950–51	Maneuver, overconfidence in Korea	MacArthur, plus Marshall, Bradley	Success, then failure
1951–53	Return to infantry basics in Korea	Ridgway	Partial success
1965–69	Search and destroy, bomb and interdict	Westmoreland, McNamara, LeMay	Failure
1969–73	Counterinsurgency methods, deescalation	Abrams, Marines	Partial failure
1991	Decisive force, maneuver, precision versus Iraq	Cheney, Powell, Schwarzkopf (antecedents in AirLand Battle)	Success
2001	Regime overthrow in Afghanistan	CIA, Special Forces	Success
2003	Regime overthrow in Iraq	Rumsfeld, Franks, Perkins	Success
2002–8	Light footprint, counterterrorism in Afghanistan	Rumsfeld, NATO	Failure

2003–6	Heavy rules of engagement in Iraq	Rumsfeld, Franks, Casey, Odierno	Failure
2007–8	Surge in Iraq	Petraeus, Odierno, McChrystal	Success
2009–11	Drawdown in Iraq, after combat mission	Austin, Gates, Panetta, Obama	Success, then failure
2009–14	Surge, drawdown in Afghanistan	Petraeus, Mullen, McChrystal, Gates	Mixed
2014–19	Counter-ISIS in Iraq and Syria	Austin, Votel, Hagel, Carter, Mattis (continues at lesser scale today)	Success
2015–20	Support mission in Afghanistan	Campbell, Nicholson, Miller, others	Mixed, then failure

Notes: * The Confederacy was not the United States yet is included here since it had been part of the United States before secession; it kept the same strategy in 1863–65 but of course lost over that period. The terms *defense strategy* and *military strategy* are used interchangeably here and elsewhere in this book; I do not make the distinction between them that current DoD semantics usually do.

on the battlefield. Again, because these difficult conflicts were generally in faraway places that were not central to American security (even if they were sometimes seen as such at the time), the nation could afford to lose or fight to a draw in some of these cases and still thrive in protecting core overseas allies and interests, as well as its own territory. That is not quite the same thing as saying that the country fought with one hand tied behind its back; efforts were very substantial, and sustained, in Korea, Vietnam, Iraq, and Afghanistan. But when the wars proved difficult to win outright, American policy makers had the luxury of ultimately reassessing whether the conflicts needed to be continued.

Considering cases where multiple strategies were employed within a given war, another point emerges: it has generally required a change in military leadership, uniformed or civilian or both, to turn around a losing effort.[16] Sometimes it has required an election as well. In the list as presented above, among military leaders, only Washington was able to learn from his own mistakes in real time and adopt a different approach to the fight. Some might argue that MacArthur did, too, in both World War II and Korea, but he tended then to make big new additional mistakes of different types.

In making this observation, I do not mean to suggest of course that Washington was the only successful innovator in U.S. military history, only that he was the clearest example of a prominent leader who had been personally associated with an unsuccessful strategy to then make a dramatic change for the better. Several secretaries of war or defense were able to oversee a major improvement in strategy—Edwin Stanton in the Civil War, George Marshall in Korea, Robert Gates in Iraq—but they were often one step further removed from the action than the top military leadership of the day.

Why have individual military leaders in particular had a hard time learning on the job, so to speak? I doubt it is an American trait or tendency per se. Humans are often a stubborn lot, and it can be particularly difficult to rethink decisions and strategies that have led to the loss of large numbers of troops under one's command. Organizations also display inertia. They often need a substantial prodding—and perhaps the fear of defeat or the observed reality of losing an ongoing struggle—to undertake fundamental change, as students of military reform including Barry Posen, Stephen Rosen, David Barno, Nora Bensahel, Frank Hoffman, Mick Ryan, and Eliot Cohen have argued and observed.[17] Also, fighting war is physically, psychologically, emotionally, and intellectually draining. As General Stanley McChrystal once observed, given these challenges, it is hard even for senior commanders to rise above the immediate tactical and materiel demands of combat and set their sights on bigger questions.[18] Thankfully, even when individuals or organizations do not learn enough to make major shifts in strategy, political leaders can sometimes do so.[19] Or voters can hold presidents and their military leaders accountable at the ballot box.

Successful wartime defense strategies always had a competent, and sometimes brilliant, military leader associated with them. But civilians have often had important roles, including not just secretaries of defense or war or the Navy but presidents as well, as Eliot Cohen has persuasively argued.[20] If nothing else, those civilian leaders had to find and empower the right military leaders, as with Lincoln and Grant, FDR and Marshall, Truman and Ridgway, Bush and Petraeus. Scientists and technologists and industrialists have also been crucial throughout American history in the development and implementation of sound U.S. defense strategies, perhaps most notably in World War II.

Now consider peacetime defense strategies of the United States, with "peacetime" being a relative term. Again, I argue that these strategies should be assessed against three criteria: how well they helped the country handle crises and small military operations of the day, how well they anticipated and deterred high-end war, and how well they prepared the American armed forces for future high-end war in the event that conflicts could not be or were not deterred.

The most striking conclusion to flow from this list is that, to the extent one accepts my coding, American peacetime defense strategies have been very successful over the years. Of my seventeen distinct peacetime strategies, none

TABLE 2. MAJOR U.S. DEFENSE STRATEGIES IN RELATIVE PEACETIME

Key Years	Essence of the Strategy	Origins	Outcome
1783–93	Comprehensive, complete demobilization	Founders	Success
1794–1800	"6 frigates" but no big federal army	Washington, Adams	Success
1801–11	Inward focus, plus Barbary pirates	Jefferson	Success
1815–45, 1848–60	As before, plus great power rumblings (Monroe Doctrine, creation of West Point)	Monroe, Jackson	Success
1865–98	Complete the country, build a navy	Mahan, Custer, McKinley	Success
1902–17	Institutionalize the Army, grow the Navy	Roosevelt, successors	Mixed
1919–39	Major drawdown (failure mitigated by Naval War College and USMC innovation: carriers, amphibious vehicles)	GOP Senate, then GOP presidents	Mixed
1946–49	Major but managed drawdown	Truman, Forrestal	Partial success
1950s	NSC-68, buildup, NATO, New Look	Truman, Eisenhower, Dulles	Success
Late 1950s	Pentomic divisions, Massive retaliation	Eisenhower, LeMay, Army	Mixed
1960s	Flexible Response, PPBE, 2½ wars	McNamara	Mixed
1969–73	Guam Doctrine, 1½ wars	Nixon, Laird	Partial success
1973–80	Early era of the all-volunteer force ("hollow force" but also AirLand Battle)	Ford, Carter, Schlesinger, Brown	Mixed
1981–90	Reagan buildup (quality, not size of force, plus Goldwater-Nichols reforms)	Reagan, Weinberger	Success
1991–2000	Post–Cold War drawdown, 2-theater wars	Bush, Clinton, Cheney, Aspin, Perry	Partial success
2011–16	Gradual shift toward third offset, Asia	Obama, Panetta, Hagel, Carter	Mixed
2017–present	Return to great power competition	Mattis, Esper, Austin	Partial success

has been an abject failure or even a "partial failure." Six were of mixed effectiveness. Even those that failed to prevent great power war, as with the strategies of the early twentieth century, were not the fundamental cause of the war—rather, it was the wrong grand strategy of the nation, quasi-isolationism (especially in regard to Europe and Asia), that got us into trouble. Defense strategy, the servant of grand strategy, could not be expected to succeed when the broader national security objectives and approaches of the day were so flawed. Indeed, the defense strategies of the 1930s in particular helped mitigate the harm done by bad grand strategy and left the armed forces ready to embark on a rapid and successful buildup once the country went to war.

In other cases, even when peacetime defense strategies failed to prepare the nation well for the next war, as in the periods leading up to Vietnam and Iraq and Afghanistan, they helped deter high-end warfare and keep the great power peace. In other words, if we view the defense strategies of the Eisenhower and Kennedy years as responsible for *both* the nation's unpreparedness for Vietnam but also its successful deterrence of the Soviet Union in Europe and the Middle East and much of the Indo-Pacific, the net record is more good than bad, despite the calamities.

Earlier in the nation's history, when expansionism was the preeminent grand strategy (whether described as such or not), the nation's "defense" strategies were quite efficient in helping enlarge and consolidate the country. They were not always defensible ethically, but they served the grand strategy of the day with effectiveness, sometimes admittedly ruthless effectiveness.

Good peacetime defense strategies tended to have multiple architects and authors, in and out of uniform. Since they typically needed to last more than two, four, or eight years, and often much longer than that, they also generally required bipartisan support, including in the Congress. This leads me to another broad conclusion, in contradiction to what is often observed about the United States. This country actually does have strategic patience and tenacity—and, to date, at least in most eras, a degree of bipartisan cooperation—when it comes to the most fundamental questions of how to protect the nation and advance its power.

LESSONS FOR FUTURE GRAND STRATEGY AND DEFENSE STRATEGY

What does all of this mean for American grand strategy, and defense strategy, today? What lessons can the United States learn from understanding its own history as well as its own strategic character and culture?

To summarize, any such analysis should begin with twin observations. One, there is no single American way of war or of defense strategy more broadly, nor can there be such going forward. Just as in the past, different challenges call for different possible solutions. Second, Americans are an assertive people, bordering on aggressive. That does not make them bad; often, a willingness to fight and fight hard has reaped the world huge benefits, including the deterrence of conflict. But no one should think about the country's future strategic options with some subconscious belief that Americans will always seek the peaceful way out.

And there are other troubling realities to contend with. Whereas there remains considerable respect for the military among the American public, that respect is not what it used to be. In addition, it does not necessarily translate into a sense of closeness or camaraderie with the men and women of the nation's armed forces. Such is the consequence of having a relatively small, all-volunteer military.[21] There are real risks from these realities—in terms of how Americans empower their leaders to make decisions on the use of force, and in terms of how America's armed forces relate to the society that they serve and protect and from which they emanate.[22]

America's system of government cannot be counted on to provide brakes and boundaries on the use of military force, even though the Constitution divides war-making powers more or less equally between the executive and legislative branches in an effort to create such checks and balances. On matters of war and peace, Democrats and Republicans, as well as Congresses and presidents, have often been quite unified—whether their collective decisions have wound up looking good from the perspective of the historian or not.[23] Sometimes, the unity binds the country together constructively in times of national peril, as noted above. Sometimes, however, the tendency toward agreement reinforces groupthink and even bad decision-making. Sometimes, partisan politics lead issues to be oversimplified; often, competitive political dynamics push leaders on both sides of the aisle toward more muscular policies since the costs of being seen as weak are perceived as greater than those of being aggressive.[24]

These proclivities toward, if anything, *too much consensus* on the use of force are evident throughout much of American history. There was, for example, strong bipartisan support for the resolution in 2002 authorizing the invasion of Iraq, with votes of support of 77–23 in the Senate and 296–133 in the House (the vote had been closer in 1991 before Operation Desert Storm, 52–47 and 250–183, respectively). The Gulf of Tonkin Resolution was passed overwhelmingly in 1964. The only close vote in the Senate in history on a declaration of war was the 19–13 margin giving President Madison authority to fight what would become known as the War of 1812; in the other ten cases, there were never more than six votes against the declaration.[25] The House vote in 1812 was 79–49; the only other time that the House produced any real opposition to a proposed declaration of war was in the 373–50 vote declaring war with Germany in 1917.[26] Of course, Congress has not always been supportive of possible military interventions. In a number of cases to include Vietnam, Lebanon, and Somalia in modern times, it helped force an end to operations it found unpromising or unneeded. But the degree of bicameral bipartisanship in big decisions on the use of force in American history is nonetheless striking. Congress has had a very important and generally constructive role in the making of U.S. defense strategy over the history of the nation, including its work on reform and restructuring of the defense establishment, particularly since World War II, as well as its debates and actions concerning the size and shape of defense budgets.[27] Yet our politics and institutions do not always provide adequate and reliable checks and balances on decisions concerning the use of force, it would appear. Unless something changes, we will have to rely on people, and our own smarts and ethics, not the structure of our government or the competitive nature of partisan politics, to make prudent choices on war and peace.

Put more positively, the United States through its history has been better at "waging peace" than waging major war. Its defense strategies in times of relatively less fighting were on balance more successful than its wartime strategies; the latter demonstrably failed more than a third of the time, whereas the former by my estimation had no categorical failures at any point in American history. This conclusion is of course debatable; evaluating the effectiveness of defense strategy in relative peacetime requires a more complex calculus than doing so in times of major combat. But controversial coding decisions aside, the overall narrative seems compelling. Defense strategies focused on territorial acquisition and enlargement achieved what the nation asked of them through the nineteenth century. Defense strategies before the world wars could not overcome the albatross that a national grand strategy of quasi-isolationism or regionalism imposed on them. But they mitigated the ostrichlike behavior of strategists and produced a military that was able to deliver results relatively fast in both world wars, once the United States engaged the fights. Cold War and post–Cold War "peacetime" defense strategies did not get the American armed forces as ready for Korea, Vietnam, Iraq (excepting Desert Storm), or Afghanistan as they might have. But they have produced the greatest period of great power peace, through effective preparedness and deterrence, in world history to date.

In the end, this history as well as the characteristics of the current global security environment lead me to advocate a grand strategy of resolute restraint. The United States should seek to be dependable in defense of core allies and interests but highly hesitant to take on more security obligations. It should also be as deescalatory as possible in managing future crises, especially those involving other great or nuclear powers. It should be quickly underscored, however, that resoluteness is just as important in the above equation as restraint. Indeed, if the United States has generally been successful in its defense strategies for relative peacetime, that is partly because its strength and its commitment to defend core interests have generally been respected by would-be rivals or adversaries. Getting resolute restraint right is a matter of balance, and it is easier to advocate in the abstract than to achieve in practice.

Thus, I do not employ the term *restraint* in the way that a certain school of thought in American political science uses it today.[28] Many "restrainers" are in fact "retrenchers" who would prefer to change the nation's grand strategy and break off a number of alliances and other overseas commitments. President Trump may wind up belonging in this intellectual tradition as well; he was tempted to end various alliances during his first term, even if he never actually did so.

A grand strategy of resolute restraint suggests a relatively straightforward path ahead in dealing with Russia, at least conceptually, but a harder one in dealing with a rising China. This is not the place for detailed policy recommendations but rather one for bearing in mind some of America's persistent proclivities, and occasional mistakes of strategic culture, as we chart a path ahead. It is possible that the country will do too little by way of effective military strategy for dealing with Moscow and Beijing, but it seems more likely that we may overreact.

In dealing with Russia, the first principle must be that NATO territory must be resolutely protected, and there can be no doubt about this in Russian minds.[29] Among its other implications, that means that American combat forces should remain in the Baltic states—NATO's most exposed eastern flank—even after the war in Ukraine is over. A second principle, more controversially, is that the United States should be less wed to insisting that Ukraine (and Georgia) someday join NATO than has often been the assumption in official U.S. policy as well as the broader American security debate. If other security architectures can help anchor Ukraine to the West and prevent a recurrence of war with Russia, they may prove to be less inflammatory in terms of Western relations with Russia and thus more prudent choices. In particular, the idea that Lise Howard and I have developed for an Atlantic-Asian Security Community that would effectively flood Ukraine with uniformed Western (including American) trainers may prove a more negotiable possibility. One need not blame the West for the war over Ukraine or question the noble motivations of those in favor of NATO expansion—I certainly do neither—to question the strategic wisdom of continuing to expand the membership and geographic scope of the North Atlantic Treaty Organization.

The United States can probably tolerate an outcome in which Kyiv does not regain control of all of its pre-2014 territory. Some will see such an outcome as rewarding Putin for his aggression. But he will have paid a huge price in blood and treasure for the war, and Russia will continue to suffer from its consequences in terms of reduced engagement and economic interaction with the outside world for years if not decades to come. And Ukraine need not abandon its aspirations to recover the land politically, someday, just as the Baltic states never abandoned their hopes to be liberated from the Soviet yoke during the half century that Moscow controlled them.[30]

In dealing with China, the United States and partners certainly need ways to help Taiwan thwart any invasion attempt. A range of capabilities should be expanded for this purpose. However, for a wider range of military scenarios, including possible spats over land formations in the South China Sea and East China Sea, as well as possible blockade scenarios concerning Taiwan, the United States working with allies and partners needs a deeper and better range of nonmilitary tools. The general notion of integrated deterrence as articulated by Secretary of Defense Lloyd Austin is the right way to think about the problem. Quick recourse to military response even in the face of Chinese provocation will often not be the wisest path forward. Nor should the United States deviate from its one-China policy or change its stated view that any mutually agreeable and peaceful resolution of the China-Taiwan division would be acceptable to the United States. Yes, any reunification would strengthen China further. But avoiding war is the preeminent concern American policy makers should emphasize in future dealings with Beijing. The Taiwan issue should be handled in that broader context.[31] American history shows that, at the time of a crisis, the United States sometimes exaggerates the inherent importance of a given piece of faraway territory: Korea, Vietnam. Taiwan is not the Korea of 1950 or the Vietnam of 1965, to be sure. And Washington should not waver in its commitment to seeing the Taiwan question resolved peacefully. But neither should it move the goalposts in comparison with earlier policy.

American strategic confidence, engagement, and assertiveness have over the centuries created a great nation that has done great things in this world. For the most part, they have proven desirable traits in the American strategic DNA. But we are often blind to these characteristics in ourselves, and that has sometimes gotten us into trouble. At times, we have dared mighty things that have not always been practical. Going forward, it is important to reflect on this history, for the past is not forgotten, in Beijing or Moscow or anywhere else—and in fact, as William Faulkner said, it is not even past. Taking American grand strategy and defense strategy in 250-year perspective, I am now persuaded that there is a much stronger and persistent American proclivity toward activism and assertiveness than I had originally believed. It seems that we do have a powerful strategic culture in the United States, even if not a distinctive American way of war.

Appendix

EXPLAINING MY CODING OF MAJOR DEFENSE STRATEGIES

The following provides brief rationales for my scoring or coding of each major U.S. defense strategy, in wartime and peacetime, presented in chapter 8.

Major U.S. Defense Strategies in Wartime

1775–76	*Head-on fight against the British, especially in New York. Washington, others. Failure.* After a good start in Boston in 1775 and early 1776, Washington could not defend New York, lost large chunks of his army, and nearly lost the war outright but for a successful escape with what remained of his forces through New Jersey.
1776–83	*Counterpunch strategy, with French assistance. Washington, Greene. Success.* Beginning with the Battle of Trenton at the turn of the new year of 1777, the colonials found their way to a successful overall strategy that had elements of irregular warfare but is probably best described as one of counterpunching—waiting for the right opportunity to hit the British hard—at places such as Saratoga, Guilford Courthouse, and of course Yorktown.
1812–15	*Head-on fight against the British on land and sea. War Department, Navy, Madison. Mixed.* The United States did not employ particularly innovative tactics or strategy in this poorly understood and largely inconclusive war. It did enjoy some good results at sea and in New

Orleans, so fighting the British directly and symmetrically did not result in catastrophe—except for the burning and ransacking of the capital! The outcome was a draw, in effect.

1846–47 *Clausewitzian showdown battles versus Mexico. War Department, Navy, Scott, others. Success.* Whatever one thinks of the ethics of this war, it is hard to quarrel with the results—a major overland campaign into Mexico, along with successful skirmishing in California, followed by an impressive amphibious assault on central Mexico and a well-engineered approach and attack on the country's capital.

1861–62 *Cautious search for a showdown. McClellan. Failure.* Although George McClellan did a nice job moving his army southward by ship to prepare his spring–summer 1862 attack on Lee's army and Richmond, he bogged down in indecision and was diagnosed by his commander in chief with a case of the "slows." Antietam in September 1862 partially salvaged his reputation, but only for a time—and given the intelligence breakthrough he happened upon in finding a copy of Lee's plans, it should have been a much more thorough rout.

1861–62 *Confederate counterpunching. Lee and Jackson.* Success. Stonewall Jackson may have been the best campaigner of the Civil War, in terms of stringing together battle victories in a way that produced important campaign-level effects, and Lee did a good job taking advantage of Union generals' mistakes and showing tactical creativity, especially through 1862 but also as late as 1863 at Chancellorsville (even if his luck had started to change at Antietam the previous fall—and even if Chancellorsville itself proved to be the kind of "victory" the Confederacy really could not afford many of, given the loss of Jackson there and the heavy casualties on both sides).

1863–65 *Grind, Anaconda, March to the Sea. Scott, Grant, Meade, Sherman. Success.* With Grant's promotion to general in chief of Union forces after his win at Vicksburg (coinciding with the Union win at Gettysburg in early July 1863); Meade in charge of the Army of the Potomac as it then undertook a campaign of tough fights in Virginia through the spring and summer of 1864 that added up to strategic success; and Sherman taking Atlanta in September 1864 as well as his fateful March to the Sea, the Union had found its successful strategy of relentlessness. (Some call it an annihilation strategy.) It complemented Scott's earlier concept of an Anaconda or squeezing strategy on the Southern economy. The North had the numbers—and, just as important, generals prepared to take advantage of those numbers—and therefore had a path to victory.

1783–1890 *Campaigns against Native Americans. Jackson, many others. (Tragic) success.* These were effective campaigns in terms of the ethically dubious goals of taking and protecting land for settlers without even necessitating a large army for the job.

1898 *Force-on-force against the Spanish. Navy, War Department, Dewey, Roosevelt. Success.* This glorious little war, to paraphrase the way it was described at the time, may even have had some positive effects for the peoples of Cuba and, eventually, even the Philippines, who gained their independence. The Battle of Manila Bay was particularly impressive as a force-on-force engagement, as were ground fights in Cuba by the Rough Riders and Buffalo Soldiers.

1898–1902 *Counterinsurgency in the Philippines. McKinley. Mixed.* In a case of be careful what you wish for, or "you take it, you own it," the United States was left in control of the Philippines after driving Spain out. There were elements of proper counterinsurgency tactics and campaigns in the strategy that was employed; the United States at least limited its losses as it discovered it had little taste for imperialism; and it did technically win the war in the sense of rendering the insurgency much weaker and sustaining control of the country—for better or worse—for decades to follow. But violence continued for a long time, too.

1917–18 *Breakthrough on the Western Front, WWI. Pershing, War Department. Success.* The United States did not boast particularly impressive tactics or field much of its own weaponry in the final year-plus of World War I, but it did mobilize huge numbers of fresh forces and get them across the ocean and put them into battle at a time when Germany had been enjoying a positive swing in momentum due to the departure of Russia from the war in the east.

1941–45 *Maneuver, innovation, attrition in WWII (carriers, amphibious vehicles, antisubmarine warfare, airpower, nuclear weapons). Marshall, King, Eisenhower, Nimitz, MacArthur. Success.* There were of course many contributors to America's largest and most complex military victory of all time, but most can be captured under the headings of mass, maneuver (whether in the Pacific or Atlantic theaters, at sea or on land), and innovation (in terms of airpower, carrier airpower, innovative antisubmarine warfare technologies and tactics, and combined-arms combat). Although it took a bit of time to build up forces and momentum, the outcome of this war was probably never in serious doubt from late 1942 or early 1943. Nor did the basic strategy waver much.

1950–51 *Maneuver, overconfidence in Korea. MacArthur, plus Marshall, Bradley. Success, then failure.* Unfortunately, brilliance at Inchon, following a successful defense in the summer of 1950 at the Pusan Perimeter, was largely superseded by disaster at the Yalu and places such as the Chosin Reservoir.

1951–53 *Return to infantry basics in Korea. Ridgway. Partial success.* On taking command of combined forces in Korea after MacArthur's firing, Ridgway could not quite win the war, but he took back key terrain and stanched the losses and stabilized the front.

1965–69 *Search and destroy, bomb and interdict. Westmoreland, McNamara, LeMay. Failure.* At both civilian and military levels of leadership, the first four years of the Vietnam War in particular may have been the poorest performance of the American armed forces in history, in terms of tactics and ethics and outcomes.

1969–73 *Counterinsurgency methods, deescalation. Abrams, Marines. Partial failure.* When General Abrams took command in Vietnam and Nixon entered the White House, it was already largely too late to turn the war around. In Lewis Sorley's words, given Abrams's much better tactics, he deserved "a better war," but it was not to be. Nixon's efforts to use bombing more aggressively had huge negative consequences in Cambodia and elsewhere; the best that can really be said about the effort at this point is that at least the United States got out when it did and turned its attention to a "peacetime" defense strategy in the form of the so-called Guam Doctrine that proved more successful for U.S. grand strategy.

1991 *Decisive force, maneuver, precision versus Iraq. Cheney, Powell, Schwarzkopf. Success.* This was of course exactly the kind of war that the American armed forces, if they ever had to fight, preferred to wage, and it employed to the hilt the recently developed techniques of AirLand Battle (or the "second offset," the first being the deployment of nuclear weapons to counter large Soviet armies in Europe). Before the fighting started, there were misgivings about how well it would go—hence the close vote authorizing the war in the U.S. Senate—but those misgivings were quickly erased, and the only real point of contention about the war became whether the United States had ended it too soon (while allowing Saddam too much free rein over the use of his military against his own people thereafter).

2001 *Regime overthrow in Afghanistan. CIA, Special Forces. Success.* The way in which special forces and CIA teams worked with the Northern Alliance as well as Western airpower was an impressive case of real-time military innovation at the tactical and campaign levels, resulting in a fast overthrow of the Taliban.

2003 *Regime overthrow in Iraq. Rumsfeld, Franks, Perkins. Success.* Culminating in Thunder Run in Baghdad and the rapid fall of Saddam's government and military, the invasion phase of the Iraq War was an impressive military feat and, as far as it went, at least partly vindicated Secretary Rumsfeld's views that a midsize force moving quickly could achieve dramatic results.

2002–8 *Light footprint, counterterrorism in Afghanistan. Rumsfeld, NATO. Failure.* Alas, the ensuing operations in Afghanistan failed to take advantage of the window of opportunity provided by the near-demise or at least disorganization of the Taliban. Security perimeters were narrowly drawn and, even more unfortunately, competent and reliable Afghan security forces were not built. NATO did a bad job understanding tribal politics as well, allowing itself to be drawn into internecine fights in one way or another while also failing to contain the corruption problem.

2003–6 *Heavy rules of engagement in Iraq. Rumsfeld, Franks, Casey, Odierno. Failure.* Sadly, lacking a serious plan for "Phase IV" and making big mistakes on such matters as failing to reach out to Sunnis, the U.S.-led coalition allowed Iraq to mutate from relative calm to anarchy to insurgency to terrorism and civil war over the space of the four years after Saddam's departure—and the killing of Zarqawi as well as the hanging of Saddam in 2006 proved to be of little net benefit either.

2007–8 *Surge in Iraq. Petraeus, Odierno, McChrystal. Success.* One of the greatest turnarounds in U.S. military history, the surge was less about an increase in U.S. forces (however important, the additional five-plus brigades amounted to less than a 25 percent increase in total American troop strength in country) and more about radical changes in force disposition and tactics, combined with a complete overhaul of Iraqi military and police leadership.

2009–11 *Drawdown in Iraq, after combat mission. Austin, Gates, Panetta, Obama. Success then failure.* This mission consolidated the gains of the surge very well at first while reducing the U.S. role and the U.S.-coalition footprint. But the fact that it culminated in a complete end of the American military presence, due to White House decisions, set the stage for renewed sectarianism within Iraq and ultimately the triumph of ISIS.

2009–14 *Surge, drawdown in Afghanistan. Petraeus, Mullen, McChrystal, Gates. Mixed.* The success of the surge in Iraq may have led to some overconfidence that a similar approach could work in a much different country with much weaker institutions and a weaker sense of national identity. That said, the surge in Afghanistan was both larger and shorter than that in Iraq and in some ways therefore was never really properly attempted. It did stem Taliban momentum, however, and led to some notable if fragile progress in places such as Helmand and Kandahar in the country's south.

2014–19 *Counter-ISIS in Iraq and Syria. Austin, Votel, Hagel, Carter, Mattis. Success.* After the huge effort it had made in Iraq from 2003 through 2011, the United States was not prepared to attempt a similar effort once ISIS took a large swath of the country's north in 2014. But it did work closely with Iraqi security forces, and tacitly even with pro-Iranian militias, to stem ISIS advances through operation Inherent Resolve. America then helped rebuild the Iraqi security forces and ultimately used airpower to help them take back occupied parts of the country. It is hard to call the operation a brilliant success given how much tragedy took place on the ground over its half-decade-long implementation, but on its own terms it was nonetheless a success.

2015–20 *Support mission in Afghanistan. Campbell, Nicholson, Miller, others. Mixed, then failure.* After the International Security Assistance Force mission ended in Afghanistan and was replaced by Operation Freedom's Sentinel as well as Operation Resolute Support, a gradual deterioration in the security environment took place—even as the government, aided by NATO forces, held all the major cities. Casualties were high for Afghan security forces and Taliban ranks; the Taliban, however, benefited from leadership sanctuary across the border in Pakistan. Civilian casualties were generally not nearly as high as in the Iraq War, but there is no escaping the fact that the blood toll was high for those doing the fighting. Of course, it is not possible to know what would have happened had the same fight continued; President Trump's and President Biden's decisions to end the U.S. (and thus, inevitably, the NATO) role in the war without much notice or time for preparation for the Afghan government led to its rapid collapse in the summer of 2021. In military terms, there is no other word for the outcome than defeat.

MAJOR U.S. DEFENSE STRATEGIES IN RELATIVE PEACETIME

1783–93 *Comprehensive, complete demobilization. Founders. Success.* Only militias remained—really no federal army or navy just a small federal force to man forts out west—within a couple short years of the end of the Revolution. But there were no real threats to the country, and for the moment, its ambitions were limited to establishing the country within existing territory, more of a political and economic project than a military one.

1794–1800 *"6 Frigates" but no big federal army. Washington, Adams. Success.* With the political changes in France and the rekindling of British-French hostilities even as the United States and Britain patched up some remaining differences, America's European concerns turned to privateers and pirates who were encouraged by France to challenge shipping involved in American commerce with England. That plus Barbary pirates led to a modest U.S. naval buildup, and talk of rebuilding a federal army, to be put under the field command of Hamilton—an idea loathed and feared by Adams as well as his vice president, Jefferson. Adams sought to make peace with Paris as soon as he could to stem the political momentum toward creation of such an army. The naval buildup proceeded partway; the federal army buildup did not.

1801–11 *Inward focus, plus Barbary pirates. Jefferson. Success.* Jefferson continued in much the same vein as latter-day Adams, despite their political and personal differences (though these, too, would diminish with time, as they established a remarkable post-presidential letter-writing friendship that continued until both died on the same day, July 4, 1826). Jefferson avoided reigniting any squabbles with European powers and allowed the westward expansion of the country to take place without raising much of an army.

1815–45, 1848–60 *As before, plus great power rumblings (Monroe Doctrine, creation of West Point). Monroe, Jackson. Success.* Having survived the War of 1812 and expanded the country considerably with the Louisiana Purchase, the United States was starting to feel its oats. Without building a large standing army, it was also starting to think it needed to train a cadre of professional military officers. Under Andrew Jackson and others, it drove Native Americans westward to consolidate control of the eastern and central parts of the country and increased its appetite for more land to the west and southwest that would soon lead to war with Mexico.

1865–98 *Complete the country, build a navy. Mahan, Custer, McKinley. Success.* Although the federal army role in Reconstruction proved short-lived and largely ineffective, the main military strategies of the post–Civil War quarter century were effective, as measured against their own objectives. The West was "won," however brutally, and with the creation of the Naval War College as well as shipbuilding projects that proceeded in fits and starts, the United States started to enter the ranks of major powers in a way that would soon manifest itself in a major "war of choice": the Spanish-American War.

1902–17 *Institutionalize the Army, grow the Navy. Roosevelt, successors. Mixed.* With the Spanish-American and Philippines Wars over, and Teddy

Roosevelt in the White House, the era of "speak softly but carry a big stick" began. Of course, the U.S. stick was really not so big, but there did remain a respectable navy (at least when measured against naval needs near America's coasts), and the Army, while still very small, started to become more organized and regularized—and active in Mexico as well as some points farther south.

1919–39 *Major drawdown. GOP Senate, then GOP presidents. Mixed.* America's decision to choose isolationism as a grand strategy was a catastrophic failure, as World War II ensued. But the defense strategy of the day had silver linings. These were largely in the Department of the Navy. The Naval War College developed new concepts for employing aircraft carriers; the Marine Corps started to figure out amphibious warfare. These ideas would benefit the country greatly in World War II. Antisubmarine warfare did not make as good strides; neither did practical theories of airpower, since the Billy Mitchell and Giulio Douhet visions of quick victory from the skies did not translate into practical plans or capabilities. Although industrial growth was not primarily a conscious strategy (though the Army did create the Industrial College in 1924 to think through such matters), the country's rapid development of its industrial base wound up creating the foundation for a rapid pivot to a wartime defense strategy in the 1940s undergirded by the world's best technology and manufacturing base.

1946–49 *Major but managed drawdown. Truman, Forrestal. Partial success.* Even though the defense drawdown of the late 1940s failed to prevent the debacle of "Task Force Smith" in Korea in 1950, and even though the grand strategy of the day failed to prevent the Korean War in general, it is important to measure both grand strategy and defense strategy against realistic benchmarks. The drawdown was more measured and managed than those after the Civil War or World War I. During this period, some of the political and economic foundations were established upon which NATO and the U.S.-Japan alliance would soon be built—and enough military capacity was retained that it could be dusted off fairly fast once the world of the 1950s required it.

1950s *NSC-68, buildup, NATO, New Look. Truman, Eisenhower, Dulles. Success.* The Korean War was not a brilliant military success for the United States, but the defense buildup that the United States undertook after the blockade of Berlin, fall of China, and North Korean invasion of South Korea was what the Cold War world would require, and Eisenhower made sure that it did not get completely out of hand budgetarily. The creation of NATO and permanent stationing of combat-credible U.S. military forces in Europe, Japan, and Korea were crucial to Cold

War grand strategy and defense strategy—these decisions on alliances and global military posture were arguably more meaningful conceptually than the simple but vague concept of containment.

Late 1950s *Pentomic divisions, massive retaliation. Eisenhower, LeMay, Army. Mixed.* By the end of the 1950s, some troubling ideas had taken root in American defense circles, not least the overreliance on nuclear weapons in various elements of defense strategy. These ways of thinking left the military fundamentally unready for the actual big war it would soon have to fight. But the defense strategy allowed Eisenhower to reduce defense spending as a share of the nation's GDP and helped keep the peace in Europe.

1960s *Flexible Response, PPBS, 2½ wars. McNamara. Mixed.* It is hard to give any aspect of 1960s defense policy or strategy a good grade, and certainly the Vietnam War was an abject failure. But the introduction of a stronger and more integrated system of civilian control of the military and defense planning, programming, and budgeting under McNamara brought some degree of rationality to areas of defense planning that were on the verge of getting completely out of hand—such as the Air Force proposal for 10,000 Minuteman ICBMs! And great power peace was sustained.

1969–73 *Guam Doctrine, 1½ wars. Nixon, Laird. Partial success.* Nixon's wartime behavior toward Southeast Asia was morally and legally unredeeming, as well as militarily ineffective, but the shift in priorities away from the Southeast Asian theater, and the general proclivity to try to avoid land wars in Asia, was overdue and essential for the country's broader interests.

1973–80 *Early era of the all-volunteer Force ("hollow force" but also AirLand Battle). Ford, Carter, Schlesinger, Brown. Mixed.* The U.S. military was in poor shape in this period, especially in terms of personnel and morale and readiness, and many of the problems that would lead to the reforms and redresses of the 1980s were becoming evident, not least the failed Iran hostage mission. Yet at the level of technology, many of the key ingredients to the precision-strike "revolution" were taking form under the prodding and watchful eyes of Harold Brown and Bill Perry.

1981–90 *Reagan buildup (quality, not size of force, plus Goldwater-Nichols reforms). Reagan/Weinberger. Success.* The 1980s were an excellent decade for the American armed forces. Reagan was the key driver, but even on matters where he and Secretary Weinberger got things wrong, notably the issue of military reform, Congress stepped in and played its role, most of all with Goldwater-Nichols reforms and with efforts to keep the nuclear arms competition with the Soviet Union within certain bounds.

1991–2000 *Post–Cold War drawdown, 2-theater wars. Bush, Clinton, Cheney, Aspin, Perry. Partial success.* The post–Desert Storm period did not represent the salad days that the 1980s had been for the American armed forces, but the downsizing that took place was nonetheless the best managed in the nation's history, with readiness standards remaining high and operations in places such as the Balkans and the skies over Iraq generally going fine. Two major caveats, however: the American armed forces continued to downplay the possibility of counterinsurgency operations, hoping, ostrichlike, that ignoring such operations would prevent policy makers from engaging in them, and when al Qaeda started to raise its head in the late 1990s, American responses were generally tepid and lacking in resoluteness.

2011–16 *Gradual shift toward Third Offset, Asia. Obama, Panetta, Hagel, Carter. Mixed.* After the Afghanistan surge, the United States under President Obama decided to downgrade the importance of stabilization missions in U.S. defense strategy, to leave Iraq (and stay out of Syria, once war began there), and to rebalance or pivot to Asia with all elements of foreign policy. The steps towards these latter goals were modest, however. On balance the international security environment deteriorated over this period to some extent—though certainly the presence of Xi Jinping and Vladimir Putin had a lot to do with that. The United States did lower the demands on its military and avoid getting involved in any new wars—no mean feats—and kept military readiness fairly strong even as the Budget Control Act bit.

2017–Present *Return to great power competition. Mattis, Esper, Austin. Partial success.* The renewed focus on great power competition under first Secretary of Defense Jim Mattis, then Mark Esper, then Lloyd Austin has led to a reprioritization of modernization and investment accounts in a defense budget that grew substantially under Donald Trump. The major effort to help Ukraine yet without sending U.S. or NATO combat troops to its rescue since 2022, though not without flaws and mistakes, has nonetheless achieved the twin goals of protecting NATO's eastern flank while avoiding superpower war. It is too soon, of course, to know whether efforts to deter China near Taiwan and the South and East China Seas will succeed, but there has been a clarity in purpose on that front in defense strategy circles, as well as some significant redirection of resources to bolster deterrence.

Notes

CHAPTER 1. AMERICAN WAYS OF WAR AND (RELATIVE) PEACE

1. See Lawrence Freedman, *Strategy: A History* (Oxford: Oxford University Press, 2013), ix–xvi.
2. Aaron L. Friedberg, *In the Shadow of the Garrison State: America's Anti-Statism and Its Cold War Grand Strategy* (Princeton, N.J.: Princeton University Press, 2000).
3. Theodore Roosevelt, *The Strenuous Life: Essays and Addresses* [1902], repr. ed. (Middletown, Del.: Vigeo, 2017), 2; Robert Kagan, *Dangerous Nation: America's Foreign Policy from Its Earliest Days to the Dawn of the Twentieth Century* (New York: Vintage, 2006), 3.
4. Sun Tzu, *The Art of War,* translated by Samuel B. Griffith (Oxford: Oxford University Press, 1963), 84.
5. Congressional Research Service, "Intelligence Community Spending Trends," Washington, D.C., September 26, 2024, https://sgp.fas.org/crs/intel/R44381.pdf.
6. Here I use the term *grand strategy* to refer specifically to security-related matters rather than to a wider and more sweeping definition of foreign policy. Others sometimes use broader definitions; Hal Brands, for example, defines *grand strategy* as "the intellectual architecture that gives form and structure to foreign policy." See Hal Brands, *What Good Is Grand Strategy? Power and Purpose in American Statecraft from Harry S. Truman to George W. Bush* (Ithaca, N.Y.: Cornell University Press, 2014), 3; Joshua Rovner, *Strategy and Grand Strategy* (London: International Institute for Strategic Studies, 2025); and Christopher Layne, *The Peace of Illusions: American Grand Strategy from 1940 to the Present* (Ithaca, N.Y.: Cornell University Press, 2006), 1–38. As noted in the text, however, I do not think that grand strategy is only about security and survival—it is also about power and influence, and it often reflects ambition as much as

fear. As such, I do not subscribe fully to the offensive realism school of thought that explains away pursuit of greater power and influence as inherently a defensive response to an anarchical international society.

7. Defense strategy can be thought of as one part of broader national security strategy; both are designed to serve the nation's grand strategy, or big and broad concept for how to protect the nation and promote its power. Even though, within the modern Pentagon, there is sometimes a distinction between national defense strategy and national military strategy, in terms of which office writes each one and what level of detail they attempt to achieve with each document, I make no such distinction here. *Defense strategy* and *military strategy* are used interchangeably.
8. Colin S. Gray, *Modern Strategy* (Oxford: Oxford University Press, 1999), 17.
9. For more on America's history with isolationism, see Charles Kupchan, "The Deep Roots of Trump's Isolationism: Democrats Need Their Own 'America First' Agenda," *Foreign Affairs,* September 9, 2024, https://www.foreignaffairs.com/united-states/deep-roots-trumps-isolationism. Kupchan elsewhere defines isolationism as "a grand strategy aimed at disengagement with foreign powers and the avoidance of enduring strategic commitments beyond the North American homeland." See Charles A. Kupchan, *Isolationism: A History of America's Efforts to Shield Itself from the World* (Oxford: Oxford University Press, 2020), 6.
10. Evan Mawdsley, *The War for the Seas: A Maritime History of World War II* (New Haven: Yale University Press, 2019), 179.
11. Stephen Wertheim, *Tomorrow, the World: The Birth of U.S. Global Supremacy* (Cambridge, Mass.: Harvard University Press, 2022).
12. See Kupchan, *Isolationism.*
13. Kagan, *Dangerous Nation,* 5–6.
14. Sean M. Zeigler, Sarah Harting, Sebastian Joon Bae, Julia Brackup, and Alan J. Vick, *Aligning Roles and Missions for Future Multidomain Warfare* (Santa Monica, Calif.: RAND, 2021), 67.

CHAPTER 2. THE REVOLUTION AND ITS AFTERMATH, 1775–1815

1. Ron Chernow, "Alexander Hamilton," in David M. Rubenstein, ed., *The American Story: Conversations with Master Historians* (New York: Simon and Schuster, 2019), 85–86.
2. See Joseph J. Ellis, *His Excellency, George Washington* (New York: Vintage, 2004), 245–55; and Richard H. Kohn, *Eagle and Sword: The Beginnings of the Military Establishment in America* (New York: Free Press, 1975), 256–303.
3. Robert Kagan, *Dangerous Nation: America's Foreign Policy from Its Earliest Days to the Dawn of the Twentieth Century* (New York: Random House, 2006).
4. Kagan, *Dangerous Nation,* 17–38.
5. Felix Gilbert, *To the Farewell Address: Ideas of Early American Foreign Policy* (Princeton, N.J.: Princeton University Press, 1961), 19–43.
6. Kagan, *Dangerous Nation,* 39–52.

7. Stephen Daggett, "Costs of Major U.S. Wars," Congressional Research Service, Washington, D.C., 2010, https://fas.org/sgp/crs/natsec/RS22926.pdf. Military fatalities for each conflict are estimated by the Congressional Research Services as about 4,400 for the Revolutionary War. See David A. Blum and Nese DeBruyne, "American War and Military Operations Casualties: Lists and Statistics," Congressional Research Service, Washington, D.C., July 29, 2020, https://sgp.fas.org/crs/natsec/RL32492.pdf.
8. Veterans Museum at Balboa Park, "Revolutionary War (War for Independence), 1775–1783," San Diego, Calif., 2024, https://veteranmuseum.net/research-revolutionary-war.
9. Blum and DeBruyne, "American War and Military Operations Casualties"; Larry H. Addington, *The Patterns of War Since the Eighteenth Century,* 2nd ed. (Bloomington: Indiana University Press, 1994), 12–19.
10. Don Higginbotham, *The War of American Independence: Military Attitudes, Policies, and Practice, 1763–1789* (Bloomington: Indiana University Press, 1971), 150.
11. James Kirby Martin and Mark Edward Lender, *"A Respectable Army": The Military Origins of the Republic, 1763–1789,* 3rd ed. (West Sussex, England: John Wiley and Sons, 2015), 48.
12. Joel Achenbach, *The Grand Idea: George Washington's Potomac and the Race to the West* (New York: Simon and Schuster, 2004), 10.
13. Theodore Ropp, *War in the Modern World* (Baltimore: Johns Hopkins University Press, 2000), 90.
14. Stephen Brumwell, *George Washington: Gentleman Warrior* (New York: Quercus, 2012), 380.
15. Charles Royster, *A Revolutionary People at War: The Continental Army and American Character, 1775–1783* (Chapel Hill: University of North Carolina Press, 1979), 61–66.
16. Martin and Lender, *"Respectable Army,"* 66–138.
17. Williamson Murray, "The American Revolution: Hybrid War in America's Past," in Williamson Murray and Peter R. Mansoor, eds., *Hybrid Warfare: Fighting Complex Opponents from the Ancient World to the Present* (Cambridge: Cambridge University Press, 2012), 72–103.
18. John Shy, *A People Numerous and Armed: Reflections on the Military Struggle for American Independence,* rev. ed. (Ann Arbor: University of Michigan Press, 1990), 126–45.
19. Martin and Lender, *"Respectable Army,"* 1–3.
20. Martin and Lender, *"Respectable Army,"* 36–39.
21. Stephen Van Evera, *Causes of War: Power and the Roots of Conflict* (Ithaca, N.Y.: Cornell University Press, 1999), 17.
22. John R. Alden, *A History of the American Revolution* (New York: De Capo, 1969), 194–200.
23. Alden, *History of the American Revolution,* 200–210.
24. Rick Atkinson, *The British Are Coming: The War for America, Lexington to Princeton, 1775–1777* (New York: Henry Holt, 2019), 257–71.
25. John Keegan, *A History of Warfare* (New York: Vintage, 1993), 347–48.
26. Ron Chernow, *Washington: A Life* (New York: Penguin, 2010), 229–33.

27. Atkinson, *British Are Coming,* 373.
28. Chernow, *Washington,* 264.
29. Chernow, *Washington,* 87–93.
30. Russell F. Weigley, *The American Way of War: A History of United States Military Strategy and Policy* (Bloomington: Indiana University Press, 1973), 3–17.
31. Atkinson, *British Are Coming,* 530–54.
32. Martin and Lender, *"Respectable Army,"* 78–83.
33. See Kevin J. Weddle, *The Compleat Victory: Saratoga and the American Revolution* (Oxford: Oxford University Press, 2021), 4.
34. Martin and Lender, *"Respectable Army,"* 78–83.
35. Weddle, *Compleat Victory,* 301.
36. Alden, *History of the American Revolution,* 309–27.
37. Weddle, *Compleat Victory,* 1–6, 361–78.
38. Technically von Steuben was named inspector general at Valley Forge. See Glenn A. Fine, *Watchdogs: Inspectors General and the Battle for Honest and Accountable Government* (Charlottesville: University of Virginia Press, 2024), 1–30.
39. Mark Edward Lender and Garry Wheeler Stone, *Fatal Sunday: George Washington, the Monmouth Campaign, and the Politics of Battle* (Norman: University of Oklahoma Press, 2016), xi–xviii.
40. Higginbotham, *War of American Independence,* 352–60.
41. Shy, *People Numerous and Armed,* 196–212; Higginbotham, *War of American Independence,* 364–76; Weigley, *American Way of War,* 18–39.
42. Lawrence E. Babits, *A Devil of a Whipping: The Battle of Cowpens* (Chapel Hill: University of North Carolina Press, 1998), 1–10, 81–123.
43. See also Dave R. Palmer, *George Washington's Military Genius* (Washington, D.C.: Regnery, 2012), 224–25.
44. Brumwell, *George Washington,* 249–70; Weigley, *American Way of War,* 3–17.
45. Gregory J. Dehler, "Fabian Strategy," Mount Vernon Ladies' Association, Mount Vernon, Va., 2023, https://www.mountvernon.org/library/digitalhistory/digital-encyclopedia/article/fabian-strategy.
46. Weigley, *American Way of War,* 18–39.
47. Brumwell, *George Washington,* 421.
48. Achenbach, *Grand Idea,* 1–8.
49. Farewell Address of George Washington, 1796, available at http://avalon.law.yale.edu/18th_century/washing.asp.
50. Some, like Alexander Hamilton, were further along in this thought process than others; see Robert B. Zoellick, *America in the World: A History of U.S. Diplomacy and Foreign Policy* (New York: Twelve, 2020), 16–26. See also Kagan, *Dangerous Nation,* 52–70.
51. Zoellick, *America in the World,* 23.
52. Gilbert, *To the Farewell Address,* 115–36.
53. On the Northwest Territory, see J. E. Kaufmann and H. W. Kaufmann, *Fortress America: The Forts That Defended America, 1600 to the Present* (Cambridge, Mass.: De Capo, 2004), 133–41.

54. Office of the Historian, "U.S. Debt and Foreign Loans, 1775–1795," Department of State, Washington, D.C., 2023, https://history.state.gov/milestones/1784–1800/loans.
55. Alden, *History of the American Revolution,* 509–10.
56. Kori Schake, "Strategic Excellence: Tecumseh and the Shawnee Confederacy," in Hal Brands, ed., *The New Makers of Modern Strategy* (Princeton, N.J.: Princeton University Press, 2023), 373; Robert M. Utley and Wilcomb E. Washburn, *Indian Wars* (Boston: Houghton Mifflin, 2002), 117–26.
57. Harold Sprout and Margaret Sprout, *The Rise of American Naval Power, 1776–1918,* repr. ed. (Annapolis, Md.: Naval Institute Press, 1980), 15.
58. "Acts of the Third Congress of the United States," Philadelphia, June 1794, https://tile.loc.gov/storage-services/service/ll/llsl/llsl-c3/llsl-c3.pdf.
59. "An Act to Provide a Naval Armament," U.S. Congress, Philadelphia, March 27, 1794, https://tile.loc.gov/storage-services/service/rbc/rbpe/rbpe22/rbpe220/2200050c/2200050c.pdf.
60. Stacie L. Pettyjohn, *U.S. Global Defense Posture, 1783–2011* (Santa Monica, Calif.: RAND, 2012), 15–18; Weigley, *American Way of War,* 41–43.
61. Ian W. Toll, *Six Frigates: The Epic History of the Founding of the U.S. Navy* (New York: W. W. Norton, 2006), 1–143.
62. Sprout and Sprout, *Rise of American Naval Power,* 40; Craig L. Symonds, *The U.S. Navy: A Concise History* (Oxford: Oxford University Press, 2016), 13–17.
63. Allan R. Millett, *Semper Fidelis: The History of the United States Marine Corps,* rev. and exp. ed. (New York: Free Press, 1991), 26–30; Sprout and Sprout, *Rise of American Naval Power,* 25–49.
64. H. W. Brands, *Founding Partisans: Hamilton, Madison, Jefferson, Adams, and the Brawling Birth of American Politics* (New York: Doubleday, 2023), 357–60.
65. Joseph J. Ellis, *Founding Brothers: The Revolutionary Generation* (New York: Vintage, 2000), 185–201.
66. Here is the key part of Vandenberg's speech on January 11, 1947—a bit more nuanced than many recall: "As a junior partner I have worked with Secretary Byrnes on what is called a 'bipartisan foreign policy' in the United Nations and in planning European peace. It would be more significant to say we have sought a united American foreign policy so that, despite some inevitable dissidence at home, America could enjoy abroad the enhanced authority of a substantially united front. I dare to believe that, despite some distressing domestic interludes, it has borne rich fruits. In any event, partisan politics, for most of us, stopped at the water's edge.

    "I hope they stay stopped—for the sake of America—regardless of what party is in power. This does not mean that we cannot have earnest, honest, even vehement domestic differences of opinion on foreign policy. It is no curb on free opinion or free speech. But it does mean that they should not root themselves in partisanship. We should ever strive to hammer out a permanent American foreign policy, in basic essentials, which serves all America and deserves the approval of all American-minded parties at all times." See Sen. Arthur Vandenberg, "Address to the Cleveland Foreign Affairs Forum," Cleveland, Ohio, January 11, 1947, https://www.americanrhetoric.com/speeches/arthurvandenbergclevelandforeignaffairsforum.htm.

67. Gian Gentile, Jameson Karns, Michael Shurkin, and Adam Givens, *The Evolution of U.S. Military Policy from the Constitution to the Present,* vol. 2 (Santa Monica, Calif.: RAND, 2020), 9–27; Martin and Lender, *Respectable Army,* 208–10.
68. Congressional Research Service, "Declarations of War and Authorizations for the Use of Military Force: Historical Background and Legal Implications," Washington, D.C., April 18, 2014, https://www.everycrsreport.com/reports/RL31133.html.
69. Robert W. Love Jr., *History of the U.S. Navy,* vol. 1: *1775–1941* (Harrisburg, Pa.: Stackpole, 1992), 72–85.
70. Sprout and Sprout, *Rise of American Naval Power,* 50–72; Glenn Tucker, *Dawn Like Thunder* (North Haven, Conn.: Bowsprit, 2019), 473.
71. Sprout and Sprout, *Rise of American Naval Power,* 58.
72. Adam Millett, *Semper Fidelis: The History of the United States Marine Corps,* rev. and exp. ed. (New York: Free Press, 1991), 43.
73. Weigley, *American Way of War,* 41–46.
74. Donald R. Hickey, *The War of 1812: A Forgotten Conflict* (Urbana: University of Illinois Press, 2012), 25–27.
75. Michael Beschloss, *Presidents of War: The Epic Story, from 1807 to Modern Times* (New York: Crown, 2018), 91.
76. Gentile et al., *Evolution of U.S. Military Policy,* 1:35.
77. John M. Owen, *Liberal Peace, Liberal War: American Politics and International Security* (Ithaca, N.Y.: Cornell University Press, 1997), 90–97.
78. Beschloss, *Presidents of War,* 1–96; Walter R. Borneman, *1812: The War That Forged a Nation* (New York: HarperCollins, 2004), 1–3.
79. Henry Adams, *The War of 1812* (New York: Cooper Square, 1999), 3.
80. Toll, *Six Frigates,* 332.
81. Hickey, *War of 1812,* 284–301; Toll, *Six Frigates,* 459.
82. Weigley, *American Way of War,* 40–55.
83. Borneman, *1812,* 99–135.
84. Government of Canada, "Discover Canada—Canada's History," Ottawa, October 26, 2015, https://www.canada.ca/en/immigration-refugees-citizenship/corporate/publications-manuals/discover-canada/read-online/canadas-history.html.
85. Hickey, *War of 1812,* 230–55.
86. Hickey, *War of 1812,* 66–99, 123–61, 183–228.
87. Weigley, *American Way of War,* 59.
88. Toll, *Six Frigates,* 461–67.
89. Frederick C. Leiner, *The End of Barbary Terror: America's 1815 War Against the Pirates of North Africa* (Oxford: Oxford University Press, 2006); Office of the Historian, "Barbary Wars, 1801–1805 and 1815–1816," Department of State, Washington, D.C., January 21, 2024, https://history.state.gov/milestones/1801-1829/barbary-wars.
90. David McCullough, *John Adams* (New York: Simon and Schuster, 2001), 484–567.
91. Frederic L. Paxson, *History of the American Frontier, 1763–1893,* repr. ed. (Middletown, Del.: n.p., 2022), 70–89.

CHAPTER 3. FROM 1815 UNTIL 1900

1. Carl Sandburg, *Abraham Lincoln: The Prairie Years and the War Years* (New York: Galahad, 1954), 231.
2. James M. McPherson, *Battle Cry of Freedom* (Oxford: Oxford University Press, 1988), 264.
3. Sandburg, *Abraham Lincoln,* 259.
4. Bruce Catton, *Grant Takes Command: 1863–1865,* new ed. (Boston: Back Bay, 1990), 139.
5. Theodore Roosevelt, *The Strenuous Life: Essays and Addresses* [1902], repr. ed. (Middletown, Del.: Vigeo, 2017), 1–4.
6. Max Boot, *The Savage Wars of Peace: Small Wars and the Rise of American Power* (New York: Basic, 2002). Boot's time horizon is longer than the nineteenth century, but he includes several conflicts from that period in his seminal work.
7. Michael E. O'Hanlon, *The Future of Land Warfare* (Washington, D.C.: Brookings Institution Press, 2015), 9.
8. Paul Kennedy, *The Rise and Fall of the Great Powers: Economic Change and Military Conflict from 1500 to 2000* (New York: Random House, 1987), 99, 154, 203; O'Hanlon, *Future of Land Warfare,* 9–11.
9. Angus Maddison, *Monitoring the World Economy, 1820–1992* (Paris: Organisation for Economic Co-operation and Development, 1995), 65.
10. Robert Kagan, *Dangerous Nation: America's Foreign Policy from Its Earliest Days to the Dawn of the Twentieth Century* (New York: Vintage, 2006), 131.
11. Kagan, *Dangerous Nation,* 71–156.
12. Michael J. Green, *By More Than Providence: Grand Strategy and American Power in the Asia Pacific Since 1783* (New York: Columbia University Press, 2017), 31.
13. Robert W. Love Jr., *History of the U.S. Navy,* vol. 1: *1775–1941* (Harrisburg, Pa.: Stackpole, 1992), 72–85, 130–31; Ian W. Toll, *Six Frigates: The Epic History of the Founding of the U.S. Navy* (New York: W. W. Norton, 2006), 205–11; James Tertius de Kay, Michael Fazio, Osborne Phinizy Mackie, and Katherine Malone-France, *The Stephen Decatur House: A History* (Washington, D.C.: White House Historical Association, 2018), 1–142.
14. Brian McAllister Linn, *The Echo of Battle: The Army's Way of War* (Cambridge, Mass.: Harvard University Press, 2007), 10–39.
15. Frederic L. Paxson, *History of the American Frontier, 1763–1893,* repr. ed. (Middletown, Del.: n.p., 2022), 214.
16. Paxson, *History of the American Frontier,* 383–84.
17. Kori Schake, "Strategic Excellence: Tecumseh and the Shawnee Confederacy," in Hal Brands, ed., *The New Makers of Modern Strategy* (Princeton, N.J.: Princeton University Press, 2023), 370.
18. Gian Gentile, Jameson Karns, Michael Shurkin, and Adam Givens, *The Evolution of U.S. Military Policy from the Constitution to the Present,* vol. 1 (Santa Monica, Calif.: RAND, 2020), 29–40.
19. Dee Brown, *Bury My Heart at Wounded Knee: An Indian History of the American West* (New York: Henry Holt, 1970); West, *Continental Reckoning,* 35–172.

20. Schake, "Strategic Excellence"; Paxson, *History of the American Frontier,* 125–30; White House, "William Henry Harrison: The 9th President of the United States," Washington, D.C., 2024, https://www.whitehouse.gov/about-the-white-house/presidents/william-henry-harrison.
21. Ulysses S. Grant, *The Complete Personal Memoirs of Ulysses S. Grant* (Lexington, Ky.: Seven Treasures, 2010), 27.
22. K. Jack Bauer, *The Mexican War, 1846–1848* (Lincoln: University of Nebraska Press, 1992), xxv.
23. Beschloss, *Presidents of War,* 97–120.
24. Bauer, *Mexican War,* 1–45.
25. Bauer, *Mexican War,* 52–57.
26. Bauer, *Mexican War,* 100.
27. John S. D. Eisenhower, *So Far from God: The U.S. War with Mexico, 1846–1848* (Norman: University of Oklahoma Press, 2000), 182–86; Bauer, *Mexican War,* 208–20.
28. Bauer, *Mexican War,* 164–72.
29. Eisenhower, *So Far from God,* 205–32.
30. Grant, *Memoirs,* 52–56.
31. Eisenhower, *So Far from God,* 312–42.
32. Russell F. Weigley, *The American Way of War: A History of United States Military Strategy and Policy* (Bloomington: Indiana University Press, 1973), 75.
33. Gentile et al., *Evolution of U.S. Military Policy,* 36–45.
34. Weigley, *American Way of War,* 65–76.
35. Gentile et al., *Evolution of U.S. Military Policy,* 38.
36. Weigley, *American Way of War,* 77–91.
37. Sprout and Sprout, *Rise of American Naval Power,* 86.
38. J. E. Kaufmann and H. W. Kaufmann, *Fortress America: The Forts That Defended America, 1600 to the Present* (Cambridge, Mass.: De Capo, 2004), 205–27.
39. Craig L. Symonds, *The U.S. Navy: A Concise History* (Oxford: Oxford University Press, 2016), 33.
40. Allan R. Millett, *Semper Fidelis: The History of the United States Marine Corps,* rev. and exp. ed. (New York: Free Press, 1991), 52–86.
41. Sprout and Sprout, *Rise of American Naval Power,* 86–150.
42. Green, *By More Than Providence,* 31–32.
43. Weigley, *American Way of War,* 59–65.
44. Sprout and Sprout, *Rise of American Naval Power,* 97, 118.
45. Williamson Murray and Wayne Wei-Siang Hsieh, *A Savage War: A Military History of the Civil War* (Princeton, N.J.: Princeton University Press, 2016).
46. Eliot A. Cohen, *Supreme Command: Soldiers, Statesmen, and Leadership in Wartime* (New York: Free Press, 2002), 15–51.
47. Cohen, *Supreme Command,* 279, 283.
48. Murray and Hsieh, *Savage War,* 7.
49. Michael E. O'Hanlon, *Military History for the Modern Strategist: America's Major Wars Since 1861* (Washington, D.C.: Brookings Institution Press, 2023), 1–52.

50. Joseph G. Dawson III, "Jefferson Davis and the Confederacy's 'Offensive-Defensive' Strategy in the U.S. Civil War," *Journal of Military History* 73, no. 2 (April 2009): 591–607.
51. Russell Weigley, *A Great Civil War: A Military and Political History, 1861–1865* (Bloomington: Indiana University Press, 2000), 29–35.
52. See Donald Stoker, *The Grand Design: Strategy and the U.S. Civil War* (Oxford: Oxford University Press, 2010), 405–16.
53. Emory M. Thomas, *Robert E. Lee* (New York: W. W. Norton, 1997), 287.
54. Weigley, *Great Civil War,* 358–67.
55. Jefferson Davis, *The Rise and Fall of the Confederate Government* (Middletown, Del.: Pantianos Classics, 1881), 140.
56. Daniel T. Canfield, "Opportunity Lost: Combined Operations and the Development of Union Military Strategy, April 1861–April 1862," *Journal of Military History* 79, no. 3 (July 2015): 657–90; Cohen, *Supreme Command,* 31–33.
57. McPherson, *Battle Cry of Freedom,* 324–25.
58. Murray and Hsieh, *Savage War,* 511.
59. Michael Walzer, *Just and Unjust Wars* (New York: Basic, 1977), 32–33.
60. Weigley, *American Way of War,* 159.
61. Gentile et al., *Evolution of U.S. Military,* 1:52.
62. Max Boot, *Invisible Armies: An Epic History of Guerrilla Warfare from Ancient Times to the Present* (New York: W. W. Norton, 2013), 218–25.
63. Paxson, *History of the American Frontier,* 329.
64. Elliott West, *Continental Reckoning: The American West in the Age of Expansion* (Lincoln: University of Nebraska Press, 2023), 144.
65. Boot, *Invisible Armies,* 153.
66. Weigley, *American Way of War,* 153–63.
67. Robert M. Utley and Wilcomb E. Washburn, *Indian Wars* (New York: Mariner, 2002), 290.
68. Linn, *Echo of Battle,* 75–77.
69. West, *Continental Reckoning,* 59.
70. Nathaniel Philbrick, *The Last Stand: Custer, Sitting Bull, and the Battle of the Little Bighorn* (New York: Viking, 2010), xv–xxii, 250–303.
71. Philbrick, *Last Stand,* xvii–xviii.
72. Utley and Washburn, *Indian Wars,* 294.
73. Linn, *Echo of Battle,* 40–67.
74. Evan Thomas, *The War Lovers: Roosevelt, Lodge, Hearst, and the Rush to Empire, 1898* (New York: Back Bay, 2011).
75. Kagan, *Dangerous Nation,* 224–45.
76. Kagan, *Dangerous Nation,* 301–56.
77. Boot, *Savage Wars of Peace,* 60.
78. Kagan, *Dangerous Nation,* 357–74.
79. Green, *By More Than Providence,* 56–77; Kagan, *Dangerous Nation,* 301–56, 363–67.
80. Green, *By More Than Providence,* 56–77.
81. Kennedy, *Rise and Fall of the Great Powers,* 199–203.

82. Weigley, *American Way of War,* 171.
83. Philip A. Crowl, "Alfred Thayer Mahan: The Naval Historian," in Peter Paret, ed., *Makers of Modern Strategy: From Machiavelli to the Nuclear Age* (Princeton, N.J.: Princeton University Press, 1986), 444–77.
84. John H. Maurer, "Alfred Thayer Mahan and the Strategy of Sea Power," in Hal Brands, ed., *The New Makers of Modern Strategy* (Princeton, N.J.: Princeton University Press, 2023), 169.
85. Love, *History of the U.S. Navy,* 1:378.
86. Francis J. McHugh, *U.S. Navy Fundamentals of War Gaming* (New York: Skyhorse, 2013), 58–59.
87. Francis J. McHugh, "Gaming at the Naval War College," *Proceedings* 90, no. 3 (March 1964): 773, https://www.usni.org/magazines/proceedings/1964/march/gaming-naval-war-college; McHugh, *U.S. Navy Fundamentals,* 56–67.
88. McHugh, *U.S. Navy Fundamentals,* 58–61.
89. Symonds, *U.S. Navy,* 55–56.
90. Symonds, *U.S. Navy,* 60.
91. Sprout and Sprout, *Rise of American Naval Power,* 213.
92. Kagan, *Dangerous Nation,* 342–50; Kennedy, *Rise and Fall of the Great Powers,* 203.
93. Symonds, *U.S. Navy,* 55–64; Weigley, *American Way of War,* 167–91.
94. Beschloss, *Presidents of War,* 259.
95. See David F. Trask, *The War with Spain in 1898* (Lincoln: University of Nebraska Press, 1981), 1–177.
96. Edward M. Coffman, *The Regulars: The American Army, 1898–1941* (Cambridge, Mass.: Harvard University Press, 2004), 1–5; Sean M. Zeigler, Alexandra Evans, Gian Gentile, and Badreddine Ahtchi, *The Evolution of U.S. Military Policy from the Constitution to the Present,* vol. 2: *The Formative Years for U.S. Military Policy, 1898–1940* (Santa Monica, Calif.: RAND, 2020), 13; Graham A. Cosmos, *An Army for Empire: The United States Army in the Spanish-American War* (College Station: Texas A&M Press, 1994).
97. Cosmas, *Army for Empire,* 103–32.
98. Doris Kearns Goodwin, *The Bully Pulpit: Theodore Roosevelt, William Howard Taft, and the Golden Age of Journalism* (New York: Simon and Schuster, 2013), 227–31.
99. Trask, *War with Spain,* 257–69.
100. Robert Kagan, *The Ghost at the Feast: America and the Collapse of World Order, 1900–1941* (New York: Alfred A. Knopf, 2023), 44.
101. Trask, *War with Spain,* 466–86.
102. Boot, *Savage Wars of Peace,* 99–128.
103. Coffman, *Regulars,* 34–39.
104. David J. Silbey, *A War of Frontier and Empire: The Philippine-American War, 1899–1902* (New York: Hill and Wang, 2007), 207–12.
105. For a good account of the Boxer Rebellion and the events of 1900, see Boot, *Savage Wars of Peace,* 69–98. The United States contributed about 5,000 troops to the effort,

out of a total international force of around 30,000. See Beschloss, *Presidents of War,* 285.

106. Robert B. Zoellick, *America in the World: A History of U.S. Diplomacy and Foreign Policy* (New York: Twelve, 2020), 96–111.

CHAPTER 4. FROM QUASI-ISOLATIONISM TO HEGEMONY, 1901–1945

1. Theodore Roosevelt, "What a Dreadful Creature Wilson Is!," New York, April 17, 1916, https://www.shapell.org/manuscript/theodore-roosevelt-criticizes-president-woodrow-wilson-cowardice.
2. Office of the Historian, "The League of Nations, 1920," Washington, D.C., Department of State, March 2024, https://history.state.gov/milestones/1914-1920/league.
3. Robert Kagan, *The Ghost at the Feast: America and the Collapse of World Order, 1900–1941* (New York: Alfred A. Knopf, 2023), 229–34.
4. Walter Lippmann, *U.S. Foreign Policy: Shield of the Republic* (New York: Little, Brown and Company, 1943), 3.
5. Lippmann, *U.S. Foreign Policy.*
6. Charles A. Kupchan, *Isolationism: A History of America's Efforts to Shield Itself from the World* (Oxford: Oxford University Press, 2020).
7. Eliot A. Cohen, *The Big Stick: The Limits of Soft Power and the Necessity of Military Force* (New York: Basic, 2016), ix–x.
8. Kagan, *Ghost at the Feast,* 85–95.
9. Stacie L. Pettyjohn, *U.S. Global Defense Posture, 1783–2011* (Santa Monica, Calif.: RAND, 2012), 36.
10. Edward S. Miller, *War Plan Orange: The U.S. Strategy to Defeat Japan, 1897–1945* (Annapolis, Md.: Naval Institute Press, 1991); Kagan, *Ghost at the Feast,* 48.
11. Kagan, *Ghost at the Feast,* 23; Paul Kennedy, *The Rise and Fall of the Great Powers* (New York: Random House, 1987), 203.
12. Weigley, *American Way of War,* 187; Kennedy, *Rise and Fall of the Great Powers,* 203.
13. Max Boot, *The Savage Wars of Peace: Small Wars and the Rise of American Power,* rev. ed. (New York: Basic, 2014), 132.
14. David J. Silbey, *A War of Frontier and Empire: The Philippine-American War, 1899–1902* (New York: Hill and Wang, 2007), 3–208.
15. Boot, *Savage Wars of Peace,* 126–27.
16. Kagan, *Ghost at the Feast,* 51–84.
17. Boot, *Savage Wars of Peace,* 136.
18. Office of the Historian, "Roosevelt Corollary to the Monroe Doctrine, 1904," Department of State, Washington, D.C., 2024, https://history.state.gov/milestones/1899-1913/roosevelt-and-monroe-doctrine; Kagan, *Ghost at the Feast,* 70–72.
19. Boot, *Savage Wars of Peace,* 155, 199.
20. Edward M. Coffman, *The Regulars: The American Army, 1898–1941* (Cambridge, Mass.: Harvard University Press, 2007), 199.
21. Kagan, *Ghost at the Feast,* 103–70.
22. Boot, *Savage Wars of Peace,* 169.

23. Office of the Historian, Foreign Service Institute, "The Treaty of Portsmouth and the Russo-Japanese War, 1904–1905," Department of State, Washington, D.C., April 2024, https://history.state.gov/milestones/1899-1913/portsmouth-treaty.
24. Michael J. Green, *By More Than Providence: Grand Strategy and American Power in the Asia Pacific Since 1783* (New York: Columbia University Press, 2017), 78–108.
25. Harold and Margaret Sprout, *The Rise of American Naval Power, 1776–1918* (Annapolis, Md.: Naval Institute Press, 1980), 250–53; Capt. John Stapler, "The Naval War College: A Brief History," *Proceedings* 58, no. 8 (August 1932): 1157–63, https://www.usni.org/magazines/proceedings/1932/august/naval-war-college-brief-history.
26. Russell F. Weigley, *The American Way of War: A History of United States Military Strategy and Policy* (Bloomington: Indiana University Press, 1973), 171–72.
27. Coffman, *Regulars,* 197.
28. Boot, *Savage Wars of Peace,* 182–204.
29. Office of the Historian, "Biographies of the Secretaries of State: Elihu Root (1845–1937)," Department of State, Washington, D.C., 2024, https://history.state.gov/departmenthistory/people/root-elihu.
30. Coffman, *Regulars,* 43–49.
31. Coffman, *Regulars,* 191.
32. Coffman, *Regulars,* 163, 168.
33. Brian McAllister Linn, *The Echo of Battle: The Army's Way of War* (Cambridge, Mass.: Harvard University Press, 2007), 93–115.
34. Kagan, *Ghost at the Feast,* 103–70.
35. Elizabeth N. Saunders, *The Insiders' Game: How Elites Make War and Peace* (Princeton, N.J.: Princeton University Press, 2024).
36. Michael S. Neiberg, *The Path to War: How the First World War Created Modern America* (Oxford: Oxford University Press, 1916), 66–94.
37. Neiberg, *Path to War,* 152, 175, 209.
38. Coffman, *Regulars,* 203.
39. Kagan, *Ghost at the Feast,* 139–44.
40. Craig L. Symonds, *The U.S. Navy: A Concise History* (Oxford: Oxford University Press, 2016), 70; Weigley, *American Way of War,* 181.
41. Antulio J. Echevarria II, *Reconsidering the American Way of War: U.S. Military Practice from the Revolution to Afghanistan* (Washington, D.C.: Georgetown University Press, 2014), 116.
42. Sean M. Zeigler, Alexandra Evans, Gian Gentile, and Badreddine Ahtchi, *The Evolution of U.S. Military Policy from the Constitution to the Present,* vol. 2: *The Formative Years for U.S. Military Policy, 1898–1940* (Santa Monica, Calif.: RAND, 2020), 63; Robert B. Zoellick, *America in the World: A History of U.S. Diplomacy and Foreign Policy* (New York: Twelve, 2020), 147–49.
43. Zoellick, *America in the World,* 350–54.
44. Neiberg, *Path to War,* 206–37.
45. B. H. Liddell Hart, *Strategy,* 2nd rev. ed. (New York: Penguin, 1991), 187–204.
46. Colin S. Gray, *Modern Strategy* (Oxford: Oxford University Press, 1999), 89.

47. Edward A. Gutierrez with Michael S. Neiberg, "The Elusive Lesson: U.S. Army Unpreparedness from 1898 to 1938," in Jason W. Warren, ed., *Drawdown: The American Way of Postwar* (New York: New York University Press, 2016), 137–54.
48. See Zeigler et al., *Evolution of U.S. Military Policy,* 63–78.
49. Peter T. Underwood, "General Pershing and the U.S. Marines," *Marine Corps History* 5, no. 2 (Winter 2019): 7; Keegan, *First World War,* 372–73, 410; Coffman, *Regulars,* 203.
50. Julian E. Zelizer, *Arsenal of Democracy: The Politics of National Security—from World War II to the War on Terrorism* (New York: Basic, 2010), 28.
51. Harold and Margaret Sprout, *The Rise of American Naval Power, 1776–1918* (Princeton, N.J.: Princeton University Press, 1980), 359–77; Robert W. Love Jr., *History of the U.S. Navy,* vol. 1: *1775–1941* (Harrisburg, Pa.: Stackpole, 1992), 479–515.
52. Weigley, *American Way of War,* 173–95.
53. Sprout, *Rise of American Naval Power,* 354.
54. Massie, *Castles of Steel,* 738.
55. Love, *History of the U.S. Navy,* 497.
56. Keegan, *First World War,* 374; Edward A. Gutierrez with Michael Neiberg, "The Elusive Lesson: U.S. Army Unpreparedness from 1898 to 1938," in Jason W. Warren, ed., *Drawdown: The American Way of Postwar* (New York: New York University Press, 2016), 137–54.
57. Robert A. Doughty, *Pyrrhic Victory: French Strategy and Operations in the Great War* (Cambridge, Mass.: Belknap Press of Harvard University Press, 2005), 511.
58. Paddy Griffith, *Battle Tactics of the Western Front: The British Army's Art of Attack, 1916–18* (New Haven: Yale University Press, 1994), 84–93.
59. Michael S. Neiberg, *The Second Battle of the Marne* (Bloomington: Indiana University Press, 2008), 65; Stephen Biddle, *Military Power: Explaining Victory and Defeat in Modern Battle* (Princeton, N.J.: Princeton University Press, 2004), 78–107.
60. Timothy T. Lupfer, "The Dynamics of Doctrine: The Changes in German Tactical Doctrine During the First World War," *Leavenworth Papers* 4 (Fort Leavenworth, Kans.: U.S. Army Command and General Staff College, July 1981), 37–58.
61. Neiberg, *Second Battle of the Marne,* 73.
62. Stephen Wertheim, *Tomorrow the World: The Birth of U.S. Global Supremacy* (Cambridge, Mass.: Harvard University Press, 2020), 109.
63. Biddle, *Military Power,* 82.
64. Neiberg, *Second Battle of the Marne,* 182–90.
65. See Marine Corps History Division, "Brief History of U.S. Marine Corps Action in Europe During World War I," 2017, https://www.usmcu.edu/Research/Marine-Corps-History.
66. Robert Doughty et al., *Warfare in the Western World,* vol. 2: *Military Operations Since 1871* (Lexington, Mass.: D. C. Heath, 1996), 621.
67. Underwood, "General Pershing," 5.
68. Underwood, "General Pershing," 85.
69. Ropp, *War in the Modern World,* 260–61; Doughty et al., *Warfare in the Western World,* 601.

70. Doughty et al., *Warfare in the Western World,* 624–26.
71. Weigley, *American Way of War,* 202–3.
72. Doughty et al., *Warfare in the Western World,* 626–31.
73. Keegan, *First World War,* 407–11.
74. Echevarria, *Reconsidering the American Way of War,* 116–17.
75. Maurice Matloff, "Allied Strategy in Europe, 1939–1945," in Peter Paret, ed., *Makers of Modern Strategy: From Machiavelli to the Nuclear Age* (Princeton, N.J.: Princeton University Press, 1986), 696.
76. Kagan, *Ghost at the Feast,* 244–60.
77. Michael S. Neiberg, *The Treaty of Versailles: A Concise History* (Oxford: Oxford University Press, 2017), 53–68.
78. Adam Tooze, *The Deluge: The Great War, America and the Remaking of the Global Order, 1916–1931* (New York: Viking, 2014), 369.
79. Patricia O'Toole, *The Moralist: Woodrow Wilson and the World He Made* (New York: Simon and Schuster, 2018), 370–71; Tooze, *Deluge,* 333–73.
80. Michael Beschloss, *Presidents of War: The Epic Story, from 1807 to Modern Times* (New York: Crown, 2018), 330–58.
81. John Lewis Gaddis, *On Grand Strategy* (New York: Penguin, 2018), 274–75.
82. See, e.g., Green, *By More Than Providence,* 125–30.
83. Zelizer, *Arsenal of Democracy,* 34.
84. O'Toole, *Moralist,* 307; Beschloss, *Presidents of War,* 317–58; Tooze, *Deluge,* 120.
85. Donald Kagan, *On the Origins of War and the Preservation of Peace* (New York: Anchor, 1995), 415.
86. See Alain C. Enthoven and K. Wayne Smith, *How Much Is Enough? Shaping the Defense Program, 1961–1969* (Santa Monica, Calif.: RAND, 2005), 31–72; Trevor N. Dupuy, *Numbers, Predictions, and War: The Use of History to Evaluate and Predict the Outcome of Armed Conflict,* rev. ed. (Fairfax, Va.: Hero, 1985); Joshua M. Epstein, *Strategy and Force Planning: The Case of the Persian Gulf* (Washington, D.C.: Brookings Institution Press, 1987); and Michael E. O'Hanlon, *Defense 101: Understanding the Military of Today and Tomorrow* (Ithaca, N.Y.: Cornell University Press, 2021).
87. Echevarria, *Reconsidering the American Way of War,* 111, 118.
88. Weigley, *American Way of War,* 244.
89. Kagan, *Ghost at the Feast,* 275–76, 312, 332.
90. Green, *By More Than Providence,* 173–81.
91. Kagan, *Ghost at the Feast,* 278–80.
92. Johnson, *Fast Tanks and Heavy Bombers,* 176, 229; Allan R. Millett, *Semper Fidelis: The History of the United States Marine Corps,* rev. and exp. ed. (New York: Free Press, 1991), 336.
93. Love, *History of the U.S. Navy,* 615.
94. Kagan, *Ghost at the Feast,* 347–98.
95. Kagan, *Ghost at the Feast,* 417–20.
96. Kagan, *Ghost at the Feast,* 399–416.
97. Weigley, *American Way of War,* 246–47.
98. Green, *By More Than Providence,* 131–42.

99. Stephen Peter Rosen, *Winning the Next War: Innovation and the Modern Military* (Ithaca, N.Y: Cornell University Press, 1991), 76–80.
100. Francis J. McHugh, "Gaming at the Naval War College," *Proceedings* 90, no. 3 (March 1964): 733, https://www.usni.org/magazines/proceedings/1964/march/gaming-naval-war-college.
101. See Peter Perla, "Introduction," in John Curry, ed., *Peter Perla's The Art of Wargaming: A Guide for Professionals and Hobbyists* (Annapolis, Md.: United States Naval Institute, 2012), 1–15; see also prologues by Adm. Thomas B. Hayward, ret., and James F. Dunnigan.
102. Geoffrey Till, "Adopting the Aircraft Carrier: The British, American, and Japanese Case Studies," in Williamson Murray and Allan R. Millett, eds., *Military Innovation in the Interwar Period* (Cambridge, Mass.: Cambridge University Press, 1996), 210–26.
103. Weigley, *American Way of War,* 253–65.
104. Coffman, *Regulars,* 277.
105. Max Boot, *War Made New: Weapons, Warriors, and the Making of the Modern World* (New York: Gotham, 2006), 272–80.
106. Lawrence Freedman, *Strategy: A History* (Oxford: Oxford University Press, 2013), 124–29.
107. Allan R. Millett, "Assault from the Sea: The Development of Amphibious Warfare Between the Wars—the American, British, and Japanese Experiences," in Murray and Millett, *Military Innovation in the Interwar Period,* 77–80.
108. Millett, *Semper Fidelis,* 319–43; Weigley, *American Way of War,* 258–65; Merrill L. Bartlett, "Ben Hebard Fuller and the Genesis of a Modern United States Marine Corps, 1891–1934," *Journal of Military History* 69, no. 1 (January 2005): 73–91.
109. Rosen, *Winning the Next War,* 80–85.
110. Montgomery C. Meigs, *Slide Rules and Submarines: American Scientists and Subsurface Warfare in World War II* (Honolulu, Hawaii: University Press of the Pacific, 2002), 3–96, 211–20; H. A. Feiveson, *Scientists Against Time: The Role of Scientists in World War II* (Bloomington, Ind.: Archway, 2018), 87–103.
111. Coffman, *Regulars,* 263–66.
112. David E. Johnson, *Fast Tanks and Heavy Bombers: Innovation in the U.S. Army, 1917–1945* (Ithaca, N.Y.: Cornell University Press, 1998), 136.
113. Johnson, *Fast Tanks and Heavy Bombers,* 116–52, 176–229.
114. Coffman, *Regulars,* 280–81, 283.
115. Linn, *Echo of Battle,* 149–50.
116. Linn, *Echo of Battle,* 119–50.
117. Coffman, *Regulars,* 286.
118. Zeigler, Evans, Gentile, and Ahtchi, *Evolution of U.S. Military Policy,* 91; Coffman, *Regulars,* 234.
119. Coffman, *Regulars,* 326.
120. Coffman, *Regulars,* 341, 351, 358.
121. D. Clayton James, "American and Japanese Strategies in the Pacific War," in Paret, *Makers of Modern Strategy,* 709–11.
122. Wertheim, *Tomorrow the World,* 47–79.

123. Under Secretary of Defense (Comptroller), *National Defense Budget Estimates for Fiscal Year 2025* (Washington, D.C.: Department of Defense, April 2024), 294, https://comptroller.defense.gov/Portals/45/Documents/defbudget/FY2025/fy25_Green_Book.pdf.
124. Michael Fullilove, *Rendezvous with Destiny: How Franklin D. Roosevelt and Five Extraordinary Men Took America into the War and into the World* (New York: Penguin), 134.
125. Fullilove, *Rendezvous with Destiny,* 135; Rick Atkinson, *An Army at Dawn: The War in North Africa, 1942–1943* (New York: Henry Holt, 2002), 7.
126. Beschloss, *Presidents of War,* 359–91.
127. Zelizer, *Arsenal of Democracy,* 51.
128. See, e.g., Atkinson, *Army at Dawn,* 54, 293–98; Beschloss, *Presidents of War,* 359–94.
129. Kennedy, *Rise and Fall of the Great Powers,* 202, 355; Raymond W. Goldsmith, "The Power of Victory: Munitions Output in World War II," *Military Affairs* 10, no. 1 (March 1946): 69–80.
130. Freedman, *Strategy,* 144.
131. Richard Overy, *Why the Allies Won* (New York: W. W. Norton, 1997), 190–92; Victor Davis Hanson, *The Second World War: How the First Global Conflict Was Fought and Won* (New York: Basic, 2017), 422; Jim Lacey, *Keep from All Thoughtful Men: How U.S. Economists Won World War II* (Annapolis, Md.: Naval Institute Press, 2011).
132. Boot, *War Made New,* 277–87.
133. Paul Kennedy, *Engineers of Victory: The Problem Solvers Who Turned the Tide in the Second World War* (New York: Random House, 2013).
134. See, e.g., Green, *By More Than Providence,* 188–90.
135. William P. Mako, *U.S. Ground Forces and the Defense of Central Europe* (Washington, D.C.: Brookings Institution Press, 1983), 5.
136. David L. Roll, *George Marshall: Defender of the Republic* (New York: Dutton Caliber, 2020), 195–202.
137. Chuck Steele, "America's Greatest Great-War Flag Officer," *Proceedings* 27, no. 3 (May 2013): 1382, https://www.usni.org/magazines/naval-history-magazine/2013/may/americas-greatest-great-war-flag-officer.
138. Green, *By More Than Providence,* 188–201; Weigley, *American Way of War,* 269–85; Richard B. Frank, *Tower of Skulls: A History of the Asia-Pacific War, July 1937–May 1942* (New York: W. W. Norton, 2020), 494–99.
139. Phillips Payson O'Brien, *How the War Was Won* (Cambridge: Cambridge University Press, 2015), 201–4, 215.
140. Weigley, *American Way of War,* 271.
141. Evan Mawdsley, *The War for the Seas: A Maritime History of World War II* (New Haven: Yale University Press, 2020), 374–75.
142. Churchill Archive for Schools, "Was Churchill Really Worried About the Battle of the Atlantic? And If So, Why?," 2024, https://www.churchillarchiveforschools.com/themes_key-questions_battle-of-the-atlantic.
143. Eliot A. Cohen and John Gooch, *Military Misfortunes: The Anatomy of Failure in War* (New York: Free Press, 1990), 59–94.

144. Wertheim, *Tomorrow the World,* 61.
145. Coffman, *Regulars,* 373–74; Rick Atkinson, *The Day of Battle: The War in Sicily and Italy, 1943–1944* (New York: Henry Holt, 2007), 12–13.
146. Russell A. Hart, *Clash of Arms: How the Allies Won in Normandy* (Boulder, Colo.: Lynne Rienner, 2001), 69–100.
147. Atkinson, *Army at Dawn,* 10–16.
148. Atkinson, *Army at Dawn,* 269–89.
149. James Holland, *Normandy '44: D-Day and the Epic 77-Day Battle for France* (New York: Atlantic Monthly, 2019), 23–41; Weigley, *American Way of War,* 312–59; Overy, *Why the Allies Won,* 100–130.
150. O'Brien, *How the War Was Won,* 485.
151. Alex Kershaw, *The First Wave: The D-Day Warriors Who Led the Way to Victory in World War II* (New York: Penguin, 2019), 5.
152. Kennedy, *Engineers of Victory,* 250–70; Keegan, *Second World War,* 373–87.
153. Overy, *Why the Allies Won,* 156–66.
154. Rick Atkinson, *The Guns at Last Light: The War in Western Europe, 1944–1945* (New York: Henry Holt, 2013), 383–89.
155. Atkinson, *Guns at Last Light,* 256–89.
156. Atkinson, *Guns at Last Light,* 375, 490.
157. Toll, *Conquering Tide,* 226.
158. Green, *By More Than Providence,* 210–18; Weigley, *American Way of War,* 282.
159. James, "American and Japanese Strategies," 722, 726; Green, *By More Than Providence,* 201, 203.
160. Weigley, *American Way of War,* 282–83.
161. Feiveson, *Scientists Against Time,* 84–86.
162. Walter R. Borneman, *The Admirals: Nimitz, Halsey, Leahy, and King—The Five-Star Admirals Who Won the War at Sea* (Boston: Back Bay, 2013), 258.
163. O'Brien, *How the War Was Won,* 391.
164. Weigley, *American Way of War,* 285; Toll, *Conquering Tide,* 402.
165. O'Brien, *How the War Was Won,* 397–402.
166. O'Brien, *How the War Was Won,* 412–44.
167. Debi Unger, Irwin Unger, and Stanley Hirshson, *George Marshall: A Biography* (New York: HarperCollins, 2014), 352–53.
168. O'Hanlon, *Defense 101,* 85–133; Enthoven and Smith, *How Much Is Enough?,* 1–72.
169. Richard B. Frank, *Downfall: The End of the Imperial Japanese Empire* (New York: Penguin, 1999), 186–87, 190–93, 194–96, 338–41, 356–58.
170. Ian W. Toll, *Twilight of the Gods: War in the Western Pacific, 1944–1945* (New York: W. W. Norton, 2020), 644–744.
171. Rosen, *Winning the Next War,* 130–47.
172. O'Brien, *How the War Was Won,* 430–44.
173. Office of the Under Secretary of Defense (Comptroller), *National Defense Budget Estimates for Fiscal Year 2025,* 288, 294.

CHAPTER 5. THE COLD WAR

1. Rosemary Foot, *The Wrong War: American Policy and the Dimensions of the Korean Conflict, 1950–1953* (Ithaca, N.Y.: Cornell University Press, 1985), 204–46.
2. McGeorge Bundy, *Danger and Survival: Choices About the Bomb in the First Fifty Years* (New York: Vintage, 1988), 273–87.
3. Stephen Kinzer, *All the Shah's Men: An American Coup and the Roots of Middle East Terror* (New York: John Wiley and Sons, 2003).
4. Gordon M. Goldstein, *Lessons in Disaster: McGeorge Bundy and the Path to War in Vietnam* (New York: Henry Holt, 2008), 189.
5. One window into this world can be found at Ben R. Rich and Leo Janos, *Skunk Works* (Boston: Little, Brown, 1994).
6. See, e.g., Thomas G. Mahnken, ed., *Net Assessment and Military Strategy: Retrospective and Prospective Essays* (Amherst, N.Y.: Cambria, 2020).
7. John Lewis Gaddis, *Strategies of Containment: A Critical Appraisal of American National Security Policy During the Cold War,* rev. ed. (Oxford: Oxford University Press, 2005).
8. Stephen Sestanovich, *Maximalist: America in the World from Truman to Obama* (New York: Vintage, 2014), 10.
9. Richard Bennet and Alex Noyes, *War at Arm's Length: How to Build Effective Partners Through Military Assistance* (New Haven: Yale University Press, 2025).
10. Lindsey A. O'Rourke, *Covert Regime Change: America's Secret Cold War* (Ithaca, N.Y.: Cornell University Press, 2018), 97–124.
11. Stephen Wertheim, *Tomorrow the World: The Birth of U.S. Global Supremacy* (Cambridge, Mass.: Harvard University Press, 2020); G. John Ikenberry, *After Victory: Institutions, Strategic Restraint, and the Rebuilding of Order After Major Wars* (Princeton, N.J.: Princeton University Press, 2000). See also Eliot A. Cohen, *The Big Stick: The Limits of Soft Power and the Necessity of Military Force* (New York: Basic, 2016), 1–5.
12. Stacie L. Pettyjohn, *U.S. Global Defense Posture, 1783–2011* (Santa Monica, Calif.: RAND, 2012), 50–51.
13. The debate on this issue stretches back at least four decades. See Robert O. Keohane, *After Hegemony: Cooperation and Discord in the World Political Economy* (Princeton, N.J.: Princeton University Press, 1984).
14. See Robert Kagan, *The World America Made* (New York: Alfred A. Knopf, 2012).
15. Dean Acheson, *Present at the Creation: My Years in the State Department* (New York: W. W. Norton, 1987).
16. Barry Blechman and Stephen Kaplan count 215 instances where force was used to signal between 1946 and 1975; of the cases they examine in detail, favorable outcomes were witnessed in about three-fourths in the six months following the initial force movement but in fewer than half if one played out the history over three years. See Barry M. Blechman and Stephen S. Kaplan, *Force Without War: U.S. Armed Forces as a Political Instrument* (Washington, D.C.: Brookings Institution Press, 1978), 23, 87; Keren Yarhi-Milo, *Who Fights for Reputation? The Psychology of Leaders in International Conflict* (Princeton, N.J.: Princeton University Press, 2018), 121, 267; and Daryl G. Press, *Calculating Credibility: How Leaders Assess Military Threats* (Ithaca, N.Y.: Cornell University Press, 2005).

17. For sophisticated treatments of how, when, and why deterrence works, see Alexander L. George and Richard Smoke, *Deterrence in American Foreign Policy: Theory and Practice* (New York: Columbia University Press, 1974), 519–32; and Bruce Bueno de Mesquita, *The War Trap* (New Haven: Yale University Press, 1981).
18. Henry Kissinger, *World Order* (New York: Penguin, 2014), 265–66.
19. Samuel P. Huntington, *The Soldier and the State: The Theory and Politics of Civil-Military Relations* (Cambridge, Mass.: Harvard University Press, 1957); Alexander L. George and Richard Smoke, *Deterrence in American Foreign Policy: Theory and Practice* (New York: Columbia University Press, 1974), 1–8.
20. On these kinds of questions about the purposes and value of grand strategy, see, e.g., Hal Brands, *What Good Is Grand Strategy? Power and Purpose in American Statecraft from Harry S. Truman to George W. Bush* (Ithaca, N.Y.: Cornell University Press, 2014), 17–58.
21. James M. Goldgeier, "A Complex Man with a Simple Idea," in Michael Kimmage and Matthew Rojansky, eds., *A Kennan for Our Times: Revisiting America's Greatest 20th Century Diplomat in the 21st Century* (Washington, D.C.: Wilson Center, 2019), 25–35; David Callahan, *Between Two Worlds: Realism, Idealism, and American Foreign Policy After the Cold War* (New York: HarperCollins, 1994), 18–29; Barton Gellman, *Contending with Kennan: Toward a Philosophy of American Power* (New York: Praeger, 1984); Kinzer, *All the Shah's Men,* 1–16.
22. Raymond L. Garthoff, *Détente and Confrontation: American-Soviet Relations from Nixon to Reagan,* rev. ed. (Washington, D.C.: Brookings Institution Press, 1994), 1160–74; Stephen Kinzer, *Overthrow: America's Century of Regime Change from Hawaii to Iraq* (New York: Henry Holt, 2006).
23. Tony Judt, *Postwar: A History of Europe Since 1945* (New York: Penguin, 2005), 29–49.
24. Stephen Rodgers, "Winston Churchill's Iron Curtain Speech—March 5, 1946," National World War II Museum, New Orleans, La., March 5, 2021, https://www.nationalww2museum.org/war/articles/winston-churchills-iron-curtain-speech-march-5-1946.
25. Lawrence J. Haas, *Harry and Arthur: Truman, Vandenberg, and the Partnership That Created the Free World* (Lincoln: University of Nebraska Press, 2016), 152.
26. Sestanovich, *Maximalist,* 31.
27. Julian E. Zelizer, *Arsenal of Democracy: The Politics of National Security—From World War II to the War on Terrorism* (New York: Basic, 2012), 1–80; Haas, *Harry and Arthur,* 95–225; James M. Lindsay, *Congress and the Politics of U.S. Foreign Policy* (Baltimore: Johns Hopkins University Press, 1994), 12.
28. Michael J. Green, *By More Than Providence: Grand Strategy and American Power in the Asia Pacific Since 1783* (New York: Columbia University Press, 2017), 193–94.
29. Ian W. Toll, *Twilight of the Gods: War in the Western Pacific, 1944–1945* (New York: W. W. Norton, 2020), 763.
30. John W. Dower, *Embracing Defeat: Japan in the Wake of World War II* (New York: W. W. Norton, 2000), 108–10; U.S. Army Center of Military History, "The U.S. Constabulary in Post-War Germany (1946–1952)," Carlisle, Pa., April 2000, https://

history.army.mil/Unit-History/Force-Structure-Support/The-US-Constabulary-in-Post-War-Germany-1946-52.

31. Sean M. Zeigler et al., *Aligning Roles and Missions for Future Multidomain Warfare* (Santa Monica, Calif.: RAND, 2021), 70–80; Morton H. Halperin and David Halperin, “Rewriting the Key West Accord,” in Robert J. Art, Vincent Davis, and Samuel Huntington, eds., *Reorganizing America’s Defense: Leadership in War and Peace* (McLean, Va.: Pergamon-Brassey’s, 1985), 344–58.
32. James Dobbins et al., *America’s Role in Nation-Building from Germany to Iraq* (Santa Monica, Calif.: RAND, 2003), 10, 34; Office of the Under Secretary of Defense (Comptroller), *National Defense Budget Estimates for FY 2025* (Washington, D.C.: Department of Defense, April 2024), 294, https://comptroller.defense.gov/Portals/45/Documents/defbudget/FY2025/fy25_Green_Book.pdf; Bureau of the Census, *Historical Statistics of the United States, Colonial Times to 1957* (Washington, D.C.: U.S. Government, 1960), 736, https://www2.census.gov/library/publications/1960/compendia/hist_stats_colonial-1957/hist_stats_colonial-1957-chY.pdf.
33. Office of the Under Secretary of Defense (Comptroller), *National Defense Budget Estimates for FY 2025*, 138.
34. Sestanovich, *Maximalist,* 44–45.
35. Charles A. Stevenson, *Secdef: The Nearly Impossible Job of Secretary of Defense* (Washington, D.C.: Potomac, 2007), 9–10.
36. Brian McAllister Linn, *The Echo of Battle: The Army’s Way of War* (Cambridge, Mass.: Harvard University Press, 2007), 151–61.
37. Office of the Under Secretary of Defense (Comptroller), *National Defense Budget Estimates for FY 2025*, 279.
38. Russell F. Weigley, *The American Way of War: A History of United States Military Strategy and Policy* (Bloomington: Indiana University Press, 1977), 388–89.
39. Weigley, *American Way of War,* 397.
40. See Bruce Cumings, *The Korean War: A History* (New York: Modern Library, 2011), 149–61.
41. Conrad C. Crane, “Raiding the Beggar’s Pantry: The Search for Air Power Strategy in the Korean War,” *Journal of Military History* 63, no. 4 (October 1999): 885–920.
42. Robert A. Pape, *Bombing to Win: Air Power and Coercion in War* (Ithaca, N.Y.: Cornell University Press, 1996), 159–65.
43. Pape, *Bombing to Win,* 148–50.
44. Kenneth P. Werrell, “Across the Yalu: Rules of Engagement and the Communist Air Sanctuary During the Korean War,” *Journal of Military History* 72, no. 2 (April 2008): 470.
45. Mira Rapp-Hooper, *Shields of the Republic: The Triumph and Peril of America’s Alliances* (Cambridge, Mass.: Harvard University Press, 2020).
46. Gaddis, *Strategies of Containment,* 25, 30–31, 70, 78–86, 90–93, 106–12.
47. Sestanovich, *Maximalist,* 29.
48. William I. Hitchcock, *The Struggle for Europe: The Turbulent History of a Divided Continent* (New York: Doubleday, 2002), 64–65.

49. Office of the Legal Advisor, "U.S. Collective Defense Arrangements," Department of State, Washington, D.C., 2017, https://2009-2017.state.gov/s/l/treaty/collectivedefense.
50. Ryan Hass, Bonnie Glaser, and Richard Bush, *U.S.-Taiwan Relations: Will China's Challenge Lead to a Crisis?* (Washington, D.C.: Brookings Institution Press, 2023), 17.
51. Green, *By More Than Providence,* 289–91.
52. Pettyjohn, *U.S. Global Defense Posture,* 65.
53. Gaddis, *Strategies of Containment,* 112.
54. Weigley, *American Way of War,* 397.
55. See Judt, *Postwar,* 50; on "the art of commitment," see Thomas C. Schelling, *Arms and Influence,* new ed. (New Haven: Yale University Press, 2008), 35–91, esp. 36–49.
56. Alain C. Enthoven and K. Wayne Smith, *How Much Is Enough? Shaping the Defense Program, 1961–1969* (Santa Monica, Calif.: RAND, 2005), 117–42; Judt, *Postwar,* 245–46.
57. Richard D. Lawrence and Jeffrey Record, *U.S. Force Structure in NATO: An Alternative* (Washington, D.C.: Brookings Institution Press, 1974), 13; Enthoven and Smith, *How Much Is Enough?,* 117–42.
58. William P. Mako, *U.S. Ground Forces and the Defanse of Central Europe* (Washington, D.C.: Brookings Institution Press, 1983), 8.
59. Mako, *U.S. Ground Forces,* 17.
60. Lawrence and Record, *U.S. Force Structure in NATO,* 48.
61. Mako, *U.S. Ground Forces,* 17.
62. Frances M. Lussier, "U.S. Ground Forces and the Conventional Balance in Europe," Congressional Budget Office, Washington, D.C., June 1988, 9, https://www.cbo.gov/sites/default/files/100th-congress-1987-1988/reports/doc01b-entire.pdf.
63. Mako, *U.S. Ground Forces,* 18, 26.
64. Frances M. Lussier, "Budgetary and Military Effects of a Treaty Limiting Conventional Forces in Europe," Congressional Budget Office, Washington, D.C., September 1990, 14–15, https://apps.dtic.mil/sti/tr/pdf/ADA464681.pdf; Lawrence and Record, *U.S. Force Structure in NATO,* 36, 84–88; Douglas I. Bell, "Just Add Soldiers: Army Prepositioned Stocks and Agile Force Projection," Army Heritage and Education Center, Carlisle, Pa., 2023, https://ahec.armywarcollege.edu/documents/Bell_POMCUS%20_Modernization_Study%20_Complete.pdf.
65. Lawrence and Record, *U.S. Force Structure in NATO,* 42–43.
66. Lawrence Freedman, *The Evolution of Nuclear Strategy* (New York: St. Martin's, 1983), xv; see also Janne E. Nolan, *Guardians of the Arsenal: The Politics of Nuclear Strategy* (New York: Basic, 1989).
67. Brands, *What Good Is Grand Strategy?,* 53.
68. Freedman, *Evolution of Nuclear Strategy,* 54–75.
69. Christopher J. Bowie, "Air Power Metamorphosis: Rethinking Air Force Combat Force Modernization," Center for Strategic and Budgetary Assessments, Washington, D.C., 2023, 7–9, https://csbaonline.org/uploads/documents/CSBA8342_(Air_Power_Metamorphosis_Report)_FINAL_web.pdf.
70. Freedman, *Evolution of Nuclear Strategy,* 76–86.

71. Robert R. Bowie and Richard H. Immerman, *Waging Peace: How Eisenhower Shaped an Enduring Cold War Strategy* (Oxford: Oxford University Press, 1998), 108, 248; Samuel F. Wells, *Fearing the Worst: How Korea Transformed the Cold War* (New York: Columbia University Press, 2019).
72. Bernard Brodie, *Strategy in the Missile Age* (Princeton, N.J.: Princeton University Press, 1959), 396.
73. David Mosher, Michael O'Hanlon, and Raymond Hall, "The START Treaty and Beyond," Congressional Budget Office, Washington, D.C., October 1991, 62; Stephen I. Schwartz, "Introduction," in Stephen I. Schwartz, ed., *Atomic Audit: The Costs and Consequences of U.S. Nuclear Weapons Since 1940* (Washington, D.C.: Brookings Institution Press, 1998), 1–5.
74. Mosher, O'Hanlon, and Hall, "START Treaty and Beyond," 10; Desmond Ball, "The Development of the SIOP, 1960–1983," in Desmond Ball and Jeffrey Richelson, eds., *Strategic Nuclear Targeting* (Ithaca, N.Y.: Cornell University Press, 1986), 66–70; David Alan Rosenberg, "The Origins of Overkill: Nuclear Weapons and American Strategy, 1945–1960," in Steven E. Miller, *Strategy and Nuclear Deterrence* (Princeton, N.J.: Princeton University Press, 1984), 116–17.
75. Bruce G. Blair, John E. Pike, and Stephen I. Schwartz, "Targeting and Controlling the Bomb," in Stephen I. Schwartz, ed., *Atomic Audit: The Costs and Consequences of U.S. Nuclear Weapons Since 1940* (Washington, D.C.: Brookings Institution Press, 2008), 206.
76. G. Philip Hughes, "Planning U.S. General Purpose Forces: The Theater Nuclear Forces," Congressional Budget Office, Washington, D.C., January 1977, 1–11, https://apps.dtic.mil/sti/tr/pdf/ADA593862.pdf.
77. Kevin O'Neill, "Building the Bomb," in Stephen I. Schwartz, ed., *Atomic Audit: The Costs and Consequences of U.S. Nuclear Weapons Since 1940* (Washington, D.C.: Brookings Institution Press, 1998), 46; Robert S. Norris, Steven M. Kosiak, and Stephen I. Schwartz, "Deploying the Bomb," in Stephen I. Schwartz, ed., *Atomic Audit: The Costs and Consequences of U.S. Nuclear Weapons Since 1940* (Washington, D.C.: Brookings Institution Press, 1998), 187.
78. Bundy, *Danger and Survival,* 273–87.
79. O'Neill, "Building the Bomb," 46.
80. Freedman, *Evolution of Nuclear Strategy,* 109–38; on the evolution of conventional and nuclear Army doctrine over the years, as well as the priority accorded to planning for European war rather than regional war, see Ingo Trauschweizer, *The Cold War U.S. Army: Building Deterrence for Limited War* (Lawrence: University Press of Kansas, 2008).
81. Blair, Pike, and Schwartz, "Targeting and Controlling the Bomb," 205.
82. David N. Schwartz, *NATO's Nuclear Dilemmas* (Washington, D.C.: Brookings Institution Press, 1983), 62–81, 179–92; Freedman, *Evolution of Nuclear Strategy,* 303–29, 383–87; Fred Kaplan, *The Wizards of Armageddon* (New York: Touchstone, 1983), 283–85.
83. Enthoven and Smith, *How Much Is Enough?*, 121–32, 165–96, 207–10.
84. O'Neill, "Building the Bomb," in Stephen I. Schwartz, ed., *Atomic Audit: The Costs and Consequences of U.S. Nuclear Weapons Since 1940* (Washington, D.C.: Brookings Institution Press, 1998), 52.

85. Blair, Pike, and Schwartz, "Targeting and Controlling the Bomb," 208.
86. Herman Kahn, *On Thermonuclear War,* 2nd ed. (Princeton, N.J.: Princeton University Press, 1961), 20; Kaplan, *Wizards of Armageddon,* 220–31.
87. Thomas C. Schelling, *The Strategy of Conflict,* new ed. (Cambridge, Mass.: Harvard University Press, 1980), 187–203.
88. Carl H. Builder, *The Masks of War: American Military Styles in Strategy and Analysis* (Baltimore: Johns Hopkins University Press, 1989), 196–98; Freedman, *Evolution of Nuclear Strategy,* 127–34, 215–33.
89. Eric S. Edelman, "Nuclear Strategy in Theory and Practice: The Great Divergence," in Hal Brands, ed., *The New Makers of Modern Strategy: From the Ancient World to the Digital Age* (Princeton, N.J.: Princeton University Press, 2023), 667; Frances J. Gavin, "The Elusive Nature of Nuclear Strategy," in Brands, *New Makers of Modern Strategy,* 692.
90. See Bruce Riedel, *JFK's Forgotten Crisis: Tibet, the CIA, and the Sino-Indian War* (Washington, D.C.: Brookings Institution Press, 2015), 180–81.
91. Bruce Riedel, *Beirut 1958: How America's Wars in the Middle East Began* (Washington, D.C.: Brookings Institution Press, 2023); Craig L. Symonds, *The U.S. Navy: A Concise History* (Oxford: Oxford University Press, 2016), 100; Robert W. Love Jr., *History of the U.S. Navy,* vol. 2: *1942–1991* (Harrisburg, Pa.: Stackpole, 1992), 693–701.
92. Sestanovich, *Maximalist,* 30–31.
93. Andrei Cherny, *The Candy Bombers: The Untold Story of the Berlin Airlift and America's Finest Hour* (New York: G. P. Putnam's Sons, 2008), 252–53, 543.
94. Bundy, *Danger and Survival,* 273–86.
95. Richard K. Betts, *Nuclear Blackmail and Nuclear Balance* (Washington, D.C.: Brookings Institution Press, 1987), 83–92; Bundy, *Danger and Survival,* 358–90.
96. Betts, *Nuclear Blackmail and Nuclear Balance,* 92–109.
97. Frederick Kempe, *Berlin 1961: Kennedy, Khrushchev, and the Most Dangerous Place on Earth* (New York: G. P. Putnam's Sons, 2011).
98. Bundy, *Danger and Survival,* 367.
99. Kempe, *Berlin 1961,* 482–502.
100. Zelizer, *Arsenal of Democracy,* 149–51.
101. Raymond L. Garthoff, "The Cuban Missile Crisis: An Overview," in James A. Nathan, ed., *The Cuban Missile Crisis Revisited* (New York: St. Martin's, 1992), 41–53.
102. Michael Dobbs, *One Minute to Midnight: Kennedy, Khrushchev, and Castro on the Brink of Nuclear War* (New York: Alfred A. Knopf, 2008), 58–63.
103. Richard Ned Lebow, *Between Peace and War: The Nature of International Crisis* (Baltimore: Johns Hopkins University Press, 1981), 299–303.
104. See also Riedel, *JFK's Forgotten Crisis,* 180–81.
105. Dobbs, *One Minute to Midnight;* Betts, *Nuclear Blackmail and Nuclear Balance,* 109–23, 144–79.
106. Bruce Jones, "Instrument of Order: Does the U.N. Security Council Matter in an Era of Global South Diplomacy and Major Power Tensions?" Brookings, June 3, 2024, https://www.brookings.edu/articles/instrument-of-order/.
107. Robert F. Hale, "Financing the Fight: A History and Assessment of Department of Defense Budget Formulation Processes," Brookings Institution, Washington, D.C., April

2021, https://www.brookings.edu/wp-content/uploads/2021/04/FP_20210429_financing_the_fight_hale.pdf.

108. Builder, *Masks of War.*
109. Enthoven and Smith, *How Much Is Enough?,* 1–50.
110. Philip Odeen, "A Critique of the PPB System," in Art, Davis, and Huntington, *Reorganizing America's Defense,* 375–80.
111. General David Petraeus and Andrew Roberts, *Conflict: The Evolution of Warfare from 1945 to Ukraine* (New York: HarperCollins, 2023), 78.
112. Henry Kissinger, *Diplomacy* (New York: Simon and Schuster, 1994), 620–42.
113. See John R. Galvin, *Fighting the Cold War: A Soldier's Memoir* (Lexington: University of Kentucky Press, 2015), 154.
114. Kenneth M. Pollack, *Armies of Sand: The Past, Present, and Future of Arab Military Effectiveness* (Oxford: Oxford University Press, 2019), 174–204.
115. Stanley Karnow, *Vietnam: A History* (New York: Penguin, 1997), 372–402.
116. Robert S. McNamara, *In Retrospect: The Tragedy and Lessons of Vietnam* (New York: Vintage, 1996), 186.
117. Karnow, *Vietnam,* 695–97.
118. Pettyjohn, *U.S. Global Defense Posture,* 72–73.
119. Weigley, *American Way of War,* 467.
120. Andrew F. Krepinevich Jr., *The Army and Vietnam* (Baltimore: Johns Hopkins University Press, 1986), 143.
121. James T. Quinlivan, "Force Requirements in Stability Operations," *Parameters* 25, no. 1 (Winter 1995): 56–69; Lt. Gen. David H. Petraeus and Lt. Gen. James F. Amos, *Field Manual 3-24: Counterinsurgency* (Washington, D.C.: U.S. Army, December 2006). For an empirically based critique, see Jeffrey A. Friedman, "Manpower and Counterinsurgency: Empirical Foundations for Theory and Doctrine," *Security Studies* 20, no. 4 (2011): 556–91.
122. Max Boot, *Invisible Armies: An Epic History of Guerrilla Warfare from Ancient Times to the Present* (New York: W. W. Norton, 2013), 420.
123. Krepinevich, *Army and Vietnam,* 157–63. Phase one consists of party formation and organization.
124. Thomas E. Ricks, *The Generals: American Military Command from World War II to Today* (New York: Penguin, 2012), 232.
125. Pierre Asselin, *We Don't Want a Munich: Hanoi's Diplomatic Strategy, 1965–1968* (Carlisle, Pa.: U.S. Army Center of Military History, 2012); John M. Carland, "Studies in the Exercise of Power: Secretaries of Defense and the Vietnam War, 1961–1973," *Army History,* no. 120 (Summer 2021): 32–44.
126. Karnow, *Vietnam,* 450–69.
127. Edward J. Drea, *McNamara, Clifford, and the Burdens of Vietnam* (Washington, D.C.: Historical Office of the Office of the Secretary of Defense, 2011), 127–30; Max Hastings, *Vietnam: An Epic Tragedy, 1945–1975* (New York: Harper, 2018), 322.
128. Krepinevich, *Army and Vietnam,* 200–201, 210–13.
129. McNamara, *In Retrospect,* 244.
130. Enthoven and Smith, *How Much Is Enough?,* 304.

131. Michael E. O'Hanlon, *Military History for the Modern Strategist: America's Major Wars Since 1861* (Washington, D.C.: Brookings Institution Press, 2023), 228.
132. Robert A. Pape, *Bombing to Win: Air Power and Coercion in War* (Ithaca, N.Y.: Cornell University Press, 1996), 183–95.
133. George C. Herring, *America's Longest War: The United States and Vietnam, 1950–1975,* 2nd ed. (New York: Alfred A. Knopf, 1986), 146–48.
134. See Boot, *Invisible Armies,* 199–200.
135. Bing West, *The Village* (New York: Pocket, 2003).
136. Krepinevich, *Army and Vietnam,* 172–80.
137. See, e.g., Cavender S. Sutton, review of Ted N. Easterling, *War in the Villages: The U.S. Marine Corps Combined Action Platoons in the Vietnam War* (Denton: University of North Texas Press, 2021), in *Journal of Military History* 85, no. 4 (October 2021): 1143–45.
138. John A. Nagl, *Learning to Eat Soup with a Knife: Counterinsurgency Lessons from Malaya and Vietnam* (Chicago: University of Chicago Press, 2005), 152–57.
139. Karnow, *Vietnam,* 616.
140. Petraeus and Roberts, *Conflict,* 77–134.
141. Mark Moyar, *A Question of Command: Counterinsurgency from the Civil War to Iraq* (New Haven: Yale University Press, 2009), 161–67.
142. Herring, *America's Longest War,* 225.
143. Lewis Sorley, *A Better War: The Unexamined Victories and Final Tragedy of America's Last Years in Vietnam* (New York: Harcourt, 1999), 204–10.
144. Sorley, *Better War,* 243–60; Hastings, *Vietnam,* 572–84.
145. Sorley, *Better War,* 217.
146. Karnow, *Vietnam,* 672.
147. Pape, *Bombing to Win,* 197–205.
148. Office of the Under Secretary of Defense (Comptroller), *National Defense Budget Estimates for FY 2025,* 288.
149. Office of the Under Secretary of Defense (Comptroller), *National Defense Budget Estimates for FY 2025,* 279.
150. Jerald G. Bachman, John D. Blair, and David R. Segal, *The All-Volunteer Force: A Study of Ideology in the Military* (Ann Arbor: University of Michigan Press, 1977), 30.
151. M. Wade Markel et al., *The Evolution of U.S. Military Policy from the Constitution to the Present,* vol. 4: *The Total Force Policy Era, 1970–2015* (Santa Monica, Calif.: RAND, 2020), xx–35; James Kitfield, *Prodigal Soldiers: How the Generation of Officers Born of Vietnam Revolutionized the American Style of War* (Washington, D.C.: Potomac, 1995), 350.
152. Kitfield, *Prodigal Soldiers,* 146–51, 348–52.
153. Conrad C. Crane, "Post-Vietnam Drawdown: The Myth of the Abrams Doctrine," in Jason W. Warren, ed., *Drawdown: The American Way of Postwar* (New York: New York University Press, 2016), 241–52.
154. Markel et al., *Evolution of U.S. Military Policy,* 33–34.
155. Martin Binkin and William W. Kaufmann, *U.S. Army Guard and Reserve: Rhetoric, Realities, Risks* (Washington, D.C.: Brookings Institution Press, 1989), 9.

156. Charles A. Sorrels, "Planning U.S. General Purpose Forces: Forces Related to Asia," Congressional Budget Office, Washington, D.C., June 1977, 66, https://www.cbo.gov/sites/default/files/95th-congress-1977-1978/reports/1977_06_asia.pdf.
157. Sorrels, "Planning U.S. General Purpose Forces," 55–63.
158. Beth Bloomfield, "Force Planning and Budgetary Implications of U.S. Withdrawal from Korea," Congressional Budget Office, Washington, D.C., May 1978, 10–15, https://www.cbo.gov/sites/default/files/95th-congress-1977-1978/reports/78-cbo-004.pdf; Green, *By More Than Providence,* 377–80.
159. Green, *By More Than Providence,* 336–45; Under Secretary of Defense (Comptroller), *National Defense Budget Estimates for FY 2025,* 291.
160. Green, *By More Than Providence,* 394–97.
161. Martin Indyk, *Master of the Game: Henry Kissinger and the Art of Middle East Diplomacy* (New York: Alfred A. Knopf, 2021), 170–99; Betts, *Nuclear Blackmail and Nuclear Balance,* 123–29.
162. Austin Carson, *Secret Wars: Covert Conflict in International Politics* (Princeton, N.J.: Princeton University Press, 2018), 238–82.
163. Thomas L. McNaugher, *Arms and Oil: U.S. Military Strategy and the Persian Gulf* (Washington, D.C.: Brookings Institution Press, 1985), 11–18.
164. William W. Kaufmann, *Defense in the 1980s* (Washington, D.C.: Brookings Institution Press, 1981), 23.
165. See Barry M. Blechman and Stephen S. Kaplan, *Force Without War: U.S. Armed Forces as a Political Instrument* (Washington, D.C.: Brookings Institution Press, 1978), 33. Another Brookings scholar, Joshua Epstein, later demonstrated how difficult it would have been logistically for the Soviet Union to reach Iran's Persian Gulf coast and sustain a fighting force there—especially if the United States properly prepared to interfere with its relatively few options to establish and sustain logistics and supply lines through mountainous northern Iran—in what remains a classic work of defense analysis. See Joshua M. Epstein, *Strategy and Force Planning: The Case of the Persian Gulf* (Washington, D.C.: Brookings Institution Press, 1987), 1–7, 107–16.
166. Rachel Schmidt, "Moving U.S. Forces: Options for Strategic Mobility," Congressional Budget Office, Washington, D.C., February 1997, 1–25, 80–81, https://www.cbo.gov/publication/10337. Moving 1,000 tons of equipment 1,000 miles per day (allowing time for the return trip, plus loading and unloading and maintaining aircraft) would constitute 1 million ton-miles per day, for example. Moving an entire brigade of the Eighty-Second Airborne Division, with a weight of around 10,000 tons, all at once could in theory be handled by this fleet.
167. Mako, *U.S. Ground Forces,* 17.
168. Robert P. Haffa Jr., *The Half War: Planning U.S. Rapid Deployment Forces to Meet a Limited Contingency, 1960–1983* (Boulder, Colo.: Westview, 1984), 17–79, esp. 38, 42, 47.
169. James Graham Wilson, *America's Cold Warrior: Paul Nitze and National Security from Roosevelt to Reagan* (Ithaca, N.Y.: Cornell University Press, 2024), 172–91.
170. Freedman, *Evolution of Nuclear Strategy,* 377–83; Kaplan, *Wizards of Armageddon,* 364–73.

171. Blair, Pike, and Schwartz, "Targeting and Controlling the Bomb," 205.
172. Bundy, *Danger and Survival,* 559–67.
173. See, e.g., Jonathan Schell, *The Fate of the Earth* (New York: Alfred A. Knopf, 1982); Carl Sagan and Richard Turco, *A Path Where No Man Thought: Nuclear Winter and the End of the Arms Race* (New York: Random House, 1990); and Strobe Talbott, *Deadly Gambits: The Reagan Administration and the Stalemate in Nuclear Arms Control* (New York: Alfred A. Knopf, 1984).
174. Mosher, O'Hanlon, and Hall, "START Treaty and Beyond," 14–15.
175. Joshua M. Epstein, *The 1987 Defense Budget* (Washington, D.C.: Brookings Institution Press, 1986), 14–15.
176. William W. Kaufmann, *Glasnost, Perestroika, and U.S. Defense Spending* (Washington, D.C.: Brookings Institution Press, 1990), 64.
177. Center for Arms Control and Nonproliferation, "Fact Sheet: The Soviet False Alarm Incident and Able Archer 83," Washington, D.C., 2024, https://armscontrolcenter.org/the-soviet-false-alarm-incident-and-able-archer-83.
178. Walter Slocombe, "The Countervailing Strategy," in Miller, *Strategy and Nuclear Deterrence,* 245–54; Wilson, *America's Cold Warrior,* 13; Kaplan, *Wizards of Armageddon,* 383–84; John Newhouse, *The Nuclear Age: From Hiroshima to Star Wars* (London: Michael Joseph, 1989), 286.
179. Robert Jervis, *The Illogic of American Nuclear Strategy* (Ithaca, N.Y.: Cornell University Press, 1984), 64–65.
180. Mosher and O'Hanlon, "START Treaty and Beyond," 2; Arms Control Association, "Strategic Arms Limitations Talks (SALT I): Treaties and Agreements," Washington, D.C., 2017, https://www.armscontrol.org/treaties/strategic-arms-limitation-talks.
181. Garthoff, *Détente and Confrontation,* 213–23.
182. See, e.g., Galvin, *Fighting the Cold War,* 351.
183. Thomas B. Cochran, William M. Arkin, Robert S. Norris, and Jeffrey I. Sands, *Nuclear Weapons Databook,* vol. 4: *Soviet Nuclear Weapons* (New York: Harper and Row, 1989), 22.
184. Stephen I. Schwartz, "Introduction," in Stephen I. Schwartz, ed., *Atomic Audit: The Costs and Consequences of U.S. Nuclear Weapons Since 1940* (Washington, D.C.: Brookings Institution Press, 1998), 23.
185. Kitfield, *Prodigal Soldiers,* 229.
186. Frederick W. Kagan, *Finding the Target: The Transformation of American Military Policy* (New York: Encounter, 2007), 66.
187. Office of the Under Secretary of Defense (Comptroller), *National Defense Budget Estimates for FY 2025,* 141, 280; Kitfield, *Prodigal Soldiers,* 199–277.
188. Bernard Rostker, *I Want You! The Evolution of the All-Volunteer Force* (Santa Monica, Calif.: RAND, 2006), 512–29.
189. Martin Binkin, *America's Volunteer Military: Progress and Prospects* (Washington, D.C.: Brookings Institution Press, 1984), 9.
190. Markel et al., *Evolution of U.S. Military Policy,* 57.
191. Defense Casualty Analysis System, "U.S. Active Duty Military Deaths by Year and Manner," Department of Defense, Washington, D.C., August 23, 2023, https://dcas.dmdc.osd.mil/dcas/app/summaryData/deaths/byYearManner.

192. Edward C. Keefer, *Harold Brown: Offsetting the Soviet Military Challenge, 1977–1981* (Washington, D.C.: Historical Office, Department of Defense, 2017), 575–600.
193. On the Army programs, see, e.g., TRADOC History and Heritage Office, "TRADOC and the Development of a New Generation of Weapons: TRADOC 50th Anniversary Series," U.S. Army, June 6, 2023, https://www.army.mil/article/267325/tradoc_and_the_development_of_a_new_generation_of_weapons_tradoc_50th_anniversary_series.
194. Richard K. Betts, *Military Readiness: Concepts, Choices, Consequences* (Washington, D.C.: Brookings Institution Press, 1995), 111.
195. Deborah Clay-Mendez, Richard L. Fernandez, and Amy Belasco, "Trends in Selected Indicators of Military Readiness, 1980–1993," Congressional Budget Office, Washington, D.C., April 1994, 68–71, https://www.cbo.gov/sites/default/files/103rd-congress-1993-1994/reports/doc13.pdf.
196. Markel et al., *Evolution of U.S. Military Policy,* 52.
197. Norman Friedman, *The U.S. Maritime Strategy* (London: Jane's, 1988), 182–205.
198. See Linton F. Brooks, "Naval Power and National Security: The Case for the Maritime Strategy," in Steven E. Miller and Stephen Van Evera, eds., *Naval Strategy and National Security* (Princeton, N.J.: Princeton University Press, 1988), 16–46; and Barry R. Posen, "Inadvertent Nuclear War? Escalation and NATO's Northern Flank," in Miller and Evera, *Naval Strategy and National Security,* 332–58.
199. Michael H. Berger, "The Costs of the Administration's Plan for the Navy Through the Year 2010," Washington, D.C., Congressional Budget Office, 1991, 2, https://www.cbo.gov/sites/default/files/102nd-congress-1991-1992/reports/1991_12_thecostoftheadminnavy.pdf; Robert F. Hale, "Testimony Before the Subcommittee on Projection Forces and Regional Defense, Senate Armed Services Committee," Congressional Budget Office, Washington, D.C., May 22, 1990, https://www.cbo.gov/sites/default/files/102nd-congress-1991-1992/reports/1991_12_thecostoftheadminnavy.pdf; Kitfield, *Prodigal Soldiers,* 275.
200. Peter T. Tarpgaard, "Building a 600-Ship Navy: Costs, Timing, and Alternative Approaches," Congressional Budget Office, Washington, D.C., March 1982, 4, https://apps.dtic.mil/sti/tr/pdf/ADA474788.pdf.
201. For instance, in recent times, a carrier battle group has had roughly the following notional cycle: thirty-two weeks of maintenance, forty-seven weeks of training, thirty to forty-three weeks of deployment, and seventeen to thirty weeks of sustainment during which it is available for short missions but back in port. See Eric J. Labs, "Preserving the Navy's Forward Presence with a Smaller Fleet," Congressional Budget Office, March 2015, 9, https://www.cbo.gov/sites/default/files/114th-congress-2015-2016/reports/49989-forwardpresence-2.pdf. See also Dov S. Zakheim, "The U.S. Sea Control Mission: Forces, Capabilities, and Requirements," Congressional Budget Office, Washington, D.C., June 1977, 40–45, https://www.cbo.gov/sites/default/files/95th-congress-1977-1978/reports/77doc581.pdf; Michael B. Berger, "Moving the Marine Corps by Sea in the 1990s," Congressional Budget Office, Washington, D.C., 1989, 21, https://www.cbo.gov/sites/default/files/101st-congress-1989-1990/reports/89-cbo-040.pdf; Dov S. Zakheim and Andrew Hamilton, "U.S. Naval Forces:

The Peacetime Presence Mission," Congressional Budget Office, Washington, D.C., December 1978, 75–81, https://www.cbo.gov/sites/default/files/95th-congress-1977-1978/reports/78-cbo-044.pdf; and Eric J. Labs, "Increasing the Mission Capability of the Attack Submarine Force," Congressional Budget Office, Washington, D.C., March 2002, ix, https://apps.dtic.mil/sti/pdfs/ADA400687.pdf.

202. Lussier, "Budgetary and Military Effects," 7.
203. For a brief summary of how this debate played out through the late 1980s and even into the early 1990s, see Michael E. O'Hanlon, *The Art of War in the Age of Peace: U.S. Military Posture for the Post–Cold War World* (Westport, Conn.: Praeger, 1992), 1–15.
204. Lussier, "Budgetary and Military Effects," 2.
205. Lussier, "Budgetary and Military Effects," 2.
206. William P. Mako, *U.S. Ground Forces and the Defense of Central Europe* (Washington, D.C.: Brookings Institution Press, 1983); Lussier, "U.S. Ground Forces," 19, 85–86; Lussier, "Budgetary and Military Effects," 11–15.
207. Lawrence and Record, *U.S. Force Structure in NATO,* 16.
208. Joshua M. Epstein, *Conventional Force Reductions: A Dynamic Assessment* (Washington, D.C.: Brookings Institution Press, 1990), 1–70.
209. Barry R. Posen, "Measuring the European Conventional Balance: Coping with Complexity in Threat Assessment," in Steven E. Miller, ed., *Conventional Forces and American Defense Policy* (Princeton, N.J.: Princeton University Press, 1986), 79–120; John J. Mearsheimer, "Why the Soviets Can't Win Quickly in Central Europe," in Miller, *Conventional Forces and American Defense Policy,* 121–57.
210. Stephen M. Walt, *The Origins of Alliances* (Ithaca, N.Y.: Cornell University Press, 1987), 282–85.
211. Barry D. Watts, "Net Assessment in the Era of Superpower Competition," in Thomas G. Mahnken, ed., *Net Assessment and Military Strategy: Retrospective and Prospective Essays* (Amherst, N.Y.: Cambria, 2020), 58–62.
212. Max Boot, *Reagan: His Life and Legend* (New York: Liveright, 2024), 585; Kitfield, *Prodigal Soldiers,* 269.
213. James R. Locher III, *Victory on the Potomac: The Goldwater-Nichols Act Unifies the Pentagon* (College Station: Texas A&M Press, 2007), 3–11.
214. Kitfield, *Prodigal Soldiers,* 283–84.
215. See Locher, *Victory on the Potomac.*
216. Harold Brown with Joyce Winslow, *Star Spangled Security: Applying Lessons Learned over Six Decades Safeguarding America* (Washington, D.C.: Brookings Institution Press, 2012), 81–82.
217. Gary Sick, *All Fall Down: America's Tragic Encounter with Iran* (New York: Random House, 2005), 300–302.
218. Edward C. Keefer, *Caspar Weinberger and the U.S. Military Buildup: 1981–1985* (Washington, D.C.: Historical Office of the Department of Defense, 2023), 271–310.
219. Kitfield, *Prodigal Soldiers,* 215–31, 237.
220. See William J. Lynn, "The Wars Within: The Joint Military Structure and Its Critics," in Art, Davis, and Huntington, *Reorganizing America's Defense,* 168–204; and Kitfield, *Prodigal Soldiers,* 197–318.

221. Max Boot, *War Made New: Technology, Warfare, and the Course of History, 1500 to Today* (New York: Gotham, 2006), 318; Stephen Biddle, *Military Power: Explaining Victory and Defeat in Modern Battle* (Princeton, N.J.: Princeton University Press, 2004), 28; Kagan, *Finding the Target.*

CHAPTER 6. THE POST–COLD WAR WORLD

1. Indeed, one group found that over the first three decades of the post–Cold War era, the United States used military force for coercive purposes more than 100 times, with about a 50 percent success rate. See Jacob Aronson, Daniel Tuke, Paul Huth, and Melanie Sisson, "Making Use of History," in Melanie W. Sisson, James A. Siebens, and Barry M. Blechman, eds., *Military Coercion and U.S. Foreign Policy: The Use of Force Short of War* (New York: Routledge, 2020), 33–37.
2. On this issue, see M. E. Sarotte, *Not One Inch: America, Russia, and the Making of Post–Cold War Stalemate* (New Haven: Yale University Press, 2021); William J. Burns, *The Back Channel: A Memoir of American Diplomacy and the Case for Its Renewal* (New York: Random House, 2019), 232–33; and Richard K. British, *American Force: Dangers, Delusions, and Dilemmas in National Security* (New York: Columbia University Press, 2012), 188–96.
3. Derek Chollet and James Goldgeier, *America Between the Wars: From 11/9 to 9/11; The Misunderstood Years Between the Fall of the Berlin Wall and the Start of the War on Terror* (New York: Public Affairs, 2009).
4. See John M. Owen IV, *Liberal Peace, Liberal War: American Politics and International Security* (Ithaca, N.Y.: Cornell University Press, 1997); and for a recent articulation of Doyle's thinking on the subject, see Michael Doyle, *Cold Peace: Avoiding the New Cold War* (New York: Liveright, 2023), 67.
5. Sarotte, *Not One Inch.*
6. See George F. Will, "A Dog in That Fight?," *Newsweek,* June 11, 1995. For a fuller explanation of Baker's thinking and role in the conflict, see James A. Baker III with Thomas M. DeFrank, *The Politics of Diplomacy: Revolution, War and Peace, 1989–1992* (New York: G. P. Putnam's Sons, 1995), 634–51.
7. On the George H. W. Bush administration grand strategy, see, e.g., Stephen Sestanovich, *Maximalist: America in the World from Truman to Obama* (New York: Vintage, 2014), 243–72; Julian E. Zelizer, *Arsenal of Democracy: The Politics of National Security—from World War II to the War on Terrorism* (New York: Basic, 2010), 355–82; Baker, *Politics of Diplomacy;* Michael J. Green, *By More Than Providence: Grand Strategy and American Power in the Asia Pacific Since 1783* (New York: Columbia University Press, 2017), 429–52; and Robert B. Zoellick, *America in the World: A History of U.S. Diplomacy and Foreign Policy* (New York: Twelve, 2020), 418–42.
8. Richard H. Ullman, "Enlarging the Zone of Peace," *Foreign Policy,* no. 80 (Fall 1990): 102–20.
9. James Goldgeier, *Not Whether but When: The U.S. Decision to Enlarge NATO* (Washington, D.C.: Brookings Institution Pres, 1999); Sestanovich, *Maximalist,* 259–72.

10. "The 'Clinton Apology" of March 25, 1998, audio clip, History.com, https://www.history.com/speeches/the-clinton-apology.
11. Ivo H. Daalder and Michael E. O'Hanlon, *Winning Ugly: NATO's War to Save Kosovo* (Washington, D.C.: Brookings Institution Press, 2000).
12. Chollet and Goldgeier, *America Between the Wars;* Charles Krauthammer, "The Unipolar Moment," *Foreign Affairs* 70, no. 1 (1990–91): 23–33; Madeleine Albright, "The Today Show," February 19, 1998, https://1997-2001.state.gov/statements/1998/980219a.html.
13. John J. Lis and Zachary Selden, "NATO Burdensharing After Enlargement," Congressional Budget Office, Washington, D.C., August 2001, 5, https://apps.dtic.mil/sti/tr/pdf/ADA452609.pdf.
14. Joe Bosco, "Two U.S. Carriers Through the Taiwan Strait in 48 Years—Time for More," *The Hill,* July 21, 2020, https://thehill.com/opinion/international/508167-two-us-carriers-through-the-taiwan-strait-in-48-years-time-for-more.
15. An important work at the time was Samantha Power, *A Problem from Hell: America and the Age of Genocide* (New York: Basic, 2002).
16. Richard N. Haass, *The Reluctant Sheriff: The United States After the Cold War* (New York: Council on Foreign Relations, 1997); Jean-Marie Guehenno, *The Fog of Peace: A Memoir of International Peacekeeping in the 21st Century* (Washington, D.C.: Brookings Institution Press, 2015); David Petraeus and Andrew Roberts, *Conflict: The Evolution of Warfare from 1945 to Ukraine* (New York: HarperCollins, 2023); Richard K. British, *American Force: Dangers, Delusions, and Dilemmas in National Security* (New York: Columbia University Press, 2012), 50–80; Yahya M. Sadowski, *The Myth of Global Chaos* (Washington, D.C.: Brookings Institution Press, 1998).
17. Ron Suskind, *The One Percent Doctrine: Deep Inside America's Pursuit of Its Enemies Since 9/11* (New York: Simon and Schuster, 2006).
18. George Packer, *The Assassins' Gate: America in Iraq* (New York: Farrar, Straus and Giroux, 2006); Sestanovich, *Maximalist,* 273–99; Hal Brands, *What Good Is Grand Strategy? Power and Purpose in American Statecraft from Harry S. Truman to George W. Bush* (Ithaca, N.Y.: Cornell University Press, 2014), 144–89.
19. Francis Fukuyama, *The End of History and the Last Man* (New York: Free Press, 1992).
20. Chollet and Goldgeier, *America Between the Wars;* Francis Fukuyama, "The End of History?," *National Interest* 16 (Summer 1989): 3–18.
21. John Lewis Gaddis, *Surprise, Security, and the American Experience* (Cambridge, Mass.: Harvard University Press, 2004), 110.
22. On this history, see William J. Burns, *The Back Channel: A Memoir of American Diplomacy and the Case for Its Renewal* (New York: Random House, 2019), 200–242; Steven Pifer, *The Eagle and the Trident: U.S.-Ukraine Relations in Turbulent Times* (Washington, D.C.: Brookings Institution Press, 2017), 212–90; and Fiona Hill and Clifford G. Gaddy, *Mr. Putin: Operative in the Kremlin,* new and exp. ed. (Washington, D.C.: Brookings Institution Press, 2015), 261–388.
23. See Martin S. Indyk, Kenneth G. Lieberthal, and Michael E. O'Hanlon, *Bending History: Barack Obama's Foreign Policy* (Washington, D.C.: Brookings Institution Press, 2012); Kurt M. Campbell, *The Pivot: The Future of American Statecraft in Asia* (New

York: Twelve, 2016); Jeffrey A. Bader, *Obama and China's Rise: An Insider's Account of America's Asia Strategy* (Washington, D.C.: Brookings Institution Press, 2013); and Susan Rice, *Tough Love: My Story of the Things Worth Fighting For* (New York: Simon and Schuster, 2019), 241–42, 449–52, 471–72.

24. On the state of the world toward the end of the Obama presidency, see Thomas Wright, *All Measures Short of War: The Contest for the 21st Century and the Future of American Power* (New Haven: Yale University Press, 2017); and Paul B. Stares, *Preventive Engagement: How America Can Avoid War, Stay Strong, and Keep the Peace* (New York: Columbia University Press, 2018).

25. See Office of Technology Assessment, "New Technology for NATO: Implementing Follow-on Forces Attack," Washington, D.C., June 1987, https://www.princeton.edu/~ota/disk2/1987/8718/8718.PDF.

26. Thomas A. Keaney and Eliot A. Cohen, *Gulf War Air Power Survey Summary Report* (Washington, D.C.: Government Printing Office, 1993), 7; Les Aspin and William Dickinson, *Defense for a New Era: Lessons of the Persian Gulf War* (Washington, D.C.: Brassey's, 1992), 79; James A. Winnefeld, Preston Niblack, and Dana J. Johnson, *A League of Airmen: U.S. Air Power in the Gulf War* (Santa Monica, Calif.: RAND, 1994), 290.

27. Aspin and Dickinson, *Defense for a New Era,* 90.

28. Rick Atkinson, *Crusade: The Untold Story of the Persian Gulf War* (New York: Houghton Mifflin, 1993), 13–49.

29. Kenneth Pollack, *Iraq,* forthcoming.

30. See Jaganath Sankaran, *Bombing to Provoke: Rockets, Missiles, and Drones as Instruments of Fear and Coercion* (Oxford: Oxford University Press, 2024).

31. Michael R. Gordon and Bernard E. Trainor, *The Generals' War: The Inside Story of the Conflict in the Gulf* (New York: Back Bay, 1995), 227–48.

32. Colin Powell with Joseph E. Persico, *My American Journey* (New York: Random House, 1995), 511–12; Aspin and Dickinson, *Defense for a New Era,* 25.

33. Atkinson, *Crusade,* 416–21.

34. Keaney and Cohen, *Gulf War Air Power Survey,* 13.

35. Aspin and Dickinson, *Defense for a New Era,* 10–11; Keaney and Cohen, *Gulf War Air Power Survey,* 21.

36. Barry D. Watts, "Friction in the Gulf War," *Naval War College Review* 48, no. 4 (Fall 1995): 94, https://digital-commons.usnwc.edu/nwc-review/vol48/iss4/10.

37. Keaney and Cohen, *Gulf War Air Power Survey,* 65, 103–17, 203; Government Accountability Office, "Operation Desert Storm: Evaluation of the Air Campaign," Washington, D.C., June 1997, 178, https://www.gao.gov/assets/nsiad-97-134.pdf. Air power used in isolation is not always so effective; see Anthony M. Schinella, *Bombs Without Boots: The Limits of Air Power* (Washington, D.C.: Brookings Institution Press, 2019). On tank plinking, see Winnefeld, Niblack, and Johnson, *League of Airmen,* 170.

38. Keaney and Cohen, *Gulf War Air Power Survey,* 184–85.

39. Keaney and Cohen, *Gulf War Air Power Survey,* 174.

40. Aspin and Dickinson, *Defense for a New Era,* 21, 34–42; Winnefeld, Niblack, and Johnson, *League of Airmen,* 271.

41. Aspin and Dickinson, *Defense for a New Era,* 17; Congressional Budget Office, "Trends in Selected Indicators of Military Readiness, 1980 through 1993," Washington, D.C., March 1994, 68–71, https://www.cbo.gov/sites/default/files/103rd-congress-1993-1994/reports/doc13.pdf.
42. Winnefeld, Niblack, and Johnson, *League of Airmen,* 308–9; Brig. Gen. Robert H. Scales Jr., *Certain Victory: The U.S. Army in the Gulf War* (Washington, D.C.: Brassey's, 1994), 161.
43. Winnefeld, Niblack, and Johnson, *League of Airmen,* 169–71; Gordon and Trainor, *Generals' War,* 335, 465, 474; Keaney and Cohen, *Gulf War Air Power Survey,* 106.
44. Atkinson, *Crusade,* 394–403.
45. Gordon and Trainor, *Generals' War,* 371–74.
46. Aspin and Dickinson, *Defense for a New Era,* 13, 28–29.
47. Stephen Biddle, "The Past as Prologue: Assessing Theories of Future Warfare," *Security Studies* 8, no. 1 (Autumn 1998): 1–74.
48. Keaney and Cohen, *Gulf War Air Power Survey,* 109; Fletcher Burton, "Letters to the Editor," *Princeton Alumni Weekly,* November 2024, 4.
49. Kenneth M. Pollack, *Armies of Sand: The Past, Present, and Future of Arab Military Effectiveness* (Oxford: Oxford University Press, 2019), 161; Gordon and Trainor, *Generals' War,* 375–432; Stephen Biddle, *Military Power: Explaining Victory and Defeat in Modern Battle* (Princeton, N.J.: Princeton University Press, 2004), 132–49.
50. Caitlin Talmadge, *The Dictator's Army: Battlefield Effectiveness in Authoritarian Regimes* (Ithaca, N.Y.: Cornell University Press, 2015).
51. Stephen Biddle, "Victory Misunderstood: What the Gulf War Tells Us About the Future of Conflict," *International Security* 21, no. 2 (Fall 1996): 139–79; Biddle, *Military Power,* 132–49.
52. Pollack, *Armies of Sand,* 158–62.
53. See Keaney and Cohen, *Gulf War Air Power Survey,* 21, 58–64, 155; and Aspin and Dickinson, *Defense for a New Era,* 1–41. For data on Arab-Israeli wars, see Barry R. Posen, "Measuring the European Conventional Balance: Coping with Complexity in Threat Assessment," in Steven E. Miller, ed., *Conventional Forces and American Defense Policy* (Princeton, N.J.: Princeton University Press, 1986), 113; and Trevor N. Dupuy, *Numbers, Predictions, and War: Using History to Evaluate Combat Factors and Predict the Outcome of Battles* (Washington, D.C.: Hero, 1985), 118–39.
54. Scales, *Certain Victory,* 81.
55. Gordon and Trainor, *Generals' War,* 370.
56. Gordon and Trainor, *Generals' War,* 430–31.
57. Atkinson, *Crusade,* 9, 489–90.
58. Aspin and Dickinson, *Defense for a New Era,* 35; Keaney and Cohen, *Gulf War Air Power Survey,* 105–6; General Accounting Office, *Operation Desert Storm: Evaluation of the Air Campaign,* GAO/NSIAD-97-134 (Washington, D.C.: General Accounting Office, 1997), 100–159.
59. Civilian casualty estimates based on briefing by William Arkin of Greenpeace to Gulf War Air Power Survey project members, October 31, 1991, cited in Keaney and Cohen, *Gulf War Air Power Survey,* 75 (for other data, see 102–19).

60. Defense Casualty Analysis System, "U.S. Active Duty Military Deaths by Year and Manner," Department of Defense, Washington, D.C., August 2023, https://dcas.dmdc.osd.mil/dcas/app/summaryData/deaths/byYearManner; Congressional Research Service, "American War and Military Operations Casualties: Lists and Statistics," Washington, D.C., July 2020, https://sgfas.org/crs/natsec/RL32492.pdf.
61. Michael R. Gordon, "Cheney's Wary First Step," *New York Times,* January 31, 1990.
62. CBS News, "Cheney Turns Up the Volume," CBSNews.com, October 16, 2000, https://www.cbsnews.com/news/cheney-turns-up-the-volume.
63. Gordon and Trainor, *Generals' War.*
64. Fred Kaplan, "Powell: The U.S. Is 'Running Out of Demons,' " *Seattle Times,* April 9, 1991.
65. Michael O'Hanlon, *Defense Planning for the Late 1990s: Beyond the Desert Storm Framework* (Washington, D.C.: Brookings Institution Press, 1995), 1–25.
66. See, e.g., Conrad Crane, "Phase Four Operations: Where Wars Are Really Won," *Military Review,* May–June 2005, 27–36, https://www.armyupress.army.mil/Portals/7/military-review/Archives/English/MilitaryReview_2008CRII0831_art006.pdf; and U.S. Marine Corps, "Send in the Marines: A Marine Corps Operational Employment Concept to Meet an Uncertain Security Environment," Washington, D.C., January 2008, https://www.marines.mil/Portals/1/Publications/The%20Long%20War_1.pdf.
67. Les Aspin, "Report on the Bottom-Up Review," Department of Defense, Washington, D.C., October 1993, 13, 19, https://history.defense.gov/Portals/70/Documents/dod_reforms/Bottom-upReview.pdf.
68. For a critique of the RMA movement, see Michael E. O'Hanlon, *Technological Change and the Future of Warfare* (Washington, D.C.: Brookings Institution Press, 2000); see also Schinella, *Bombs Without Boots;* and Biddle, *Military Power.*
69. Christopher Bowie et al., *The New Calculus: Analyzing Airpower's Changing Role in Joint Theater Campaigns* (Santa Monica, Calif.: RAND, 1993).
70. O'Hanlon, *Defense Planning for the Late 1990s,* 9; Michael E. O'Hanlon, *Healing the Wounded Giant: Maintaining Military Preeminence While Cutting the Defense Budget* (Washington, D.C.: Brookings Institution Press, 2013), 19.
71. Secretary of Defense William J. Perry, *Annual Report to the President and the Congress* (Washington, D.C.: Department of Defense, 1995), 275; O'Hanlon, *Defense Planning for the Late 1990s,* 9.
72. John T. Correll, "Back to 'Win-Hold-Win,' " *Air and Space Forces Magazine,* October 1, 1999, https://www.airandspaceforces.com/article/1099edit/; Michael E. O'Hanlon, "Lighten Up on Rumsfeld," *Los Angeles Times,* May 24, 2001.
73. On U.S. troop strength in Iraq, see Sam Gollob and Michael O'Hanlon (based on earlier versions of the Iraq Index that included Adriana Lins de Albuquerque, Nina Kamp, Jason Campbell, Ian Livingston, and Adam Twardowski), "Iraq Index: Tracking Variables of Reconstruction and Security in Post–Saddam Hussein Iraq," Brookings Institution, Washington, D.C., August 25, 2020, https://www.brookings.edu/wp-content/uploads/2020/08/FP_20200825_iraq_index.pdf. On U.S. troop strength in Afghanistan, see Sam Gollob and Michael O'Hanlon (based on earlier work by the

same additional coauthors and Jeremy Shapiro), "Afghanistan Index," Brookings Institution, Washington, D.C., August 2020, https://www.brookings.edu/articles/afghanistan-index.

74. Frederick W. Kagan, *Finding the Target: The Transformation of American Military Policy* (New York: Encounter, 2006), 144–75; Under Secretary of Defense (Policy) Paul Wolfowitz, "Defense Planning Guidance, FY 1994–1999," Department of Defense, Washington, D.C., April 1992, 2, https://www.archives.gov/files/declassification/iscap/pdf/2008-003-docs1-12.pdf; Patrick E. Tyler, "U.S. Strategy Plan Calls for Insuring No Rivals Develop," *New York Times,* March 8, 1992.
75. Sadowski, *Myth of Global Chaos.*
76. For an entertaining rendition of this exchange, offered by Albright and Powell together (very amicably) more than two decades later, see "Madeleine Albright and Colin Powell: Finding Shared Values for U.S. Foreign Policy," conversation with Ann Compton, Library of Congress, Washington, D.C., July 8, 2015, https://www.loc.gov/item/2021689839/. See also Colin L. Powell, "U.S. Forces: Challenges Ahead," *Foreign Affairs* 71, no. 5 (Winter 1992/93): 32.
77. Center for Military History, "United States Forces, Somalia: After Action Report, and Historical Overview: The United States Army in Somalia, 1992–1994," U.S. Army, Washington, D.C., 2003, https://history.army.mil/html/documents/somalia/SomaliaAAR.pdf; Mark Bowden, *Black Hawk Down: A Story of Modern War* (New York: Grove, 2010).
78. Kenneth Pollack, *Iraq,* forthcoming.
79. John Miller, "Greetings, America, My Name Is Osama Bin Laden . . . ," *Frontline,* PBS News, 1999, https://www.pbs.org/wgbh/pages/frontline/shows/binladen/who/miller.html.
80. Benjamin S. Lambeth, *The Transformation of American Air Power* (Ithaca, N.Y.: Cornell University Press, 2000); Daalder and O'Hanlon, *Winning Ugly;* Schinella, *Bombs Without Boots.*
81. Daalder and O'Hanlon, *Winning Ugly,* 1–5, 137–237; Benjamin S. Lambeth, *NATO's Air War for Kosovo: A Strategic and Operational Assessment* (Santa Monica, Calif.: RAND, 2001), 88.
82. Lambeth, *NATO's Air War for Kosovo,* 220–22.
83. On the RMA debate, see, e.g., Andrew F. Krepinevich Jr., "Cavalry to Computer: The Pattern of Military Revolutions," *National Interest,* no. 37 (Fall 1994): 30–42; Biddle, *Military Power;* MacGregor Knox and Williamson Murray, eds., *The Dynamics of Military Revolution, 1300–2050* (Cambridge: Cambridge University Press, 2001); F. G. Hoffman, *Decisive Force: The New American Way of War* (Westport, Conn.: Praeger, 1996); Michael G. Vickers and Robert C. Martinage, *The Revolution in War* (Washington, D.C.: Center for Strategic and Budgetary Assessments, 2004); and O'Hanlon, *Military Technology and the Future of Warfare.*
84. Historical Office, Office of the Secretary of Defense, "Quadrennial Defense Review," Department of Defense, Washington, D.C., August 2024, https://history.defense.gov/Historical-Sources/Quadrennial-Defense-Review.

85. National Defense Panel, "Transforming Defense: National Security in the 21st Century," Arlington, Va., December 1997, https://www.govinfo.gov/content/pkg/GOVPUB-D-PURL-LPS15419/pdf/GOVPUB-D-PURL-LPS15419.pdf; Wayne Glass, "Closing Military Bases: An Interim Assessment," Congressional Budget Office, Washington, D.C., December 1996, https://www.cbo.gov/sites/default/files/104th-congress-1995-1996/reports/1996doc33.pdf.
86. O'Hanlon, *Technological Change.*
87. Commission to Assess the Ballistic Missile Threat to the United States, "Executive Summary," Washington, D.C., July 1998, https://irfas.org/threat/bm-threat.htm.
88. United States Commission on National Security/21st Century, "Road Map for National Security: Imperative for Change," Washington, D.C., January 2001, https://irfas.org/threat/nssg.pdf. For two forward-looking assessments of the new threat environment, published before the 9/11 attacks, see John D. Steinbruner, *Principles of Global Security* (Washington, D.C.: Brookings Institution Press, 2000); and Anthony Lake, *Six Nightmares: Real Threats in a Dangerous World and How America Can Meet Them* (New York: Little, Brown, 2000).
89. Dickie Davis, David Kilcullen, Greg Mills, and David Spencer, *A Great Perhaps? Colombia: Conflict and Convergence* (London: C. Hurst, 2016).
90. See Ivo H. Daalder and James M. Lindsay, *America Unbound: The Bush Revolution in Foreign Policy* (Washington, D.C.: Brookings Institution Press, 2005).
91. Bruce Hoffman, *Inside Terrorism,* 3rd ed. (New York: Columbia University Press, 2017), 88–90; 9/11 Commission, "The 9/11 Commission Report," Washington, D.C., 2004, 71–107, https://dpcld.defense.gov/Portals/49/Documents/Civil/911Report.pdf.
92. Kagan, *Finding the Target,* 293.
93. Michael E. O'Hanlon, "A Flawed Masterpiece," *Foreign Affairs* 81, no. 3 (March–April 2002): 47–63.
94. Sean Naylor, *Not a Good Day to Die: The Untold Story of Operation Anaconda* (New York: Berkley, 2005), 14.
95. Senate Foreign Relations Committee Majority Staff, "Tora Bora Revisited: How We Failed to Get bin Laden and Why It Matters Today," Government Printing Office, Washington, D.C., November 2009, https://www.govinfo.gov/content/pkg/CPRT-111SPRT53709/html/CPRT-111SPRT53709.htm; Boot, *War Made New,* 379.
96. Brands, *What Good Is Grand Strategy?,* 170.
97. Seth G. Jones, *Graveyard of Empires: America's War in Afghanistan* (New York: W. W. Norton, 2009), 110–15.
98. Ambassador James F. Dobbins, *After the Taliban: Nation-Building in Afghanistan* (Washington, D.C.: Potomac, 2008), 161–63.
99. Gollob and O'Hanlon, "Afghanistan Index."
100. Jones, *Graveyard of Empires,* 142–45.
101. James Dobbins, "Afghanistan Was Lost Long Ago: Defeat Wasn't Inevitable, but Early Mistakes Made Success Unlikely," *Foreign Affairs,* August 30, 2021, https://www.foreignaffairs.com/articles/afghanistan/2021-08-30/afghanistan-was-lost-long-ago.

102. See Michael E. O'Hanlon and Hassina Sherjan, *Toughing It Out in Afghanistan* (Washington, D.C.: Brookings Institution Press, 2011), 19–30, 129–56.
103. Ronald E. Neumann, *The Other War: Winning and Losing in Afghanistan* (Washington, D.C.: Potomac, 2009), 58, 109; Carter Malkasian, *The American War in Afghanistan: A History* (Oxford: Oxford University Press, 2021), 129–56.
104. Malkasian, *American War in Afghanistan,* 133, 456.
105. Malkasian, *American War in Afghanistan,* 101, 129–56.
106. Thomas Barfield, *Afghanistan: A Cultural and Political History,* 2nd ed. (Princeton, N.J.: Princeton University Press, 2022), 319; Gollob and O'Hanlon, "Afghanistan Index."
107. Jones, *Graveyard of Empires,* 213–20.
108. Antonio Giustozzi, "Conclusion," in Antonio Giustozzi, ed., *Decoding the New Taliban: Insights from the Afghan Field* (New York: Columbia University Press, 2009), 298.
109. David Kilcullen, *The Accidental Guerrilla: Fighting Small Wars in the Midst of a Big One* (Oxford: Oxford University Press, 2009), 48–49.
110. See "Strategic Geography" maps in Toby Dodge and Nicholas Redman, *Afghanistan to 2015 and Beyond* (London: International Institute for Strategic Studies, 2011), 166.
111. The Asia Foundation, *A Survey of the Afghan People: Afghanistan in 2009* (San Francisco: The Asia Foundation, 2009), 15–41.
112. Malkasian, *American War in Afghanistan,* 200.
113. Stanley McChrystal, *My Share of the Task: A Memoir* (New York: Penguin, 2013), 331; Petraeus and Amos, *Field Manual 3-24,* 1–13. Some believe that the range of twenty to twenty-five should have a substantially higher upper bound; see R. Royce Kneece Jr. et al., "Force Sizing for Stability Operations," Institute for Defense Analysis, Alexandria, Va., March 2010, https://apps.dtic.mil/sti/pdfs/ADA520942.pdf.
114. Vanda Felbab-Brown, *Aspiration and Ambivalence: Strategies and Realities of Counterinsurgency and State-Building in Afghanistan* (Washington, D.C.: Brookings Institution Press, 2012), 27–28.
115. Gollob and O'Hanlon, "Afghanistan Index." Brookings Institution, Washington, D.C., August 2020, https://www.brookings.edu/wp-content/uploads/2020/08/FP_20200825_afganistan_index.pdf.
116. Felbab-Brown, *Aspiration and Ambivalence,* 22–32.
117. For one critique, of not only Obama but the policy process writ large, see Daniel Bolger, *Why We Lost: A General's Inside Account of the Iraq and Afghanistan Wars* (Boston: Houghton Mifflin Harcourt, 2014), 420–34.
118. McChrystal, *My Share of the Task,* 361.
119. John Pike, "Afghan National Army (ANA)—Order of Battle," Globalsecurity.org, Washington, D.C., 2012, https://www.globalsecurity.org/military/world/afghanistan/ana-orbat.htm; C. J. Radin, "Afghan Security Forces Order of Battle," *Long War Journal,* May 2011, Foundation for Defense of Democracies, Washington, D.C., 2007, https://www.longwarjournal.org/oobafghanistan.
120. NATO Headquarters, "International Security Assistance Force: Key Facts and Figures," Brussels, August 1, 2013, https://www.nato.int/isaf/placemats_archive/2013-08-01-ISAF-Placemat.pdf.

121. Bolger, *Why We Lost,* 435.
122. Livingston and O'Hanlon, "Afghanistan Index," February 10, 2015.
123. Seth G. Jones and Arturo Munoz, *Afghanistan's Local War: Building Local Defense Forces* (Santa Monica, Calif.: RAND, 2010); Felbab-Brown, *Aspiration and Ambivalence,* 138–60, 268–70.
124. Malkasian, *American War in Afghanistan,* 300.
125. Malkasian, *American War in Afghanistan,* 384–403.
126. Special Inspector General for Afghanistan Reconstruction, "Divided Responsibility: Lessons from U.S. Security Sector Assistance Efforts in Afghanistan," Arlington, Va., 2019, 19–25, Divided Responsibility: Lessons from U.S. Security Sector Assistance Efforts in Afghanistan (sigar.mil).
127. Malkasian, *American War in Afghanistan,* 384–403, 457.
128. Malkasian, *American War in Afghanistan,* 404–22.
129. Harleen Gambhir, "Afghanistan Partial Threat Assessment: February 23, 2016," Institute for the Study of War, February 24, 2016, https://www.understandingwar.org/map/afghanistan-partial-threat-assessment-february-23-2016.
130. Arturo Munoz, Rebecca Zimmerman, and Jason H. Campbell, "RAND Experts Q&A on the Fighting in Kunduz," RAND Blog, October 2, 2015, https://www.rand.org/blog/2015/10/rand-experts-qampa-on-the-fighting-in-kunduz.html.
131. Jonathan Schroden, "Lessons from the Collapse of Afghanistan's Security Forces," *CTC Sentinel* 14, no. 8 (October 2021): 45–61, based on data from Kate Clark, "Menace, Negotiation, Attack: The Taliban Take More District Centers Across Afghanistan," Afghanistan Analysts Network, Kabul, July 16, 2021, https://www.ecoi.net/en/document/2057178.html.
132. Robert Jervis, "The Trump Experiment: An Assessment," in Robert Jervis, Diane N. Labrosse, Stacie E. Goddard, and Joshua Rovner, eds., *Chaos Reconsidered: The Liberal Order and the Future of International Politics* (New York: Columbia University Press, 2023), 20.
133. Michael E. O'Hanlon, *Defense 101: Understanding the Military of Today and Tomorrow* (Ithaca, N.Y.: Cornell University Press, 2021), 58–61; Congressional Budget Office, "Funding for Overseas Contingency Operations and Its Impact on Defense Spending," Washington, D.C., October 2018, https://www.cbo.gov/publication/54219.
134. Air Force Public Affairs, "Combined Forces Air Component Commander 2013–2019 Airpower Statistics," December 31, 2019, https://www.afcent.af.mil/Portals/82/Documents/Airpower%20summary/(U)%20APPROVED%20Dec%202019%20APS%20Data.pdf; Jared Keller, "The U.S. Dropped More Munitions on Afghanistan Last Year Than Any Other Time in the Last Decade," *Task and Purpose,* January 27, 2020, https://taskandpurpose.com/news/the-us-dropped-more-munitions-on-afghanistan-last-year-than-any-other-time-in-the-last-decade.
135. Amy McGrath and Michael O'Hanlon, "Were U.S. Losses in Vain?," *USA Today,* August 15, 2021.
136. See Michael O'Hanlon, *Military History for the Modern Strategist: America's Major Wars Since 1861* (Washington, D.C.: Brookings Institution Press, 2023), 47–75, 194, 319–21.

137. Michael R. Gordon and Bernard E. Trainor, *Cobra II: The Inside Story of the Invasion and Occupation of Iraq* (New York: Pantheon, 2006), 164–81.
138. Walter L. Perry, Richard E. Darilek, Laurinda L. Rohn, and Jerry M. Sollinger, eds., *Operation Iraqi Freedom: Decisive War, Elusive Peace* (Santa Monica, Calif.: RAND, 2015), 53, 59, 344; Bob Woodward, *Plan of Attack* (New York: Simon and Schuster, 2004), 329.
139. Gordon and Trainor, *Cobra II,* 26.
140. Perry et al., *Operation Iraqi Freedom,* 151–57.
141. Rick Atkinson, *In the Company of Soldiers: A Chronicle of Combat* (New York: Henry Holt, 2004), 297–303.
142. See Thomas Donnelly, *Operation Iraqi Freedom: A Strategic Assessment* (Washington, D.C.: American Enterprise Institute, 2004), 52–84; and Williamson Murray and Robert H. Scales, *The Iraq War: A Military History* (Cambridge, Mass.: Belknap Press of Harvard University Press, 2003), 99–100.
143. Stephen Biddle, "Speed Kills: Reassessing the Role of Speed, Precision, and Situation Awareness in the Fall of Saddam," *Journal of Strategic Studies* 30, no. 1 (February 2007): 3–46; Gordon and Trainor, *Cobra II,* 374–410.
144. Kenneth Adelman, " 'Cakewalk' Revisited," *Washington Post,* April 10, 2003.
145. Perry et al., *Operation Iraqi Freedom,* 100.
146. Charles H. Ferguson, *No End in Sight: Iraq's Descent into Chaos* (New York: Public Affairs, 2008), 104–38.
147. Hilary Synnott, *Bad Days in Basra: My Turbulent Time as Britain's Man in Southern Iraq* (London: I. B. Tauris, 2008), 250.
148. In addition to a number of other books cited already, on this basic situation in 2003, see Rajiv Chandrasekaran, *Imperial Life in the Emerald City: Inside Iraq's Green Zone* (New York: Alfred A. Knopf, 2007); and Don Eberly, *Liberate and Leave: Fatal Flaws in the Early Strategy for Postwar Iraq* (Minneapolis, Minn.: Zenith, 2009).
149. Thomas E. Ricks, *Fiasco: The American Military Adventure in Iraq* (New York: Penguin, 2006), 159.
150. Toby Dodge, *Inventing Iraq: The Failure of Nation Building and a History Denied* (New York: Columbia University Press, 2003); Ambassador L. Paul Bremer III, *My Year in Iraq: The Struggle to Build a Future of Hope* (New York: Simon and Schuster, 2006), 161–65, 220–97; George Tenet, *At the Center of the Storm: My Years at the CIA* (New York: HarperCollins, 2007), 416–30.
151. David Rieff, "Who Botched the Occupation?," *New York Times Magazine,* November 2, 2003.
152. Gordon and Trainor, *Cobra II,* 489.
153. On the multifaceted insurgency, see Ahmed S. Hashim, *Insurgency and Counter-Insurgency in Iraq* (Ithaca, N.Y.: Cornell University Press, 2006). See also Omer Taspinar, *What the West Is Getting Wrong About the Middle East* (London: I. B. Tauris, 2021), 109–34.
154. Ian Livingston and Michael E. O'Hanlon, "Iraq Index: Tracking Variables of Reconstruction and Security in Post-Saddam Iraq," Brookings Institution, Washington, D.C., January 31, 2011, https://www.brookings.edu/wp-content/uploads/2016/07/index20110131.pdf.

155. Michael R. Gordon and Gen. Bernard E. Trainor, *The Endgame: The Inside Story of the Struggle for Iraq, from George W. Bush to Barack Obama* (New York: Alfred A. Knopf, 2012), 351–68.
156. McChrystal, *My Share of the Task,* 231–36.
157. Peter W. Rodman, *Presidential Command: Power, Leadership, and the Making of Foreign Policy from Richard Nixon to George W. Bush* (New York: Alfred A. Knopf, 2009), 266–67.
158. Gordon and Trainor, *Endgame,* 282–311.
159. Peter R. Mansoor, *Surge: My Journey with General David Petraeus and the Remaking of the Iraq War* (New Haven: Yale University Press, 2013); Kimberly Kagan, *The Surge: A Military History* (New York: Encounter, 2008).
160. Special Inspector General for Iraq Reconstruction, *Hard Lessons: The Iraq Reconstruction Experience* (Washington, D.C.: U.S. Government Printing Office, 2009), 295–319.
161. Mansoor, *Surge,* 148–76. For broader histories of Joint Special Operations Command, see Sean Naylor, *Relentless Strike: The Secret History of Joint Special Operations Command* (New York: St. Martin's, 2015); Linda Robinson, *One Hundred Victories: Special Ops and the Future of American Warfare* (New York: Public Affairs, 2013); and Mark Moyar, *Oppose Any Foe: The Rise of America's Special Operations Forces* (New York: Basic, 2017). For a sensational historical perspective with a focus on World War II, see William H. McRaven, *Spec Ops: Case Studies in Special Operations Warfare* (San Francisco: Presidio, 1996).
162. See Peter A. Clement, "Impact of Intelligence Integration on CIA Analysis," *Studies in Intelligence* 65, no. 3 (September 2021): 25–33; and Jim Clapper and Trey Brown, "Reflections on Integration in the Intelligence Community," *Studies in Intelligence* 65, no. 3 (September 2021): 1–4.
163. Stanley McChrystal, *Team of Teams: New Rules of Engagement for a Complex World* (New York: Portfolio, 2015).
164. See W. Singer, *Corporate Warriors: The Rise of the Privatized Military Industry* (Ithaca, N.Y.: Cornell University Press, 2003); and Congressional Budget Office, "Contractors' Support of U.S. Operations in Iraq," U.S. Congress, Washington, D.C., August 12, 2008, https://www.cbo.gov/sites/default/files/110th-congress-2007-2008/reports/08-12-iraqcontractors.pdf.
165. Jason H. Campbell and Michael E. O'Hanlon, "Iraq Index: Tracking Variables of Reconstruction and Security in Post-Saddam Iraq," Brookings Institution, Washington, D.C., December 18, 2008, https://www.brookings.edu/wp-content/uploads/2016/07/index20081218.pdf.
166. Gordon and Trainor, *Endgame,* 358–65.
167. Kagan, *The Surge,* 97–204.
168. Emma Sky, *The Unraveling: High Hopes and Missed Opportunities in Iraq* (New York: Public Affairs, 2015), 329–42, 360; Pollack, *Iraq.*
169. Philip H. Gordon, *Losing the Long Game: The False Promise of Regime Change in the Middle East* (New York: St. Martin's, 2020), 134–44.
170. Joel Rayburn, *Iraq After America: Strongmen, Sectarians, Resistance* (Stanford, Calif.: Hoover Institution Press, 2014), 209–64.

171. Sky, *Unraveling,* 360; Pollack, *Armies of Sand,* 167–68.
172. Daniel Byman, *Al Qaeda, the Islamic State, and the Global Jihadist Movement: What Everyone Needs to Know* (Oxford: Oxford University Press, 2015), 166–77.
173. See Will McCants, *The ISIS Apocalypse: The History, Strategy, and Doomsday Vision of the Islamic State* (New York: St. Martin's, 2015). See also Jessica Stern and J. M. Berger, *ISIS: The State of Terror* (New York: HarperCollins, 2015); and Ash Carter, *Inside the Five-Sided Box: Lessons from a Lifetime of Leadership in the Pentagon* (New York: Penguin, 2020), 227–29.
174. Tim Arango, "Maliki Agrees to Relinquish Power in Iraq," *New York Times,* August 14, 2014; Becca Wasser et al., *The Air War Against the Islamic State: The Role of Air Power in Operation Inherent Resolve* (Santa Monica, Calif.: RAND, 2021), xiv.
175. Michael R. Gordon, *Degrade and Destroy: The Inside Story of the War Against the Islamic State, from Barack Obama to Donald Trump* (New York: Farrar, Straus and Giroux, 2022).
176. Benjamin S. Lambeth, *Air Power in the War Against ISIS* (Annapolis, Md.: Naval Institute Press, 2021), 146, 245–46; Wasser et al., *Air War Against the Islamic State,* 297, 410.
177. See, e.g., Bruce Riedel, *The Search for al Qaeda: Its Leadership, Ideology, and Future* (Washington, D.C.: Brookings Institution Press, 2008); Paul R. Pillar, *Terrorism and U.S. Foreign Policy* (Washington, D.C.: Brookings Institution Press, 2001); Michael Morrell and Bill Harlow, *The Great War of Our Time: The CIA's Fight Against Terrorism—from al Qa'ida to ISIS* (New York: Twelve, 2015); and Tenet, *Center of the Storm.*
178. For a thoughtful study reflective of much of the debate of the 1990s into the 2000s, see Thomas P. M. Barnett, *The Pentagon's New Map: War and Peace in the Twenty-First Century* (New York: G. P. Putnam's Sons, 2004).
179. See Juan C. Zarate, *Treasury's War: The Unleashing of a New Era of Financial Warfare* (New York: Public Affairs, 2013); Michael d'Arcy et al., *Protecting the Homeland, 2006/2007* (Washington, D.C.: Brookings Institution Press, 2006); and Richard A. Clarke, *Against All Enemies: Inside America's War on Terror* (New York: Free Press, 2004).
180. Michael E. O'Hanlon, *The Art of War in the Age of Peace: U.S. Military Posture for the Post–Cold War World* (Westport, Conn.: Praeger, 1992), 75.
181. Eric V. Larson et al., *Defense Planning in a Time of Conflict: A Comparative Analysis of the 2001–2014 Quadrennial Defense Reviews, and Implications for the Army* (Santa Monica, Calif.: RAND, 2018), 28.
182. Donald H. Rumsfeld, "2001 Quadrennial Defense Review Report," Department of Defense, Washington, D.C., September 30, 2001, 17–18, https://history.defense.gov/Portals/70/Documents/quadrennial/QDR2001.pdf; Larson et al., *Defense Planning in a Time of Conflict.*
183. O'Hanlon, *Healing the Wounded Giant,* 25.
184. Petraeus and Roberts, *Conflict,* 318.
185. M. Wade Markel et al., *The Evolution of U.S. Military Policy from the Constitution to the Present,* vol. 4: *The Total Force Policy Era, 1970–2015* (Santa Monica, Calif.: RAND, 2020), 125–71.

186. Catherine Dale and Pat Towell, "In Brief: Assessing the 2012 Defense Strategic Guidance (DSG)," Congressional Research Service, Washington, D.C., August 13, 2013, https://sgfas.org/crs/natsec/R42146.pdf.
187. Donald H. Rumsfeld, "2006 Quadrennial Defense Review Report," Department of Defense, Washington, D.C., February 6, 2006; Robert M. Gates, "2010 Quadrennial Defense Review Report," Department of Defense, Washington, D.C., February 2010; Chuck Hagel, "2014 Quadrennial Defense Review Report," Department of Defense, Washington, D.C., March 2014; all at https://history.defense.gov/Historical-Sources/Quadrennial-Defense-Review.
188. Vice Admiral James Syring, Missile Defense Agency, "Ballistic Missile Defense System Update," Center for Strategic and International Studies, Washington, D.C., January 19, 2016, https://www.csis.org/events/ballistic-missile-defense-system-update; Tom Karako, "The 2022 Missile Defense Review: Still Seeking Alignment," Center for Strategic and International Studies, Washington, D.C., October 27, 2022, https://www.csis.org/analysis/2022-missile-defense-review-still-seeking-alignment; Matthew R. Costlow and Robert M. Soofer, "U.S. Homeland Missile Defense: Room for Expanded Roles," Atlantic Council, Washington, D.C., November 2023, https://www.atlanticcouncil.org/in-depth-research-reports/issue-brief/us-homeland-missile-defense-room-for-expanded-roles.
189. See, e.g., National Defense Strategy Commission, "Providing for the Common Defense: The Assessments and Recommendations of the National Defense Strategy Commission," Washington, D.C., November 2018, https://www.usip.org/publications/2018/11/providing-common-defense; and Andrew F. Krepinevich Jr., *The Origins of Victory: How Disruptive Military Innovation Determines the Fate of Great Powers* (New Haven: Yale University Press, 2023), 3–6.
190. Natalya Anfilofyeva, "Majority of U.S. MRAPs to Be Scrapped or Stored," Center for Strategic and Budgetary Assessments, Washington, D.C., January 5, 2014, https://csbaonline.org/about/news/majority-of-us-mraps-to-be-scrapped-or-stored; International Institute for Strategic Studies, *The Military Balance 2023* (London: Routledge, 2023), 37.
191. Robert M. Gates, *Duty: Memoirs of a Secretary at War* (New York: Alfred A. Knopf, 2014), 239–45; John A. Tirpak, "Gates Versus the Air Force," *Air and Space Forces Magazine,* March 1, 2014, https://www.airandspaceforces.com/article/0314gates.
192. Congressional Research Service, "U.S. Military Overseas Basing: New Developments and Oversight Issues for Congress," U.S. Congress, Washington, D.C., January 26, 2006, https://www.everycrsreport.com/reports/RL33148.html.
193. International Institute for Strategic Studies, *Military Balance 2023*, 47–49; Michael J. Lostumbo et al., *Overseas Basing of U.S. Military Forces: An Assessment of Relative Costs and Strategic Benefits* (Santa Monica, Calif.: RAND, 2013), 20–35.
194. On the concept of responsibility to protect, see Gareth Evans, *The Responsibility to Protect: Ending Mass Atrocity Crimes Once and for All* (Washington, D.C.: Brookings Institution Press, 2008).
195. See, e.g., Eileen Rivers, *Beyond the Call: Three Women on the Front Lines in Afghanistan* (New York: Da Capo, 2018); Kate Germano with Kelly Kennedy, *Fight Like a Girl:*

The Truth Behind How Female Marines Are Trained (Amherst, N.Y.: Prometheus, 2018); Paula G. Thornhill, *Demystifying the American Military: Institutions, Evolution, and Challenges Since 1789* (Annapolis, Md.: Naval Institute Press, 2019); and O'Hanlon, *Defense 101*, 26–31.

196. See Dana Priest, *The Mission: Waging War and Keeping Peace with America's Military* (New York: W. W. Norton, 2003), 29.

197. The original requirement was for a ten-year gap, as specified in the National Security Act of 1947; see Congressional Research Service, "The Position of Secretary of Defense: Statutory Restrictions and Civilian-Military Relations," January 2021, https://www.everycrsreport.com/files/2021-01-06_R44725_6022705d08d81f812052a96606f91626d6f9e2cd.pdf.

198. Homi Kharas and Kristofer Hamel, "A Global Tipping Point: Half the World Is Now Middle Class or Wealthier," Brookings Institution, Washington, D.C., September 27, 2018, https://www.brookings.edu/blog/future-development/2018/09/27/a-global-tipping-point-half-the-world-is-now-middle-class-or-wealthier.

CHAPTER 7. DEFENSE PLANNING IN THE NEW ERA OF GREAT POWER RIVALRY

1. Walter Russell Mead, "The Return of Hamiltonian Statecraft," *Foreign Affairs* 103, no. 5 (September/October 2024): 52–66.
2. See David E. Sanger, *New Cold Wars: China's Rise, Russia's Invasion, and America's Struggle to Defend the West* (New York: Random House, 2024); David Petraeus and Andrew Roberts, *Conflict: The Evolution of Warfare from 1945 to Ukraine* (New York: HarperCollins, 2023), 350–404; Kathryn E. Stoner, *Russia Resurrected: Its Power and Purpose in a New Global Order* (Oxford: Oxford University Press, 2021); and Michael O'Hanlon, *The Art of War in an Age of Peace: U.S. Grand Strategy and Resolute Restraint* (New Haven: Yale University Press, 2021).
3. Tanvi Madan, "Riding the Roller Coaster: India and the Trump Years," in Robert Jervis, Diane N. Labrosse, Stacie E. Goddard, and Joshua Rovner, eds., *Chaos Reconsidered: The Liberal Order and the Future of International Politics* (New York: Columbia University Press, 2023), 222–35.
4. See Robert D. Blackwill and Jennifer M. Harris, *War by Other Means: Geoeconomics and Statecraft* (Cambridge, Mass.: Harvard University Press, 2016); Juan Zarate, *Treasury's War: The Unleashing of a New Era of Financial Warfare* (New York: Public Affairs, 2013); and Richard Nephew, *The Art of Sanctions: A View from the Field* (New York: Columbia University Press, 2017).
5. Thomas J. Christensen, "No New Cold War: Why U.S.-China Strategic Competition Will Not Be Like the U.S.-Soviet Cold War," Asan Institute, Seoul, South Korea, September 2020, http://en.asaninst.org/contents/no-new-cold-war-why-us-china-strategic-competition-will-not-be-like-the-us-soviet-cold-war/.
6. Secretary of State Antony Blinken, "A Foreign Policy for the American People," Department of State, Washington, D.C., March 3, 2021, https://2021-2025.state.gov/a-foreign-policy-for-the-american-people.

7. Secretary of State Antony Blinken, "The Administration's Approach to the People's Republic of China," George Washington University, Washington, D.C., May 26, 2022, https://2021-2025.state.gov/the-administrations-approach-to-the-peoples-republic-of-china.
8. Aaron L. Friedberg, *Getting China Wrong* (Cambridge: Polity, 2022); James Stavridis, *Sea Power: The History and Geopolitics of the World's Oceans* (New York: Penguin, 2017), 165–97; Chris Cillizza, "It's Time to Admit It: Mitt Romney Was Right About Russia," CNN.com, February 27, 2022, https://www.cnn.com/2022/02/22/politics/mitt-romney-russia-ukraine/index.html.
9. Stoner, *Russia Resurrected,* 181–91.
10. Fiona Hill and Clifford G. Gaddy, *Mr. Putin: Operative in the Kremlin,* rev. and exp. ed. (Washington, D.C.: Brookings Institution Press, 2015), 334–41, 390–91.
11. See Daryl G. Kimball, "The Intermediate-Range Nuclear Forces (INF) Treaty at a Glance," Arms Control Association, August 2019, https://www.armscontrol.org/factsheets/intermediate-range-nuclear-forces-inf-treaty-glance. For hopeful words on a nuclear-free world, see William J. Perry, *My Journey at the Nuclear Brink* (Stanford, Calif.: Stanford University Press, 2015). For good and concise histories of nuclear weapons technology and policy, see Stephen M. Younger, *The Bomb: A New History* (New York: HarperCollins, 2009); and Francis J. Gavin, *Nuclear Weapons and American Grand Strategy* (Washington, D.C.: Brookings Institution Press, 2020).
12. Susan L. Shirk, *Overreach: How China Derailed Its Peaceful Rise* (Oxford: Oxford University Press, 2023), 207–8, 224–25; Rush Doshi, *The Long Game: China's Grand Strategy to Displace American Order* (Oxford: Oxford University Press, 2021), 184–205; Lynn Kuok, "How China's Actions in the South China Sea Undermine the Rule of Law," in Tarun Chhabra, Rush Doshi, Ryan Hass, and Emilie Kimball, eds., *Global China: Assessing China's Growing Role in the World* (Washington, D.C.: Brookings Institution Press, 2021), 75–85.
13. Joseph Dunford, "Joint Chiefs' Chairman Dunford on the '4+1' Threat Framework and Meeting Transnational Threats," Brookings Institution, Washington, D.C., February 24,2017,https://www.brookings.edu/articles/joint-chiefs-chairman-dunford-transnational-threats/.
14. Andrew F. Krepinevich Jr., *The Origins of Victory: How Disruptive Military Innovation Determines the Fate of Great Powers* (New Haven: Yale University Press, 2023), 3–6, 43–84.
15. Aaron L. Friedberg, *Beyond Air-Sea Battle: The Debate over U.S. Military Strategy in Asia* (New York: Routledge, 2014). Jan van Tol, a retired Navy captain, and others at the Center for Strategic and Budgetary Assessments were instrumental in the process. See Friedberg, *Beyond Air-Sea Battle,* 79; and Jan van Tol, Mark Gunzinger, Andrew F. Krepinevich, and Jim Thomas, "AirSea Battle: A Point-of-Departure Operational Concept," Center for Strategic and Budgetary Assessments, Washington, D.C., 2010, https://csbaonline.org/research/publications/airsea-battle-concept.
16. Bob Work, "Remarks by Deputy Secretary Work on Third Offset Strategy," Brussels, April 28, 2016, https://www.defense.gov/News/Speeches/Speech/Article/753482/remarks-by-deputy-secretary-work-on-third-offset-strategy; Friedberg, *Beyond Air-Sea*

Battle; Jose Diaz de Leon, "Understanding Multi-Domain Operations in NATO," *Three Swords Magazine* 37 (2001): 91–94; Department of Defense, "Summary of the Joint All-Domain Command and Control (JADC2) Strategy," March 2022, https://media.defense.gov/2022/Mar/17/2002958406/-1/-1/1/SUMMARY-OF-THE-JOINT-ALL-DOMAIN-COMMAND-AND-CONTROL-STRATEGY.PDF.

17. Derek Chollet, *The Long Game: How Obama Defied Washington and Redefined America's Role in the World* (New York: Public Affairs, 2016).
18. Three very useful books discussing aspects of Trump security policy are John Bolton, *The Room Where It Happened: A White House Memoir* (New York: Simon and Schuster, 2020); Mark T. Esper, *A Sacred Oath: Memoirs of a Secretary of Defense During Extraordinary Times* (New York: HarperCollins, 2022); and H. R. McMaster, *Battlegrounds: The Fight to Defend the Free World* (New York: HarperCollins, 2020).
19. For a good account of McMaster's views, see McMaster, *Battlegrounds,* 89–149.
20. Secretary of Defense Jim Mattis, "Summary of the 2018 National Defense Strategy of the United States: Sharpening the American Military's Competitive Edge," Department of Defense, Washington, D.C., January 2018, https://dod.defense.gov/Portals/1/Documents/pubs/2018-National-Defense-Strategy-Summary.pdf.
21. Secretary of Defense Lloyd Austin, "2022 National Defense Strategy of the United States of America," Department of Defense, Washington, D.C., October 2022, https://media.defense.gov/2022/Oct/27/2003103845/-1/-1/1/2022-NATIONAL-DEFENSE-STRATEGY-NPR-MDR.PDF; "The 2022 National Defense Strategy: A Conversation with Colin Kahl," Brookings Institution, Washington, D.C., November 4, 2022, https://www.brookings.edu/events/the-2022-national-defense-strategy-a-conversation-with-colin-kahl.
22. See, e.g., "Keynote Conversation with General Joseph Dunford," Knight Forum on Geopolitics, Brookings Institution, Washington, D.C., October 2, 2024, https://www.brookings.edu/events/the-2024-knight-forum-on-geopolitics.
23. Under Secretary of Defense (Comptroller), *National Defense Budget Estimates for FY 2025* (Washington, D.C.: Department of Defense, April 2024), 141–45, https://comptroller.defense.gov/Portals/45/Documents/defbudget/FY2025/fy25_Green_Book.pdf.
24. Secretary of Defense Lloyd Austin, "2022 Nuclear Posture Review," Department of Defense, Washington, D.C., October 2022, https://media.defense.gov/2022/Oct/27/2003103845/-1/-1/1/2022-NATIONAL-DEFENSE-STRATEGY-NPR-MDR.PDF.
25. Michael J. Green, "The Real Asia Hands: What Washington Can Learn from Its Asian Allies," *Foreign Affairs* 101, no. 6 (November/December 2022).
26. Renanah M. Joyce and Becca Wasser, "All About Access: Solving America's Force Posture Puzzle," *Washington Quarterly* 44, no. 3 (Fall 2021): 50.
27. U.S. Marine Corps, "Force Design 2030: Annual Update," Washington, D.C., June 2023, https://www.marines.mil/Portals/1/Docs/Force_Design_2030_Annual_Update_June_2023.pdf; see also "Force Design: A Conversation with General Eric Smith," Brookings Institution, Washington, D.C., July 2, 2024, https://www.brookings.edu/events/force-design-a-conversation-with-general-eric-smith-39th-commandant-of-the-us-marine-corps.

28. See Michael J. Mazarr, "Defending Without Dominance: Accelerating the Transition to a New U.S. Defense Strategy," RAND, Santa Monica, Calif., September 2023, https://www.rand.org/content/dam/rand/pubs/perspectives/PEA2500/PEA2555–1/RAND_PEA2555-1.pdf; David A. Ochmanek and Michael O'Hanlon, "Preventing China from Taking Taiwan," *The Hill,* December 8, 2021, https://thehill.com/opinion/national-security/584370-heres-the-strategy-to-prevent-china-from-taking-taiwan/.
29. Mark A. Milley and Eric Schmidt, "America Isn't Ready for the Wars of the Future," *Foreign Affairs* 103, no. 5 (September/October 2024); see also David Petraeus and Andy Yakulis, "Ukraine's Lessons for the Pentagon," *Wall Street Journal,* September 19, 2024,https://www.wsj.com/opinion/the-u-s-can-fight-yesterdays-war-but-not-tomorrows-4b7bca66.
30. For a solid critique of the track record, see Robert D. Blackwill and Richard Fontaine, *Lost Decade: The U.S. Pivot to Asia and the Rise of Chinese Power* (Oxford: Oxford University Press, 2024), 224–38.
31. Michael O'Hanlon, "Can China Take Taiwan? Why No One Really Knows," Brookings, August2022,https://www.brookings.edu/articles/can-china-take-taiwan-why-no-one-really-knows.
32. Seth Jones, "China Is Ready for War, and Thanks to a Crumbling Defense Industrial Base, America Is Not," *Foreign Affairs,* October 2, 2024, https://www.foreignaffairs.com/china/china-ready-war-america-is-not-seth-jones.
33. John Hudson and Dan Lamothe, "Biden Sends Antimissile System and 100 Troops to Israel, Deepening U.S. Role," *Washington Post,* October 13, 2024.
34. See Michael Kofman, "The Russia-Ukraine War: Military Operations and Battlefield Dynamics," in Hal Brands, ed., *War in Ukraine: Conflict, Strategy, and the Return of a Fractured World* (Baltimore: Johns Hopkins University Press, 2024), 99–120; Dara Massicot, "Russian Military Resilience and Adaptation: Implications for the War in Ukraine and Beyond," in Brands, *War in Ukraine,* 121–38; and Francis J. Gavin, "Nuclear Lessons and Dilemmas from the War in Ukraine," in Brands, *War in Ukraine,* 173–86.
35. William Brooks and Michael O'Hanlon, "Who Is Winning in Ukraine? These Maps Tell the Real Story," *Washington Post,* September 26, 2024.
36. Michael O'Hanlon, Constanze Stelzenmuller, and David Wessel, with Alejandra Rocha, Sophie Roehse, and Mallika Yadwad, "The Ukraine Index: Tracking Developments in the Ukraine War," Brookings Institution, Washington, D.C., January 22, 2025, https://www.brookings.edu/articles/ukraine-index-tracking-developments-in-the-ukraine-war/.
37. Jessica T. Mathews, "What Was the Biden Doctrine?," *Foreign Affairs* 103, no. 5 (September–October 2024): 38–51.
38. Danielle L. Lupton, *Reputation for Resolve: How Leaders Signal Determination in International Politics* (Ithaca, N.Y.: Cornell University Press, 2020).
39. Constanze Stelzenmuller, "The Return of the Enemy: Putin's War on Ukraine and a Cognitive Blockage in Western Security Policy," Brookings Institution, Washington,

D.C., August 2023, https://www.brookings.edu/articles/the-return-of-the-enemy. On Ukraine's long history with Russia, see Serhii Plokhy, *The Gates of Europe: A History of Ukraine* (New York: Basic, 2021); and Eugene Finkel, *Intent to Destroy: Russia's Two-Hundred-Year Quest to Dominate Ukraine* (New York: Basic, 2024).

40. Elbridge A. Colby, *The Strategy of Denial: American Defense in an Age of Great Power Conflict* (New Haven: Yale University Press, 2021).
41. Roger Cliff, *China's Future Military Capabilities* (Carlisle, Pa.: U.S. Army War College Press, 2023), 60–61.
42. Chas Danner, "Biden Says U.S. Will Defend Taiwan Against Taiwan—Or Maybe Not," *Intelligencer,* May 23, 2022, https://nymag.com/intelligencer/2022/05/biden-vows-to-defend-taiwan-against-china-or-did-he.html.
43. Ryan Hass, Bonnie Glaser, and Richard Bush, *U.S.-Taiwan Relations: Will China's Challenge Lead to a Crisis?* (Washington, D.C.: Brookings Institution Press, 2023), 127–30.
44. David Vergun, "Official Says Integrated Deterrence Key to National Defense Strategy," DoD News, Department of Defense, Washington, D.C., December 6, 2022, https://www.defense.gov/News/News-Stories/Article/Article/3237769/official-says-integrated-deterrence-key-to-national-defense-strategy/.
45. See also Mara Karlin, "The Return of Total War," *Foreign Affairs* 103, no. 6 (November/December 2024): 8–19.
46. See, e.g., Paul R. Pillar, "Export Controls and the Junction of Economics and National Security: A Review Article," *Political Science Quarterly* 139, no. 3 (Fall 2024): 445–58.
47. See "A Conversation with Commander of US Indo-Pacific Command Admiral Samuel Paparo," Brookings Institution, Washington, D.C., November 19, 2024, https://www.brookings.edu/events/a-conversation-with-commander-of-us-indo-pacific-command-admiral-samuel-paparo.
48. Department of Justice, "Court-Authorized Operation Disrupts Worldwide Botnet Used by the People's Republic of China State-Sponsored Hackers," Washington, D.C., September 18, 2024, https://www.justice.gov/opa/pr/court-authorized-operation-disrupts-worldwide-botnet-used-peoples-republic-china-state; Cybersecurity and Infrastructure Security Agency, "PRC State-Sponsored Actors Compromise and Maintain Persistent Access to U.S. Critical Infrastructure," February 7, 2024, https://www.cisa.gov/news-events/cybersecurity-advisories/aa24-038a.
49. See, e.g., Bruce D. Jones, *To Rule the Waves: How Control of the World's Ocean's Shapes the Fate of Superpowers* (New York: Scribner, 2021), 220–28; Michael Glynn, "Bring Analytics Back to Theater ASW," *Proceedings* 144, no. 4 (April 2018), https://www.usni.org/magazines/proceedings/2018/april/bring-analytics-back-theater-asw; Caitlin Talmadge, "The U.S.-China Nuclear Relationship: Growing Escalation Risks and Implications for the Future," Testimony Before the U.S.-China Economic and Security Review Commission, Washington, D.C., June 7, 2021, https://www.uscc.gov/sites/default/files/2021-06/Caitlin_Talmadge_Testimony.pdf; and O'Hanlon, "Can China Take Taiwan?"
50. See Keir A. Lieber and Daryl G. Press, *The Myth of the Nuclear Revolution: Power Politics in the Atomic Age* (Ithaca, N.Y.: Cornell University Press, 2020), 115–19; Vipin Narang,

Nuclear Strategy in the Modern Era: Regional Powers and International Conflict (Princeton, N.J.: Princeton University Press, 2014), 305–6; Sukjoon Yoon and Yongweon Yu, "How Will South Korea and the U.S. Rewrite Their Operational Plan?," *Diplomat,* December 22, 2021, https://thediplomat.com/2021/12/how-will-south-korea-and-the-us-rewrite-their-operational-plan; Michael Peck, "Introducing U.S. Operations Plan 5015 (Or the Plan to Crush North Korea in a War)," *National Interest,* April 9, 2019, https://nationalinterest.org/blog/buzz/introducing-us-operations-plan-5015-or-plan-crush-north-korea-war-51627; and Walter Pincus, "U.S. and South Korea Back to Pre-Trump Strategies on North Korea," *Cipher Brief,* February 7, 2023, https://www.thecipherbrief.com/column_article/u-s-and-south-korea-back-to-pre-trump-strategies-on-north-korea.

51. Commission on the National Defense Strategy, "Commission on the National Defense Strategy," Washington, D.C., July 2024, https://www.rand.org/content/dam/rand/pubs/misc/MSA3057-4/RAND_MSA3057-4.pdf.
52. See Congressional Budget Office, "The U.S. Military's Force Structure: A Primer, 2021 Update," Washington, D.C., May 2021, 120–21, https://www.cbo.gov/system/files/2021-05/57088-Force-Structure-Primer.pdf; and Michael E. O'Hanlon, *Defense 101: Understanding the Military of Today and Tomorrow* (Ithaca, N.Y.: Cornell University Press, 2021), 70–80.
53. Congressional Budget Office, "U.S. Military's Force Structure," 120–21; O'Hanlon, *Defense 101,* 70–80.
54. Congressional Budget Office, "U.S. Military's Force Structure," 120–21; O'Hanlon, *Defense 101,* 70–80.
55. John D. Maurer and John H. Maurer, "The Challenge of Tripolar Arms Competition: Lessons from the Washington Treaty," *War on the Rocks,* November 10, 2023, https://warontherocks.com/2023/11/the-challenge-of-tripolar-arms-competition-lessons-from-the-washington-treaty/.
56. Congressional Commission on the Strategic Posture of the United States, "America's Strategic Posture," Washington, D.C., October 2023, https://www.ida.org/-/media/feature/publications/a/am/americas-strategic-posture/strategic-posture-commission-report.ashx; Study Group at the Center for Global Security Research, "China's Emergence as a Second Nuclear Peer: Implications for U.S. Nuclear Deterrence Strategy," Lawrence Livermore National Laboratory, Livermore, Calif., Spring 2023, https://cgsr.llnl.gov/sites/cgsr/files/2024-08/CGSR_Two_Peer_230314.pdf; Commission on the National Defense Strategy, "Commission on the National Defense Strategy," 44–45; Matthew Costlow and Robert M. Soofer, "U.S. Homeland Missile Defense: Room for Expanded Roles," Atlantic Council, Washington, D.C., November 2023,https://www.atlanticcouncil.org/wp-content/uploads/2023/11/Costlow-Soofer-Homeland-Missile-Defense.pdf.

CHAPTER 8. AMERICA THE ASSERTIVE

1. Dexter Filkins, *The Forever War* (New York: Vintage, 2009). See also Rosa Brooks, *How Everything Became War and the Military Became Everything* (New York: Simon and Schuster, 2016).

2. Robert Kagan, *The World America Made* (New York: Alfred A. Knopf, 2012). See also G. John Ikenberry, *Liberal Leviathan: The Origins, Crisis, and Transformation of the American World Order* (Princeton, N.J.: Princeton University Press, 2011); Michael E. O'Hanlon, *Military History for the Modern Strategist: America's Major Wars Since 1861* (Washington, D.C.: Brookings Institution Press, 2024), 315–25; Fareed Zakaria, *The Post-American World* (New York: W. W. Norton, 2008); Charles A. Kupchan, *No One's World: The West, the Rising Rest, and the Coming Global Turn* (Oxford: Oxford University Press, 2012); and Michael Beckley, *Unrivaled: Why America Will Remain the World's Sole Superpower* (Ithaca, N.Y.: Cornell University Press, 2018).
3. See Antulio J. Echevarria II, *Reconsidering the American Way of War: U.S. Military Practice from the Revolution to Afghanistan* (Washington, D.C.: Georgetown University Press, 2014), 162–77.
4. Russell F. Weigley, *The American Way of War: A History of United States Military Strategy and Power* (Bloomington: Indiana University Press, 1973), xxii.
5. F. G. Hoffman, *Decisive Force: The New American Way of War* (Westport, Conn.: Praeger, 1996).
6. For similar views, see Echevarria, *Reconsidering the American Way of War;* and Brian McAllister Linn, *The Echo of Battle: The Army's Way of War* (Cambridge, Mass.: Harvard University Press, 2009).
7. Indeed, Hoffman's own subsequent writings emphasize the importance of adaptability in war more than following a certain script or style—see Frank G. Hoffman, *Mars Adapting: Military Change During War* (Annapolis, Md.: Naval Institute Press, 2021). For a related argument about the complexities and unpredictabilities of modern warfare, see Mick Ryan, *War Transformed: The Future of Twenty-First-Century Great Power Competition and Conflict* (Annapolis, Md.: Naval Institute Press, 2022). On the challenges of counterinsurgency, see John A. Nagl, *Learning to Eat Soup with a Knife: Counterinsurgency Lessons from Malaya and Vietnam* (Chicago: University of Chicago Press, 2005).
8. Talk of a revolution in military affairs was common in the 1990s, especially after Operation Desert Storm and then the Kosovo War, but even then, it was often overhyped. See Michael E. O'Hanlon, *Technological Change and the Future of Warfare* (Washington, D.C.: Brookings Institution Press, 2000); and Stephen Biddle, *Military Power: Explaining Victory and Defeat in Modern Battle* (Princeton, N.J.: Princeton University Press, 2004).
9. Thomas E. Ricks, *Making the Corps* (New York: Simon and Schuster, 1997), 19.
10. Micah Zenko, "100% Right 0% of the Time," *ForeignPolicy.com,* October 16, 2012, https://foreignpolicy.com/2012/10/16/100-right-0-of-the-time.
11. Ben Connable et al., "Will to Fight: Returning to the Human Fundamentals of War," RAND Research Brief, Santa Monica, Calif., September 13, 2019, https://www.rand.org/pubs/research_briefs/RB10040.html.
12. See Geoffrey Blainey, *The Causes of War* (New York: Free Press, 1973), 35–56, 186–227; and Williamson Murray, "The Strategy of Decisive War Versus the Strategy of Attrition," in Hal Brands, ed., *The New Makers of Modern Strategy* (Princeton, N.J.: Princeton University Press, 2023), 495–96.

13. Lawrence Freedman, *Strategy: A History* (Oxford: Oxford University Press, 2013), 87–136; Carl von Clausewitz, *On War,* translated by J. J. Graham (Middletown, Del.: n.p., 2021), 1–42; Sun Tzu, *The Art of War,* translated by Thomas Cleary (Boulder, Colo.: Shambhala, 2005).
14. Williamson Murray and Wayne Wei-Siang Hsieh, *A Savage War: A Military History of the Civil War* (Princeton, N.J.: Princeton University Press, 2016), 12.
15. David Barno and Nora Bensahel, *Adaptation Under Fire: How Militaries Change in Wartime* (Oxford: Oxford University Press, 2020).
16. On this point, see Eliot A. Cohen, *Supreme Command: Soldiers, Statesmen, and Leadership in Wartime* (New York: Anchor, 2003).
17. Barno and Bensahel, *Adaptation Under Fire,* 10–17; Barry R. Posen, *The Sources of Military Doctrine: France, Britain, and Germany Between the World Wars* (Ithaca, N.Y.: Cornell University Press, 1984), 220–44; Stephen Peter Rosen, *Winning the Next War: Innovation and the Modern Military* (Ithaca, N.Y.: Cornell University Press, 1991), 251–62; Cohen, *Supreme Command;* Hoffman, *Mars Adapting;* Ryan, *War Transformed.*
18. Stanley McChrystal, Remarks at Brookings Event, "Military History for the Modern Strategist: America's Major Wars Since 1861," Brookings Institution, Washington, D.C., January 27, 2023, https://www.brookings.edu/events/military-history-for-the-modern-strategist-americas-major-wars-since-1861.
19. Hoffman, *Mars Adapting.*
20. Cohen, *Supreme Command.*
21. Kori Schake and Jim Mattis, "Ensuring a Civil-Military Connection," in Kori Schake and Jim Mattis, eds., *Warriors and Citizens: American Views of Our Military* (Stanford, Calif.: Hoover Institution Press, 2016), 287–320.
22. Mara Karlin, *The Inheritance: America's Military After Two Decades of War* (Washington, D.C.: Brookings Institution Press, 2022), 38–48.
23. See Jordan Tama, *Bipartisanship and U.S. Foreign Policy: Cooperation in a Polarized Age* (Oxford: Oxford University Press, 2024).
24. Elizabeth N. Saunders, *The Insiders' Game: How Elites Make War and Peace* (Princeton, N.J.: Princeton University Press, 2024).
25. United States Senate, "About Declarations of War by Congress," 2024, https://www.senate.gov/about/powers-procedures/declarations-of-war.htm.
26. Congressional Research Service, "Declarations of War and Authorizations for the Use of Military Force: Historical Background and Legal Implications," Congressional Research Service, Washington, D.C., April 18, 2014, https://crsreports.congress.gov/product/pdf/RL/RL31133; O'Hanlon, *Military History for the Modern Strategist,* 264; "U.S. Involvement in the Vietnam War: The Gulf of Tonkin and Escalation, 1964," Department of State, Washington, D.C., 2024, https://history.state.gov/milestones/1961-1968/gulf-of-tonkin.
27. Barry M. Blechman, *The Politics of National Security: Congress and U.S. Defense Policy* (Oxford: Oxford University Press, 1990).
28. For an excellent example of the so-called restraint school, see Barry R. Posen, *Restraint: A New Foundation for U.S. Grand Strategy* (Ithaca, N.Y.: Cornell University Press, 2014). For a view closer to mine, see Paul D. Miller, *American Power and Liberal Order:*

A Conservative Internationalist Grand Strategy (Washington, D.C.: Georgetown University Press, 2018).

29. For a good discussion of the Ukraine crisis and conflict, and its origins, see the essays in Hal Brands, ed., *War in Ukraine: Conflict, Strategy, and the Return of a Fractured World* (Baltimore: Johns Hopkins University Press, 2024).
30. William J. Burns, *The Back Channel: A Memoir of American Diplomacy and the Case for Its Renewal* (New York: Random House, 2019), 54–56, 107–11, 225–42; Lise Morjé Howard and Michael O'Hanlon, "Backstopping Ukraine's Long-Term Security: An Alternative to NATO Membership," *Washington Quarterly* 47, no. 2 (Summer 2024): 143–57.
31. Ryan Hass, Bonnie Glaser, and Richard Bush, *U.S.-Taiwan Relations: Will China's Challenge Lead to a Crisis?* (Washington, D.C.: Brookings Institution Press, 2023), 127–30; Michael O'Hanlon, "Could the United States and China Really Go to War? Who Would Win?," Brookings Institution, Washington, D.C., August 2024, https://www.brookings.edu/articles/could-the-united-states-and-china-really-go-to-war-who-would-win.

Acknowledgments

Many people have contributed to my lifelong education, and thus to everything I write; most of them I have already thanked publicly for help with previous projects. For this book, I feel a special gratitude to Herb and Herbert Allen, John Allen, Bill Antholis, Steve Biddle, Natalie Britton, Chris Cavoli, Bridge Colby, John Colby, Emma Corbett, Walter Cronkite, Hank Crumpton, A.J. Dilts, Jeffrey Feltman, Mike Green, Edward Guttierez, Martin Indyk, Bruce Jones, Mara Karlin, Phil Knight, Tanvi Madan, Stan McChrystal, Jabari Miller, Wes Moore, Alex Noyes, John Owen, Juliano Perczek, David Petraeus, Ken Pollack, Mike Poznansky, John Reece, Bruce Riedel, the amazing Alejandra Rocha, Kara Savitt, Chris Schroeder, Tammy Schultz, Melanie Sisson, Aidan Smyth, Conor Smyth, Tom Stefanick, Caitlin Talmadge, George Tenet, Louis Weiner, four very thoughtful anonymous reviewers, my students from 2023 to 2025 at Georgetown and Columbia, and all of my colleagues in the Foreign Policy program at Brookings as well as Ceci Rouse for her inspiring and energetic leadership of Brookings since January 2024.

Index